Microsoft FrontPage 98

No experience required.

Microsoft®
FrontPage® 98

No experience required.™

Gene Weisskopf

SYBEX®

San Francisco • Paris • Düsseldorf • Soest

Associate Publisher: Amy Romanoff
Acquisitions Manager: Kristine Plachy
Acquisitions & Developmental Editor: Suzanne Rotondo
Editor: Dana Gardner
Project Editor: Kim Crowder
Technical Editor: Rob Sanfilippo
Book Designers: Patrick Dintino and Catalin Dulfu
Electronic Publishing Specialist: Bill Gibson
Production Coordinator: Katherine Cooley
Indexer: Lynnzee Elze
Cover Designer: Ingalls + Associates

Screen reproductions produced with Collage Complete.

Collage Complete is a trademark of Inner Media Inc.

SYBEX, is a registered trademark of SYBEX Inc.

No experience required. is a trademark of SYBEX Inc.

TRADEMARKS: SYBEX has attempted throughout this book to
distinguish proprietary trademarks from descriptive terms by
following the capitalization style used by the manufacturer.

Netscape Communications, the Netscape Communications logo,
Netscape, and Netscape Navigator are trademarks of Netscape
Communications Corporation.

Microsoft is a registered trademark, and the Microsoft Internet
Explorer logo is a trademark of Microsoft Corporation

The author and publisher have made their best efforts to prepare
this book, and the content is based upon final release software
whenever possible. Portions of the manuscript may be based
upon pre-release versions supplied by software manufacturer(s).
The author and the publisher make no representation or war-
ranties of any kind with regard to the completeness or accuracy of
the contents herein and accept no liability of any kind including
but not limited to performance, merchantability, fitness for any
particular purpose, or any losses or damages of any kind caused
or alleged to be caused directly or indirectly from this book.

Photographs and illustrations used in this book have been downloaded from publicly accessible file archives and are used in this
book for news reportage purposes only to demonstrate the variety
of graphics resources available via electronic access. Text and
images available over the Internet may be subject to copyright and
other rights owned by third parties. Online availability of text and
images does not imply that they may be reused without the permission of rights holders, although the Copyright Act does permit
certain unauthorized reuse as fair use under 17 U.S.C. Section 107.

Library of Congress Card Number: 97-61958
ISBN: 0-7821-2188-8

Manufactured in the United States of America

10 9 8 7 6 5 4 3 2 1

To my mother and father.

Acknowledgments

I would like to thank *everyone* at Sybex for all their talent, good spirits, and willingness to help out when needed. Producing a book with them is always a very gratifying experience.

There are several people at Sybex who played a major role in bringing this book to life. My thanks go to Kristine Plachy, acquisitions manger, whose pleasant demeanor and willingness to help are always appreciated. Many thanks to editor Dana Gardner, project editor Kim Crowder, and technical editor Rob Sanfilippo. I'd also like to thanks the electronic publishing specialist Bill Gibson, production coordinator Katherine Cooley, and indexer Lynnzee Elze.

Many thanks to Suzanne Rotondo, acquisitions and developmental editor, who organized the schedule and arranged for the talented writing team who made extensive revisions to this book to update it for the latest version of FrontPage.

I offer an extremely special thank you to that rewriting team, Gini Courter and Annette Marquis. Their schedule was challenging to say the least, and their results were timely and commendable.

Contents at a Glance

Table of Contents

Introduction

In the early days of the PC revolution, if you wanted to underline or boldface text in a document, you might very well have had to look up the control codes for those effects in your printer manual. Unless you were something of a programmer type (and there were plenty of them back then, by necessity), your word processor offered little more than an IBM Selectric Typewriter. Less than 20 years later, feature-rich word processors, such as Microsoft Word, have transformed the PC into a lot more than the glamorous typewriter it was when the PC was in its infancy.

In the 1990s, the Internet and the World Wide Web have created another dramatic spark in the computer revolution. And once again, a major contender in the PC revolution is struggling to move out of its infancy. In the earliest years, only those users who were willing to master the Hypertext Markup Language (HTML) using a text editor and a lot of code were able to publish their ideas to this remarkable new medium.

Thankfully, the early days of the Web are waning quickly, and Microsoft FrontPage 98 is one of the primary reasons. With FrontPage in hand, you don't need a deep understanding of HTML to produce attractive and informative Web pages that work together to create well-designed, fully functional Web sites. With *Microsoft FrontPage 98: No experience required* in your other hand, you'll be well-prepared to set out on the Information Highway.

Who Should Read This Book

The Internet is, by far, the fastest growing component in the computer industry today. As a result, the demand for Internet-savvy professionals is skyrocketing. The No Experience Required series from Sybex is designed to teach you the skills that are essential to being successful in some aspect of this revolutionary field. This book, which focuses on Microsoft FrontPage 98, gives you the skills you need to become a player in the Internet revolution.

Microsoft FrontPage 98: No experience required introduces you to Microsoft FrontPage 98 while at the same time introducing you to the process of designing Web sites and Web pages. Whether you're building a home page for your personal Web site on the Internet or a departmental Web site on your corporate intranet, this book and FrontPage will help you get the job done quickly and easily, impressing your co-workers, your best friend, or maybe even your boss.

This book helps you in two important ways:

- If you are new to publishing on the Web, you'll gain a solid grounding in the basics of Web design while learning how to apply the powerful features of FrontPage 98 to build an attractive, well-coordinated Web site.

- If you are already familiar with the Web and HTML, you'll see how to use FrontPage 98 to cut your development in half, taking advantage of its highly regarded Web-site management and page-editing tools.

You certainly don't need to be a computer expert to use this book, but you should have a general working knowledge of Windows and Windows-based word processing. Creating Web pages in the FrontPage Editor is really not all that different from creating documents in your word processor. Understanding folders and file management helps you work with the FrontPage Explorer, where creating and managing Web sites become very straightforward tasks.

What's Inside

The best way to start reading this book is from the beginning. Skill 1, *Web Publishing with FrontPage 98*, is an introduction to the Internet and the World Wide Web. It explains how FrontPage is a well-rounded solution to the issues involved with creating, running, and managing a Web site, and creating Web pages for that site.

Skill 2, *Creating a Web and Web Pages*, shows you how to create a new Web site in the FrontPage Explorer and gives you an overview of the FrontPage Editor, where you create your Web pages. You can save your pages in a FrontPage web, or use them elsewhere. Skills 3 and 4, and 6 through 13 all cover various page-creation issues in the Editor.

Skill 3, *Working with Lists and Headings* and Skill 4, *Formatting Your Pages* both focus on the basics of editing and formatting your Web pages, including the ways you can change the appearance of a page by formatting text, paragraphs, or the entire page.

Skill 5, *Managing Webs in the Explorer*, shows you how to manage files and folders in a web and the ways the Explorer helps you understand the hyperlinks in the files in your site. Most importantly, it shows you how to add pages to your web's structure that are automatically linked to other pages.

Perhaps the most important feature of any Web site—creating and using hyperlinks—is covered in Skill 6, *Linking Your Pages to the Web*. You'll learn how to create hyperlinks from text or images, and specify the target files and bookmarks.

You'll also learn how to apply shared borders and navigation bars to make your web easy to get around.

The HTML table is discussed in Skill 7, *Using Tables to Add Structure*. You can use tables to organize data within its orderly rows and columns. You also learn how to take advantage of the structure of a table as a valuable page layout and design tool.

Skill 8, *Displaying Images in Your Pages*, covers another important feature in any Web site: the images it displays. You'll learn the differences between GIF and JPEG image files, and you'll learn how to convert images to other formats. You'll see how to insert images and video clips into a page and how to change their size and appearance. Skill 9, *Getting Graphic with Image Composer* takes you on a grand tour through Microsoft Image Composer, the dramatically re-designed image-editing program that comes with FrontPage.

Skill 10, *Creating a Consistent Look for Your Web*, shows you how to create new pages in the Editor using templates or Wizards and apply themes that provide backgrounds, colors, and buttons for all the pages of your web. One of the newest HTML features, cascading style sheets, is introduced in this Skill, in addition to information on how to import and export files between webs.

Skill 11, *Automating and Activating Your Web*, covers some of the exciting new dynamic HTML and other automated features incorporated into FrontPage 98. You learn how to create Hover buttons, banner ads, and scrolling marquees, and how to add automated features such as a table of contents and hit counter to your Web pages.

Skill 12, *Letting Users Interact with Forms*, introduces you to building forms in Web pages. You'll see how easy it is in the FrontPage Editor to create text fields, check-boxes, radio buttons, drop-down menus, and other form controls. In Skill 13, *Getting Fancier with Frames*, you'll learn about a frames page, which is a single page that displays other pages, each within a separate frame, or window. You'll also examine the question of when to use frames most effectively and when not to use them.

Finally, Skill 14, *Publishing Your Web Site*, covers some of the Web administration tasks you can perform in FrontPage, such as assigning access rights to a Web site. Following this Skill is Appendix A, *Installing and Starting FrontPage*, which discusses the issues you need to consider when installing FrontPage.

For readers who would like more grounding in HTML coding, Appendix B is a valuable guide to keep next to your computer. This HTML reference covers every tag from the HTML 4 Document Type Definition.

You'll find plain language whenever possible in this book, which was a pretty daunting task considering that acronyms and jargon are rampant in the language of the Internet. Appendix C, *Glossary of Terms,* helps you over the humps.

Other features you'll find in this book include helpful Notes, Tips, and Warnings, which serve as adjuncts to the main body of text. All the sample Web pages and examples of HTML features in this book are simple, uncluttered, and to the point. You won't have any trouble following along with the exercises and explanations.

This book utilizes some typographical elements you'll find useful to help distinguish certain aspects of the text. Text you enter with your keyboard is in **boldface**, while file names and URLs are in a monospaced `program font`. All letters in file names are capitalized when the name appears within a paragraph, but when the name appears within a path or URL, the letters are lowercased.

I hope you find *Microsoft FrontPage 98: No experience required* to be helpful as well as enjoyable to read, and that it becomes a valuable tutorial and reference guide as you build your Web pages and sites. If you have any comments about this book, please send them to me in care of Sybex; they will be much appreciated.

Web Publishing with FrontPage 98

- ❑ Understanding the Internet

- ❑ Accessing the World Wide Web (WWW)

- ❑ Using an intranet as an in-house Web site

- ❑ Understanding Web publishing

- ❑ Using FrontPage as your Web site publishing solution

The explosive growth of the Internet in the past few years is ample evidence of how a simple concept—a network that can connect every computer on Earth—can fulfill countless needs. This Skill first introduces you to the Internet, the World Wide Web, and subsets of the Internet called intranets. Then you'll see how Microsoft FrontPage 98 offers the tools you need to set up and manage a site on the Web, create Web pages, and leap over many of the hurdles you'll encounter while publishing on the Web.

If you are already familiar with the World Wide Web and want to get right to work creating Web pages with the FrontPage Editor, you can skip ahead to Skill 2. Skill 5 shows you how to access the files and hyperlinks in an existing Web site using the newly designed FrontPage Explorer. If you want to focus on creating and editing graphics, Skill 9 describes how to work with the Microsoft Image Composer. For help installing FrontPage, turn to Appendix A, *Installing and Starting FrontPage*. And if you're brand new to the role of web designer, follow right along and you'll soon be a pro.

Understanding the Internet, the Web, and Intranets

The *Internet* was originally conceived, designed, and implemented in the 1960s as a United States Defense Department strategy to protect lines of communication and access to vital databases in the event of a nuclear attack. The early version of the Internet, called ARPANet, connected computers in military installations and universities in the United States; this network was then expanded to Canada and Western Europe. It was only in the 1990s, however, that the Internet moved out of university research centers and into the homes and businesses of millions of people around the world. This phenomenon is the result of the *World Wide Web (WWW)*—an amazing development that transformed a boring, text-based communications system into a dynamic, colorful, multimedia-rich environment.

One of the strengths of the Internet has always been that it is platform-independent: regardless of the type of computer and operating system you have, you can connect to the Internet. This means that a Macintosh user living in Great Britain can post information on a computer in London that runs the Windows NT operating system. Then, someone in Framingham using a PC running Windows 3.1 can connect to a computer in Boston that runs the UNIX operating system, have that computer connect to the computer in London, and receive the information they need. In a matter of seconds, information is literally transported halfway around the world.

Of course, the original designers of the Internet did not envision the innumerable uses that people of the 90s have found for this incredible communications tool. But the need to make any sort of file available to remote users, regardless of which computer they use, is exactly why the Internet was created.

Clients, Servers, and Networks

The Internet consists of three fundamental elements:

- **Servers**   Computers and software that make data available to other programs on the same or other computers, also called hosts.

- **Clients**   Computers that request data from servers.

- **Networks**   Groups of computers that can communicate with each other, such as clients requesting and receiving data from a server. The communication can be over copper wire, coaxial cable, fiber-optic cable, microwave relay, satellite transmission, and so on.

 NOTE   When you connect to a server halfway around the world, you might use any or all of these network communication methods. Of course, it doesn't really matter to you; the system simply follows the most advantageous route over the network until it reaches the computer you want to access.

Internet Protocols

Although the Internet is a network, you shouldn't think of it as a single network. It's really a collection of countless smaller networks, all of which agree to send and receive data according to a set of standards called *protocols* to communicate across the Internet.

Transmission Control Protocol/Internet Protocol (TCP/IP) is the means by which these computer networks communicate. *TCP* specifies how messages should be split up into packets for transmission. *IP* addresses the packets and routes them to their destination. It's the combined TCP/IP protocol that makes the Internet the Internet, because it allows any computer or network using TCP/IP to access and exchange information with other TCP/IP computers.

There are many ways to get data from the Internet. For example, *File Transfer Protocol (FTP)*, a program that transfers files from one computer to another, is one of the original Internet services; mailing lists for users who were interested in specific topics were another early Internet tool. But there's one Internet access method that has taken the world by storm; it allows companies and individuals to publish newspapers and magazines, open online retail stores, offer online catalogs and reference material, and even broadcast live audio and video from around the world. This latest addition to the Internet family is called the World Wide Web.

The World Wide Web

The rocket fuel for the Internet's dizzying rise is the World Wide Web (WWW, or simply, the Web). Tim Berners-Lee created the graphical-based Web in 1992 to make it easier to search for documents. The rapid international adoption of the Web has vastly improved the way you access data on the Internet.

 NOTE   In this book, you'll see the word web used frequently in different contexts. The word Web (capitalized) refers to the World Wide Web; the term Web site, or just plain site, refers to a collection of files on the Web that you access with a browser. A FrontPage web (lowercase), or simply a web, is a Web site that you've created in FrontPage. Realize that it's not always easy, or even necessary, to distinguish between a Web site and the Web because the network and the computers connected to it must all function together.

Understanding Internet Addresses

Each file, or resource, on the Web is identified by its *Uniform Resource Locator (URL)*, which is its address or location on the Web. URLs begin with the name of the protocol used by the URL's server. *Hypertext Transfer Protocol*, or *HTTP*, is the protocol designed for the World Wide Web. The protocol is followed by a colon, two slashes, and the site type. The site type is usually World Wide Web (www), but could be File Transfer Protocol (ftp) or Gopher (gopher). The site type is followed by the address of the host computer, called a *domain address.* The domain address includes the site name, followed by the *domain,* which indicates the type of organization that owns the server. The URL for the HTTP server owned by Sybex looks like this:

```
http://www.sybex.com
```

http is the server protocol; *www* is the site type; *sybex* is the site name; and *com* is the domain.

> **NOTE**
> Don't confuse URL (Uniform Resource Locator) with IRL, which is online short-hand for "In Real Life".

Domain Names   Until recently, there were only six root (top level) domain names used in the United States:

- COM - for commercial companies, like Sybex in the URL listed above
- EDU - for schools, colleges, and universities
- GOV - for federal, state, and local government entities
- MIL - reserved for the military
- NET - for companies that administer or provide access to the Internet
- ORG - for non commercial organizations, like non-profits

Countries outside the United States use a two letter country code as the domain name: for example, UK for the United Kingdom, and JP for Japan. Due to the rapid expansion of the World Wide Web, seven new domains have been approved for use on the Web:

- FIRM - for commercial businesses
- STORE - for retail and mail order businesses
- WEB - for organizations that deal with the World Wide Web
- ARTS - for cultural and entertainment organizations
- REC - for organizations emphasizing recreation/entertainment activities
- INFO - for companies that provide information services, like information brokers and libraries
- NOM - (as in *nomenclature)* for individuals who want their own Web server

Accessing Resources on the Internet

The software you use to access data on the Web is the *browser,* which is essentially a file viewer that can use HTTP to communicate with servers. There are several popular browsers available, including Microsoft Internet Explorer (which is included with FrontPage 98) and Netscape Navigator.

Here's the overview of how you open a resource (file) on the Web:

- In your browser, you specify the complete URL of the Web resource you want to access.
- The browser sends your request to the server with which you're communicating.
- Your server forwards the request to the server you specified in the URL.
- That server locates the resource and sends it back to your server.
- Finally, your server sends the resource to your browser.

It may sound complicated, but all this usually happens in a matter of seconds, no matter where on the Internet the resource may be located. It's really no different (at least, from your perspective) than picking up the telephone, dialing a phone number, and having the phone system make the connection.

Once you open a resource in your browser, you can view it, print it, or save it on a disk. Basically, it's yours to play with. Note that when a Web browser receives a file it can't handle, such as an audio or video file, it may ask you if you'd like to save that file on a disk so you can work with it later on. Otherwise, it passes the file along to the computer's operating system, which then opens the appropriate program (assuming there is one) for that file.

Web Sites, Pages, and Links

When you want to create documents, or pages, that Web browsers can read, you use the *Hypertext Markup Language (HTML)*, the language used to format Web pages. You use HTML to create the content and specify the structure and format of the Web page. HTML files are always plain text files, so you can send a page to virtually any type of computer in the world (as long as it's connected to the Internet, of course).

Each user's browser interprets the HTML code and displays the page. A page may not appear exactly the same when displayed in different browsers. This is because the precise appearance of a page is not explicitly included in the HTML code. Rather, the page's appearance is broadly described and the browser is responsible for coming up with a suitable representation. This may sound like a weakness of the Web, but it's actually a great strength—browsers on completely dissimilar computers can present reasonable renditions of the same page.

A *Web site* is a collection of Web pages and other resources that have something in common, and can be considered as one body of information, like a set of encyclopedias. The resources in a Web site are often all located on one server, but they don't need to be. The Web site's *home page* is the initial page that you see when you access a Web site without specifying the name of a specific file at that location. For example, www.sybex.com is Sybex's home page, shown in Figure 1.1. The home page usually serves as a welcome mat or a table of contents, and may give instructions for accessing the other resources in the site.

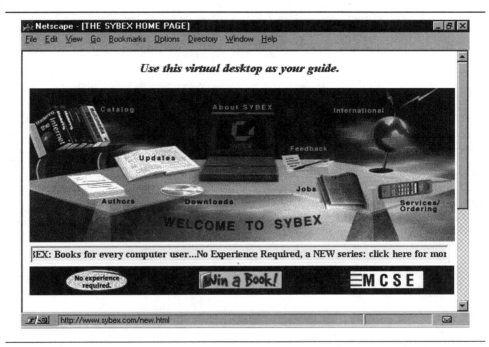

FIGURE 1.1: The Sybex Home Page has hotspots for user navigation.

The best aspect of the Web is the ability to embed links within pages so users can move easily between pages in a Web site, or jump to another related site with a single click. A *hyperlink,* or link, is text (usually signified by being underlined and in a different color) or a graphic image called a hotspot that you can click on to access the target resource of that link anywhere on the Web. In Figure 1.1, the virtual desktop includes links that take the user to Catalog, Authors, and several other areas on the Sybex Web site. Text hyperlinks and hotspots are a quick, easy, and very effective way to let you jump from one URL to another.

The Internet and Intranets

All the issues discussed in the previous sections relate to the global Internet and the World Wide Web. However, you can also set up a local TCP/IP network that takes advantage of HTML pages, links, URLs, Web sites, and the rest, but isn't necessarily connected to the global Internet. Such a network is called an *intranet*, and differs from the Internet only because it is not accessible to every Internet-connected computer in the world. The term *I*net* refers to both the Internet and intranets.

Thousands of businesses are realizing the low costs and numerous benefits of using an intranet to distribute information within an organization. Even older computers can run some type of browser, and it's quite likely that the computers on a local network already have Web-browsing software installed, so there's no additional investment needed on the client end. Many users of those computers are probably already familiar with browsing the Web and can browse an intranet with little or no additional training. Once you've set up an intranet, it's easy to publish just part of it to the Internet at large because all the resources on the intranet are already in a Web-ready format.

 NOTE   The trick is making sure that outside users can't access your company's intranet through the public pages that you open to the Internet. Companies use a variety of software packages called *firewalls* to prevent unauthorized access from the Internet to an intranet – or to keep employees from surfing the Internet on company time.

Finally, the browsing and linking concept of the Web effectively allows multiple users at client computers to share the same server resources via their browsers. And it works just as well for interoffice communications within a company as it does between countries on separate continents. For more information and examples of intranets created with FrontPage, visit the Site Developer Network at `http://www.microsoft.com`.

The FrontPage Solution to Web Publishing

You can create a Web site from scratch using any text editor. However, this makes the job of creating and running a Web site difficult and time consuming. Enter the Web-smart components of FrontPage 98:

- **Personal Web Servers**   Two "personal-sized" Web servers that let you create, test, revise, and host a Web site.

- **Server Extensions**   Add-on programs for Web server software that make the server "FrontPage-aware" and able to interact more closely with FrontPage webs.

- **Explorer**   A Web-site management tool that shows you all the resources in the site, lets you add, remove, and rename resources, and keeps all the hyperlinks up to date.

- **Editor**   A powerful HTML editor that lets you produce Web-ready pages while working in what is really an easy-to-use word processor.

- **Tasks List**   A convenient way to keep track of all the large and small chores that need to be completed on your FrontPage web.

- **Image Composer**   An image editor that lets you create images for any Web site, import them, modify them, adjust them, embellish them, and otherwise slop paint on the old electronic canvas.

In the sections that follow, we'll take a short look at these FrontPage components so you can see how each one simplifies your task of creating and running a Web site.

 NOTE   Don't confuse the FrontPage Explorer with the other Explorers that Microsoft produces. The Internet Explorer is a Web browser, and the Windows Explorer is the disk and file navigation tool for Windows 95, 98, and NT. (Internet Explorer 4.0 integrates seamlessly with the Windows Explorer, so you effectively end up with one Windows Explorer.)

Personal Web Servers

FrontPage 98 comes with two *Personal Web Servers (PWSs)* that can host your Web site as you build, test, and maintain it. The FrontPage Personal Web Server has always been a part of the FrontPage package. The Microsoft Personal Web Server is a newer, more sophisticated server that is actually a subset of the Internet Information Server (IIS) used with Windows NT. It will eventually supplant the FrontPage PWS.

Both of the Personal Web Servers fulfill three important functions:

- **Local Server**   With a Personal Web Server running on your PC, you can build and test your Web site on a single computer without being connected to a network and a server. This means you are free to work on your Web site on a portable computer, for example, seated comfortably in a beach chair miles from any telephone lines. It also means that while you're working on a construction copy of your web site, users can still access an intact, fully functional copy running on another server.

- **Server Functions**   The Personal Web Servers work hand-in-hand with the other components in FrontPage while you build your Web site. For example, they let the FrontPage Explorer access any of the Web sites that are located under the PWS and provide password security, as well.

- **Host Server**   You can host your entire Web site with a PWS, which may be all the server you need.

With a PWS, you can use a Web browser to test your Web site on a local computer. The PWS checks a user's access authorization if needed, fetches requested pages, and responds to clicks on hotspots and hyperlinks. The PWSs are important FrontPage components, since it is most convenient to work on your Web site on a computer running a web server. FrontPage makes this easy; if you're using the FrontPage PWS, the FrontPage Explorer starts it automatically when the server is needed, such as when you want to open a FrontPage web. If you use the Microsoft PWS, it's launched when you start your computer. More information about both Personal Web Servers is found in Skill 14.

 NOTE   You should avoid making changes to a FrontPage web or its pages, links, or other files while outside of FrontPage Explorer or when the server is not running. FrontPage keeps track of the files and folders that make up a web. If those files are changed outside of FrontPage, at best, those changes would go unnoticed by FrontPage; at worst, they could throw the web into disarray.

The FrontPage Server Extensions

You'll get the most out of your FrontPage webs when your Web server is set up to work with FrontPage. The two personal Web servers discussed in the previous section are FrontPage-ready (why else would Microsoft include them with FrontPage?).

However, you may want to use FrontPage to develop Web pages and sites for other servers. For example, you may want to create content for your company's intranet which uses the Microsoft Internet Information Server, or hang your personal Web site on your Internet Service Provider's Netscape Communications server.

If you want to take advantage of all of FrontPage's features with other servers, you need to install the FrontPage Server Extensions on the server. FrontPage includes these server extensions for widely used servers like the Microsoft Internet Information Server (IIS), Apache, O'Reilly WebSite, and Netscape Communications Server, and you can download more extensions from Microsoft's Web site free of charge:

```
http://www.microsoft.com/frontpage/
```

If you can't find server extensions for the server you need, don't worry. You can still use FrontPage 98 with a PWS to create your Web site, then publish or post your Web site on the server.

The FrontPage Explorer

You use the FrontPage Explorer for creating, revising, and managing a Web site; the Explorer is covered in detail in Skills 5 and 14. In the Explorer, you can open any FrontPage web (to which you have access rights) on any server available to the Explorer. Figure 1.2 shows the Explorer in Hyperlinks view with an open web.

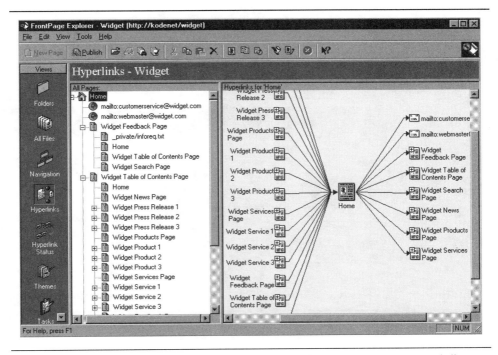

FIGURE 1.2: The FrontPage Explorer lists the files in a Web site and displays them as a map based on their links.

The left side of the Explorer lists all the pages and other files that make up the resources of the web. It displays their page titles or, if they have no titles, their file names. At the top of the list of Web resources is the home page, the file named INDEX.HTM when the server is the FrontPage PWS. The resources are arranged based on the links each page contains. You can manipulate the outline in the usual Windows Explorer manner—click on the plus sign to expand a level of the outline to show more detail, or click on the minus sign to hide the detail.

The right side of the Explorer in Figure 1.2 displays a model of the web, with lines connecting a page to any resources it includes or links to. This is a real peek behind the scenes of your web because it reveals the normally hidden relationships among its resources.

In addition to Hyperlinks view, you can work with a web in:

- **Folder view**   Shows how your web is organized by displaying each folder and file in the web, along with its size, the date and time it was last modified, the person who modified it, its URL, and any comments that have been attached to it. It's easy to create, delete, copy and move folders in this view.

- **All Files View**   Lists only the files in the web, along with the information provided in Folder view.

- **Navigation view**   Allows you to examine and change the structure of a web by dragging and dropping pages into the structure of the web (see Figure 1.3).

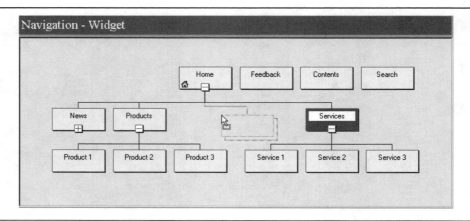

FIGURE 1.3: In Navigation view, changing the structure of a web is as easy as dragging and dropping.

Together, these views let you examine and manipulate the FrontPage web as a whole, instead of your having to work with and keep track of many separate and seemingly unrelated files.

The FrontPage Editor

The FrontPage solution for creating Web pages is the FrontPage Editor. We begin discussing The Editor in Skill 2. It is essentially a WYSIWYG word processor that is designed to work specifically with HTML pages, and offers you all the common page layout options that are available in the most recent version of HTML.

Figure 1.4 shows the Editor and a Web page open for editing. The Editor has many of the tools and features you expect in a Windows word processor. For example, you can open multiple documents in the Editor, and copy and paste data between them in the usual ways.

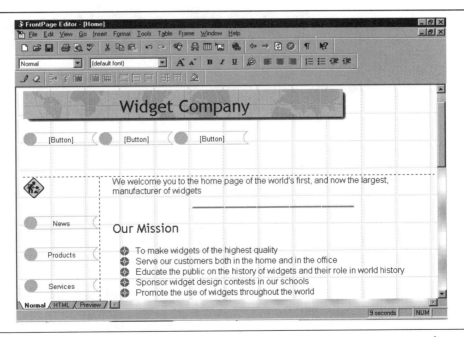

FIGURE 1.4: The FrontPage Editor is like a Windows word processor for editing HTML pages.

NOTE   If you use Microsoft Word or other programs in Microsoft Office, you'll find that the Editor is carved from the same block of granite. The Editor even shares the Office spelling dictionary and thesaurus. You'll recognize many of the Editor's features and commands, and you should find it a comfortable place to work.

The FrontPage Task List

Creating and maintaining a Web site is no small feat, at least not if you want to do the job well. You need to attend to countless Web related assignments, large and small. To help you keep track of these jobs, FrontPage offers the Task List, which is discussed in Skill 5 and shown in Figure 1.5.

	Tasks - Widget					
Status	Task	Assigned...	Priority	Linked To	Modified Date	Description
Not Started	Customize Home Page	Annette	High	Widget Company	8/21/97 8:23:20...	replace generic text with some
● Not Started	Customize Feedback Form	Annette	Medium	Widget Feedback Page	8/21/97 8:23:22...	adjust input areas in the form
● Not Started	Customize News Page	Annette	High	Widget News Page	8/21/97 8:23:22...	add your own public relations
● Not Started	Customize Products Page	Annette	High	Widget Products Page	8/21/97 8:23:22...	create data sheets for your ow
● Not Started	Customize Search Page	Annette	Medium	Widget Search Page	8/21/97 8:23:22...	explain how to search for com
● Not Started	Customize Services Page	Annette	High	Widget Services Page	8/21/97 8:23:22...	describe your service offerings
● Not Started	Customize TOC Page	Annette	Medium	Widget Table of Conte...	8/21/97 8:23:23...	describe sections in more deta

FIGURE 1.5: The FrontPage Task List helps you manage Web-related tasks.

When you invoke the Edit ➤ Add Task command in the Editor or click on the New Task button in the Explorer, the task you create in the Task List is automatically linked to the page or file that is active in the Editor or selected in the Explorer. When you later open the linked task in the Task List and click on the Do Task button, the linked file automatically opens so you can complete the task.

There is a single Task List for tracking in every FrontPage web. Anyone working on the site can create a new entry for a task and include information such as a name for the task, to whom it's assigned, its priority, the resource to which it's linked, and a description of the task. You can sort the items in the Task List by clicking a column-title button at the top of any of the columns.

When you actually finish a task, you can mark it as completed in the Task List, and either delete it from the list or retain that task as part of a history of jobs completed.

Microsoft Image Composer

The World Wide Web would not be the exciting place that it is if it weren't for the rich and varied use of graphical images in the millions of pages on the Web.

Because images play such a crucial role in bringing a Web site to life, FrontPage 98 comes with Microsoft Image Composer 1.5. With the Image Composer, you can create images, add clip art and photos, open many different image file formats, and add a wide range of special effects to your work. You'll find it discussed in Skill 9.

Now that you've had an introduction to the Internet, the World Wide Web, Web sites, and FrontPage 98, we'll look at how you can create a web and add content to a web page.

Are You Experienced?

Now you can:

- ☑ **Speak the language of the Internet**
- ☑ **Describe the process for creating a web page**
- ☑ **Outline the functions of web servers**
- ☑ **Differentiate between the FrontPage Explorer and the FrontPage Editor**

S K I L L

2

two

Creating a Web and Web pages

The FrontPage Explorer is your Web site navigation center, the place where you start and finish your work on a web site. This Skill shows you how to create a web in the Explorer and use the FrontPage Editor to design exciting web pages to house in your web. The overview of the Editor and the features presented in this skill prepares the way for the Skills that follow, where you'll learn about a wide variety of HTML elements you can create in your pages.

Creating a New Web

In the FrontPage Explorer, you work with one FrontPage web at a time, which is called the current or active web. You create individual pages in the FrontPage Explorer or Editor, and work with all the pages in the Web site with the Explorer. New pages you create and save in the Editor become part of the active web unless you specify otherwise.

When you start the FrontPage Explorer, the Getting Started dialog box is displayed (see Figure 2.1).

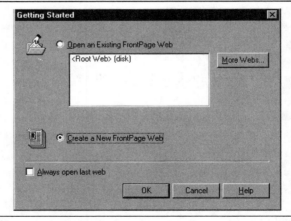

FIGURE 2.1: The Getting Started with Microsoft FrontPage dialog box lets you open an existing Web or create a new one.

In this dialog, you can open an existing web, or create a new web by selecting Create a New FrontPage Web and clicking on OK to open the New FrontPage Web dialog, shown in Figure 2.2.

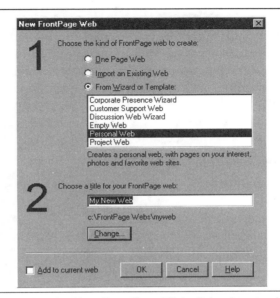

FIGURE 2.2: Use the New FrontPage Web dialog box to choose a web type and location.

There are three choices in the New FrontPage Web dialog box:

- **One Page Web**   Although most webs ultimately have more than one page, this is a simple place to start creating a web from scratch.

- **Import an Existing Web**   Choose this option if you want to base a new web on another web.

- **From Wizard or Template**   FrontPage has six templates and wizards that contain basic structural elements you can use to create webs. The Personal Web template is the default.

TIP   If you are new to FrontPage, you may want to start out by creating a one-page web and then build from there. This gets you familiar with working with a Web page before moving on to more complex webs. If you are already familiar with FrontPage and want to import an existing web or create a web with a Wizard or a template, you may want to skip to Skill 10, *Creating a Consistent Look for your Web,* before returning to this skill and *Creating Pages in the Editor.*

Choosing a Location for the Web

After you choose the kind of web you want to create, you need to specify a name for the web and may need to change the location where the web is stored. The default name for your web is *My New Web*. You can give your web any name you want using spaces and upper and lower case letters. Although the full name is available in the Explorer, FrontPage takes the first 14 letters and numbers to create a folder name for the web. For example, *Gini's First Web Page* would be converted into *ginisfirstwebp* (see Figure 2.3).

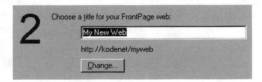

FIGURE 2.3:   When creating a new web, you need to specify a name.

The default location for your web is generally in the folder called WebShare (if you are using the Microsoft Personal Web Server) or FrontPage Webs (if you are using the FrontPage Personal Web Server). While you are creating your web, you might want to store it on a folder you create on your local drive. When the web is ready to be published for all the world to see, you can transfer the web to its permanent location (See *Publishing a Web to a Server* in Skill 14).

To change the location of the web, click on the Change button below the title to open the Change Location dialog box:

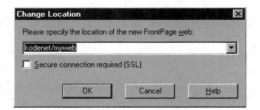

Click on the drop-down arrow to the right of the text box to choose from one of the established server locations. If you want to save the web to a folder on a local or network drive outside the control of a web server, type the entire path to the folder in the text box. If the folder does not already exist, FrontPage asks if you want to create it. If the folder does exist but it isn't already a FrontPage web, you're asked whether you want to convert the folder to a FrontPage web:

Click on Yes, and FrontPage creates the folders and files it needs to treat the folder as a web.

The Folders in a FrontPage Web

A FrontPage web contains not only the files you create, but several other folders and files that are created by FrontPage 98 when you create a new web. These are used by FrontPage to manage and run your web. The names of most of these folders begin with an underscore, such as _VTI_PVT, and are invisible in the FrontPage Explorer (you can view them in the Windows Explorer).

Most of these folders are strictly for FrontPage's own use, so you shouldn't change or delete them. However, there are two folders that you are free to use as you need them:

- **Images**   This is a convenient folder in which to store image files, such as GIF and JPEG files.

- **Private**   This folder is not visible to browsers, so any files in it are invisible as well. Once your site is up and running, this might be a place to keep pages that are under construction, reference files, and other documents you want to be available for your use only. Unlike the other FrontPage folders that begin with the underscore character, the contents of this folder are visible in the FrontPage Explorer.

Viewing a Web in the Explorer

After you specify a name and location for your web, you are taken directly into the FrontPage Explorer, shown in Figure 2.4.

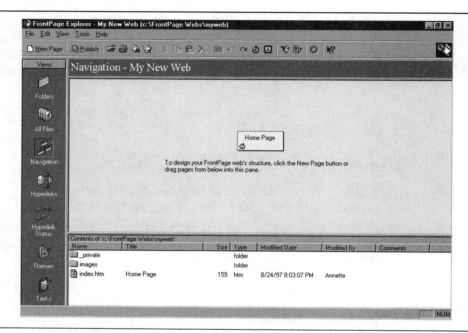

FIGURE 2.4: Viewing a web in the FrontPage Explorer.

The web's home page is prominently displayed in the middle of the window. If you create a more complex web, you see all the pages of the web and how they relate to each other. At the bottom of the window, you see the visible folders and files that make up your newly created web. This view, called Navigation view, is one of several ways to view a web. See Skill 5 for information about other views and how to work with webs in the Explorer.

Saving Your Web

One bonus of the FrontPage Explorer is that you don't have to worry about saving your work. There is no File ➤ Save command in the Explorer; any changes you make to a web are saved automatically when you exit the Editor. If you close the Explorer before closing the Editor, FrontPage 98 will reopen the Explorer to save your changes.

Opening and Closing Existing Webs

To open an existing FrontPage web in the Explorer, use the File ➤ Open FrontPage Web command or click on the Open FrontPage Web button on the toolbar. The Open FrontPage Web dialog box is similar to the one you find when you are creating a new web, as discussed earlier in this chapter in *Choosing a Location for the Web.*

To open an existing web, choose File ➤ Open FrontPage Web, select a server or folder from the list or type in the name of one, and click on the List Webs button. This displays a list of the titles of all the available FrontPage webs on the chosen server or folder. Select the one you want and then click on OK to open that web.

As always, if the web has security controls placed on it, you may have to enter your username and password before you can open the web. See Skill 14, *Publishing Your Web Site,* for more information about security.

You can choose File ➤ Close FrontPage Web at any time to close the active FrontPage web in the Explorer. You don't have to worry about losing any changes you've made because the Explorer saves them automatically. (If you have the Editor open, it's best to close it before closing the web in the Explorer; otherwise, FrontPage will have to reload the Explorer to save the web.) Because you can only have one web open at a time in the Explorer, the active web is automatically closed when you open another web.

Creating Pages in the Editor

You usually use the FrontPage Editor in conjunction with the FrontPage Explorer and a Web server such as a Personal Web Server. For example, you open HTML pages from the active web in the Explorer, modify them in the Editor, and save them back in the web.

NOTE   Earlier in this Skill you were introduced you to the concept of the *active web,* which is the web currently open in the FrontPage Explorer. When you choose File ➤ Open in the Editor, you see the pages in the active web by default. The same is true when you save a page in the Editor—it will save the page in the active web by default.

There are several ways to start the FrontPage Editor. From within the Explorer you can choose Tools ➤ Show FrontPage Editor or click on the button on the toolbar. Once the Editor is open, you can choose to create a new page or open an existing one.

You can also open an existing page in the Editor from the Explorer window using the Navigation, All Files, Folders, or Hyperlinks views:

- Double-click on a page name or icon.

- Select the page name or icon and choose Edit ➤ Open (Ctrl+O), or right-click and choose the Open command from the shortcut menu.

- If the Editor window is visible on the screen, drag the page name or icon into the Editor's desktop (not into another open page, which creates a link within that page). You can't use this drag and drop technique in Navigation view.

 When you are working in the Editor, you can switch to the Explorer at any time by choosing Tools ➤ Show FrontPage Explorer or by clicking on the FrontPage Explorer button on the toolbar. Of course, you can switch to either program by selecting it from the Windows taskbar.

When you're finished with the Editor, you can close it with the File ➤ Exit command. As recommended earlier, you should close any open documents in the Editor before you close the active web in the Explorer or close the Explorer itself. This ensures that the Explorer keeps its web up to date by recording any changes you make to the pages in the active web.

Creating a New Page

Let's take a quick look at how you create a new page in the Editor. To create a new blank page, just click on the New button on the toolbar and you're ready to get to work. You can have multiple pages open at the same time, switching between them as needed.

You can also create a new page from a FrontPage template, which is a ready-built page that serves as the basis for the new page. You choose a template when you use the File ➤ New command. The Normal Page template is the standard blank page that opens when you click on the New button. Templates are discussed in Skill 10.

 NOTE Just as in your word processor, you must save your work in the Editor to keep it. You can choose to save a document either in the active web or in another location.

To close the active document, choose File ➤ Close or click on the document's Close button on the right side of its title bar (or on the right side of the menu bar, if the document's window is maximized).

Entering and Editing Text

The FrontPage Editor looks very much like a typical WYSIWYG word processor, where "what you see is what you get." In this case, what you see in the Editor is pretty much what the rest of the world sees in their Web browsers when they view the current page on your Web site (see Figure 2.5).

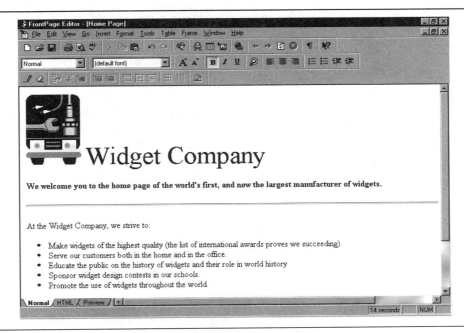

FIGURE 2.5: You create your Web pages in the FrontPage Editor.

If you are a Microsoft Word user, you may notice the Editor looks suspiciously similar to Word. The similarities are not accidental. Microsoft has worked very hard to have all its Office products—Word, Excel, PowerPoint, and FrontPage—share the same look and even the same program resources. For example, you'll find the same toolbar buttons for commands such as New, Open, Save, Cut, and Paste. Those commands also appear in the same menus, so if you're already familiar with Microsoft Word, you won't have any trouble getting started in the FrontPage Editor.

TIP   Paste Special is also available in the Editor, so you can insert formatted text from within FrontPage or from other applications.

Let's take a quick look at some of the features of the Editor in Figure 2.5:

- At the top of the screen, beneath the Editor's title bar, is the menu bar, the Standard toolbar, and the Formatting toolbar. Several other toolbars are available as well. You can turn the display of a toolbar on or off by selecting it from the View menu.

- At the bottom of the screen is the Editor's status bar, which displays useful information as you work in the Editor. For example, the left side of the status bar displays a description of the currently selected command on the menu, and it displays the target address of a hyperlink when you point to a link in the page.

- Just above the status bar are three tabs that switch you between views of your document: Normal, HTML, and Preview views (more about those later).

- The web page that you're editing appears in the window beneath the toolbars. You can open multiple documents pages in the Editor, and you can switch between them in the usual ways: for example, selecting the page name from the Window menu or pressing Ctrl+F6.

- The horizontal and vertical scroll bars offer one way to scroll through your document; you can also use the usual keyboard keys, such as PgUp and PgDn. If your mouse has a scrolling wheel, such as Microsoft's IntelliMouse, you can use the wheel to scroll up or down through the page.

Basic Editing Procedures

The best way to familiarize yourself with the Editor is to start typing. Most of the basic procedures you've already learned in your word processor are applicable in the FrontPage Editor:

- You can have multiple documents open at the same time in the Editor, but only one is active. The active page receives the text you enter, and is the target of any commands you issue.

- In the active document, enter text just as you would in your word processor; press Enter only to create a new paragraph.

- Press Del to delete the character to the right of the insertion point; press Backspace to delete the character to its left. Press Ctrl+Del to delete the word to the right of the insertion point, and press Ctrl+Backspace to delete the word to its left.

- Press Ctrl+Home to go to the top of the document and Ctrl+End to go to the bottom.

- Using the standard Windows commands, you can change the size of the active document's window, minimize it to an icon, or maximize it so it is as large as possible.

- Select text by dragging over it with your mouse or by pressing the Shift key while you use a keyboard arrow key to select the material.

- Once you select a portion of the document, you can act on the selection by making choices from the menu, a toolbar, or a shortcut menu. For example, choose Edit ➤ Cut from the menu, click on the Cut button on the toolbar, or right click and choose Cut from the shortcut menu to remove the selection from the document and send it to the Windows Clipboard.

- You can transfer text or images between FrontPage and other programs in the usual ways by using Copy or Cut and Paste with the Clipboard.

- Choose Edit ➤ Undo from the menu, click the Undo button on the standard toolbar, or press Ctrl+Z to undo your most recent action in the document. You can "undo an undo" by choosing Edit ➤ Redo or by clicking on the Redo button.

You can add comments in a page by selecting Insert ➤ FrontPage Component from the menu and choosing Comment from the Insert FrontPage Component dialog box. The text you enter is displayed in the page in the Editor, but not when the page is viewed in a browser. A comment can explain an area in the page or serve as a reminder to you or another author.

Inserting Paragraphs and Line Breaks

When you want to create a new paragraph in a document, simply press Enter, just as you would in your word processor. Behind the scenes, this inserts new <P> and </P> opening and closing tags in the underlying HTML code, defining the beginning and end of the new paragraph.

A new paragraph not only begins on a new line, it also has its own formatting, just as in Word. For example, if you press Enter at the end of a left-aligned paragraph (the default alignment), you can center the new paragraph, right align it, or add other paragraph formatting without changing the formatting for the previous line.

NOTE   The Editor also places the HTML code for a non-breaking space (CTRL+SHIFT+ Space) between the two paragraph tags, so the code created when you press Enter looks like this: <P>(your text) (your text)</P>. If you don't add any text to the paragraph, the non-breaking space forces a browser to display a blank line, where it might otherwise ignore the "empty" paragraph.

You can force a line to break without creating a new paragraph by pressing Shift+Enter instead of Enter. This inserts the single line-break tag,
 (you can also choose Normal Line Break from the dialog box of the Insert ➤ Line Break command). The text that follows the line break appears on a new line, but is otherwise still a part of the current paragraph and carries all of its formatting.

Most browsers insert some extra space between two paragraphs of text, so there are instances when you'd rather use the <BR> tag than the <P> tag to create a new line. For example, when you display your name and address in a page, you don't want extra space between each line of the address.

Shown below are two addresses in a table in the Editor. In the address on the left, Enter is pressed at the end of each line to insert a line break. In the address on the right, Shift+Enter is pressed.

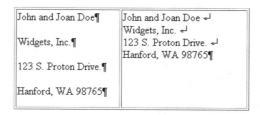

Notice that the Editor displays a right-angle arrow for the line break and a paragraph mark between regular paragraphs. You can turn the display of line breaks and some other on-screen marks on or off by choosing View ➤ Format Marks, or by clicking on the Show/Hide button on the Standard toolbar.

Inserting Special Characters

Your computer's keyboard is limited to a standard set of letters, numbers, and punctuation. But there are a lot of other characters that simply are not included on your keyboard. For example, there's the degree symbol (100°), the copyright symbol (©1997), and the fraction symbol for one-half ($1/2$).

In the FrontPage Editor, you insert symbols into your page just as you do in Word: with the Insert ➤ Symbol command, which displays the Symbol dialog box (see Figure 2.6). Select the symbol you want and click on the Insert button to place that symbol into your document at the insertion point. You can continue to select other symbols in the dialog box and click the Insert button. When you are finished, click on the Close button.

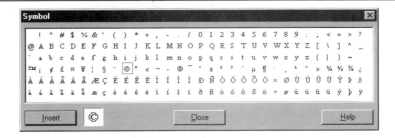

FIGURE 2.6: The Insert ➤ Symbol command lets you pick a symbol to include in your page.

Check Your Spelling

The FrontPage Editor lets you check the spelling in your Web pages, just as your word processor lets you do in your documents. To check the spelling in the active page, choose Tools ➤ Spelling (F7) or click on the Check Spelling button on the toolbar. If you have experience with any of the applications in Microsoft Office, this routine is quite familiar.

The spell-checker checks the spelling of the active page or the spelling of the highlighted text. Note that the spell-checker does not check the spelling of any included pages in the active page. These are pages that appear as the result of the Include FrontPage Component, which is discussed in *Including Another Web Page Automatically* in Skill 11. You must open these pages separately to check their spelling.

TIP   You can check the spelling in all pages in the web by choosing the Tools ➤ Spelling command in the Explorer.

If the spell-checker finds no misspelled words in the page, a dialog box notifies you of the success. If it finds a misspelled word (or rather, a word not in the spelling dictionary), you see the Spelling dialog box (shown in Figure 2.7) with the suspect word displayed in the Not in Dictionary field.

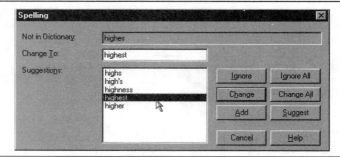

FIGURE 2.7:   The Spelling dialog box displays a suspected misspelled word and offers a list of suggested replacements.

If the Word Is Spelled Correctly

The spell-checker flags many words that are actually correct, especially proper names and technical or medical terms. When the suspect word is correct, you can do any of the following:

- Choose the Ignore button to bypass this word and continue to check the spelling; if the suspect word appears again, it's flagged again.

- Choose the Ignore All button, bypassing all occurrences of the suspect word during this spell-checking session.

- Choose the Add button to add this word to the custom dictionary. In the future, FrontPage will recognize that the word is spelled correctly.

If the Word Is Misspelled

If the word in question is not correct, you can either type the correct spelling into the Change To field or select one of the words from the Suggestions list (which then appears in the Change To field). At this point you have some options:

- Choose the Change button to replace the misspelled word with the word in the Change To field.

- Choose Change All to change all occurrences of the misspelled word in the active page.

You can also choose the Cancel button at any time to end the spell-checking session.

Finding and Replacing Text

You use the Edit ➤ Find command to find all occurrences of text you specify in the active page. If you want to search through all the pages in a multi-page web, use the Tools ➤ Find command in the Explorer.

In the Find dialog box, shown below, enter the characters you want to find. You can choose to find those characters only when they are a complete word or when the case (UPPER or lower) exactly matches the case of the text you entered. You can also choose to search up or down the page, starting from the insertion point.

To begin the search, choose the Find Next button. The first occurrence of the specified text is selected in the page. At this point you can:

- Choose Find Next to find the next occurrence.

- Click Cancel to close the Find dialog box.

- Click on the page in the Editor so you can continue to work in it, perhaps to edit the text that was found. The Find dialog box remains open.

For the Edit ➤ Replace command, specify the text to search for as well as the text with which to replace it. If you leave the Replace With field empty, the text that is found is deleted.

You perform the Replace operation with three buttons in the Replace dialog box:

- **Find Next** finds the next occurrence of the specified text but does not replace it.

- **Replace** replaces the current occurrence, then moves on to find the next occurrence.

- **Replace All** replaces every occurrence of the text without further action on your part.

 NOTE   Practice safe computing by saving the page before using the Replace All command on the entire page.

When you're finished finding and replacing text, you can click on the page to leave the dialog box open and continue working on the page, or click the Cancel button to close the dialog box and return to the page.

HTML and Browsers—The Start and End of Your Work

All of the pages in the Editor are built from HTML code. However, the Editor does such a good job of displaying the page and letting you manipulate it that you often just work along without even thinking about the underlying code that the Editor is creating.

Nonetheless, HTML is there and waiting if you need it, and the more you work with Web pages, the more often you may want to take a peek at the HTML code. The Editor gives you several ways to interact with a page's HTML code:

- You can view the code at any time, making changes to it as though you're working on the page in a text editor.

- You can insert HTML tags that the Editor does not support.

- You can view your page in any available Web browser, so you can see exactly how the HTML in the page will be interpreted by various browsers.

Seeing the HTML Source Code

When you want to see the HTML code behind the active page in the Editor, click on the HTML tab on the bottom left of the window. The display in the Editor window switches to show the actual HTML code for your page—the same code that is saved on disk when you save your page.

Figure 2.8 shows the HTML view for the page that was displayed in the Editor in Figure 2.5. If you're just viewing the code and do not want to make any changes to it, you can return to the page in the Editor by clicking on the Normal Tab.

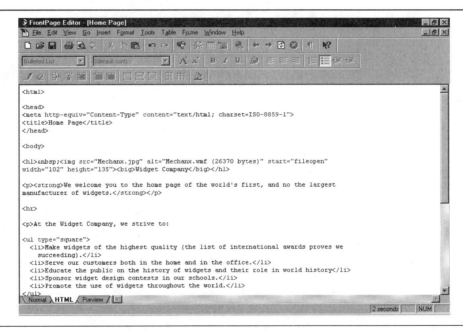

FIGURE 2.8: Clicking on the HTML tab lets you view or edit the underlying HTML code for a page.

The HTML view is just another way to display your web page. Use caution when making changes to the HTML code, as they're reflected in the page when you return to the Editor. If, for example, you accidentally delete one of the angle brackets for an HTML tag, you'll see the result reflected on the page when you switch back to Normal view.

NOTE   Although many of the Editor's menu choices are disabled while you are in HTML view, you can still use Cut, Copy, and Paste to move or copy text. Find and Replace are also still active so you can, for example, search for all occurrences of the <STRONG> tag (bold) and replace them with the <EM> tag (italics).

HTML view not only displays the underlying HTML for the active page, it also helps you interpret it by color-coding it:

- The text you enter is shown in the normal black.

- HTML tags are shown in purple.

- The attribute or argument names within tags are shown in red.

- The actual attributes you enter (via the Editor) are shown in blue.

The different colors make it a lot easier to make sense of the code as you scroll through it. Viewing the underlying code is always a good exercise to help you get a feel for the ins and outs of HTML.

Previewing Your Work in a Browser

The ultimate outcome for a Web page is to be viewed within a Web browser. Although the FrontPage Editor does a very good job of showing you how a page will appear within a browser, it can never offer the final and absolutely definitive view of a page. No editor can.

The primary reason for this is that HTML is designed to be very flexible in the way its pages are formatted. The same HTML code can be interpreted somewhat differently in different browsers.

On top of that inherent flexibility is the fact there are just too many variables that affect the ultimate appearance of a page within a browser. For example, a browser running within a screen resolution of 800 by 600 pixels displays over 50 percent more of a page than one running within a screen resolution of 640 by 480.

The only way to be sure how your web looks is to view it within a browser or, preferably, in several of the more popular browsers. You can also view a single page, right from the Editor, so you can immediately see how it appears in that browser. Click on the Preview tab at the bottom of the editing window to view the page. (This requires that you have Microsoft Internet Explorer 3.0 or higher installed on your system. If you do not, you won't have a Preview tab.)

To open an actual browser such as Microsoft Internet Explorer or Netscape Navigator, choose File ➤ Preview in Browser. The Preview in Browser dialog box, shown in Figure 2.9, opens so you can choose which browser you want to use.

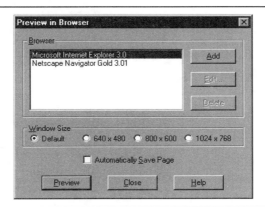

FIGURE 2.9: The Preview in Browser dialog lets you choose a browser to view your page.

When you initially install FrontPage, it searches for browsers on your computer and automatically adds installed browsers to the list in the Preview in Browser dialog. If you add other browsers after you install FrontPage 98, you can add them to the list by clicking on the Add button in the Preview in Browser dialog box. You enter a name for the browser, which appears in the list of browsers, then enter the command that opens that browser. Use the Browse button to select the program from a typical Windows files dialog box.

Once the new browser appears in the list, you can select it to preview the active page in the Editor. Use the Edit or Delete buttons in the Preview in Browser dialog box to revise the settings for a browser or to remove a browser from the list.

If you have not saved the page you want to view, click on the Automatically Save Page check box. (If you don't, you'll be told that you can't view the page until you save it.) FrontPage opens a Save As dialog box if you haven't saved the page. If you've previously saved the page, it just goes ahead and saves it again before displaying it in the browser.

Before clicking on the Preview button, select a size for the browser's window in the Window Size group of options. For example, if your computer's resolution is 800 by 600, you can choose the 640 by 480 option to see how the page looks in a browser that has been maximized to full-screen size on a computer whose screen resolution is 640 by 480. Choose the Default option to open the browser without specifying a size.

Now you're ready to click on the Preview button to open the Save As dialog box. If you've already saved your page, this action takes you directly to the browser you selected.

Saving a Page for the First Time

When you see the Save As dialog box for the first time, shown in Figure 2.10, you'll notice right away that it looks different than in other Windows applications. The dialog box shows all the files in the current web and asks for a URL. Because FrontPage already knows the protocol you are using and the path location is selected in the listbox above, all you have to enter here is the file name you want to use. Press Tab to move to the Title field and enter the title you want to use for your page. The title appears in the Title bar and in the Explorer views of your web.

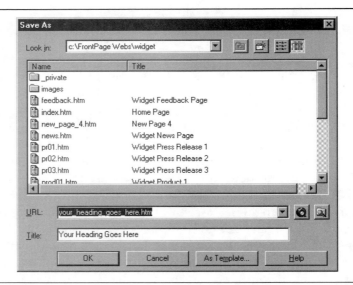

FIGURE 2.10: The FrontPage Save As dialog box asks for a URL rather than a file name.

As soon as you click on the OK button in the Save As dialog box, the dialog box closes and the page opens in the designated browser so you can see how your page actually looks when others view it on the Web. You can see how the page looks when displayed within the specified window size and how the features within the page compare to the way they appear in the Editor. When you're ready to go back to work on the page, switch back to the Editor in one of the usual Windows ways: Alt+Tab, click on the Editor on the Task bar, minimize the browser, or close the browser completely. When you are ready to view the page again in the same browser, all you have to do is click the Preview in Browser button on the toolbar.

Printing Your Page

You can print the active page in the Editor the same way you print a document in your word processor. Of course, the need to print arises only rarely, since a page is meant to reside on a Web site and be viewed by a browser. Nonetheless, you may wish to print pages to proof them for accuracy, hang them on your refrigerator, or show them to others when you can't access a computer.

To print the active page using the current print settings, choose File ➤ Print or click on the Print button on the toolbar. This displays the standard Print dialog box, in which you can specify the number of copies to print, the range of pages to print, and the printer to which the job should be sent.

Defining the Page Layout

Before you print, you can modify the page layout via the File ➤ Page Setup command; its dialog box is shown here. You can specify the margins for the printout, as well as the text that should appear in the header and footer on each page.

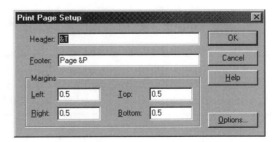

You can enter any text you want in the header and footer, but there are two special codes the Editor includes by default— &T displays the page's title (the same title you gave the page when you saved it—choose File ➤ Page Properties if you want to change it) and &P displays the page number in the printout (there are no page numbers within the context of the web).

> Unlike your word processor, the settings in the Page Setup dialog box affect all the pages (files) you print within the Editor, and remain in effect until you change them.

Previewing the Printout

Before you print a page, take a few seconds to preview what your printout will look like on paper by choosing File ➤ Print Preview. The buttons on the preview toolbar perform the following tasks:

- **Print**   Closes the preview but opens the Print dialog box, where you can print as usual to a printer.

- **Next Page**   Displays the next page of a multipage printout; you can also use PgDn. The left side of the status bar shows the current page number.

- **Previous Page**   Displays the previous page; you can also use PgUp.

- **Two Page/One Page**   Toggles between displaying a single page or two pages of the printout.

- **Zoom In**   Magnifies the preview so you can see more detail on the page, but less of the entire page.

- **Zoom Out**   Shows you more of the page but shrinks the size of the characters on it.

> Here's a fast way to zoom in on a specific portion of the page without having to hunt for it after the screen is magnified. Just point to the portion of the preview you want to see and click. Click again to zoom out again.

- **Close**   Closes the preview and returns to the active page; you can also press Esc.

Again, your Web pages are meant to be viewed within your Web site by a browser, so you'll probably print pages only when you're developing the web and want input from others, or want to lay it all out and see how the pages fit together.

This chapter has introduced you to the FrontPage Explorer and Editor, and has shown you some of the basic editing tools FrontPage offers. In the next chapter, you'll learn how to add some of the bells and whistles that Web pages are famous for.

Are You Experienced?

Now you can...

- ☑ **Create a new web**
- ☑ **Open, close, and save a web**
- ☑ **Switch between the Explorer and the Editor**
- ☑ **Add content to a web page**
- ☑ **Add special characters**
- ☑ **Check the spelling of a page**
- ☑ **Find and replace text**
- ☑ **View the underlying HTML code**
- ☑ **Save a web page**
- ☑ **Preview a web page in a browser**
- ☑ **Print a page you are working on**

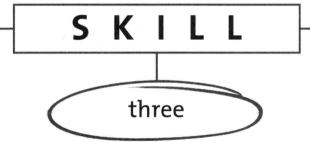

S K I L L

three

Working with Lists and Headings

- ❑ Dividing a page with a horizontal line
- ❑ Changing the properties of a line
- ❑ Creating an outline structure with headings
- ❑ Creating and working with bulleted and numbered lists
- ❑ Changing the look of a list, including using Image Bullets
- ❑ Nesting lists
- ❑ Creating collapsible lists
- ❑ Creating other types of lists

In this Skill, you learn how the FrontPage Editor lets you organize your pages into logical sections with horizontal lines, headings, and lists. These features can make your Web page more attractive and easier for users to browse.

Creating Sections with Horizontal Lines

Perhaps the simplest way to add definition to a Web page is by inserting a horizontal line with the Insert ➤ Horizontal Line command. This adds the HTML tag <HR>, and is often referred to as a horizontal rule. By default, the line spans the entire width of the page in the Editor or in a browser. It is a simple but very effective way to delineate one section from another, as shown in Figure 3.1.

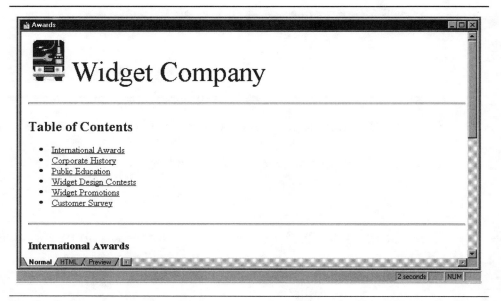

FIGURE 3.1: You can use horizontal lines to divide sections within a page.

In this case, the page has a banner headline and graphic across the top, with a horizontal line separating the banner and graphic from a hyperlinked table of contents. Beneath the table of contents is another line, followed by the main body of the page (which you cannot see in Figure 3.1). The lines create obvious divisions between logical sections of the page.

Changing the Look of a Line

The default horizontal line is thin. To modify the look of a horizontal line, open its Properties dialog box (shown here) by right-clicking on the line and choosing Horizontal Line Properties from the shortcut menu. You can change the width, height, alignment, and color of the line.

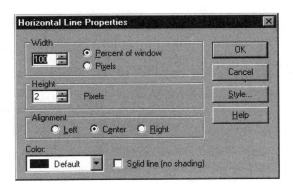

- **Width**   The width of a default line is 100 percent of the width of the Editor or browser window, so it always spans the page. Change the percentage to 50 for a line half the width of the window. Choose Pixels to specify an exact width for the line, no matter how wide the window may be. If the resulting line is longer than the width of window, the portion that extends beyond the edge of the window is simply hidden from view.

NOTE   A *pixel* is an individual display element on a screen. For example, if your monitor's display *resolution* is 640 × 480, there are 640 pixels across and 480 pixels down the screen. If you need a graphic element like a line to span the screen, you shouldn't specify its width in pixels because some users may have their display set at a different resolution.

- **Height**   The default height, or thickness, of the line is two pixels; increase or decrease the height as needed.

- **Alignment**   If you specify a width other than 100 percent for the line, you can align the line to the left or right side of the window or center it within the window. You can choose different alignments even if the line is set to 100 percent, but the effect won't be noticeable.

- **Color**   Select a color for the line; you can also choose to have the line displayed with a shadow effect or as a solid line.

> The Style button on the Horizontal Line Properties dialog box, and numerous other dialog boxes, takes you to the cascading style sheet properties, a new feature in FrontPage 98. For more about cascading style sheets, see Skill 10: *Creating a Consistent Look for Your Web.*

Using Images as Lines

Another common way to create a dividing line in a page is to use a graphic image as a line. Lines and horizontal images both serve the same purpose, but the image can include multiple colors, patterns, or a picture.

> One small disadvantage of a graphic image is that it takes time for an image to download, while horizontal lines are quickly created "on site" by the browser's interpretation of the HTML <HR> tag. However, most line image files are small, and if you reuse the image elsewhere in the page or in the Web site, the browser only needs to download it once.

FrontPage comes with a collection of clip art images, several of which are suitable for horizontal lines. You'll read more about using clip art images within your pages in Skill 8: *Displaying Images on Your Pages.*

Creating a Hierarchy with Headings

A very common and quite efficient way to add structure to a Web page is through the use of headings. Just take a look at the table of contents of this book to see headings in action; a Skill is divided into several main headings, each of which may contain several subheadings. Those subheadings may contain yet other subsubheadings. It's essentially the structure of an outline, only with a lot of text and graphics between the headings.

A Web page can have up to six levels of headings, which you create by applying paragraph formats. Because headings are paragraph styles, they're applied to an entire paragraph, not just selected text. The HTML tags that FrontPage creates for the six different headings are easy to remember: <H1> for heading 1, <H2> for heading 2, and so on.

To make a heading, first click within the paragraph of text you want as the heading, and then choose one of the six headings from the Change Style list on the Format toolbar, as shown here.

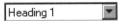

You can also pick a heading from a list of paragraph styles by opening the Format Paragraph dialog box, either by choosing the Format ➤ Paragraph command on the menu, or right-clicking on the paragraph and selecting Paragraph Properties from the shortcut menu.

If you look back at Figure 3.1, you'll see examples of three different headings. The Widget Company heading at the top of the page is level 1, the Table of Contents is a level 2 heading, and the International Awards heading is level 3. If you ignore the graphic at the top of the page and the items under the Table of Contents heading other than International Awards, the HTML code for the headings and the horizontal lines between them looks like this:

```
<H1>Widget Company</H1>
<HR>
<H2>Table of Contents</H2>
<HR>
<H3>International Awards</H3>
```

As with all HTML codes, there is no built-in style for headings—different Web browsers might interpret the look of a heading in a different way. In general, a level 1 heading is in a larger, bolder font than a lower-level heading and may have a blank line above and below it. In the FrontPage Editor, the headings look the same way they do in Microsoft's Internet Explorer Web browser. A sample of the six headings within that browser is shown here.

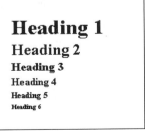

Although headings help organize a page, FrontPage has no rules about how you use them. You are free to turn any text into a heading and use the various levels of headings in any order you choose. For example, you could choose to use level 5 headings for titles and level 1 headings for subtitles. But, it makes very good sense to use them as you would in an outline, relying on the fact that all browsers make higher level headings look "more important" than lower level headings.

For example, the first heading you use on the page should usually be the highest level that appears in that page, although you don't have to start with level 1 (you may choose to start with level 2 and go on from there). Once you pick the highest level for a particular page, you'll probably want to continue using lower levels for subsequent headings.

Organizing Data within Lists

A very practical way to organize groups of items on a page is to arrange them in a list. There are several built-in lists in HTML. The two most useful are:

- **Bulleted list**   Prefaces each item (paragraph) in the list with a bullet. Bulleted lists begin with the <UL> tag because they are also called *unordered lists*.

- **Numbered list**   Numbers each item in the list. The <OL> tag begins the list, which is also called an *ordered list*. The browser applies the appropriate number to each line when it opens the page, so you can add or delete items from the list while you create the page without having to worry about updating the numbering.

You can create a list before you enter the items or after. Each item in the list is a separate paragraph.

Creating a List from Existing Text

Suppose you have text that you've already entered on a page, and you want to turn it into a bulleted list. For example, the left side of Figure 3.2 shows the table of contents from Figure 3.1 before it was changed to a bulleted list.

Table of Contents	Table of Contents	Table of Contents
International Awards	• International Awards	1. International Awards
	• Corporate History	2. Corporate History
Corporate History	• Public Education	3. Public Education
	• Widget Design Contests	4. Widget Design Contests
Public Education	• Widget Promotions	5. Widget Promotions
	• Customer Survey	6. Customer Survey
Widget Design Contests		
Widget Promotions		
Customer Survey		

FIGURE 3.2: You can turn multiple paragraphs into a bulleted list

To turn paragraphs like these into a bulleted list, simply select them all and click on the Bulleted List button on the Editor's Format toolbar or select Bulleted List from the Change Style list on the Format toolbar. The resulting bulleted list is shown in the middle of Figure 3.2.

It's just as easy to turn existing text into a numbered list. With the text selected, click on the Numbered List button on the Format toolbar or choose Numbered List from the Change Style drop-down list on the Format toolbar. The result is shown on the right side of Figure 3.2. You can switch back and forth between the two list styles at any time.

In both examples shown in Figure 3.2, the six selected paragraphs are reduced to a single paragraph when they are converted to a list. List styles, like headings, are paragraph styles, so you don't have to select all the entries in a list to switch to the other type of list. Just click anywhere in the list before clicking on the Numbered List or Bulleted List button.

Here's the HTML code for the bulleted list in Figure 3.2. (The list in Figure 3.2 includes hyperlinks, but they're left out of this code so that you just see the code for the list.)

```
<H2>Table of Contents</H2>
<UL>
    <LI>International awards</LI>
    <LI>Corporate history</LI>
    <LI>Public education</LI>
    <LI>Widget design contests</LI>
    <LI>Widget promotions</LI>
    <LI>Customer survey</LI>
</UL>
```

The code for the numbered list is the same, except that the beginning and ending tags for the unordered list are replaced with those for an ordered list: <OL> and </OL> appear in place of the <UL> and </UL> tags, respectively. As always with HTML, the way a browser formats the list, such as the amount of indentation and the style of the bullets, varies from browser to browser. On the other hand, graphics look the same in every browser. Later in this Skill, you'll find out how to use graphic images as bullets.

Creating a List As You Type

You can also create a list as you type the items into the list. Here's how to create the table of contents bulleted list shown in the center of Figure 3.2:

1. On a new blank line in the page, click on the Bulleted List button. You'll see a bullet appear next to this line, which is now the first line in the list.

2. Type the text you want to appear on this line; in the list shown in Figure 3.2, the first entry is **International Awards**.

3. Press Enter to move to the second line in the bulleted list. Type the item text, and press Enter. Continue with each new line in the list.

4. When you have typed the last item in the list, either press Enter twice or press Ctrl+Enter to finish the list.

The first new line following the list is in the Normal style.

Working in a List

Let's look at how to perform some typical tasks in a bulleted or numbered list:

-   To add an item within a list, place the insertion point at the beginning of a line and begin typing. The text you type is inserted in front of the existing text. Press Enter to move the existing text to the next line.

-   To add an item to the end of a list, place the insertion point at the end of the last item in the list and press Enter to create a new list item.

-   To select one item in the list, move the mouse pointer to the left of the item's bullet or number and click.

-   To select the entire list, move the mouse pointer to the left of the bullets or numbers and double-click.

- To delete an item, select it, then press Del or choose Edit ➤ Clear from the menu.

- To change a list to another list type, select the entire list and either click a list button on the Format toolbar, choose a different list style from the Change Style drop down list, or choose a list style in the Bullets and Numbering dialog box (Format ➤ Bullets and Numbering).

Changing the Look of a Bulleted or Numbered List

The Bulleted List and Numbered List buttons on the Format toolbar create lists in the default style, but you can choose other types of bullets or numbering for lists. The easiest way to see the effects of changing the list style is by selecting an existing list, and then choosing Format ➤ Bullets and Numbering, or by right-clicking on the list and choosing List Properties from the shortcut menu.

The List Properties dialog box contains four tabs:

- **Image Bullets**   Use an existing image as the bullet character. Click the Browse button to locate the file. In FrontPage 98, you can even use animated images as bullets. If you have a theme applied to the page, you can click the Use Images from Current Theme button. For more about themes, see Skill 10: *Creating a Consistent Look for Your Web.*

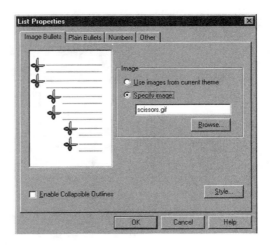

- **Plain Bullets**   Choose the style of bullets you want to use in the list, such as solid or hollow round bullets. The first choice, which shows no bullets, removes the HTML list tags and returns the list to normal text.

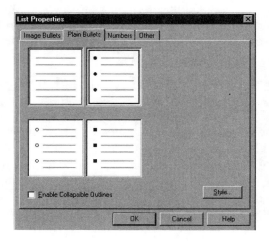

- **Numbers**   Choose the numbering style for a numbered list, such as Arabic or Roman numeral numbering, or uppercase or lowercase lettering. The first choice, which shows no numbering, returns the list to normal text. In the option labeled Start At, you can specify the starting number for the list (the default is 1).

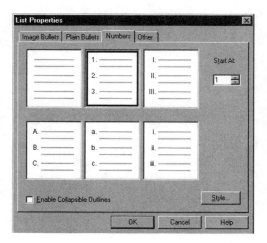

- **Other**   Choose a list style, such as Bulleted, Numbered, or Definition (see "Creating Other Types of Lists" later in this Skill). Choose (None) to turn a list back into normal text.

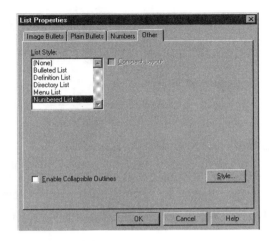

Changing the List properties from the default adds attributes to the HTML tag for the list. For example, if you select the Roman numeral numbering list and set the Start At property at V (5), the HTML tag that marks the beginning of the list looks like this:

```
<OL TYPE="I" START="5">
```

Creating a Nested List within a List

You can nest one list within another so that the second is a subordinate of the first. This lets you create tables of contents with chapter titles and section titles, or display lists of inventory items grouped by category or employee e-mail addresses by department. In short, nested lists provide a good way to display information that has to be *grouped* to make it easier to use or understand. Shown here is the original bulleted list from Figure 3.2 with a second list nested within it.

- International Awards
- Corporate History
- Public Education
    - ○ Kidz Widget Magazine
    - ○ Public Television Widget Night
    - ○ Widgets at Home Pamphlet
- Widget Design Contests
- Widget Promotions
- Customer Survey

NOTE   Although the FrontPage Editor uses different types of bullets for the main list and nested list, some browsers do not.

Here is how you create the nested list shown in the previous example:

1. At the end of the Public Education line, press Enter to create a new item in the primary list.

2. With the insertion point still on the new line, click on the Increase Indent button on the Format toolbar.

3. Now click on the Bulleted List or Numbered List button to turn this new line into a list item.

4. Enter the text for the line and press Enter to create the next item in the nested list.

5. Continue to create new items until you're finished with the nested list. Then simply move the insertion point to another location in the page.

Collapsing Outlines

On each List Properties page there is a checkbox called Enable Collapsible Outlines. If you're familiar with Outline view in Microsoft Word, or use the Windows Explorer to view files and folders, you understand the basic concept around collapsible outlines. Users can click on a bullet and the points underneath will collapse to show only the heading or expand to display all of its subpoints.

Collapsible outlines are a new feature of FrontPage 98 and require a Web browser that supports Dynamic HTML, such as Microsoft Internet Explorer 4.0. If you attempt to preview a page that has dynamic HTML elements without a supporting browser, you receive a warning like the one shown below:

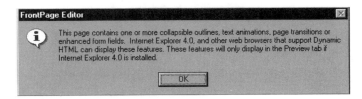

You can include collapsible outlines on your pages even if you're using a browser that doesn't support Dynamic HTML, but you won't be able to see how they affect your overall design.

NOTE It doesn't make sense to rely on collapsible outlines for Web sites until more browsers support Dynamic HTML. However, some companies that include Internet Explorer 4.0 in their standard desktop configuration are already using Dynamic HTML features on their intranets.

Creating Other Types of Lists

There are several other types of HTML lists you can create in the Editor, although they're used only rarely in Web sites. The Menu and Directory lists made early appearances in the HTML standard, but added little functionality to the basic unordered list and have essentially fallen into disuse. They look just like the bulleted list in the Editor, as well as in the most popular browsers. Instead of the <OL> tag, they use the <MENU> and <DIR> tags, respectively.

You can use the Definition list to create a glossary of terms, such as the sample shown here. This type of list is a bit different from the ones we've discussed so far, because it actually consists of two different types of elements—terms and definitions.

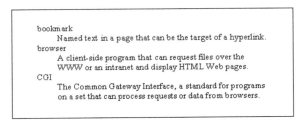

Web browsers usually display the defined term as normal text, with the definition for the term indented from it. Here's how you create a Definition list:

1. On the line where the first defined term appears, choose Defined Term from the Change Style list on the Format toolbar either before or after you type the term.

2. Press Enter; the Editor assumes that the next text you enter is the definition for the term.

3. Type the definition for the term and press Enter. When you press Enter following a definition, FrontPage assumes the next entry is a new term.

4. Continue to type terms and definitions, pressing Enter after each. When you're finished with the list of terms and definitions, press Ctrl+Enter to end the Definition list and add the appropriate HTML tag.

Here's the HTML code for the Definition list shown on the previous page:

```
<DL>
    <DT>bookmark</DT>
    <DD>Named text in a page that...</DD>
    <DT>browser</DT>
    <DD>A client-side program that...</DD>
    <DT>CGI</DT>
    <DD>The Common Gateway Interface is a...</DD>
</DL>
```

Are You Experienced?

Now you can...

- ☑ **Organize a page with horizontal lines**
- ☑ **Use styles to add various heading levels to paragraphs**
- ☑ **Create bulleted and numbered lists**
- ☑ **Modify lists and use images as bullets**
- ☑ **Create collapsible outlines**
- ☑ **Create other types of lists, such as definition lists**

Formatting Your Pages

- ❑ Changing fonts
- ❑ Changing paragraph styles
- ❑ Aligning paragraphs
- ❑ Indenting paragraphs
- ❑ Changing page titles
- ❑ Setting the background color
- ❑ Specifying a background image
- ❑ Defining a background-definition page

This Skill deals with the overall appearance of a page: the way text is displayed, and the background behind the text. You learn how to change the format of text, paragraphs, and the page itself to make your page stand out from the crowd.

Setting Text Properties

The first thing to remember about formatting your pages is that the browser determines how the HTML tags in your pages are displayed. You can play with the formatting of a page all you want, but once it's out on your Web site, all your design work and artistry may be lost when viewed on a one- or two-year-old browser that can't support the features you've included.

You could, of course, choose not to spend much time on page layout—but that would be a mistake. High quality Web browsers that render HTML beautifully are cheap or free, and many users upgrade their browsers several times a year. If a visitor to your Web site is using any recently released browser, for the most part your page should come through as you intended. The exceptions to this rule are the Dynamic HTML features such as collapsible lists (Skill 3), and text animation and page transitions, described in this Skill, which are only supported by the latest versions of top of the line browsers.

Most of the formatting you can apply to text can be found in the Font dialog box (choose Format ➤ Font from the menu). There are also equivalent buttons for many of the same features on the Format toolbar. Text properties, or attributes, include familiar buttons such as bold, italic, underline, subscript, and superscript, but also include other less familiar properties like strikethrough and typewriter.

You can also apply styles to paragraphs and pages, which often changes the default font properties for a page or paragraph. You'll read about these in the *Setting Paragraph Properties* and *Setting Page Properties* sections later in this Skill.

Choosing the Text to Format

To change the format of existing text, first select the text in any of the usual Windows ways:

- Drag the cursor over text with your mouse.

- Click at the beginning of the text you want to select, hold down the Shift key, and click on the end of the selection.

- Hold down the Shift key and make the selection using the keyboard arrow keys.

- Double-click to select a single word.

- Move the mouse pointer to the left of a paragraph (the pointer will change to an arrow instead of an I-beam) and double-click to select the entire paragraph.

- To select the entire document, press Ctrl+Home to move to the top of the document, then hold down the Shift key and press Ctrl+End (or if you're already at the end, hold down the Shift key and press Ctrl+Home).

Once you select text, you are free to modify its format. You can also move or copy it, re-align it, or if all else fails, delete it.

Changing Font Properties

Select the text you want to format, then open the Font dialog box in any of the following ways:

- Choose Format ➢ Font from the menu.

- Choose Edit ➢ Font Properties from the menu.

- Right-click on the selected text and choose Font Properties from the shortcut menu.

- Press Alt+Enter.

Of course, you can also change the formatting of selected text with the buttons and tools on the Format toolbar, shown below. For example, select text and click on the Bold button.

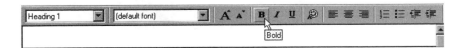

NOTE   You can return selected text to its default paragraph style by pressing Ctrl+Spacebar. This is a quick way to eliminate any changes you've applied to that text, such as a font, font size, or font attribute.

The default settings for the Font tab of the Font dialog box are shown in Figure 4.1. The default font settings lack any special formatting, so each browser displays the text using the browser's default settings. For example, the default settings for the regular text on a page are Normal size, Regular style, Default color, with no font specified. With most browsers, this results in a 12-point Times Roman font.

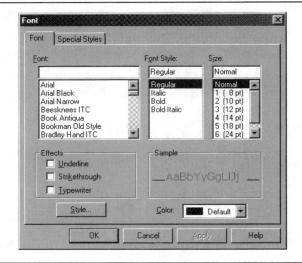

FIGURE 4.1: You can change the look of text with the options in the Font dialog box.

 NOTE Point is a typesetting measurement. One *point* is 1/72", so 12 point type is 1/6" high. (This also means that with 12 point type, there are six lines of text to a vertical inch.)

Can you assume, then, that in most browsers, unstyled text is some version of Times Roman characters about 1/6" tall? No. All but the lowliest browsers allow users to change their default font setting. Screen resolution, which users can also change, determines how large text and images appear when displayed on-screen. Therefore, you can't know whether everyone who views the page sees it exactly the same way. Part of web design is making good choices about the elements you *can* control, and learning to let go of the rest, as you'll see in the following section.

To change Font properties for selected text, make your selections in the dialog box, and preview the effect of the changes on the sample text in the dialog box. When you're finished, either click the Apply button to see the changes take effect in the page while keeping the dialog box open, or click OK to accept the changes and close the dialog box. Let's look at the font options.

 NOTE   If you are creating webs that are displayed in different languages (Japanese, French, etc.), you can open the Options dialog box (Tools ➤ Options) and use the Default Font tab to specify the default fonts that are used for different character sets.

Font

You can select a specific font from the list of all the fonts available to Windows on your computer. You can also choose a font from the Change Font list on the Format toolbar. Again, when using the Font dialog, keep your eye on the Sample pane in the dialog box to see the effect of the font change on the sample text.

The font you choose appears in the FACE attribute for the <FONT> tag in the HTML code, such as:

```
<FONT FACE="Arial">This is not the default font.</FONT>
```

Now comes one of the caveats we referred to earlier: Although you can apply any font from the list in the dialog box, browsers display fonts by loading them from the local machine. If the font you choose isn't installed on the browser's computer, the browser displays the text in its default font. (You remember, Times Roman, 12 point—boring.) The trick is to shoot for the majority of users by choosing the more common (albeit less exciting) fonts like Times New Roman and Arial that are installed on almost every computer.

When you become confident as a FrontPage user and want to dabble in HTML, you can open the HTML code by clicking on the HTML tab, then edit the code to include multiple font names in the FACE attribute. If a browser doesn't have the first font, it tries the second, and so on until it finds one it does have. If none of the fonts listed are installed locally, it uses the default font. Here's how the previous code looks with alternate fonts included:

```
<FONT FACE="Arial,Helvetica,Humana">This is...</FONT>
```

Skill 4

Font Style

The Font Style list includes the standard font style options: Regular (no bold or italic), Bold, Italic, and Bold Italic. You can also press Ctrl+B and Ctrl+I to apply or remove these styles from selected text, or use the Bold and Italic buttons on the Format toolbar to toggle text styles on or off.

NOTE   The HTML code for the text you make bold is enclosed in the <STRONG> tag; the <EM> (emphasis) tag italicizes text.

Font Size

To change the size of the font, select one of the sizes from the Size list on the Font page of the Font dialog box. The default choice, Normal, doesn't specify a size, so a browser uses the default font size, whatever that might be.

The choices in the Size list range from 1 through 7. The Editor shows a point size in parentheses next to each of those numbers, but you should only use the point sizes as a guide. Font sizes are (you guessed it) interpreted by the browser.

Size 3 is the default font size. If you choose size 4, the browser displays the text in a font one size larger than the default font. If you choose size 1, the text is displayed in a font two sizes smaller than the default. When you look at the Size list, you'll notice that the sizes change on a sliding scale, with two points between the smaller fonts (sizes 1 and 2), and up to 12 points between sizes 6 and 7. When you specify a size, the HTML code created by FrontPage looks like the code below for a font two sizes larger than the default font:

```
<FONT SIZE="5">
```

NOTE   You can also change the font size using the Increase Text Size and Decrease Text Size buttons on the Format toolbar. Click a button once to change to the next size.

Font Effects

Use the Effects options in the Font dialog box (see Figure 4.1) to apply three different effects to text: Underline <U> places a single underline under the text; Strikethrough <STRIKE> draws a line through the text; Typewriter <TT> displays the text in a non-proportional font like those used on manual typewriters. (Before you get nostalgic (or curious), read *The Formatted Paragraph Style* later in this Skill).

Browsers designate hyperlinks by underlining them. Therefore, most visitors to your Web site expect that clicking on underlined text takes them somewhere else. Unless you're creating an entry for the "Most Annoying Web Page" contest, don't underline regular text.

Another way to add interest to a web page is by making effective use of different colors for text. Simply choose a new color for selected text from the Color list in the Font dialog box. As always, choosing Default applies no specific color to the text; each browser uses its own default color to display the text. Choose Custom to create your own color.

If the only text property you want to change is color, it's faster to click the Text Color button on the Format toolbar to open the Color dialog box. Another bonus: the dialog box color palette contains more colors than the Font dialog box color list. If the color you want to use isn't displayed, click the Define Custom Colors button to expand the Color dialog box so you can mix your own color. Click on Add to Custom Colors to add the color you mixed to the Custom Colors palette in the Color dialog box so you can apply it to the selected text.

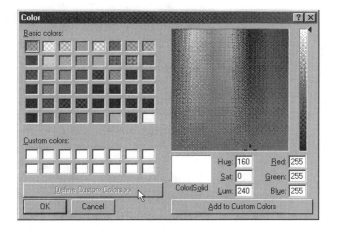

If you already have the Font dialog box open, you can choose Custom from the drop-down list of colors to open the Color dialog box.

Changing the Special Styles Properties

The Font dialog box has another tab labeled Special Styles (see Figure 4.2). This tab offers you more choices for changing the look of text. These choices often overlap other, more commonly used styles.

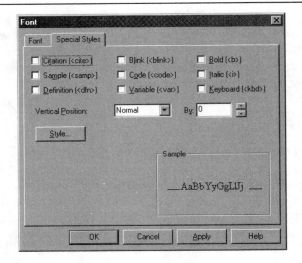

FIGURE 4.2: The Special Styles tab in the Font dialog box.

For example, when you click on the Bold button on the Format toolbar or choose that style in the Font page, FrontPage applies the HTML tag <STRONG> to the text. This code tells a browser to "do something to the text so it stands out." Browsers have traditionally displayed that text in boldface, but it's up to the browser, and some browsers might emphasize <STRONG> text by displaying it in a larger font, rather than bold face.

The Bold option in the Special Styles page applies the bold tag, <B>. This is a newer HTML tag that more specifically indicates what you expect a browser to do. Applying the <B> tag by choosing Bold from the Special Styles tab forces the browser to bold the text, whether or not it displays text that was tagged <STRONG> as boldface.

Most browsers actually have two default fonts. The default proportional font, like Times New Roman, is used for normal text, and the default typewriter font (a non-proportional font like Courier) is used for all Special Styles like the Keyboard, Code, Sample, Citation, and Definition styles. So, Keyboard text looks just like Definition text, but neither looks like regular text.

The Special Styles tab is also where you choose a subscript or superscript style for selected text. For example, suppose you want to enter the formula 6.02 times 10 to the 23rd power. (Of course, you do this at least twice a day.) Let's see how this works in the Editor:

1. Enter the characters in the formula, 6.02*1023, but don't worry about the superscript yet.

2. Select the text you want to make a superscript, in this case the 23.

3. Choose Format ➤ Font and click on the Special Styles tab.

4. In the Vertical Position list, choose Superscript.

5. In the By field, choose 1.

6. Click on the Apply button to see the effect in the page.

7. If you want to increase the height of the superscript relative to its line of text, enter a larger number in the By field (note most browsers simply ignore any height change greater than 2, perhaps because that would be such an unusual layout).

8. Click on OK when you're finished.

The formula below is shown without the superscript, with the superscript set to 1, and with the superscript set to 2.

$$6.02*1023 \qquad 6.02*10^{23} \qquad 6.02*10^{23}$$

Use the same process to create a subscript, but choose the Subscript option in the Vertical Position list. These text formats use the <SUP> and <SUB> tags, respectively.

Formatting Text as You Enter It

If you want to establish the format of text before you type it, change the properties first and then start typing—any text you type after that reflects the changes you made.

However, the default formats are still there, just beyond the insertion point. If you examine the HTML code while entering text, you see the tag to end the current format just past the insertion point, like </B> to end boldface. If you reach the end of a line and press Enter, the next text you type is still bold, because pressing Enter moves the HTML tag to the next line. If you use the down arrow to move to a new line, however, the HTML tag remains in place on the line above, and the next text you enter is in the default, unbolded style.

If you want to quit typing formatted text and enter text in the default style, press the down arrow to move to the next line, or right arrow to move past the HTML tag on the same line. To keep entering text in the current style, make sure you press Enter.

Setting Paragraph Properties

The FrontPage Editor has a variety of styles that affect entire paragraphs, not just selected text within a paragraph. You've already seen some of these styles, like headings and bulleted and numbered lists. When you apply a paragraph style anywhere in a paragraph, the entire paragraph gets formatted. If you want to change multiple paragraphs, select them all first, then apply the style.

You can access the paragraph styles from the Change Style list on the Format toolbar or by choosing Format ➢ Paragraph from the menu. The Paragraph Properties dialog box, as shown in Figure 4.3, does not include the List styles like Bulleted and Numbered. (See Skill 3 if you need more help with List Styles.) Remember that the Normal style removes all paragraph formatting and resets the paragraph back to its default style.

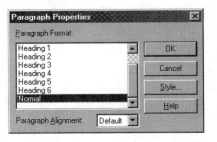

FIGURE 4.3: Change the look of paragraphs with the Paragraph Properties dialog box.

 NOTE   Paragraphs are normally preceded by the <P> tag. When you apply a style to a paragraph, however, the style tags precede and follow the paragraph (for example, the <OL> tag appears before a numbered list and at the end), so the default paragraph tag <P> is no longer required.

When you press Enter at the end of a paragraph, paragraph styles (like headings) are automatically turned off. (The exceptions are the list styles, where you must press Enter twice to turn them off.) Any text formats you applied independent of the style (bold, underline, font size) stay on. The new paragraph returns to the default paragraph format.

To split a paragraph into two that both have the same formatting, position the insertion point where you want the split and press Enter.

The Formatted Paragraph Style

The Formatted style is particularly useful. A browser displays text in this style in a monospaced font like Courier, where each character takes up exactly the same amount of space. It is the one instance in HTML when multiple spaces are displayed exactly as they appear in the code.

This style uses the <PRE> tag (for preformatted), and lets you use spaces to align text in columns or with indentations, having the characters fall exactly where you expect them to. Before the HTML language included tables (see Skill 7), the Formatted style was the only way to align columns of text on a page.

For example, Figure 4.4 shows a Web page that uses the Formatted style. It was quite easy to align the form fields with one another just by pressing the Spacebar.

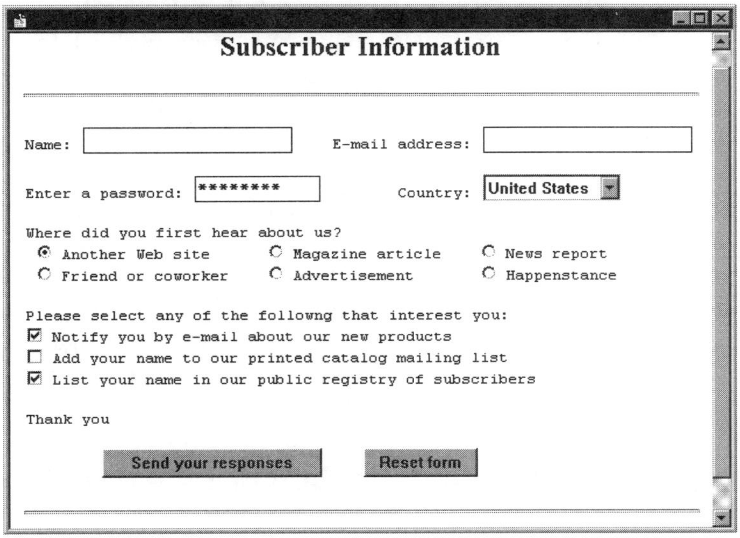

FIGURE 4.4: The Formatted style makes it easy to align the fields in this form page.

Setting Paragraph Alignment

 By default, paragraphs are aligned along the left side of the Editor or browser window. You change the alignment of the current paragraph or selected paragraphs by clicking on the appropriate button on the Format toolbar: Align Left, Center, or Align Right.

If you prefer, you can choose an alignment from the Alignment drop-down list in the Paragraph Properties dialog box. Right click in the selection and choose Paragraph Properties to open the dialog box. Choosing Default removes any other alignment setting. The default for most browsers is Align Left.

The alignment setting in the HTML code appears as an attribute of the paragraph tag, such as:

```
<P ALIGN="center">
```

Indenting Paragraphs

 The HTML indent is like a block indent used to set off a long quote from other text; both the left and right margins of the text are indented. Click on the Increase Indent button on the Format toolbar to indent the current or selected paragraphs, and FrontPage adds the <BLOCKQUOTE> tag. Each time you click on the Increase Indent button, the indentation is increased. A few browsers automatically italicize <BLOCKQUOTE> text, but indentation alone is the norm.

 To remove indentation one level at a time, click the Decrease Indent button. As described in Skill 3, you can also use the Decrease Indent button to change a selected bulleted or numbered list back to normal text.

Setting Page Properties

Each Web page has its own set of properties that you can access by choosing File ➤ Page Properties, or by right-clicking anywhere on the page and choosing Page Properties from the shortcut menu. The Page Properties dialog box has five pages: General, Background, Margins, Language, and Custom. Each is described in the sections that follow.

Changing the Title and Other General Options

We'll take a quick look at all the settings for the General page. You might choose to change some of these settings now; others you'll probably want to leave as is until you learn more about them in later Skills.

The General page of the Page Properties dialog contains the following settings (see Figure 4.5).

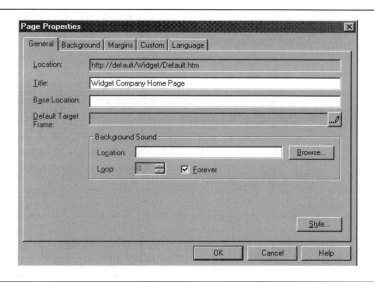

FIGURE 4.5: The General page of the Page Properties dialog box.

- **Location** Displays the page's complete URL or file name and path. You can't change a page's location in this dialog box. To move the page to a new location, use the File ➢ Save As command on the Editor menu or rename/move the page or web in the FrontPage Explorer.

- **Title** Displays and lets you revise the page's title. You usually create a title the first time you save a page (see *Saving a Page* in Skill 2). In the HTML view, you'll find the <TITLE> tag within the <HEAD> tag near the top of the page. Giving your web a good title is critical, because the title is used by Web search engines. A poorly titled page is very frustrating for users because the page shows up in search results when it shouldn't. It's also frustrating for you, because users who you wish to attract to your page won't be able to locate it by searching. The title should accurately and briefly describe the contents of your page. Web browsers display the page's title in their title bar, and offer the title as the default name when you save the page's URL as a favorite or bookmarked location, so the title needs to remind users about the contents of the page.

- **Base Location**   If you enter an absolute URL here, you ensure that any hyperlinks on this page that use relative URLs always point to the correct target. (Absolute URLs are discussed in *Understanding Links* in Skill 6.)

- **Default Target Frame**   If your page is displayed within a frame set, you can specify the name of the frame that serves as the default frame for all hyperlinks in this page that do not otherwise specify a frame. (Frame sets are discussed in Skill 13.)

- **Background Sound**   To pique a visitor's interest, you may want to specify the name of a sound file, such as a .WAV or .MIDI file, that a browser plays when it opens the page (such as Ta Da!!!!). By default, the sound file plays once. If you want it to repeat, increase the Loop number. Select the Forever checkbox, and the sound loops continuously while the page is open in a browser.

 NOTE   Playing a short, welcoming sound when a page is opened can be a nice feature. Using an annoying sound file even once can be an absolute turn off. So use discretion with background sounds—a little goes a long way.

Changing Background Settings

To set page background properties, move to the Background page of the Page Properties dialog box (see Figure 4.6). You can also open this page by choosing Format ➤ Background from the menu. Changes you make on this page are added as attributes to the page's <BODY> tag.

You can specify a color or an image file that a browser displays as a page's background. The Editor also includes a trick that lets you change the background for many pages in a web in one operation; it's a real time-saver (see *Getting Background Options from Another Page* later in this Skill).

You have two possibilities: you can choose the colors you want to use for background and text, or use the settings from an existing page. Specify Background and Colors is the default choice. The defaults are black text on a white background, which is rather boring, but you can, for example, change the screen to white text on a blue background.

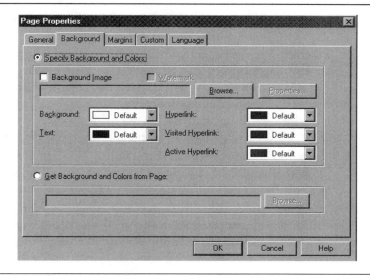

FIGURE 4.6: The Background tab of the Page Properties dialog box.

You can also change the colors used for hyperlinks, visited hyperlinks, and active hyperlinks. However, it's easier to recognize hyperlinks when you use standard colors for them throughout your web. You should probably avoid changing their colors for an individual page unless the default colors conflict with the color you've chosen for that page's background.

Specifying a Background Image

Just as you can paint or wallpaper a wall in your office or on the Windows desktop, you can add color to a page's background, or "wallpaper" it with an image file. A browser normally tiles a small image to fill the background completely, so there's no need to use a large image. In fact, the smaller the image file, the faster it loads into a browser, which is always an important consideration. Visitors to your Web site may skip over a page if it takes too long to load.

Not all images are meant to be backgrounds. For example, dropping a stunning M.C. Escher picture or a detailed graphic of the starship Enterprise may make the page almost jump out of the screen, but also makes all but the largest, boldest text unreadable.

Effective background images are small and textured and can be easily tiled together into a seamless background. They provide a muted and comfortable backdrop that does not dominate the page.

To specify an image for a page's background, select the Background Image option. Then, click on the Browse button to select an image from the Current FrontPage web (such as in the web's Images folder) in the Select Background Image dialog box, shown in Figure 4.7.

To locate a file outside the current web, click on the Use Your Web Browser to Select a Page button for web pages, or the Select a File on Your Computer button to locate a file on a local or network drive. Both of these icons are next to the URL text box. If the image isn't in the current web, but is part of another Web page, you can type a URL for the image in the URL text box.

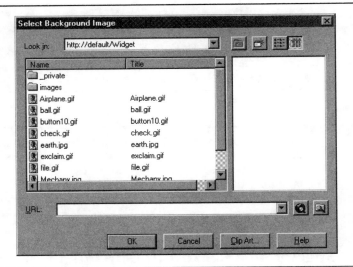

FIGURE 4.7: Choosing a Background Image from the Select Background Image dialog box.

You can access images from the Microsoft Clip Gallery, shown in Figure 4.8, by clicking on the Clip Art button. This may look familiar: FrontPage 98 uses the same clip art gallery as Microsoft Office 97. Select the piece of clip art you want to use and click on the Insert button (you'll read more about clip art in Skill 8).

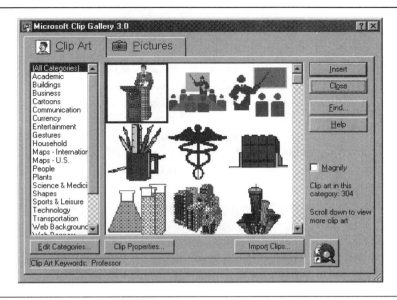

FIGURE 4.8: The Microsoft Clip Gallery offers a variety of images that are suitable page backgrounds.

Whether you choose clip art or another image file, the file's name appears on the Background page of the Page Properties dialog box. When you're finished specifying page properties and you close the dialog box, you'll find the background image you selected, tiled to completely fill the page's background in the Editor just as it would in a browser.

 NOTE When a background image is tiled to fill a page, a browser scrolls the background as you scroll the page. If you choose the Watermark option in the Background tab, browsers that support this feature leave the background image stationary while you scroll the page.

Once you specify a background image file and save it as part of your web, you can return to the Page Properties dialog box and click on Properties to view or modify the properties of this image. These and other image-editing issues are discussed in *Setting Image Properties* in Skill 8.

Saving Images with Your Page

If you include an image file from outside of the web, you should save a copy of the image with the page so that it's always available. FrontPage makes this extraordinarily easy. When you save a page that includes images or other files that came from outside the current web, the Save Embedded files dialog box (see Figure 4.9) opens, listing all the embedded files on the page. You can rename the embedded files, choose a different folder (Images is a good choice), set the action (Save or Don't Save), then click on OK. If you can't remember what a particular image looks like, you can click on the image name, and a thumbnail of image appears in the dialog box Image Preview pane.

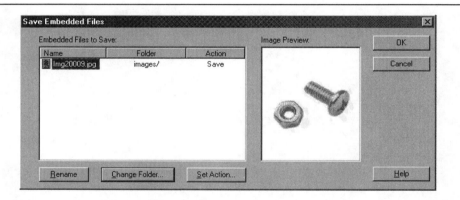

FIGURE 4.9: Setting Save Options for Embedded Files

Getting Background Options from Another Page

Imagine that your Web site has dozens of pages, and you'd like them to share a consistent look. One of the site's most noticeable features is the pale yellow background that includes a rendition of your company's logo. It's a real beauty—understated, yet attention grabbing.

Now imagine that a special someone who signs your paycheck has suggested that perhaps a soft, very light green would make a better background for these pages. This is simple enough to try if your Web site is only a one- or two-pager. Changing the look of your fifty-page work of art, however, is a daunting task.

Happily, FrontPage has a feature that can help you brush off this project single-handedly and in record time: the Get Background and Colors from Page option.

Select this option in the Page Properties' Background Page, then specify a page in your web that you want to copy the Background settings from for use on the current page. There's nothing more to it. Each time the current page is opened in a browser or the FrontPage Editor, the settings for its Background options are read from the other page. Therefore, if you simply change the background settings in the latter page, you will effectively change those settings in all the pages that refer to it.

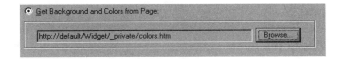

To really take advantage of the this feature, you should use it from the very beginning when building your web. Right now, you're working with a single page web. If each new page you create refers back to this page (or, perhaps, one of just a couple pages) for its colors and background, it's a snap to modify the colors and backgrounds of all the pages in your web just by modifying the few pages that all pages are based on. To find out more ways to standardize your design and make future site maintenance easy, see *Adding Pages Using Templates* in Skill 10.

Setting Page Margins

To specify a top or left margin for the page, open the Margins page of the Page Properties dialog box. By default, both margins are set to zero, so no margins are specified.

You can only define the margin in pixels, so the actual width of the blank area at the top or left side of the page in a browser depends on the screen resolution on the users' computers. For this reason (and the fact not all browsers support the TOPMARGIN and LEFTMARGIN attributes for the <BODY> tag), you should use caution when setting margins for your pages. If you are creating pages for a company intranet and there are company standards for browser software and screen resolution, you should be relatively safe adjusting margins.

Creating Meta Page Information

HTML includes the <META> tag as a way for a page's author to supply information about the page to the server that processes the page and browsers that open the page. For example, an author can include a list of keywords in a <META> tag that the server uses to index that page for Web-wide searching. A browser checks the <META> tag to find out which character set should be used to display the page, or at what interval it should automatically reload the page. When included in a page, the <META> tag appears within the page's <HEAD> tag.

In the Custom tab in the Page Properties dialog box, you add, modify, or remove what FrontPage refers to as variables, which appear within the <META> tag for a page. It's unlikely you'll need to work with variables, but it's good to know where you can access them.

By default, the Editor creates two variables for a page. The single system variable, which isn't displayed on the Custom page, tells a browser or server what type of document this is and the character set that should be used for it. The user variable simply lets the world know which program generated this page. Each variable consists of a name, such as Generator, and a value, such as Microsoft FrontPage 3.0 (the engine that FrontPage 98 uses). If you enter variables on the Custom page, the system variables you create appear as part of the HTTP-EQUIV attribute for the <META> tag, and user variables appear as their own attributes of that tag.

Animating Text and Other Page Elements

As Web designers develop more exciting Web pages by adding objects that move on the page, it becomes harder to find pages that load within a reasonable amount of time. No matter how amazing a page, if visitors get tired of waiting, they can always move on to another location. Dynamic HTML is a way to add movement to a page without compromising loading speed. (Of course, visitors to your site must have a browser, such as Microsoft Internet Explorer 4.0, that can handle Dynamic HTML.) A new Dynamic HTML feature in FrontPage 98 is Text Animation.

Text animation is a bit of a misnomer, because you can animate text, graphics, or other page elements, making them drop in from the sky or fly in from off-page. To animate text or another page element, first select it. Then, choose Format ➤ Animation and select the type of animation you want to apply from the menu shown here.

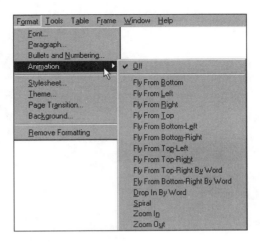

To view the animation, open the page in a browser that supports Dynamic HTML. If a user's browser doesn't support Dynamic HTML, the text or object appears in its regular position on the page.

 NOTE   If you work with Microsoft PowerPoint, you're probably already familiar with animation, called a "build" in older versions.

Are You Experienced?

Now you can...

☑ **Select text using a number of different methods**

☑ **Change text fonts and apply text formatting**

☑ **Change paragraph styles**

☑ **Align and indent paragraphs**

☑ **Change the properties of a page**

☑ **Specify a background image or color**

☑ **Add animation to text and other page elements**

Jones 356-555-3398.

PROGRAMMERS

C C VB, Cobol, exp. Call 534-555-6543 or fax 534-555-6544.

PROGRAMMING

MRFS Inc. is looking for a Sr. Windows NT developer. Reqs. 3-5 yrs. Exp. In C under Windows, Win95 & NT, using Visual C. Excl. OO design & implementation skills a must. OLE2 & ODBC are a plus. Excl. Salary & bnfts. Resume & salary history to HR. 8779 HighTech Way, Computer City, AR

PROGRAMMERS

Contractors Wanted for short & long term assignments; Visual C MFC Unix C/C SQL Oracle Dev elop ers PC Help Desk Support Windows NT & NetWareTelecommunications Visual Basic, Access, HTML, CGI, Perl MMI & Co., 885-555-9933

PROGRAMMER World Wide Web Links wants your HTML & Photoshop skills. Develop great WWW sites. Local & global customers. Send samples & resume to WWWL, 2000 Apple Road, Santa Rosa, CA.

TECHNICAL WRITER Software firm seeks writer/editor for manuals, research notes, project mgmt. Min 2 years tech writing, DTP & programming experience. Send resume & writing samples to: Software Systems, Dallas, TX.

TECHNICAL Software development firm looking for Tech Trainers. Ideal candidates have programming experience in Visual C, HTML & JAVA. Need quick self starter. Call (443) 555-6868 for interview.

TECHNICAL WRITE R/ Premier Computer Corp is seeking a combination of technical skills, knowledge and experience in the following areas: UNIX, Windows 95/NT, Visual Basic, on-line help & documentation, and the internet. Candidates must possess excellent writing skills and be comfortable working in a quality vs. deadline driven environment. Competitive salary. Fax resume & samples to Karen Fields, Premier Computer Corp, 444 Industrial Blvd. Concord, CA. Or send to our website at www.premier.com

WEB DESIGNER

BA/BS or equivalent programming/multimedia production. 3 years of experience in use and design of WWW services streaming audio and video HTML, PERL CGI, GIF, JPEG, Demonstrated interpersonal, organization, communication, multi-tasking skills. Send resume to: The Learning People at www.learning.com

WEBMASTER-TECHNICAL

BSCS or equivalent. 2 years of experience in CGI, Windows 95/NT, UNIX, C, Java, Perl. Demonstrated ability to design, code, debug and test on-line services. Send resume to The Learning People at www.learning.com.

PROGRAMMER World Wide Web Links wants your HTML & Photoshop skills. Develop great WWW sites. Local & global customers. Send sam-

ing tools. Experienced in documentation preparation & programming languages (Access, C, FoxPro) are a plus. Financial or banking customer service support is required along with excellent verbal & written communication skills with multi levels of end-users. Send resume to KKUP Enterprises. 45 Orange Blvd. Orange, CA.

COMPUTERS Small Web Design firm seeks indiv. w/NT, Webserver & Database management exp. Fax resume to 556-555-4221.

COMPUTER/ Visual C/C, Visual Basic Exp'd Systems Analysts/ Programmers for growing software dev. team in Roseburg. Computer Science or related degree preferred. Develop adv. Engineering applications for engineering firm. Fax resume to 707-555-8744.

COMPUTER Web Master for dynamic SF Internet co. Site Dev. test, coord. train. 2 yrs prog. Exp. C C Web C FTP. Fax resume to Best Staffing 845-555-7722.

COMPUTER PROGRAMMER

Ad agency seeks programmer w/exp. in UNIX/NT Platforms, Web Server, CGI/Perl. Programmer Position avail on a project basis with the possibility to move into F/T. Fax resume & salary req. to R. Jones 334-555-8332.

COMPUTERS Programmer/Analyst Design and maintain C based SQL database applications. Required skills: Visual Basic, C, SQL, ODBC. Document existing and new applications. Novell or NT exp. a plus. Fax resume & salary history to 235-555-9935.

GRAPHIC DESIGNER

Webmaster's Weekly is seeking a creative Graphic Designer to design high impact marketing collateral, including direct mail promos, CD-ROM packages, ads and WWW pages. Must be able to juggle multiple projects and learn new skills on the job very rapidly. Web design experience a big plus, technical troubleshooting also a plus. Call 435-555-1235.

GRAPHICS - ART DIRECTOR - WEB-MULTIMEDIA

Leading internet development company has an outstanding opportunity for a talented, high-end Web Experienced Art Director. In addition to a great portfolio and fresh ideas, the ideal candidate has excellent communication and presentation skills. Working as a team with innovative producers and programmers, you will create dynamic, interactive web sites and application interfaces. Some programming experience required. Send samples and resume to: SuperSites, 333 Main, Seattle, WA.

MARKETING

Fast paced software and services provider looking for MARKETING COMMUNICATIONS SPECIALIST to be responsible for its webpage, seminar coordination, and ad plac-

PROGRAMMERS Multiple short term assignments available: Visual C, 3 positions SQL ServerNT Server. 2 positions JAVA & HTML, long term NetWare. Various locations. Call for more info. 356-555-3398.

PROGRAMMERS

C, C, VB, Cobol, exp.
Call 534-555-6543
or fax 534-555-6544.

PROGRAMMING

MRFS Inc. is looking for a Sr. Windows NT developer. Reqs. 3-5 yrs. Exp. In C under Windows, Win95 & NT, using Visual C. Excl. OO design & implementation skills a must. OLE2 & ODBC are a plus. Excl. Salary & bnfts. Resume & salary history to HR. 8779 HighTech Way, Computer City, AR

PROGRAMMERS/ Contractors Wanted for short & long term assignments; Visual C MFC Unix C/C SQL Oracle Developers PC Help Desk Support Windows NT & NetWareTelecommunications Visual Basic, Access, HTML, CGI, Perl MMI & Co., 885-555-9933

PROGRAMMER World Wide Web Links wants your HTML & Photoshop skills. Develop great WWW sites. Local & global customers. Send samples & resume to WWWL, 2000 Apple Road, Santa Rosa, CA.

TECHNICAL WRITER Software firm seeks writer/editor for manuals, research notes, project mgmt. Min 2 years tech. writing, DTP & programming experience. Send resume & writing samples to: Software Systems, Dallas, TX.

COMPUTER PROGRAMMER

Ad agency seeks programmer w/exp. in UNIX/NT Platforms, Web Server, CGI/Perl. Programmer Position avail on a project basis with the possibility to move into F/T. Fax resume & salary req. to R. Jones 334-555-8332.

TECHNICAL WRITER Premier Computer Corp is seeking a combination of technical skills, knowledge and experience in the following areas: UNIX, Windows 95/NT, Visual Basic, on-line help & documentation, and the internet. Candidates must possess excellent writing skills, and be comfortable working in a quality vs. deadline driven environment. Competitive salary. Fax resume & samples to Karen Fields, Premier Computer Corp, 444 Industrial Blvd. Concord, CA. Or send to our website at www.premier.com

WEB DESIGNER

BA/BS or equivalent programming/multimedia production. 3 years of experience in use and design of WWW services streaming audio and video HTML, PERL CGI, GIF, JPEG, Demonstrated interpersonal, organization, communication, multi-tasking skills. Send resume to The Learning People at www.learning.com

WEBMASTER-TECHNICAL

BSCS or equivalent, 2 years of experience in CGI, Windows 95/NT, UNIX, C, Java, Perl, Demonstrated

COMPUTERS Small Web Design firm seeks indiv. w/NT, Webserver & Database management exp. Fax resume to 556-555-4221.

COMPUTER Visual C/C, Visual Basic Exp'd Systems Analysts/ Programmers for growing software dev. team in Roseburg. Computer Science or related degree preferred. Develop adv. Engineering applications for engineering firm. Fax resume to 707-555-8744.

COMPUTER Web Master for dynamic SF Internet co. Site. Dev. test, coord., train. 2 yrs prog. Exp. C C Web C FTP. Fax resume to Best Staffing 845-555-7722.

COMPUTERS/ QA SOFTWARE TESTERS Qualified candidates should have 2 yrs exp. performing integration & system testing using automated testing tools. Experienced in documentation preparation & programming languages (Access, C FoxPro) are a plus. Financial or banking customer service support is required along with excellent verbal & written communication skills with multi levels of end-users. Send resume to KKUP Enterprises, 45 Orange Blvd. Orange, CA.

COMPUTERS Programmer/Analyst Design and maintain C based SQL database applications. Required skills. Visual Basic, C, SQL, ODBC. Document existing and new applications. Novell or NT exp. a plus. Fax resume & salary history to 235-555-9935.

GRAPHIC DESIGNER

Webmaster's Weekly is seeking a creative Graphic Designer to design high impact marketing collateral, including direct mail promo's, CD-ROM packages, ads and WWW pages. Must be able to juggle multiple projects and learn new skills on the job very rapidly. Web design experience a big plus, technical troubleshooting also a plus. Call 435-555-1235.

GRAPHICS - ART DIRECTOR - WEB-MULTIMEDIA

Leading internet development company has an outstanding opportunity for a talented, high-end Web Experienced Art Director. In addition to a great portfolio and fresh ideas, the ideal candidate has excellent communication and presentation skills. Working as a team with innovative producers and programmers, you will create dynamic, interactive web sites and application interfaces. Some programming experience required. Send samples and resume to: SuperSites, 333 Main, Seattle, WA.

COMPUTER PROGRAMMER

Ad agency seeks programmer w/exp. in UNIX/NT Platforms, Web Server, CGI/Perl. Programmer Position avail on a project basis with the possibility to move into F/T. Fax resume & salary req. to R. Jones 334-555-8332.

PROGRAMMERS / Established software company seeks programmer with extensive knowledge in

ment. Must be a self-starter, energetic, organized. Must have 2 web experience. Programming plus. Call 985-555-9854

PROGRAMMERS Multiple term assignments available: C, 3 positions SQL ServerNT S 2 positions JAVA & HTML, long NetWare. Various locations. C more info. 356-555-3398.

PROGRAMMERS

C C VB, Cobol, exp. Call 534 6543 or fax 534-555-6544.

PROGRAMMING

MRFS Inc. is looking for a Windows NT developer. Req yrs. Exp. In C under Win Win95 & NT using Visual C. OO design & implementation a must. OLE2 & ODBC are a Excl. Salary & bnfts. Resum salary history to HR. 8779 Hig Way, Computer City, AR

PROGRAMMERS/ Contr Wanted for short & long term a ments: Visual C, MFCUnix C/C Oracle Developers PC Help Support Windows NT & Net Telecommunications Visual Access, HTML, CGI, Perl MMI 885-555-9933

PROGRAMMER World Wide Links wants your HTML & Phot skills. Develop great WWW Local & global customers. Send ples & resume to WWWL, Apple Road, Santa Rosa, CA.

TECHNICAL WRITER Software seeks writer/editor for man research notes, project mgmt. years tech. writing, DTP & pro ming experience. Send resum writing samples to: Son Systems, Dallas, TX.

TECHNICAL Software develo firm looking for Tech Trainers, candidates have programming rience in Visual C HTML & Need quick self starter. Call 555-6868 for interview.

TECHNICAL WRITER Pr Computer Corp is seeking a c nation of technical skills, know and experience in the follo areas: UNIX, Windows 95/NT, Basic, on-line help & documen and the internet. Candidates possess excellent writing skills be comfortable working in a q vs. deadline driven environ Competitive salary. Fax resu samples to Karen Fields, Pr Computer Corp. 444 Industria Concord, CA. Or send to our we at www.premier.com

WEB DESIGNER

BA/BS or equivalent prog ming/multimedia product years of experience in use design of WWW services strea audio and video HTML, PERL GIF, JPEG. Demonstrated inte sonal, organization, commun multi-tasking skills. Send resu The Learning People at www.lea ing.com.

WEBMASTER-TECHNIC

Managing Webs in the Explorer

❑ Adding pages with the Explorer's Navigation view

❑ Rearranging pages in Navigation view

❑ Working in the Explorer's Hyperlink and Folder views

❑ Updating links when you rename or move a file

❑ Working with file properties

❑ Associating files with editors or viewers

❑ Organizing chores with the Task List

Up to this point, you've been working with a single page web. Now it's time to add pages to your web and link them together so visitors can move around your site easily. The best web designers lay out the entire design for the web first, create the various pages and relationships (links) between the pages, and design the consistent elements that appear on every page before entering the actual content for each page. This process ensures consistency between different sections of the web and correct connections between the pages.

Although you can create pages in the FrontPage Editor then link them together, it is better to create the structure of your web in the FrontPage Explorer. When you construct your web in the Explorer, FrontPage 98 automatically builds links between the pages for you. The Explorer also gives you an inside look at your FrontPage web and reveals the relationships among its files. With the Explorer's ability to update hyperlinks automatically, you are free to add, move, or rename files in your web without worrying about tracking and updating individual links.

In this Skill, you learn how to create additional pages that are automatically linked to your home page; how to move pages; and how to keep track of the myriad tasks that a web designer must manage while developing a web.

Working in Navigation View

With FrontPage 98 there are four ways to view a web site, depending on what it is you want to do to the site: Navigation view, Hyperlinks view, Folders view, and All Files view. When you create a new web, you are immediately taken to *Navigation view*. Figure 5.1 shows a fully developed version of the Widget Company's web in Navigation view. As you can see, Navigation view is actually two views in one. In the top pane, you see an organizational chart of the web called a *site map*. The Home Page, called a *parent page*, is on the top level and the additional pages are shown underneath. In this example, News, Products, and Services are *child pages* to the Home page, but each is also a parent page to other, subordinate pages.

The bottom pane lists all the files and folders contained in the web. Drag the horizontal divider up or down to change the relative size of the panes.

 TIP Click on any of the icons in the Views bar on the left side of the Explorer window to switch between the different views of your web. Changing views does not change the contents of the current web.

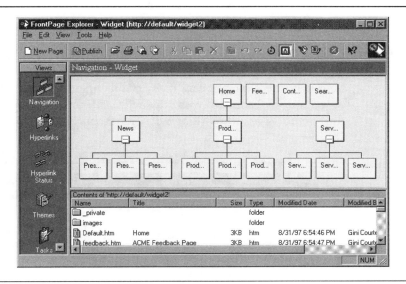

FIGURE 5.1: In Navigation view, FrontPage shows you an organization chart of your web based on the relationship between pages in the web.

 NOTE

To follow along with the activities in this Skill, use the one-page web you worked on in previous skills or create a new one by choosing File ➤ New ➤ FrontPage Web, and click on One-Page Web. Enter a title for the web (click on Change to enter a new location if you wish) and click on OK.

To add a new page to the web, click on the page in the Navigation view site map that serves as parent to the new page. In a one-page web, that's the Home page. (You can create a page on the same level as the Home page by not selecting a page, but you'd rarely want to do this.) Click on the Create New Page button on the toolbar; FrontPage asks you if you want to include Navigation bars to link the pages together and tells you that these navigation bars are placed in the borders of each page:

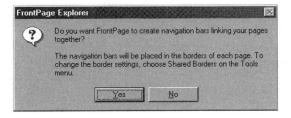

Navigation bars are sets of buttons located on each page that allow visitors to move to another page in the current web. They are typically placed in a section of a page called a *shared border*, a page area that displays the same content on each page in the web. If you're familiar with word processing, you might think of shared borders as the headers or footers of a web page. There is one difference: Shared borders can appear on any or all edges of a page—left, right, top, or bottom. Figure 5.2 shows a web page with all four shared borders turned on. You'll find out more about working with shared borders in Skill 6, *Adding Links for User Navigation*.

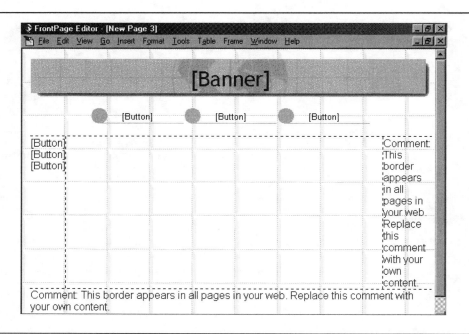

FIGURE 5.2: Shared borders on the top, bottom, left, and right sides of pages share content with other pages in the current web.

When you tell FrontPage to create navigation bars in Navigation view, it automatically adds hyperlinks where appropriate in the current web. Even if you move, delete, or add pages, FrontPage updates the links it created. If you create links yourself, you are responsible for updating them. For this reason, if you want to add pages that are linked to other pages in the current web, it is best to add them in Navigation view and have FrontPage add navigation bars.

Renaming Pages in Navigation View

When you add a new page to your web, it is called New Page *n*, where *n* is the number of new pages you've created in this session, just as new Word documents are called Document *n* and new Excel workbooks are called Book *n*. You can easily change this riveting, sequence-oriented name to something more descriptive by right-clicking on the page and choosing Rename from the shortcut menu. The background around the name in the Navigator diagram turns blue to indicate that it is selected and you can type in the new name.

Moving Pages within a Web

Once you create a page, you can change how it relates to other pages by dragging and dropping it into a new position. Click on the page you want to move, hold down the mouse button, and drag the page until the connecting line attaches to the correct page, as shown in Figure 5.3.

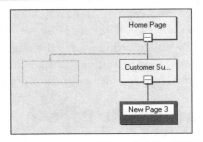

FIGURE 5.3: Change the relationship between pages by dragging and dropping a page into a new position.

If the page you want to reposition has child pages under it, moving the parent moves all the children with it. In other words, you can't break up a family unit by moving the parent—all the kids tag along.

Skill 5

Deleting Pages in Navigation View

There are two options for deleting pages from the Navigation view structure. If you select the page you want to delete and press the Delete key on the keyboard, a dialog box like the one shown here appears with the possible options.

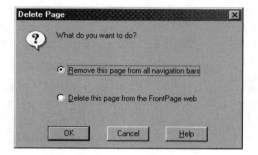

You may then choose to:

1. Remove this page from all navigation bars.

2. Delete the page from the web entirely, which means the page itself and all links to the page are deleted.

Removing a page from all navigation bars is more like hiding the page than deleting the page. FrontPage removes the page and all links to the page from the active web, but keeps the page available for future use. For example, if you have a page you want to work on or have revisions you want to make to a page on a published web, you can remove the page from navigation bars so that visitors can't access the page while it's under construction. When your work is complete, you can add the page back into the web, as you'll see in the section below.

Inserting an Existing Page in Navigation View

You may have some existing pages you want to add in Navigation view so that FrontPage is responsible for maintaining links and navigation bars for them. To add an existing page to the Navigation view site map, select the page in the Files pane and drag it into the desired position in the Navigation view site map.

Viewing All or Parts of Your Web

As your web gets bigger, you'll probably want to see just a branch of the site map at a time, rather than having to scroll through the entire map. In Navigation view, each parent page includes a Collapse button with a minus sign. Click on the Collapse button, as shown here, to hide the child pages under the parent page (and any child pages subordinate to those child pages).

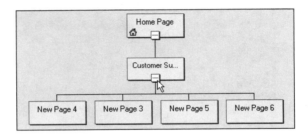

The minus sign changes to a plus sign, called the Expand button. Click on the Expand button to uncover the children of the branch. While you're working on your web, use the Expand and Collapse buttons to display the parts of the web that are relevant.

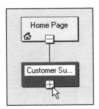

Displaying All of Your Web's Structure

When your web is fully expanded, you may not be able to see the entire site map within your screen display. However, you can easily move around the site map. Hold down the mouse button any place on the display, and when the pointer changes to a hand, drag the site map to move the portion you wish to view into the window. Or, for a fast tour, you can pan back and forth across the site map. This gives you a quick view of hidden parts of the web.

If you really want to see the entire web at once, FrontPage gives you a way to do this, too. Click on the Size To Fit button and FrontPage reduces the web to fit into the Navigator pane. However, if the web is too big, Front Page doesn't display page names in their entirety, but truncates or simply doesn't display page names, as shown in Figure 5.4.

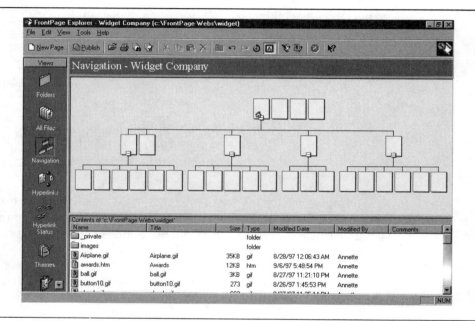

FIGURE 5.4: The Size to Fit button reduces the web so it can be shown in one pane, but you can't display full page names.

While the web is reduced, you can still use the Collapse and Expand buttons and move, insert, and delete pages. Clicking on the Size to Fit button again returns the web to full size.

Rotating the View

Depending on your web's structure, you may find that you can see more of your web if you turn it over on its side, as shown in Figure 5.5.

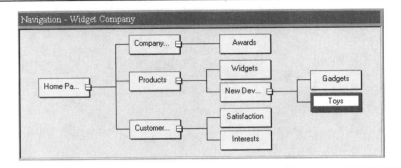

FIGURE 5.5: Rotating the web may make it easier to view.

  Click on the Rotate button on the toolbar to change the rotation. Click it again to return to a vertical rotation.

Printing the Navigation View

As you design your web, you'll find times when it's helpful to have a hard copy available to share with other team members, clients, or supervisors. At any point in the design process, choose File ➤ Print Navigation View to open the Print dialog box. Click on Print to accept the defaults and print a copy of the Navigation view site map.

If you'd rather see how the site map looks before printing it, choose File ➤ Print Preview. FrontPage doesn't give you options for adding headers or footers to the printed page, but it provides you with a printed site map for your web. Navigation view is the only view you can print in the FrontPage Explorer.

Displaying Your Web in Hyperlinks View

Hyperlinks view allows you to see the interconnectedness of your web pages. Like Navigation view, Hyperlinks view, shown in Figure 5.6, is also two views in one: a list of pages in the left pane and a model of their connections in the right pane.

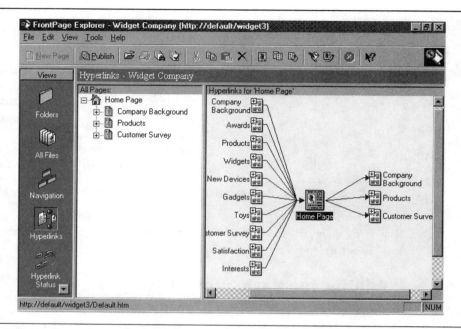

FIGURE 5.6: In Hyperlinks view, the FrontPage Explorer displays the links between web pages.

When you choose View ➤ Hyperlinks, or click on the Hyperlinks icon on the Views bar, the web is displayed according to the hyperlinks in its pages. The All Pages pane (on the left) displays a list of all the pages and other files and URLs that are part of the current web (see Figure 5.6). The right Hyperlinks pane displays a graphical representation of the web—a model that uses the selected item in the All Pages pane as its starting point. Pages and other items like URLs and images are shown as icons in this model, with arrows connecting a page to the links it contains and the files it includes.

The All Pages Pane

The All Pages pane (left pane) lists web pages by HTML page title. File names are used for graphic images and other files that don't have titles, and URLs for links to other web files or pages. Each item is displayed with the relevant icon. You can see some icons in Figure 5.6, and the various icons used by FrontPage are described in Table 5.1. The pages, images, and other items are grouped in a hierarchical manner based on the hyperlinks, images, and other files each page contains. If page A has a link to page B, page B appears as a subordinate of page A beneath it in the list and indented. Embedded items, like an image used as a page's background, are subordinates of the page they are embedded in.

TABLE 5.1: Icons Used in the FrontPage Explorer

Icon	Description
	The Web's home page
	Web page
	Graphic image file (GIF or JPEG)
	Link to an e-mail address
	Link to a URL
	Broken link (no longer valid)
	Error in Web page, usually in a WebBot

An item appears more than once in the All Page pane if it is included in multiple pages or is the target of links in other pages. In the previous example, if page B contains a link back to page A, then page A also appears as a subordinate of page B.

An item with a plus or minus sign contains embedded items or links to other pages. You can navigate through the All Pages pane and expand or collapse levels, just as you can with folders and files in the Windows Explorer:

- Click on the plus sign, or select the page and press → to expand lower levels to show subordinate items and links.

- Click on the minus sign, or select the page and press ← to collapse the item, hiding its subordinates.

- Double-click on a page to toggle between hiding and displaying subordinate items.

- Press Home or End to go to the top or bottom of the list, respectively.

- Scroll through the list using the vertical scroll bar or ↓ or ↑.

- Scroll the list from side to side using the horizontal scroll bar, or pan the list using Ctrl+→ or Ctrl+←.

Skill 5

Expanding the Hyperlink View

 You can expand or contract the scope of the Hyperlink view. Choose View ➤ Hyperlinks to Images from the menu or click on the Hyperlinks to Images button on the toolbar to hide or display image files in both panes of Hyperlinks view. If a site contains many image files, you can turn off this option so you get a better view of other types of files in the web.

 Choose View ➤ Repeated Hyperlinks from the menu or click on the Repeated Hyperlinks button on the toolbar to display or hide multiple links from one Web page to another page, file, or URL.

The default setting in FrontPage is to display only a single link; enabling repeated hyperlinks from the menu or toolbar shows each link to a file or page, even if there are several from the same page. It's not unusual to use the same image for seven different buttons on a page. Working with Repeated Hyperlinks turned off makes sure that you only see a single link from the page to the image, rather than having six extra links cluttering up the Hyperlinks pane.

 Choose View ➤ Hyperlinks Inside Page, or click on the Hyperlinks Inside Page toolbar button to hide or display links back to the page that contains the link. You should hide the internal hyperlinks when you're checking the links between pages so they aren't in the way.

 NOTE   You may often have multiple hyperlinks within a page, such as when you have a table of contents at the top of the page that contains links to locations within the page. In this case, you could use both the Repeated Hyperlinks and Hyperlinks Inside Page buttons to see all the links. You can read about bookmarks and other types of links in *Understanding Links* in Skill 6.

Remember that you can turn these view options on or off at any time, either to see more of the details of your site or to simplify the display.

The Hyperlinks Pane

The Hyperlinks pane (the right pane) of the Explorer's Hyperlink view, as seen earlier in Figure 5.6, is a model of the underlying link relationships among the pages and other items in a web. Each page or file is represented by an icon as well as its title, filename, or URL.

The item you select in the All Pages pane is given the center of focus in the Hyperlinks pane. To change the orientation of the model, right-click on an icon in the Hyperlinks pane and choose Move to Center from the shortcut menu, which shifts the center of focus to the item represented by the icon.

Figure 5.7 shows another example of the Hyperlinks view. The *Widget Product 2* page is selected in the All Pages pane, so it is the focal center in the Hyperlinks pane.

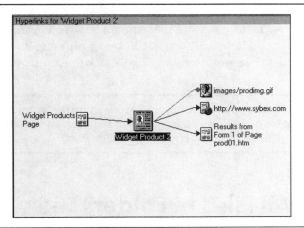

FIGURE 5.7: The Hyperlinks pane shows you the chain of links among the pages and resources in the web.

The Hyperlinks pane shows you a vast amount of information at a glance—information that's very difficult to glean and organize by combing through each page in the web. Here's what you can see in the Hyperlinks pane in Figure 5.7:

- When you're looking at links, read the Hyperlinks pane from left to right. Pages that contain hyperlinks to the page selected in the All Pages pane are shown at the left, with arrows pointing to the page selected in the All Pages pane. In Figure 5.7, the Widget Products Page contains hyperlinks to the Widget Product 2 page.

- The Widget Product 2 page contains hyperlinks to other pages, which are represented by arrows that run from the page's icon to target icons on the right.

- A link arrow that ends in a bullet indicates that the target is included in the page. The Widget Product 2 page has one link to an included resource, an image that appears on the page.

- A link arrow that ends in an arrowhead indicates a hyperlink that opens the link's target. The Widget Product 2 page has two hyperlinks that open other resources. One link is to a page within the current web (*internal link*), and one is a link to a URL outside of the current web (an *external link*).

- Icons for pages that contain links (other than the one at the center of focus) include a plus sign. Click on a plus sign to expand the links, and the plus changes to a minus sign. Click the minus sign to collapse the links.

NOTE   Don't forget that you can focus in on the specific types of links you want to see with the three commands on the View menu—Hyperlinks to Images, Repeated Hyperlinks, and Hyperlinks Inside Page.

Seeing All Files in Folders View

To view your web's folders and files in the Explorer, choose View ➤ Folders or click on the Folders button on the Views bar. The left pane displays the folders contained in the Web site, and the right pane displays all the files in the selected folder. Figure 5.8 shows the Folders view of the Widget web used in earlier examples.

Folders view is very much like the Windows Explorer view of a hard disk. The contents of the folder selected in the All Folders (left) pane are displayed in the Files pane on the right. In the All Folders pane, click on the plus sign on a folder to expand it, displaying the folders it contains. To hide the folders within a folder, click the folder's minus sign.

The Files pane displays columns of information for each file in the web: name, page title, size, type, date and time modified, modifier, and comments. This is the same information you can view and modify in the item's Properties in the Explorer, as you'll see in the next section.

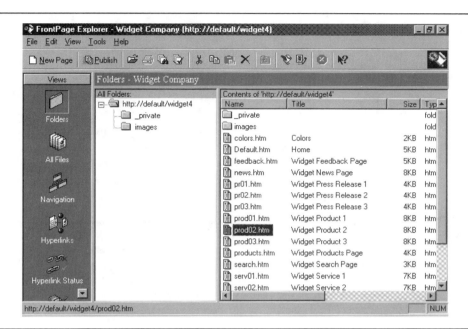

FIGURE 5.8: Folders View provides a detailed list of all the files in your web.

You can manipulate the Files list as you would in the Windows Explorer:

- Click on a column heading to sort the file list by that column. For example, click on the Modified Date column title to see the most recently edited files at the top of the list.

- Click on the column heading again to reverse the sort order.

- Resize a column by dragging the right edge of the column heading to the left or right.

- Select multiple contiguous files by selecting the first file, then holding Shift and clicking on the last file you want to select. Select multiple non-contiguous files by selecting the first file, then holding Ctrl while selecting each additional file.

You can create new folders in Folders view as long as you have administrator level permission (see Skill 14, *Publishing Your Web Site* for more about permissions). Just select the Folder in which you want to create the new subfolder and choose File ➤ New ➤ Folder.

Use subfolders to organize a web site the same way you organize files within folders and subfolders on your hard drive. For example, by default the Explorer creates a folder called Images within a new web, in which you can store all image files. Suppose your web includes many pages and images that make up a reference manual. You can put those files out of the way by placing them all in subfolders, such as /MyWeb/Manual and /MyWeb/Manual/Images.

Now let's look at the many ways you can work with items in Hyperlinks and Folder views in the Explorer.

NOTE If you include a file named with the default home page name for the web site (like INDEX.HTM) in a subfolder, you create a subweb. When a user browses the subfolder, the server sends the browser the file INDEX.HTM from that folder. This means you can have different "home pages" in a web site.

Viewing All the Files in a Web

As if Navigation, Hyperlinks, and Folders views weren't enough, FrontPage 98 provides one more way to examine and work with the files in your web: the All Files view. Choose View ➤ All Files or click on the All Files icon on the Views bar to switch to All Files view. This view, shown in Figure 5.9, closely resembles the Folders view except that everything is dumped out of its folder and listed independently.

All the file management options available in the Folders view are available to you here with one exception: You can't create folders or move files between folders. However, you can see in which folder the files are located and can also tell if the file is an *orphan*, a file that is not linked to any other files in the web. Unless you plan to use orphaned files later, you should delete them from the web or return to Folders view and move them into a subfolder so only active, connected files are visible in the various views.

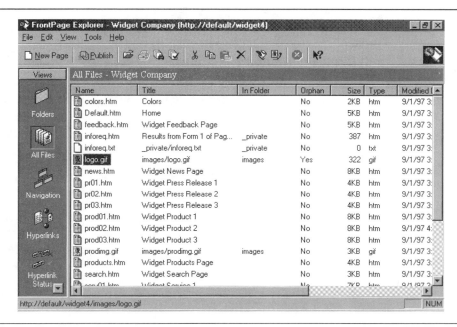

FIGURE 5.9: In All Files view, you can see if a file like logo.gif is linked to other files or is an orphan.

Manipulating Files and Their Properties

Each file has its own set of properties. You can modify some properties directly. For example, you can rename a file or edit the comments about the file. Other properties are updated automatically when the file is modified, for example, file size, modification date, and modifier name.

 NOTE   When a team is working on a site, other team members' changes are not automatically displayed in your copy of the Explorer. Choose View ➣ Refresh from the menu to have the Explorer read the web from the server and update your view of the web.

Regardless of the view you choose, there are a number of Edit commands you'll use to work with files in the Explorer. You can either select a file and choose a command from the Edit menu, or right-click on the selected file and choose a command from the shortcut menu. A few of the choices are only available in some views, and with particular types of files.

- **Open**   Opens a web page in the FrontPage Editor; opens other items in their associated application. For example, you can open and edit a .GIF or .JPEG image file in the Microsoft Image Composer, or a MIDI sound file in the Windows Sound Recorder.

- **Open With**   Lets you choose the editor or viewer in which to open the selected file. (See *Specifying Web File Editors* later in this Skill.)

- **Delete**   Removes the file from your web and deletes it (except for external files). You're prompted to confirm the deletion. In Navigation view only, you are given the option to delete navigation links but retain the file itself in the web.

- **Properties**   Displays the file's Properties dialog box.

- **Cut/Copy/Paste**   The Cut command removes the resource from the web and copies it to the Windows Clipboard. The Copy command copies the resource to the Clipboard, and the Paste command places the contents of the Clipboard into the selected folder in the active web. In Folders view, these commands let you copy or move a file to a different folder. In All Files view, use these commands to move or copy a file to the root folder only. In Navigation view, use Cut and Paste to relocate a selected page or branch, including a parent page and its child pages, to a different position in the view. Use Copy and Paste to duplicate a portion of the web.

- **Rename**   In Folders, All Files, and Navigation views, choose Rename to change the file name of the selected folder or file. You can also click on the name of a file twice with a pause between clicks and edit the name. If the file is already selected, just click once on the filename. (Don't double-click or you'll open the file!)

- **Add Task**   Creates a new entry in the FrontPage Task List that is linked to the selected file (see *Keeping Track with the Task List* later in this Skill).

The file icons in the right pane of the Explorer's Folders, All Files, and Hyperlinks views give you fast ways to open files and create links:

- Double-click on a file's icon to open the file. For example, double-click on a web page to open it in the FrontPage Editor, or on an image file to open it in an image editing program. (Double clicking to open also works in Navigation view.)

- Drag a page icon onto the Editor's desktop to open it there.

- Drag an file's icon into an open page in the FrontPage Editor to link the page to the file.

Renaming or Moving a File

Before you rename or move a file, be sure that the file is not open in another application like the Editor or Image Composer. This avoids conflicts that can occur when two programs try to access the same file, or when a file that is open is moved from its original location.

In the Explorer's Folders view, move a file to another folder simply by dragging it there, or by using Cut and Paste. For example, you can move all the images for a particular section of the web into a subfolder in the Images folder.

To copy a file or a folder, hold down the Ctrl key while you drag it, or use Copy and Paste. You can also drag a file or a folder with the right mouse button instead of the left, and then choose Copy Here, Move Here, or Cancel from the shortcut menu, just as you do in the Windows Explorer.

> **WARNING** Never change a file extension (the three characters following the period). The extension identifies the file's type, and links it to the appropriate application.

When you rename a file, you see the Rename dialog box, shown here.

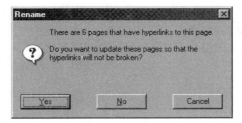

The dialog box lets you know that the Explorer is on the job, watching over your web, and tells you how many other resources are linked to the file whose name you are changing. At this point, you can do any of the following:

- Click on Yes to have the Explorer automatically revise the links to this file so they refer to the new name.

- Click on No if, for some reason, you want to rename the file without having the links to it revised; this "breaks" the links to the page or file.

- Click on Cancel to cancel the renaming operation.

 NOTE   Renaming a page file does not change the page's title. To change the title, switch to Navigation view and rename the page in the Navigation site map.

You can read more about the Explorer's link-maintenance abilities in the section called *Fixing and Verifying Links in the Explorer* in Skill 6.

Viewing and Revising File Properties

You can view or modify the properties of a file in the Explorer's right pane by right-clicking on the file's icon and choosing Properties from the shortcut menu (or choose Edit ➤ Properties from the menu.) Figure 5.10 shows both tabs of the Properties dialog box.

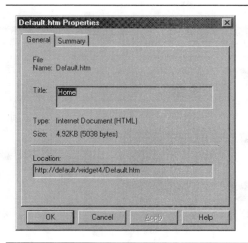 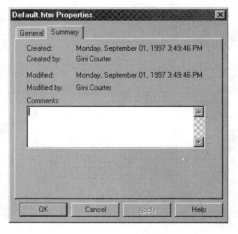

FIGURE 5.10: The General and Summary tabs of the Properties dialog box.

The General and Summary pages display all the file's properties, including the file's name, type, size, and the date and time it was last modified. These are the same properties that you see in the columns in the Files pane in Folders view. Two of the properties are user changeable:

- **Comments**   Enter comments about the file, such as its purpose in the web or when it should be updated.

- **Title**   For files that are not HTML web pages, such as image files, you can enter a more descriptive title here that only FrontPage uses to identify the resource. For example, you can change *bh10-01.gif* to *homepagebuttonimage.gif*.

You also see a Location field in the General page that displays the resource's URL, such as:

```
http://default/widget4/Default.htm
```

Specifying Web File Editors

By default, a web page is opened in the FrontPage Editor, but, you can choose to use a different editor if you prefer. You can also specify the editor or viewer you want to use to open file types other than HTML pages.

A file type is defined by its file extension, so FrontPage opens files in whatever program is associated with the file's extension. By default, several FrontPage file types are already associated with editors. For example, files with either .HTM or .HTML extensions are assigned to the FrontPage Editor; files with no extension are assigned to Notepad, the Windows text editor; and image files like .GIFs, .JPGs, and .BMPs are assigned to Microsoft Image Composer, the graphics-editing program that comes with FrontPage, if it was installed along with FrontPage.

You can add or change file and editor associations at any time in the FrontPage Explorer. For example, you can specify that files with the .WAV extension should be opened by your favorite sound editor, or that files with no extension should be opened in a text editor other than Notepad.

 NOTE   If a file type is not associated with an editor in FrontPage, you may still be able to open that file if there is an application associated with the file's extension in Windows.

Let's create an association for sound files with a .WAV extension. In a typical Windows installation, this file type is already associated with the Sound Recorder (filename SNDREC32.EXE), so we shouldn't have any problems creating the same association in this exercise in FrontPage:

1. In the Explorer, choose Tools ➤ Options.

2. In the Options dialog box, select the Configure Editors tab. This displays the current list of file and editor associations, which is shown in Figure 5.11.

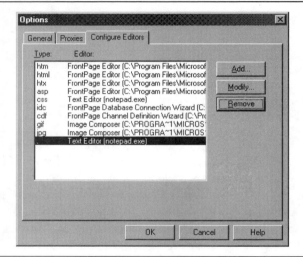

FIGURE 5.11: You assign a program to a file type in the Configure Editors page of the Options dialog box.

3. Click on the Add button, which displays the Add Editor Association dialog box.

4. In the File Type field, enter the file name extension **WAV**.

5. In the Editor Name field, enter a descriptive name like **Windows Sound Recorder**.

6. In the Command field, enter the path and program name, such as `C:\WINDOWS\SNDREC32.EXE` or click on the Browse button and select the program in the Browse dialog box.

7. Click on OK when you are finished to close the Add Editor Association dialog box. Click on OK again to close the Options dialog box.

Now when you double-click a file with the .WAV extension in the FrontPage Explorer, the file is opened in the Windows sound recorder.

You can remove a file association from the Configure Editors list by selecting it and clicking on the Remove button. To change an association, select it in the list and click on Modify. Because the width of the Options dialog box does not always allow for a display of the complete command for an associated application, you can also click the Modify button to see the entire command for an association. Click on Cancel if you don't want to make any changes.

To open a file that is not associated with an application, choose Edit ➤ Open With from the menu, or right click on the file and select Open With from the shortcut menu. This displays the Open With Editor dialog box, which lists all the current associated programs in FrontPage. Just pick the program you want to use to open this file and click on OK.

 NOTE
Note that the Open With Editor dialog box only includes the editors that have been configured in FrontPage. If, for example, you want to open an embedded video clip, there may not be an appropriate editor already configured in FrontPage. In that case, you need to follow the steps listed above to find and configure an editor before you can open the file from within FrontPage Explorer.

Finding Text and Spell-Checking throughout the Web

In your word processor, you've probably used Find, Replace, and Spelling many times. These are quick and easy ways to seek out a word, sentence, or just a few characters in the document, replace text with other text, and check the spelling of all the words in the document.

Find, Replace, and Spelling are available in the FrontPage Editor as well, which you read about in Skill 2. FrontPage offers an even more powerful way to use these tools, by applying them to every page in your entire web. This is yet another example of how FrontPage condenses huge web-management tasks down to simple, single step operations.

Finding and Replacing Text in Your Web

Suppose that the Widget Company decides to change its business focus and create a new image, including changing its name to the Technical Tools Company. Even though you redesign the web to reflect the company's new image, you also want to make sure that the company's web presence is maintained through the transition so that visitors to the web aren't disappointed. You need to find every occurrence of *Widget* in every page in the Web, and replace it with *Technical Tools*. Here's how to let the Explorer help you with this task.

1. Before you perform this operation, close any pages that are open in the FrontPage Editor to ensure that you're searching through the most recently saved versions of each page.

2. If the web is not already open in the Explorer, open it now.

3. Choose Tools ➣ Replace from the menu to open the Replace in FrontPage Web dialog box, shown below.

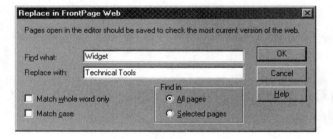

4. Enter **Widget** in the Find What field.

5. Enter **Technical Tools** in the Replace With field.

6. In this case, choose the All Pages option so that FrontPage searches every web page. If you select pages before opening the dialog box, you can choose to search Selected Pages.

7. Click on the OK button to start the process.

FrontPage begins searching through every page in your web and displays its progress in the Find Occurrences Of...dialog box shown in Figure 5.12. You'll see the title for each page in which the Find What text has been found, the number of occurrences of text in that page, and a status indicator that is red when the file is first listed, but turns to yellow once you've edited the page or added a task for that page to the Task List (see more about the Task list later in this Skill). If you need to pause, click on the Stop button to halt the Find procedure; click Resume to continue.

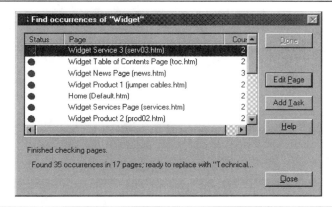

FIGURE 5.12: The Find Occurrences dialog box lists the pages that contain the text you want to replace.

    NOTE   The Replace command does not automatically replace the text it finds; you can verify each change within the page itself so you can confirm the changes.

When Find is finished (or you have stopped the process), the Find Occurrences dialog box contains a list of pages that include the Find What text string. Select the page you want to begin working with and click on the Edit Page button. The Editor opens and runs the Replace command within the selected page, as though you had started Replace from the Editor (as discussed in *Finding and Replacing Text* in Skill 2). When you're finished replacing text on the open page, save the page and continue on to the next page.

If you're not ready to make all the replacements now, you can still keep track of the pages that need more work. In the Find Occurrences dialog box, select each page you wish to work with later and click on the Add Task button. This creates a task for the page in the FrontPage Task List so you'll remember that it still needs work.

If you just want to find all occurrences of a word or phrase without replacing them, click on the Cross File Find button on the Explorer's toolbar. FrontPage checks all the pages in the web and list the pages that contain the text string.

Checking the Spelling in Your Web

When you create your web, you should make sure that all the text is spelled correctly. After you publish your web, you still need to provide periodic maintenance as new pages are added and existing pages require editing. It's easy to introduce a misspelling, even if you only spend 30 seconds on a page. FrontPage's spelling tools are designed to let you check all the pages of your web before you publish them for users to browse. To check all the pages, open the web in the Explorer and choose Tools ➤ Spelling from the menu or click the Cross File Spelling button on the toolbar. As with the Replace command discussed in the previous section, you can choose to check all pages or just those you select in the Explorer. You can also have the pages with possible misspellings automatically added to the Task List for later action.

When you click on the OK button to start the spell check, you see a dialog box similar to the one in Figure 5.12 that lists all the pages in which misspelled words have been found. To correct misspellings, select a page and click on the Edit Page button to open that page in the Editor and run through the spell-checking (which is discussed in *Checking Your Spelling* in Skill 2). When you're finished with one page, you're given the option to open the next one and continue.

You can also select a page in the list and click on the Add Task button to create an item in the Task List that reminds you to check the spelling on that page.

Keeping Track with the Task List

The number of files and links in a web site can grow astoundingly large, so getting the site ready may require many tasks, both large and small. The fact that multiple authors can work on the same web site means that you need a method to track who is responsible for completing specific tasks related to each page, link, or file.

A good web grows and changes, and someone needs to manage the tasks related to keeping the information up to date and meaningful for users. In print media, publishing something—a book, magazine, or newspaper—means that you are absolutely and completely done with it, at least until the next edition. But when you publish electronically on the Web, there's just no such thing as a final draft. What you finish and publish on Friday afternoon may be fodder for your Monday morning projects.

Now you'll see how the FrontPage Task List can help you keep track of the myriad and ever-changing jobs associated with building and maintaining a web.

Opening the Task List

The FrontPage Task List, shown in Figure 5.13, is just what its name implies—a convenient way for you to keep a list of things that need to be done in the current web. You can add tasks to the list, remove tasks, sort the list, and mark tasks as being completed. Because you can assign tasks to various individuals, departments, or teams working on a web, tasks should be self-contained units that you or someone else can make progress on in a single work session. For example, *Check links on home page* or *Create drop-down list of states* are better task descriptions than *Finish home page* or *Make drop-downs for all pages*.

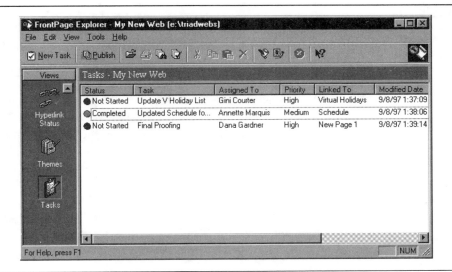

FIGURE 5.13: Use the Task List to keep track of jobs related to the current web.

To open the Task List from the FrontPage Explorer, click on the Tasks button on the Views bar or choose View ➤ Tasks from the menu.

Viewing Tasks

There are seven fields that define a task in the Task List, four of which you can modify when you create or revise a task. Each field is a column in the Task List:

- **Status**   Shows whether a task is Not Started or Completed
- **Task**   Your name for the task
- **Priority**   The importance of the task: Low, Medium, or High
- **Assigned To**   The person or team responsible for completing the task
- **Linked To**   The page, image or file to which this task applies
- **Modified Date**   The date on which the task was modified or completed
- **Description**   Your comments about the task

 TIP   You can sort the items in the Task List by clicking on a column-title button at the top of a column. For example, click on the Linked To button to sort the list by the web resources to which the tasks are linked. Or click the Priority button to put all the highest priority tasks at the top of the list.

To see all the tasks related to a web, including those that have been completed, right-click on a blank area of the Task List and choose Task History. Scanning the history of your site provides a good dose of reality about halfway through development, when you have a lot of unfinished items in the Task List.

Working with Tasks

Right-click on any task in the Task List to choose from among the following options on the shortcut menu:

- **Edit Task**   Opens the Task's Details dialog box (see below), where you can change who is assigned to the task and the description of the task.
- **Do Task**   Opens the Web page, image or file that is linked to this task in the associated editor so you can go to work.
- **Mark Complete**   Marks the task completed and changes the Modified Date to today's date.
- **Delete**   Deletes the task from the list.

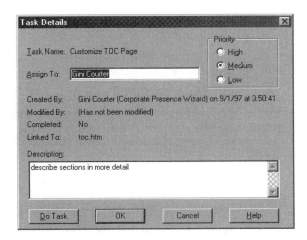

Adding a Task

If you want to add a task that is specific to a page, image, or other file, select the file in one of the Explorer views, right click, and choose Add Task from the shortcut menu. This opens a New Task dialog box, shown in Figure 5.14, linked to the selected page or file. If you are working on a page in the Editor, choose Edit ➤ Add Task to add a task related to the open page.

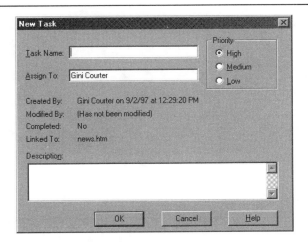

FIGURE 5.14: You create a new task in the Add Task dialog box.

In the Add Task dialog box, you can enter a name and priority for a task, revise the person responsible for the task (the default is the task's creator), and enter descriptive comments to help those responsible understand the task. Other task information, such as the date the task was created and the page, image, or file to which it is linked, is not editable.

 NOTE   Be sure you enter names in the Assign To field consistently. Otherwise, sorting the Task List by the Assigned To field won't be very useful.

When you are finished, click on the OK button and the new task appears in the Task List.

Completing and Removing Tasks

When you finish the job that is described in the Task List, right-click on the task and choose Mark Complete. The red ball in front of the task changes to green, the Status indicates Completed, and the Modified Date changes to the current date. If Task History is turned off, the task no longer appears on the list after it is refreshed.

 NOTE   When you mark a task as being completed, FrontPage doesn't check to see that you actually did the work described by the task. You're on the honor system!

Are You Experienced?

Now you can...

☑ Add pages to your web with the Explorer's Navigation view

☑ Rearrange pages in Navigation view

☑ Work with links in the Explorer's Hyperlinks view

☑ Copy, move, and delete files in the Folders and All Files view

☑ Work with file properties

☑ Associate files with editors or viewers

☑ Find and replace text and check the spelling in the entire web

☑ Organize jobs with the Task List

Linking Your Pages to the Web

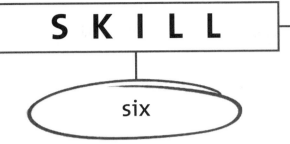

- ❑ Learning about hyperlinks
- ❑ Creating a hyperlink
- ❑ Changing or deleting a hyperlink
- ❑ Creating bookmarks
- ❑ Linking to a bookmark
- ❑ Modifying navigation bars
- ❑ Keeping links up to date

This Skill describes the feature that distinguishes Web sites from other "off-line" publications you create—hyperlinks. You'll learn about the different kinds of hyperlinks you can place in a page, how to create bookmarks and hyperlinks, how to modify navigation bars, and how to let FrontPage keep your links up to date.

Understanding Links

The feature that puts the "Web" into "World Wide Web" is the hyperlink (or link), first discussed in Skill 1. A hyperlink is a connection from a page on the World Wide Web to another page, image, e-mail address, or file at another location on the Web. A hyperlink can connect internally to a location within the current web or externally to a location half-way around the world through the World Wide Web.

There are several types of hyperlinks you can include in a page, and many different ways to create them, but every hyperlink consists of two primary parts:

- **Hyperlink** The text or image in a page that you define as a hyperlink; clicking the hyperlink in a browser opens the link's target.

- **Target** The page or file that opens when a user clicks a hyperlink; a target is usually defined by its URL.

 NOTE The hyperlinks you create in your Office 97 documents consist of these same two components. If you include linked documents in a FrontPage web, their hyperlinks appear in the Explorer just like the hyperlinks in HTML pages.

Text or Image Hyperlinks

A text hyperlink is probably the most common type of hyperlink, and can be from one word to several lines long. However, the fact that link text *can* be several lines long doesn't mean it usually is, or should be. The hyperlink text should just be enough to let the user know what they'll find when they click on the link, not a five hundred word description of every item they'll find when they arrive.

You can see two examples of hyperlinks displayed in Internet Explorer in Figure 6.1. The first hyperlink is a text hyperlink. Like most popular browsers, Internet Explorer employs several different ways to indicate that text is a hyperlink. For instance, the link text is underlined and displayed in a different color, making it stand out on the page.

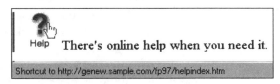

FIGURE 6.1: Many browsers display the URL of a text or graphic hyperlink in the status bar when you point to the link.

As you can see in Figure 6.1, when you move your mouse pointer over a link, the pointer changes to a hand and the name of the link's target appears on the status bar in the lower-left corner of the screen. (This also happens in the Editor, so you can see what it looks like.) This cue not only tells you this text is a hyperlink, but it also lets you know what URL you access by clicking the link.

Hyperlinks aren't limited to text; any image in a page can be used as a hyperlink, so clicking on the image activates a link. An image not only livens up a page but, used well, can be very descriptive. For example, the Ticketmaster Online site (`http://www.ticketmaster.com`) uses images of a ticket counter, an information booth, and an events calendar. Users can quickly determine which image to click on to order tickets, get more information, or find events in their area.

The bottom of Figure 6.1 shows an image hyperlink. In this case, the text next to the image merely describes the link. As with a text link, when you point to an image hyperlink in Internet Explorer, the pointer changes to a hand and the status bar displays the hyperlink's target. In this example, the target URL is the same for both the text link on the top and the image link on the bottom. You'll read more about images and their use as hyperlinks in Skill 8, *Displaying Images in Your Pages*.

Target Files and Bookmarks

You specify the target file of a hyperlink with its URL or filename, such as:

```
http://default/myweb/helpindex.htm
```

The file you list as the target is the file that a browser opens when a user activates the link by clicking on it.

Skill 6

The target can be any type of file. For example, the browser might open a Web page, a graphic image, a sound file, or a video file. The target can also be a program file that the target server runs, such as a CGI (Common Gateway Interface) script that might, for example, calculate the total number of accesses to the current Web site and then return the result to the browser. The target file doesn't have to be on the World Wide Web. For example, the target file might be located on the browser's local hard disk, a network drive, or on a local server.

When you specify a page as the target of a hyperlink, you can also include the name of a bookmark, or named location, within that page. The browser displays that location at the top of the reader's screen when the page is opened. (This allows you to create a link to a specific entry in the middle of a list, rather than forcing the user to scroll down the list after they arrive on the page.)

The HTML anchor tag, <A>, defines a link. It includes the source of the link (the text or image hyperlink) and the target file. Here is the code for the top text link shown in Figure 6.1:

```
There's <A HREF="helpindex.htm">online help</A> when you need it.
```

Now look at the code for the image link shown on the bottom of Figure 6.1:

```
<A HREF="helpindex.htm"><IMG SRC="images/help.gif" border="0"
width="46" height="51"></A> There's online help when you need it.
```

In each case, the target of the hyperlink is specified as an attribute of the <A> tag. However, you don't have to enter the HTML code; FrontPage creates it for you.

Absolute and Relative URLs

When you create a hyperlink (or otherwise refer to another file in a Web page), you can define the target (reference) in one of two ways: as an absolute reference, or a relative reference. An absolute reference uses the complete URL to specify the exact location of the file. Here are four examples of absolute URLs:

```
http://www.widget.com/
http://www.widget.com/hist-toc.htm
http://www.widget.com/images/logo.gif
file:///c:/mywebs/homepage.htm
```

As always, if a URL does not include a specific file name ending in HTM or HTML, (see the first example), the server at that location sends the default file, such as Index.htm, or may simply send a list of all the files in the specified folder.

A relative reference specifies the location of a file in relation to the location of the page that contains the hyperlink. For example, if a link in the hist-toc.htm page (see the second example) refers simply to:

```
history1-1.htm
```

the implication is that history1-1.htm is stored in the same folder as the source of the reference, hist-toc.htm. If hist-toc.htm also includes a relative reference to the file:

```
images/logo.gif
```

this means the Images folder is a subfolder of the folder that hist-toc.htm is stored in.

In general, you should use a relative reference when the target of a hyperlink is stored in the active FrontPage web (an internal reference). In many cases, you use an absolute reference only when the target is stored outside of the web (an external reference). If you use relative references, you're free to move the entire web without penalty. For example, if you rename the Widget Web site *Technical Tools*, you would have to spend hours revising absolute references to files on the former Widget site, like:

```
http://www.techtools.com/images/logo.gif
```

But you could ignore relative addresses to files, such as:

```
images/logo.gif
```

The relative URL still points to the Images folder within the source page's folder, which now happens to be TechTools instead of Widget. It's not unusual for designers to move a Web site to a new and improved server or different service provider. You can save yourself needless effort later by avoiding absolute references when relative references suffice.

Because a relative URL is based on the source page's URL, you can't create a relative hyperlink in a page until it has been saved. For example, if you're working on a new page, hyperlinks you create have absolute references. Once you save the page, however, FrontPage updates the links and makes all the internal links relative.

Skill 6

Creating a Hyperlink

As you have learned, you can create a hyperlink in the FrontPage Editor from either text or an image, and the target can be a file either within the active FrontPage web or outside of it. There are several ways to create a link, but here's the most common method:

1. In the Editor, select the text or image you want to serve as a hyperlink.

2. Choose Edit ➤ Hyperlink from the menu or click on the Create or Edit Hyperlink button on the toolbar to open the Create Hyperlink dialog box, shown in Figure 6.2. In this dialog box, you'll specify the link's target.

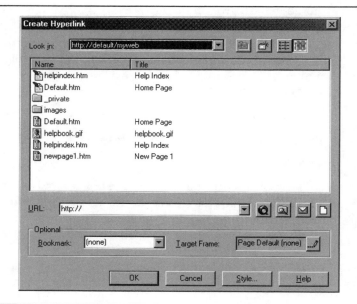

FIGURE 6.2: In the Create Hyperlink dialog box, you specify the target of the hyperlink.

3. Select a target from the current web, World Wide Web, or drives connected to your computer.

    -   **Current FrontPage Web** Use the Look In control and file list to select files in the active FrontPage web; FrontPage creates an internal link with a relative URL.

- **World Wide Web**   Type in a URL or click on the Web Browser button to locate a Web page on the World Wide Web. The external link uses an absolute URL.

- **On Your Computer**   Click on the Windows Explorer button to browse and locate a file on your computer or local area network as the target of the hyperlink.

- **E-Mail**   Click on the Make a Hyperlink that Sends E-mail button and type an e-mail address in the dialog box that opens. When a visitor clicks on this hyperlink, he or she is presented with an e-mail form to send e-mail to the address you enter.

- **New Page**   Click on the Create a Page and Link to the New Page button to create a new page. When you save the new page, it serves as the target for the link.

4.   When you are finished defining the hyperlink, click on the OK button.

When you create a text hyperlink, the selected text is underlined and displayed, by default, in blue. When you move your mouse over the text or image hyperlink, the link's target is displayed in the status bar. You can edit the hyperlink text just as you would any other text in the page.

Linking to a Page in the Current FrontPage Web

You can link to any file in the web that's currently open in the Explorer by selecting the file in the Create Hyperlink dialog box (shown in Figure 6.2). If the file you want to use is in a folder, double-click to open the folder.

Click on the Up One Level button to return to the current web folder.

Linking to a Bookmark

Just as in Word, a FrontPage *bookmark* is a specific, named location within a page that can serve as the target for a link. You'll learn about creating bookmarks and links to bookmarks a little later in this Skill.

Specifying a Target Frame

A frame set is a single page that displays other pages within frames, or windows, in that page. It allows your browser to display multiple pages, instead of having to close a page to open another one. If the current page (the one containing the hyperlink you are defining) is part of a frame set, you can specify which frame the target file opens into when the hyperlink is clicked. For example, even though the hyperlink is in a frame on the left side of the page, you might want the target displayed in a frame to the right. You'll find out how to do this and more with frames in Skill 13.

Linking to a Page on the Web

To create a link to a page on the World Wide Web, enter a URL in the URL text box or click the Use Your Web Browser to Select a Page or File button in the Create Hyperlink dialog box. This opens your default Web browser, along with a message telling you to locate the URL you want. After going to the correct URL, switch back to the Editor. The URL from the browser appears in the URL field in the Editor's Create Hyperlink dialog box.

Linking to a File on Your Computer

To create a hyperlink to a file on your computer (or your local area network) that is not part of the current web, choose Make a Hyperlink to a File on Your Computer. This opens a Select File dialog box, shown in Figure 6.3. Select the file you want and click on OK to close the dialog box and create the link.

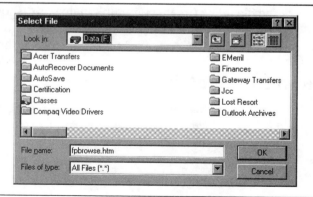

FIGURE 6.3: Select a file on your computer to serve as the target of the hyperlink.

Linking to E-mail

A standard Web feature is a "return address" – a link that allows visitors to send e-mail requesting information or giving feedback. Clicking on the Make a Hyperlink that Sends an E-mail button opens a dialog box where you can enter an e-mail address. Click on OK to enter the e-mail address in the URL text box. Notice that FrontPage inserts a "mailto" tag in front of the address.

The corresponding HTML looks like this:

```
Send mail to <a
href="mailto:webmaster@widget.com">webmaster@widget.com</a> with questions
or comments about this web site.
```

When a visitor clicks an e-mail link, an e-mail form like the one in Figure 6.4 opens so they can type their e-mail, click on the Send button, and send it through the Internet e-mail system.

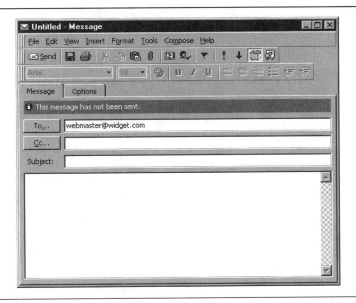

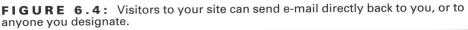

FIGURE 6.4: Visitors to your site can send e-mail directly back to you, or to anyone you designate.

Linking to a New Page

You can create a link to a Web page *and* the Web page at the same time if you choose the Create a Page and Link to the New Page button in the Create Hyperlink dialog box. This is a convenient way to create a web—you can work in one page and create all its links and targets at the same time.

Clicking on the Create a Page and Link to the New Page button opens the New dialog box as though you had chosen the File ➤ New command. Select the type of page you want to create and click on OK. FrontPage creates a new page and opens the page in the Editor. If you're not ready to work on the page yet, choose Window from the menu and switch back to the page you want to work on from the list of open pages.

If you don't even want to think about creating content for the new page now, you can click the Just Add Web Task check box before clicking on OK. This creates the new page and immediately opens the Save As dialog box. Enter a name for the new page and click on OK. FrontPage creates the page, saves it, adds a task for the page to the Task List, and closes the new page. The hyperlink to that page, however, is already in place.

Creating Links by Dragging and Copying

After you've created a few links and understand how they work, you might want to check out some other ways to create links:

- Drag a file from the FrontPage Explorer into an open page in the Editor to create a link to the dragged file. If the file is a Web page, its title appears as the link text in the page as though you had typed the title at the line where you released the mouse button. If a page is titleless, the file's name appears as the link text. (Remember that you can edit the text.)

- For absolute references, simply type the URL of the target file (it must begin with a protocol, such as HTTP), and the Editor automatically defines that text as a link to the URL you specified. If you want to link to an open page in a browser, copy the URL of the page from the browser's address field, paste it into the Editor, and press the spacebar to signal the end of the link text.

- Drag a hyperlink from a page in your browser into a page in the Editor to create an identical link in the Editor.

Revising, Deleting, and Following Hyperlinks

With FrontPage, you can change either component of a link—the text or image that a user clicks to invoke the hyperlink (the source) or the hyperlink's target. You can also disconnect the hyperlink while leaving the text or image you click to get there intact. At the click of a button (actually, several clicks), you can navigate through the hyperlink's target pages in the Editor.

Revising a Hyperlink

To change the text of a hyperlink, simply edit it as you would any other text. As long as the text you revise is still underlined, you'll know it's still a link. You can also change the image for an image hyperlink. Just right-click on the image and choose Image Properties from the shortcut menu. In the Image Properties dialog box, specify the new image in the Image Source field, shown here:

or click on the Browse button to select an image from your FrontPage web or another location. The new image in the page then serves as the image hyperlink.

To modify the hyperlink definition, select the image (click on it) or position the insertion point anywhere within the link text (you need not select any of the text), and choose Edit ➤ Hyperlink or click on the Create or Edit Hyperlink button on the toolbar. This action displays the Edit Hyperlink dialog box, which is essentially the same as the Create Hyperlink dialog box shown earlier in this Skill. You'll see the current link definition in the URL field. You can specify a different target file, page, bookmark, e-mail address, or target frame for the link, and click on OK when you're finished.

Deleting a Hyperlink

When you delete a hyperlink from a page, you are not affecting the link's target; you're only removing the reference to it. There are several ways to delete a link:

- Delete the image or all of the text for the link, and the link to the target file is deleted as well. Keep this in mind when you're editing hyperlink text, and be careful not to accidentally delete all the text. (If you do, remember Undo.)

- To delete a hyperlink but leave the link source on the page, select the link image or position the insertion point anywhere within the link text, then choose Edit ➢ Unlink from the menu.

- To remove the link definition from just some of the link text, select that text and choose Edit ➢ Unlink. (You might use this, for example, when the link text includes a whole sentence, but you'd rather just use a couple of key words as the link.)

- If you're working in the Edit Hyperlink dialog box, select the text in the URL field and delete it. Click on OK and the link is removed. If you're working in the Create Hyperlink dialog box, just click on Cancel and the hyperlink will not be created.

Following Hyperlinks in the Editor

The FrontPage Editor lets you navigate through the links in a page in much the same way you do in a browser. If a hyperlink in the Editor's current page has a web page as its target, you can open that page in the Editor by holding down the Ctrl key (the pointer changes to a pointing hand) and clicking on the link, or right-clicking and choosing Follow Hyperlink from the shortcut menu.

When you follow a link to another page, especially a page on another server, there's always a chance the server at that site is running very slowly—or not at all. To cancel an open operation, press Esc or click the Stop button, just as you do in your browser.

When you open several pages in the Editor, you can use the Back and Forward buttons on the toolbar or Go ➢ Back and Go ➢ Forward on the menu to navigate between pages.

Working with Bookmarks

Earlier in this Skill, you read about including a bookmark as the target for a hyperlink so when the target page is opened in a browser, the browser displays the bookmark location within the page. A bookmark lets you take a visitor to a specific section of text, rather than requiring them to locate it by scrolling through the page.

Defining a Bookmark

Creating a bookmark names a location so you can refer to it by name. Bookmarks are also referred to as destinations or named targets in HTML jargon. You can use bookmarks to link to a location on the same page as the hyperlink or to a specified location of another page.

Here's how to create a bookmark:

1. In the Editor, move the insertion point to the line where you want to create the bookmark.

2. Although you can create a bookmark without selecting any text, it's usually a good idea to select some text that the bookmark is related to. That way, if you add more text to the paragraph, the bookmark is still attached to the text you selected.

3. Choose Edit ➤ Bookmark, which displays the Bookmark dialog box (shown here).

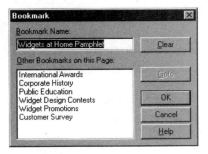

4. If you selected text before opening the dialog box, FrontPage automatically places it in the Bookmark Name field. Revise it if you wish, then click on OK to create the bookmark.

NOTE   Within a web, each bookmark must have a unique name—and using *Bookmark 1*, *Bookmark 2*, etc. is not a good idea. Bookmark names should clearly but briefly describe the bookmark's location so you or another author can easily select it from the list of bookmarks when you're creating a hyperlink.

The HTML tag for a bookmark is an attribute of the anchor tag <A>. If you select the text Widgets at Home Pamphlet and then created the bookmark name Widgets at Home, here's how the code looks:

```
<A NAME="Widgets at Home">Widgets at Home Pamphlet</A>
```

In the FrontPage Editor, the text within the opening and closing anchor tags is underlined with a dashed line so you can tell it's a bookmark:

> Widgets at Home Pamphlet

A browser, however, does not apply any special formatting to bookmarks; it simply uses them as reference points when they are included as the targets for hyperlinks.

Creating Hyperlinks to Bookmarks

Once you define bookmarks in your Web pages, you can create hyperlinks that take users right to the spot on the page you want them to see. You can use bookmarks to link to a location on the same page as the hyperlink, or to a specified location of another page.

When you are defining a hyperlink, if the target page you select is part of the active web in the Explorer, select the page where the bookmark is defined and select the desired bookmark from the Bookmark drop-down list in the Create Hyperlink dialog box. To create a link to a bookmark in the current page (the page in which you're creating the link), just open the Create Hyperlink dialog box and choose a bookmark from the drop-down list.

In Figure 6.5, the bookmark named International Awards on the `awards.htm` page is selected. In HTML, a reference to a bookmark name is preceded by a pound sign (#), so the complete reference for this link is:

```
awards.htm#International Awards
```

If the hyperlink in Figure 6.5 was also on the `awards.htm` page, the HTML code would only include the pound sign and bookmark name:

```
#International Awards
```

When a user clicks on this link in a browser, the page awards.htm opens, and the browser displays the bookmark named International Awards at the top of the screen—even if International Awards is in the middle of the page.

FIGURE 6.5: FrontPage automatically inserts a pound sign (#) in front of the URL to designate a hyperlink to a bookmark.

Revising, Deleting, and Going to Bookmarks

Within the FrontPage Editor, you can jump to any bookmark in the page by selecting it in the Bookmark dialog box (Edit ➤ Bookmark) and clicking on the Goto button. The dialog box remains open, and because the insertion point is now on a bookmark, the Clear button is enabled. Click on the Clear button to remove the bookmark from the page. Only the bookmark name is removed; text in the page isn't affected.

To revise the name of a bookmark, click anywhere within the text defined as the bookmark and choose Edit ➤ Bookmark. In the Bookmark dialog box, you see the name of that bookmark in the Bookmark Name field. Edit the name as needed and, when you're done, click on OK.

FrontPage does not automatically update bookmark references in your web as it does with file names. So, when you revise a bookmark name or delete a bookmark, FrontPage doesn't change the bookmark name or delete the reference to the bookmark in hyperlinks. You have to find and revise each link that references the bookmark. Therefore, it's best to rename bookmarks *before* you've used them as hyperlink targets—or not at all.

Using and Modifying Navigation Bars

In Skill 5, you learned that FrontPage automatically adds navigation bars to pages you create in the Explorer's Navigation view. Now that you have an understanding of how hyperlinks work, let's take a closer look at those navigation bars.

To review, navigation bars are sets of hyperlinks, located in the shared borders of each page, that connect to pages within the current web. For example, let's say you create a simple one-page web, then add three other pages in Navigation view. FrontPage automatically adds a top and left border to each page that contains hyperlinks to each of the three new pages. Figure 6.6 shows this simple web in Navigation view. Figure 6.7 shows each of the web's pages with their shared borders and hyperlinks to the other pages.

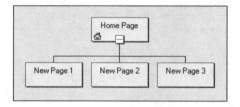

FIGURE 6.6: When pages are added to this one-page web, FrontPage inserts navigation bars on each page.

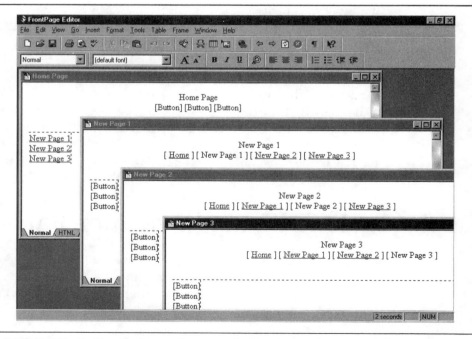

FIGURE 6.7: Each page has a navigation bar at the top and shared borders on the left to take users to other pages in the web.

Shared borders are indicated by the dotted lines that are especially visible in New Page 3 in Figure 6.7. *Shared borders* are shared because the same borders appear on each page in the site. When you click in the shared border, the dotted line becomes solid. When you click on any one of the Navigation bars in the border, the entire bar is selected and the mouse pointer changes to a robot.

The top border of the Home Page includes the word *Button* surrounded by brackets. Although the Home Page does not include any hyperlinks in the top shared border, FrontPage still represents where the buttons appear on the other pages that share the same top border. If you delete the button from the home page, none of the other pages include buttons, either.

Modifying Shared Borders

The web defaults for shared borders are set in the FrontPage Explorer. Choose Tools ➤ Shared Borders to set the borders for the entire web. You can display or hide borders for the active page by choosing shared borders from the shortcut menu and enabling the Set for this Page Only checkbox (see Figure 6.8). Then, you can then turn the Top, Left, Right, or Bottom border display on or off, or reset the page to the web shared border default settings.

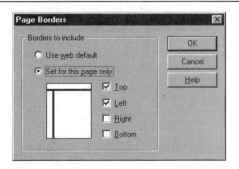

FIGURE 6.8: Set shared borders for the web in the Explorer, and for individual pages in the Editor

The shortcut menu also includes options to change Paragraph Properties and Font Properties, both of which have direct impact on the navigation bar in the shared border. You can change the paragraph format in the Paragraph Properties, and change the text font in the Font Properties. If you want to change navigation bar text, you must do so in the FrontPage Explorer's Navigation view. Any text or images that you place in a shared border appear on every page of the web.

Altering Navigation Bars

You are not limited to the default hyperlinks in the navigation bars. You can change which links appear and how many levels of links are available. To access the navigation bar properties, select a navigation bar, right-click, and choose FrontPage Component Properties from the shortcut menu. This opens the Navigation Bar Properties dialog box, shown in Figure 6.9.

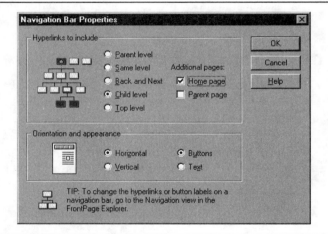

FIGURE 6.9: You can change the hyperlinks that are included in the Navigation Bar Properties dialog box.

In the Navigation Bar Properties dialog box, you can select one of five levels of pages to display in the navigation bar:

- **Parent Level**   Creates hyperlinks to the other page(s) on the same level as the parent page.

- **Same Level**   Creates hyperlinks to the other page(s) on the same level as the open page.

- **Back and Next**   Creates *Back* and *Next* hyperlinks to the adjacent page(s) on the same level as the open page.

- **Child Level**   Creates hyperlinks to the page(s) below the level of the open page.

- **Top Level**   Creates hyperlinks to the page(s) on the same level as the home page.

In addition, you can add buttons for two other pages:

- **Home Page**   Includes a hyperlink to the home page.

- **Parent Page**   Includes a hyperlink to the parent page.

There are two orientations to choose from:

- **Horizontal**   Aligns the navigation bar horizontally.

- **Vertical**   Aligns the navigation bar vertically.

Finally, choose the appearance of the hyperlinks in the navigation bar:

- **Buttons**   Displays the navigation bar as graphical buttons.

- **Text**   Displays the navigation bar as text.

As you make choices, your changes are reflected in the preview pane in the dialog box. When you are satisfied with your selections, click on OK.

If you choose hyperlinks for a level that doesn't exist (for example, choosing Child pages when there aren't any), the hyperlinks aren't created.

Inserting Navigation Bars

Creating pages in Navigation view is the easiest way to add navigation bars. However, you can enable navigation bars even if you add pages in the Editor or in another view in the Explorer. Open the page you want to add Navigation bars to, and select Insert ➤ Navigation Bar from the menu. FrontPage automatically opens the Navigation Bar Properties dialog box so you can set its properties.

Fixing and Verifying Links in the Explorer

One of the most important web-management jobs is maintaining the hyperlinks in your pages. Users quickly grow frustrated and leave your site if links take them to the wrong location, or to no location at all. If you want to keep your Web site running smoothly, you must ensure each hyperlink references the correct target. If you rename a file in your FrontPage web, for example, you must also make sure that FrontPage correctly revises the target name in any hyperlinks that reference that file.

As part of your web's regular maintenance, you should check to see that each hyperlink target's URL is still valid and works correctly. This is especially important for external links because you have no control over the location of their targets. It's easiest if you schedule a time each week to check external links: for example, every Wednesday afternoon.

Because Web sites can have so many links, these jobs can be some of the most time-consuming aspects of managing a site—unless of course, you're using FrontPage 98.

Fixing Target Names Automatically

In Skill 5, you learned how to rename a file or move it to another folder in a FrontPage web. Renaming or moving a file would normally break hyperlinks to the file, because the links would still target the original name or location. However, when you change a file's name or location in the FrontPage Explorer, the Explorer automatically updates any links to that file in the current web so they reference the new name or location. (A reminder: this *doesn't* work in the Windows Explorer.)

When you rename a file, the FrontPage Explorer displays the Rename dialog box, asking you if you want to update all the hyperlinks to this file. Choose Yes and the links are revised to reference the new name, so you don't have to worry about a "dead" link. Choose No, and the file is renamed but the links still reference the old name. You might do this when you are going to create a new file with the old name to serve as the target of those hyperlinks.

When you move a file to another folder in the FrontPage web, just sit back and let the Explorer automatically update links to the file so they refer to the new location.

Verifying Links in the Explorer

The Explorer can also help you verify the links in your FrontPage web and find any that are broken and can no longer access their targets. To verify the hyperlinks in the active FrontPage web, go to the Explorer and choose Tools ➤ Verify Hyperlinks from the menu to open the Verify Hyperlinks dialog box. Choose to verify all or selected links and click Start. When the scan is complete, the Hyperlink Status view, shown in Figure 6.10, lists all external links in all the pages of the FrontPage web, as well as any broken internal links. The Status column next to each link indicates the link's condition.

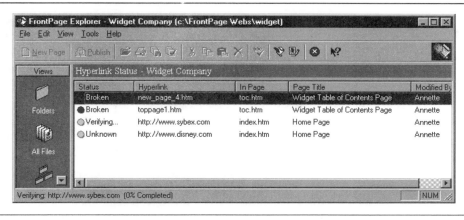

FIGURE 6.10: The Explorer's Hyperlink Status view shows you any broken internal links and allows you to verify all external links.

There are six possible conditions:

- **OK**   The link has been checked and works correctly.

- **Broken**   The link has been checked and is broken.

- **Unknown**   The link has not been checked yet (in the case of an external link).

- **Verifying**   The link is currently being verified.

- **Added Task**   The link may be broken or has not been checked yet, but a reminder has been added to the Task List to check it again later.

- **Edited**   The Link has been edited and is OK.

In Figure 6.10, you can see there are two broken internal links to the file Widget Table of Contents Page. (The source page for the broken links is displayed in the Page Title column in the Hyperlink Status view.) You know the broken links are internal links because only the file name is shown in the Hyperlink column (a relative reference), which means the file should be found in the same folder as the hyperlink's source file.

The primary cause of a broken internal link is that the target file is missing as far as the link is concerned. There are two possibilities: the file isn't there, or the target specified in the link is incorrect. The quickest way to accidentally kill an internal link is to move files in the Windows Explorer, rather than the FrontPage Explorer, resulting in links that point to the file's old location. If the target in the hyperlink is incorrect, chances are an author typed it in rather than browsing to find it. Missing a single character in a file's name or location results in a broken link.

There are two external hyperlinks listed in Figure 6.10; you know they're external because their URLs are outside of the current FrontPage web. You must have an active Web connection to verify external links, and because it may take a long time, FrontPage does not verify them automatically. Only the validity of the URL is checked—the target page won't actually be opened. If a URL is valid (includes the protocol and hostname with the proper punctuation), the link's bullet turns green and the next link is checked. External links that cannot be verified are shown as Broken or Unknown.

So, what do you do with broken links? If people are using the web, you need to clean up the links immediately. If the web is offline for design or maintenance, you may choose to delay some of the required fixes. When FrontPage is finished verifying links, you can:

- Leave things as they are and leave the Hyperlink Status view, then verify the hyperlinks again at another time.

- Select a broken link and double click on it to edit it in the Edit Hyperlink dialog box (shown in Figure 6.11). You can enter a new URL, or click on the Browse button and select a page in your browser. You can also click on Edit Page to edit the link directly in the page in which it appears. Then decide whether to change all the pages that contain that link or just those you select. Click on OK when you're finished to close the dialog box.

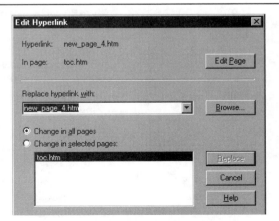

FIGURE 6.11: Use the Edit Hyperlink dialog box to fix a hyperlink that is broken or needs to be redirected.

- Select a link, right-click, and choose Add Task, which adds a task in the FrontPage Task List linked to this page, reminding you that the broken hyperlink needs your attention.

If you choose to leave the Hyperlink Status view without fixing the broken links, it's a good idea to open the Task list and create a reminder to verify the links again.

Are You Experienced?

Now you can...

- ☑ **Create internal and external hyperlinks**
- ☑ **Change or delete a hyperlink**
- ☑ **Create bookmarks**
- ☑ **Link to a bookmark**
- ☑ **Modify navigation bars**
- ☑ **Verify Hyperlinks**

Skill 6

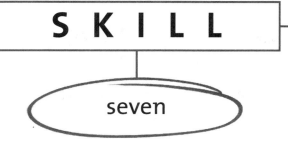

S K I L L

seven

Using Tables to Add Structure

❑ Understanding the layout of tables

❑ Creating a table

❑ Moving between the cells in a table

❑ Selecting parts of a table

❑ Adding a caption

❑ Changing table properties

❑ Changing cell properties

❑ Changing the size of a table

Tables are fast becoming one of the most powerful and versatile tools in a Web designer's toolkit. And they're not limited to their traditional role of presenting data in rows and columns. Tables permit designers to sidestep the limitations of HTML to precisely place text, data, and images on a Web page. Any attractive, graphically appealing site you run across on the Web today is probably constructed with at least a few tables lurking in the background.

The Structure of a Table

Tables provide an effective structure for a web page because they have a versatile structure of their own. In its most rudimentary form, a table is an HTML feature that helps you arrange information within rows and columns. You may have already worked with tables in a word processing program or learned about columns, rows, and cells from your spreadsheet application. Many of those skills are transferable to working with tables in FrontPage. However, you can use tables much more discreetly to provide a behind the scenes grid to help you position elements on your pages. Using tables in this way opens up a whole new world of possibilities for first class web page design.

Depending on the type of information you want to present, you may want your tables to look like a traditional table, like the example in Figure 7.1 with border lines dividing its rows, columns, and cells. Other times, you may want to turn off all the borders and use the hidden border structure to present information more graphically, as shown in Figure 7.2. What you put in a table is pretty much up to you; if you can place it on a page, you can put it in a table cell.

Work Schedule for the Week of December 14, 1997							
	Mon	Tue	Wed	Thu	Fri	Sat	Sun
Celeste	X	X	X			X	X
Gerald	X	X		X	X	X	
Gordon	X			X	X	X	X
Carol			X	X	X	X	X

(As of Nov 15, 1997)

FIGURE 7.1: A table consists of rows, columns, and cells, as well as optional border, caption, and header cells.

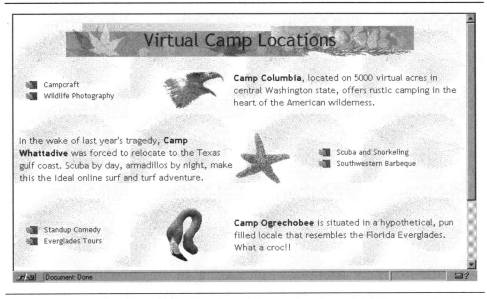

FIGURE 7.2: With the exception of the top border, all the elements in this page are in a table.

Figure 7.1 shows a typical table with standard and special features applied to it:

- The table has six rows and eight columns; at the junction of each row and column is a cell.

- The cells in the first row have been merged into a single cell.

 NOTE   By default, a column expands to include the width of its contents, and a table is, therefore, as wide as the longest entries in its cells. You can specify an exact width for a table or for any of its columns. If you don't, the table doesn't expand any wider than the window in which it is displayed; when it reaches that limit, text in cells wrap to new lines as needed.

- An optional border is displayed around the table and all its cells.

- There is a caption centered beneath the table.

- The cells with the names of the people and the days of the week are formatted as header cells, so they stand out in the table.

- The header cells have a background color.
- The days of the week and the contents of the cells beneath them are centered.

Creating a New Table

There are three ways to create a table in FrontPage 98:

- Dragging with the Insert Table Button
- Using the Table ➤ Insert Table menu option
- Drawing with the Draw table pointer

None of these is better than the others, but you'll find that you develop a preference. Even if you already know how to use one of these methods, try all three, because each might be better for creating a specific type of table.

All three methods create tables quickly and relatively painlessly. It is important, however, to think out the design of your page and how the table(s) impact that design before you start creating them. You should determine approximately how many columns and rows you need and in what cells to place the various page elements. This helps you create cells that enhance your design from the outset and require less tweaking in the end.

 TIP It's a good idea to save regularly while you are working with tables in case you make a significant change that negatively impacts your design. Of course, don't forget to use the Undo button to revert back to a previous step (you can reverse up to 30 actions in FrontPage).

The following example gives you some practice creating a simple table. The table you build here will be used in several other exercises in this Skill, so even if you've had some experience with tables it's helpful to follow along.

Using the Insert Table Button

First we'll use the most direct method of creating a table; then we'll look at the other two methods.

1. Position the insertion point where you want the upper-left corner of the table to appear in the page.

2.   Point to the Insert Table button on the toolbar, then press and hold down the mouse button.

3.   A table template appears beneath the button, which you can use to define the dimensions of the table. Drag down and to the right to expand the number of rows and columns in the table. As you do, you'll see the size noted beneath the template.

4.   The table in Figure 7.1 has six rows and eight columns, so keep dragging until you have that many highlighted in the template. Then release the mouse button to create the new table.

Using the Insert Table Command

The next method for creating a table lets you define the appearance of the table as well as its dimensions.

1.   Choose Edit ➤ Undo Insert to remove the table you just created.

2.   With the insertion point located where you want the new table, choose Table ➤ Insert Table to open the Insert Table dialog box (see Figure 7.3).

3.   Enter 6 in the Rows field and 8 in the Columns field.

4.   By default, the Border Size option is set to 1 (pixel). Even if you plan to remove the border, you might want to leave it on while you're inputting the table's contents. At this point, don't change the width of the table—it spans the page by default.

5.   Click on OK to create the table.

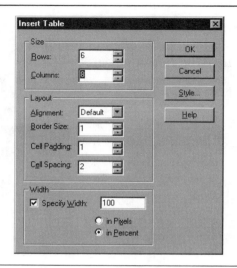

FIGURE 7.3: You can define the size and look of a table in the Insert Table dialog box.

Drawing the Table by Hand

FrontPage 98 has added a number of enhancements to Tables, including the Draw Table feature seen in Word 97. Choose Table ➤ Draw Table to view the Tables toolbar shown here.

The first tool, the Draw Table button, is depressed when the toolbar is activated, and the mouse pointer changes shape from an I-beam to a pencil. Use the pencil pointer to drag a rectangle, as seen in Figure 7.4, for the outside border of your table.

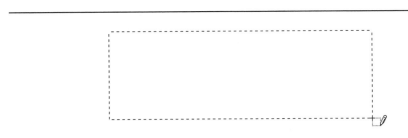

FIGURE 7.4: Position the pencil at the top left corner and hold the mouse button down to drag a rectangle to create a table cell.

Once the table's outside border is in place, use the pencil again to draw in column and row borders, as shown here. When you're ready to get your regular mouse pointer back, click on the Draw Table button to turn the pencil tool off.

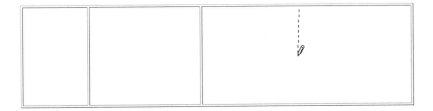

TIP   If you draw a border and it disappears, you may not be drawing a long enough line. The line needs to extend from one border to the other.

The drawing feature is very helpful when you want to add a cell or split it into smaller sections. To show or hide the Table toolbar, choose View ➢ Table Toolbar.

Viewing the HTML Code

If you want to see the code behind the tables you create, click on the HTML tab at the bottom of the Editing window. The HTML coding for a table is pretty straightforward; you really only need three tags to build a table (each has a closing tag, as well). The <TABLE> tag begins the table definition, the <TR> tag defines a new row in the table, and the <TD> tag defines a single cell within the table. Here is the code that builds a small table:

```
<TABLE BORDER="1">
  <TR>
    <TD>Cell A1</TD>   <TD>Cell B1</TD>
  </TR>
  <TR>
    <TD>Cell A2</TD>   <TD>Cell B2</TD>
  </TR>
  <TR>
    <TD>Cell A3</TD>   <TD>Cell B3</TD>
  </TR>
</TABLE>
```

The resulting table has three rows and two columns. The text within the <TD> and </TD> tags is what appears in each cell. The HTML default is a table with no borders, but the FrontPage default is a border one-pixel wide, specified in the <TABLE> tag.

Working within a Table

To move between the cells in a table:

- Use the Tab key on your keyboard to move one cell to the right. If you Tab in the last cell of a table, a new row is automatically inserted.

- Hold down the Shift key and press Tab to move to one cell the left.

- Click within a cell with your mouse.

In the empty table you just created, enter the data from the table shown in Figure 7.1.

To move out of the last cell of a table, hold Ctrl and press Enter. If you need to insert text before a table, hold Ctrl and press Home. The insertion point moves to the first cell of the table. Press Enter to insert a blank line before the table.

To move text and other elements within a table, select what you want to move and then just drag it and drop it into its new location. To copy items, hold down the Ctrl key until after you release the mouse button.

NOTE   In previous versions of FrontPage, columns started out very narrow and automatically expanded to match the longest text entry or widest image in them. FrontPage 98 creates a table that spans the page width. When you insert more than one line of text in a cell, the text wraps to the next line within the same cell. An image that is too large for a cell, however, causes the target cell to expand horizontally, vertically or both. As a result, other columns might be forced to shrink.

You can think of each cell in a table as a mini-page. You can change a cell's background color, and just about anything you put on a page can also be placed in a cell, including images, hyperlinks, and even another table!

That's right, you can nest a table within another table, as shown in Figure 7.5. In this example, four cells in the larger, surrounding table contain a two-row by two-column table. Each of the four cells in those smaller tables contains an image.

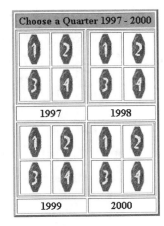

FIGURE 7.5: You can create almost any layout by nesting tables within tables.

Selecting Table Elements

To modify the look or shape of a table, you need to select one or more of its elements. To select a cell, row, column, or the entire table, move the insertion point to a cell and choose the appropriate command from the Table menu: Select Cell, Select Row, Select Column, or Select Table (from any cell).

Skill 7

You can also select various elements in the following ways:

- **Cell**   Hold down Alt and click or double-click the top border of the cell when a pointer is displayed.

- **Row or Column**   Move the mouse pointer to the far left border of the row (or top border of the column), and the mouse pointer changes to a solid arrow pointing across the row (or down the column), as shown here.

Click to select the row or column.

- **Multiple Cells**   Click in the first cell and then press shift and click in the last cell you want to select to select contiguous cells. Select one cell and then hold Ctrl and click to select non-contiguous cells. You can also drag over adjacent cells, rows, or columns to select them. To deselect individual cells, hold Ctrl and click on each one.

- **Caption**   Point to the left of the caption and click.

- **Table**   Move the pointer to the left side of the table to the area known as the selection bar, and the mouse pointer changes from an I-beam to a right-pointed arrow. Double-click on the selection bar to select the table.

You can select a cell, row, column or table from the Table menu. For example, place the insertion point anywhere in a row, and choose Table ➤ Select Row.

When you create a table without a border, the Editor displays dashed gridlines so you can see the limits of each cell. Click on the Preview tab to see the table without the gridlines.

Formatting a Table's Contents

You can format cell text as you would other text on a page. For example, you can make the title in the first row of the table a second-level heading. But before you do that, you need to merge all the cells in that row into a single cell that spans the width of the table.

1. Select the first row of the table (Table ➤ Select Row).

2. Click the Merge Cells button on the Tables toolbar or choose Table ➤ Merge Cells from the menu. The first row becomes a single cell; its width is determined by the total width of the cells that were merged.

3. With the insertion point still in the first row, select Heading 2 from the Change Style drop-down list on the Editor's Format toolbar.

With the data in the table, the top row merged into one cell, and the title displayed in the Heading 2 format, the table (shown in Figure 7.6) looks a lot more like the one in Figure 7.1.

Work Schedule for the Week of December 14, 1997							
	Mon	Tue	Wed	Thu	Fri	Sat	Sun
Celeste	X	X	X			X	X
Gerald	X	X		X	X	X	
Gordon	X			X	X	X	X
Carol			X	X	X	X	X

FIGURE 7.6: The table after adding data and merging the cells in its first row.

Adding and Aligning a Caption

You can add an optional caption to a table, which appears either directly above or below the table.

1. Select any cell in the table.

2. Choose Table ➤ Insert Caption.

3. The insertion point is centered just above the table so that you can enter the caption text.

4. Type the text for the caption, such as (As of Nov 15, 1997), as in Figure 7.1.

5. When you're finished, click outside the caption.

You can also position a normal line of text just above or below the table. But unlike a caption, the text does not stay centered above or move with the table.

You can apply text formatting, such as bold or italic, to a caption, but it does not accept paragraph formats, such as a heading. To delete a caption, select it and press Del on the keyboard twice.

By default, a caption appears centered above the table, but you can display it above or below the table. To change its position, click anywhere in the caption and choose Table ≻ Caption Properties. In the Caption Properties dialog box, choose Bottom of Table and then click on OK.

Changing the Look of a Table

Once you've created a table, you can change its appearance with the settings in the Table Properties dialog box (see Figure 7.7). Select any cell in the table and choose Table ≻ Table Properties, or right-click anywhere on the table and choose Table Properties from the shortcut menu.

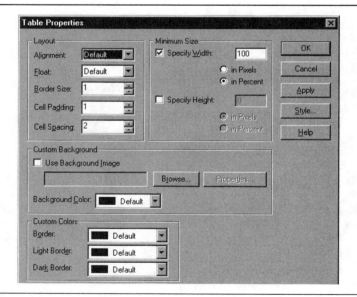

FIGURE 7.7: The Table Properties dialog box lets you adjust table format and dimensions.

Most of the options in the Table Properties dialog box affect table formatting. The Minimum Size group of options affects the overall dimensions of the table and is discussed in *Changing the Size of a Table* later in this Skill. When you change one or more of the settings in the Table Properties dialog box, you can click the Apply button to apply the new settings to the table without closing the dialog box. This lets you fine-tune the settings while you watch their effects on the table.

Changing a Table's Alignment and Layout

The Layout option group includes the following choices:

- **Alignment**   Set the horizontal alignment of the table within the width of the page. Choose Left, Center, or Right; choose Default to specify no alignment which most browsers display as left aligned. For the table you created earlier in this Skill, set its Alignment option to Center so it's centered in the page.

- **Float**   Allow other page text to wrap around the table rather than appear above or below it. Choose Left or Right to float the table to the left or right of existing text.

- **Border Size**   Set the width of the outside table border in pixels. This does not affect the width of the inner borders separating the cells; their widths can't be changed. By default, Border Size is set to 1 pixel.

- **Cell Padding**   The amount of space in pixels that separates the contents of a cell from the cell's edges (picture a padded cell) ; the default is 1.

- **Cell Spacing**   The amount of space in pixels between adjacent cells; the default is 2.

These last two options can be a little confusing until you see how they affect the cells in the table. Shown here are three copies of the same table. The one on the top has the default padding and spacing; the one in the middle has larger padding but default spacing; and the one on the bottom has larger spacing and default padding.

Sun	Mon	Tue	Wed	Thu	Fri	Sat
1	2	3	4	5	6	7

Padding -1 Spacing - 2

Sun	Mon	Tue	Wed	Thu	Fri	Sat
1	2	3	4	5	6	7

Padding - 8 Spacing - 2

Sun	Mon	Tue	Wed	Thu	Fri	Sat
1	2	3	4	5	6	7

Padding -1 Spacing - 8

Setting a Table's Background and Border Colors

The Table Properties dialog box includes two option groups that affect the table's background and borders. With the Custom Background options, you can change the table's background to distinguish it from the surrounding page. (The settings are similar to those that affect a page's background, as discussed in *Setting Page Properties* in Skill 4.)

- **Use Background Image**   Choose an image file that fills the table's background; either type a name or click on the Browse button and select an image file.

- **Background Color**   Choose a color for the table's background; the Default choice specifies no color for the table's background, so the table uses the same background as the page.

If you choose both a color and an image for a table's background, the image is displayed, not the color. However, the background color shows through a transparent color in a GIF image. If you apply background colors to individual cells (discussed in the next section), the cell background hides the table background.

 TIP   Use the Background Color button on the Table toolbar to change a table's background color without opening the Table Properties dialog box. Make sure the entire table is selected first, or you'll only change the background of the selected cells.

Use the Custom Colors options in the Table Properties dialog box to change the color of all the borders in the table. Tables are surrounded by two borders: a light border and a dark border. Choosing different colors for the two borders gives the border a 3-D effect.

- **Light Border**   Choose a color for one of the pair of lines that make up the table's border.

- **Dark Border**   Choose a color for the second in the pair of border lines.

- **Border**   Choose a color to apply to both borders when Light Border and Dark Border are set to Default, or for browsers that don't support Light Border and Dark Border options.

Experiment with the Border options to see how the Editor applies color to the border. To see how the Light and Dark Border options are interpreted, preview the page in your browser. If a browser does not support Light and Dark Border options, it applies the specified Border setting.

Changing the Look of Cells

Cells in a table have their own properties that affect alignment, background and border color, column width, and the number of columns or rows they span. We'll save the discussion of these last two items for *Changing the Size of a Table* later in this Skill.

To change the properties of a single cell, click within the cell and choose Table ➢ Cell Properties, or right-click and choose Cell Properties from the shortcut menu to open the Cell Properties dialog box (see Figure 7.8). To change the properties of multiple cells, select them before opening the dialog box.

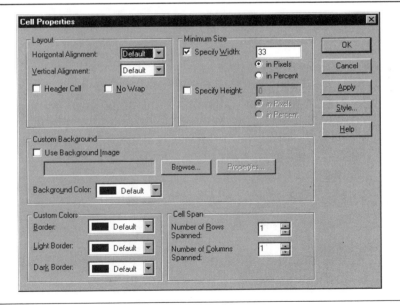

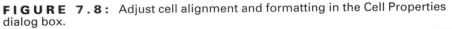

FIGURE 7.8: Adjust cell alignment and formatting in the Cell Properties dialog box.

Setting Cell Alignment and Layout

Most browsers align the contents of a cell with the left edge of the cell and center the contents vertically in the cell. You can change these alignment settings with the Horizontal Alignment and Vertical Alignment options in the Cell Properties dialog box. The horizontal choices are Left, Center, and Right, and the vertical choices are Top, Middle, Baseline, and Bottom.

 TIP To quickly adjust vertical alignment, click on the Align Top, Center Vertically or Align Bottom buttons on the Table toolbar.

By default, when text is longer than its cell is wide, the text wraps to a new line, expanding the height of the cell. Just like in an Excel worksheet or Word table, changing the height of one cell changes the height of the entire row. If you select the No Wrap option (see Figure 7.8), a browser doesn't wrap text to a new line in the cell, but expands the width of the column to display all the text.

Let's change the alignment of some cells in the table you built in the exercises earlier in this Skill. To center the contents in the cells that contain the days of the week and the cells below them:

1. Beginning with the "Mon" cell, select the cells that contain the days of the week and the cells directly below them.

2. Click on the Center button on the Format toolbar or choose Table ➤ Cell Properties, and set the Horizontal Alignment option to Center in the Cell Properties dialog box. Click on OK to align the text in the cells and close the dialog box.

Creating Header Cells

You can define any cells in a table as header cells to give them emphasis, such as when the cells are row or column titles. In the table you've been working on in this Skill, the days of the week and the names in the left column should be defined as header cells, as they are in Figure 7.1.

1. Select the days of the week.

2. Choose Table ➤ Cell Properties.

3. In the Cell Properties dialog box, select the Header Cell option. Click on OK.

4. Select the names in the left column, and set their Header Cell option.

FrontPage and most browsers display the text in header cells in boldfaced type.

Setting a Cell's Background and Border Colors

Cells have the same background and border properties as tables and pages. In the Cell Properties dialog box, you can specify an image or a color for a cell's background and the colors for the border around the cell.

When you set these options for a cell to anything but Default, the browser displays the colors or image you specify, overriding any backgrounds or borders used for the rest of the table. If there is no background specified for the cell or table, the page's background is used for the cell. This hierarchy of properties (Cell, then Table, then Page) is referred to as *cascading*.

Let's add some background color to some of the cells in the table we've been building:

1. If they are not already selected, select the cells that contain the days of the week.

2. Choose Table ➤ Cell Properties, or right click and choose Cell Properties.

3. Choose a color other than Default from the drop-down list for the Background Color (choose Silver for a light gray background).

4. Click on OK, then select and format the names in the first column.

Changing the Size of a Table

When FrontPage 98 creates a table, the default width is 100 percent of the width of the screen you are using to view it. It's possible to change the width of a table, to lock in a table's width, or allow it to expand and contract based on the entries in the cells or the size of the screen.

Changing Table Width

You can set the width of a table when you create it with the Insert Table dialog box or revise it with the Table Properties dialog box. First select the Specify Width option in either dialog box, then choose the measurement you want to use to define the width:

- **In Pixels**   Enter the exact width of the table in pixels.

- **In Percent**   Enter the width as a percentage (1 to 100) of the width of the browser's window, no matter how wide that window might be. For example, entering 100 makes the table as wide as the window; entering 50 makes the table half as wide as the window.

The method you choose depends on how you want your table displayed. For example, when you set the width of a table that has a lot of text or images in each cell (see Figure 7.2), you may want to maximize its visibility by setting the width as 100 percent. That way, no matter how large or small the display is, the table fills the screen. You might use this when you have a table on your home page displaying important information or hyperlinks for visitors to your site. By letting the table size with the window, all its contents will always be visible.

On the other hand, if the table is only a few columns with minimal text (see Figure 7.1), lock in the table's size in pixels so it doesn't interfere with the overall appearance of the page, even at higher resolutions.

Changing a Column's Width

There are several methods you can use to adjust the width of columns rather than have them automatically adjust based on the width of the window. Each of these ways may be more or less useful depending on your overall goals for the table. The methods are:

- Point to any of the cell borders and when the pointer changes to a double-headed arrow (as seen below), hold the mouse button and drag the border. This can be used both to adjust cell width and cell height.

- Select the rows or columns you want to adjust and click on the Distribute Rows Evenly or Distribute Column Evenly buttons on the Tables toolbar.

- Specify a minimum width in the Cell Properties dialog box. The choices are similar to those you use to set the width of a table, as discussed in the previous section. You can specify the minimum width either in pixels or as a percentage of the table's width (not the window's width).

In the sample table, don't worry about drastic changes in the widths of columns that could affect the look of the table; you just want seven columns (the days of the week) to be the same width. Here's how to do it:

1. Point to the top edge of the table above the Mon. column so the pointer changes to the black arrow pointing down that column; then click to select all the cells in that column.

2. Hold down the mouse button and drag to the right, straight across the top edge of the table to select all the columns until the right end of the table.

3. Click on the Distribute Columns Evenly button on the Table toolbar.

Adding and Removing Cells

Once you create a table, you are still free to add or remove cells. Note that a table need not be filled with cells; each row can have a different number of cells in it.

You can add either single cells or entire rows or columns. Before you add new cells to the table, move the insertion point to a cell that's adjacent to the new ones.

To add a single cell, choose Table ➤Insert Cell; the new cell is added to the left of the insertion point.

To add a row or column, select the row or column adjacent to where you want the new one and click on the Insert Rows or Insert Columns button on the Table toolbar. To insert multiple rows or columns, select the corresponding number of rows or columns. Rows are inserted above the selected rows; columns are inserted to the left of the selected columns.

If you want to insert rows or columns at the end of a table, choose Table ➤ Insert Rows or Columns. In the dialog box that appears, choose rows or columns, the quantity to insert, and where they should be placed in relation to the active cell. For example, to add three new rows below the active cell, choose Rows, set the Number of Rows option to 3, choose Below Selection, and click on OK.

TIP   When you insert a row or column, the new row/column contains the same number of cells as the active row/column.

Skill 7

To delete cells from a table, select one or more cells, or entire rows or columns, and click on the Delete Cells button on the Table toolbar, or choose Table ➤ Delete Cells.

Merging and Splitting Cells

You can also change the layout of a table by combining multiple cells into one and splitting one cell into multiple cells. Earlier in this Skill you merged all the cells in the top row of the table into a single, table-wide cell. Here's the general method for merging cells.

 Select the cells you want to make into a single cell (they must all be adjacent and form a rectangle), and then click on the Merge Cells button on the Table toolbar or choose Table ➤ Merge Cells. The borders between those cells dissolve. The resulting single cell takes up the same amount of room in the table if the cells were empty. The amount of space may increase if there was content in the merged cells.

 You can also merge cells using the Eraser on the Table toolbar. Click on the Eraser button to turn it on, then drag over the border you want to erase, as shown in Figure 7.9.

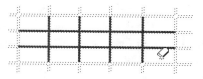

FIGURE 7.9: Drag the eraser over cells you want to merge.

 To split cells into multiple cells, select either a single cell or a rectangle of adjacent cells and click on the Split Cells button on the Table toolbar, or choose Table ➤ Split Cells. In the Split Cells dialog box (shown here), choose whether you want to split the cells into columns or rows. A diagram in the dialog box reminds you what the effect of each is. Set the number of new rows or columns you want to create and click on OK.

TIP   For a quick and easy way to split cells, click on the Draw Table tool and draw the new borders into the table.

Changing Cell Span

Here's yet another way to change the cells in a table, although this method doesn't change the number of cells, it changes the size of the cells. You select the cells you want to change and choose Table ➤ Cell Properties. You'll find the Cell Span group of options in the Cell Properties dialog box (shown here).

You can set one or both of the two options to have the selected cells span the specified number of rows or columns. For example, if you select a single cell and set its Cell Span option to 2 rows, that cell now expands downward into the row below, effectively doubling in size. The cell that had been below it, and all the cells to the right of the cell that had been below it, are pushed to the right so that the last cell in that row now extends beyond what had been the right-hand edge of the table.

Troubleshooting Table Layout

Once you've changed cell span, the table is no longer symmetrical, as some rows and columns have a different number of cells than their neighbors. The table contains dead space—areas clearly within the boundaries of the table that contain no cells. You might also create dead space when you insert columns or rows based on a column or row that contains merged cells. Figure 7.10 shows a table with dead space in the fourth column, created by changing the span of the first cell in column 2. Figure 7.11 is a browser's interpretation of the table.

Skill 7

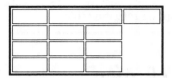

FIGURE 7.10: This table contains dead space.

FIGURE 7.11: The browser formats dead space as it would a thick border.

This isn't a problem once you realize the limitations of this empty area of a table. Dead space isn't a cell, so you can't select it. You can't place objects or text in it, or format it. The borders of the neighboring cells only have a single, light border rather than the double border surrounding other cells and the table.

You can't use the Draw Table tool to alter dead space. If you want to remove dead space from table, the easiest way is to move to the cell on the immediate left of the dead space and choose Table ➤ Insert Cell from the menu. Another option is to simply delete the column or row that contains the dead space.

Are You Experienced?

Now you can...

- ☑ Create a table in any of three ways
- ☑ Move between the cells in a table
- ☑ Select parts of a table
- ☑ Add a caption to the top or bottom of the table
- ☑ Change table properties, including layout, size and background colors
- ☑ Change cell properties
- ☑ Merge and split cells of a table
- ☑ Troubleshoot table layout problems

Skill 7

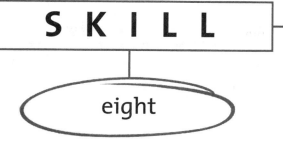

SKILL

eight

8

Displaying Images in Your Pages

- ❏ Working with GIF and JPEG images
- ❏ Inserting images and video clips
- ❏ Setting image properties
- ❏ Using interlaced images
- ❏ Creating thumbnails
- ❏ Making a color transparent
- ❏ Creating image maps

In this Skill, you see how easy it is to add sizzle to your Web site with graphic images. You bring an image into a page in the Editor, position it in the page and edit it. You learn several ways to improve image download time for crisp viewing, and use an image to fire up several hyperlinks—a snazzy effect found on many of the best Web sites.

The World of Image Formats

Images in your Web sites convey information or serve as the source for hyperlinks. You can also specify an image file as the target of a hyperlink so a browser opens and displays the image when the user clicks on its hyperlink. Images are also valuable as "window dressing"—livening up an otherwise humdrum, text-filled page. A bit of color can make a page more appealing and help distinguish one page from another, and logos clearly identify the Web site with a company or product.

An image within a Web page is called an *inline image*. Because HTML is a language for presenting text, inline images are actually stored as a separate files, which are then opened and displayed along with the HTML page in a browser.

 **NOTE**   The term *image* applies to many non-text objects displayed in a Web page: line drawings, photographs, charts, geometric shapes, and textures suitable for page backgrounds.

Computer image files come in a wide variety of formats. A *file format* defines how information is saved in a file, not the file's content. (The same is true with text, which can be saved in different formats: as a Word document, plain text (ASCII), Rich Text Format (RTF) or HTML.) Two image formats have become widely accepted standards for use on the World Wide Web: GIF and JPEG, pronounced "giff" and "jay-peg," respectively. Both file formats compress images, so the saved image is smaller than in other, noncompressed file formats. This becomes critical when the file is transferred over a network like the Internet, because smaller files take less total time to transfer.

When you place an image on a page in the FrontPage Editor, you can choose from images that were saved in other image formats. FrontPage 98 lets you import images stored in a number of common formats (see Table 8.1). When you save the page, however, FrontPage converts the image to a JPEG or GIF.

The GIF Format

CompuServe developed the Graphics Interchange Format (*GIF*) to shorten the time it takes to transfer images online. This format, which uses a .GIF file name extension, supports up to 256 colors (or 8-bit color), often the maximum number of colors that older computers can display. Because the image is compressed for network communications, then uncompressed by the browser, GIF images arrive more quickly than, say, a bitmap or PCX file format.

When an image-editing program compresses and saves an image as a GIF file, it leaves nothing behind—when you open a GIF image you'll see the original picture exactly as it looked when it was saved. This is called *lossless* compression, and gives the best compression ratios when the image has many repeating patterns, such as broad fields of the same color or repetitive lines. If you want to scan your company's black and white logo into a computer file, the GIF format is probably the one to choose.

 NOTE   A *compression ratio* relates the size of a file before and after compression. For example, if an image that occupies 400KB of the computer's memory is saved as a 100KB GIF file, then the compression ratio is 4:1.

The JPEG Format

The Joint Photographic Expert Group format (*JPEG*; the three-letter file name extension is JPG) can handle many more colors than the GIF format—up to 16.7 million colors (24-bit color). Like the GIF format, JPEG compresses files, but to achieve a higher compression ratio, it uses a *lossy* compression method, which literally strips out and loses what it considers to be expendable bits of the image. When you open a JPEG file, the image you see is of a lower quality than the original image.

The trick, however, is that the sophisticated JPEG compression algorithm takes out bits that you may not really notice are missing. This is especially true in richly colored images such as photographs, where a significant reduction in file size has only a slight effect on the quality of the image. When you save an image in the JPEG file format, you can specify the file size to image quality ratio. For example, you can choose a high-quality image with a larger file size, or you can choose a smaller file size with an image that's somewhat degraded. If you want to include a photograph of your company president on your web, the JPEG format is the one to choose.

Table 8.1 lists other common file formats you'll encounter when you work with images and other media on the World Wide Web.

INSERT TABLE 8.1: Common File Formats

Format Name	File Extension	Purpose, Internet Use
AIFF	.AIF	digital sound, commonly used
SoundEdit	.AU, .SND	digital sound, commonly used
Audio Video Interleaved	.AVI	video for Windows only, so minimally used
Windows Bitmap	.BMP	images, noncompressed format used for icons, wallpaper; FrontPage can import
Encapsulated Postscript	.EPS	images; FrontPage can import
Macromedia	.MMM	animation, commonly used
QuickTime Movie	.MOV	audio/video scaleable compression format for Windows or Mac, the Web standard for downloadable video clips
Moving Picture Experts Group (MPEG)	.MPG	audio/video compression, seeing increasing use
PCX bitmap	.PCX	images; FrontPage can import
RealMedia	.RAM	video; FrontPage can import
Raster	.RAS	images; FrontPage can import
Targa	.TGA	images; FrontPage can import
Tagged Image File Format (TIFF)	.TIF	images, noncompressed format often used for clipart; FrontPage can import
Wave	.WAV	digital sound, commonly used for opening effects at a site
Windows Metafile	.WMF	images; FrontPage can import
Virtual Reality Modeling Language (VRML)	.WRL	3-D models, used for "virtual tour" sites

Inserting Images

To bring an image file into a page in the Editor, first position the insertion point where you want the image to appear. Don't worry about too much precision. You can move the image later.

Click on the Insert Image button on the toolbar or choose Insert ➢ Image from the menu to open the Image dialog box, shown in Figure 8.1. To add an image file from the active web, locate the image in the list of image files. You can preview JPEG and GIF files; simply select the file, and FrontPage provides a preview in the Image dialog box.

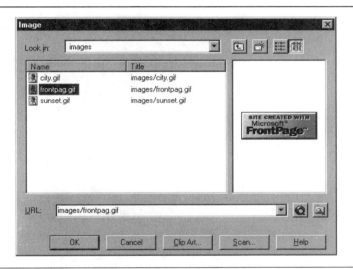

FIGURE 8.1: Specify an image to insert in the Image dialog box.

If the image isn't stored in the active web, click on the Use Your Web Browser to Select a Page or File or Select a File on Your Computer button to browse the Web or local and network drives for the image file. After you have selected an image, click on OK. FrontPage inserts the image in your page in the Editor.

 You can also insert an image using copy and paste. Select the image in its native program, copy it to the clipboard, then switch to the Editor and paste it on the page. If the Editor and the other program are both displayed on the screen, you can simply drag the image into the page in the Editor.

The HTML code for an image specifies the URL for the image and the image's size:

```
<IMG SRC="images/undercon.gif" WIDTH="40" HEIGHT="38">
```

Inserting Clip Art

The Microsoft Clip Gallery is included with FrontPage 98. Choose Insert ➢ Clip Art from the menu or click the Clip Art button in the Image dialog box to open the gallery, shown in Figure 8.2.

FIGURE 8.2: The Microsoft Clip Gallery includes bullets, backgrounds, and other Web images.

If you scroll to the bottom of the Category list, you'll find several categories designed for FrontPage 98, such as Web Buttons, Web Dividers, and Web Pictures. Choose a category, then browse the images. When you've selected the clip art image you want to use, click on Insert to close the Clip Gallery and place the image on your page. Figure 8.3 shows a new page with two images: a small piece of clip art, and a larger image of a bridge.

To insert clip art on a page:

1. Position the insertion point on the line where you want the image to appear.

2. Choose Insert ➢ Image or click on the Insert Image button.

3. In the Image dialog box, click on the Clip Art button.

4. In the Clip Gallery, select a category.

5. Choose an image, then click on Insert to place the image on your page.

The image that appears in the page is no different from any other image. You can change its properties, size, or position, or delete it from the page.

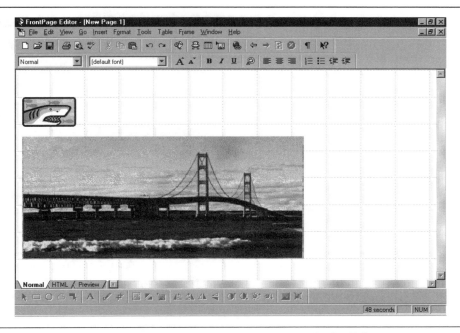

FIGURE 8.3: It's easy to place images on a page in the Editor.

Using Scanned Images

FrontPage 98 is TWAIN–compliant, so you can insert images directly onto a page from a scanner or digital camera attached to your computer. To insert a digital image from a device, click on the Scan button in the Image dialog box. The Camera/Scanner dialog box opens:

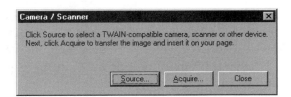

This dialog box works like a simple Wizard. First, click on the Source button to open a list of TWAIN-compliant devices attached to your computer:

Choose the device, then click on Select to return to the Camera/Scanner dialog box. Now, click on the Acquire button, and FrontPage transfers control to the device you selected, which opens its own dialog boxes to walk you through the acquisition process.

 NOTE   The Select Source dialog box is generated by Windows. If the device you want to use isn't on the list, use the software supplied with the device or the Add Hardware applet in the Windows Control Panel to add the scanner or camera to your system.

Inserting a Video Clip

You can also include a moving image in a page in the Editor—a video clip with an .AVI or .RAM extension. The process is very much the same as inserting a fixed image. Choose Insert ➢ Active Elements ➢ Video, then select the video clip.

The Editor inserts a still frame of the clip. You won't see the video running in the Editor, but you can use the File ➢ Preview in Browser command to see how it looks in a browser.

Video clips take up a lot of disk space, so even a few seconds of video can be several hundred thousand bytes. For example, the 15 second *welcome.avi* file included with Windows 95 is over 6MB. Adding the video to the page in Figure 8.3 adds 10 minutes to the time it takes a user with a 28.8 modem to load the page. The estimated time to load a page is shown in the FrontPage Editor status bar:

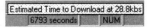

With this in mind, include a video only when its size is not a critical issue, such as when the video plays a key role in the web. Or make the video the target of a hyperlink on an otherwise unused page, and include text that tells users the estimated download time. Then, only those who are willing to wait will click the link to load the video.

Moving and Sizing Images

Before you can move or size an image, you must select it. Click on the image. A selection handle appears at each corner of the image and in the middle of each side. Not only do these indicate the image is selected, but you can use them to resize the image. When you point to any handle, the mouse pointer changes to a double arrow. Drag the handle to resize the image; if you drag a corner handle, FrontPage automatically maintains the image's *aspect ratio* (the relationship between its width and its height).

Move the selected image relative to other images and text by dragging it to a new location (drag it by the center to avoid changing its size). You can also use the Edit ➤ Cut and Paste method. Use Edit ➤ Copy and Paste, or hold Ctrl while you drag and drop, to make multiple copies of the image.

Saving Embedded Images

While you can place scanned and imported images on a page, FrontPage 98 saves all images within a web as GIFs or JPEGs (videos are saved in their original format). It chooses the file format based on the number of colors in the original image. Images created with palettes of up to 256 colors are saved as GIFs; images with more colors are saved as JPEGs. The two images in Figure 8.3 are both TIFFs. When you save the page, FrontPage saves the small shark picture as a GIF; the more complex bridge photograph is saved as a JPEG, as shown in Figure 8.4. When you insert a video clip from outside of the active web, you're given the opportunity to save the clip in the web when you save the page.

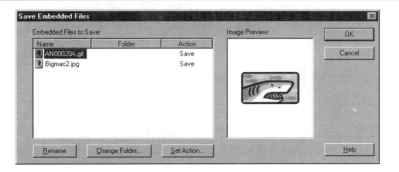

FIGURE 8.4: FrontPage saves imported images as GIFs or JPEGs.

Changing Image Properties

Select an image, then open the Image Properties dialog box by choosing Edit ➤ Image Properties or by right-clicking on the image and choosing Image Properties from the shortcut menu.

Setting General Properties

On the General Page of the Image Properties dialog box, shown in Figure 8.5, you set four properties: image source, type, alternative representations, and default hyperlink.

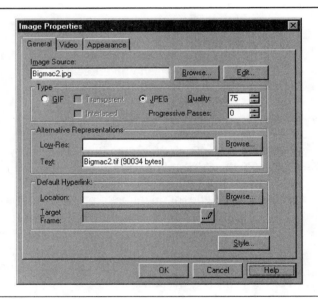

FIGURE 8.5: On the Image Properties dialog box General Page, specify a file format and default hyperlink for the image.

Setting Image Source Properties

The Image Source defines the source file for the image. If you want to replace this image with another, either enter the name and location of the new image or click on the Browse button and select the file from the Image dialog box. Selecting a different file replaces the current image in the page, so the other settings in the Image Properties dialog box now apply to that new image. Clicking on the Edit button opens the image in the image-editing program associated with GIF or JPEG files. In FrontPage, the Microsoft Image Composer is associated with these file types.

Specifying Image Type

In the Type option group, you specify whether the image should be saved in your web as a GIF or JPEG file. If the image is already a GIF or JPEG file, the appropriate option is selected. If the page has not been saved and the image is in another format, choose GIF or JPEG.

Options for GIF Images

When you select the GIF option, there are two GIF-related check boxes available: Transparent and Interlaced.

A GIF image can have one transparent color (see "Making Images Transparent" later in this Skill). If the image already has a transparent color defined, this option lets you choose whether to display that color in the image or to keep it transparent. If you make a color in a GIF image transparent, the Transparent check box is already selected when you open the dialog box. Turn Transparent off to display the color again in the image, removing the transparent definition for that color.

When you open a GIF in a browser, the image is loaded line by line, from the top to the bottom. This happens so quickly in a small image that you hardly notice how the image appears. However, if the image is large or the network connection is slow, you see the image grow from the top down. The effect can sometimes breed impatience as users watch the slow unveiling of the image.

The *Interlaced* property rearranges the order of the scan lines in the image file so the image seems to "get there" faster. With the Interlaced option enabled, the image loads in alternating sets of lines. The result is that when an interlaced image is sent to a Web browser, the picture occupies its space more quickly and seems to come into focus within that space, instead of appearing gradually from the top to the bottom.

Options for JPEG Images

When you save a JPEG image, you can specify the amount of compression to apply by adjusting the value in the Quality field. The default value in the Quality field is 75 in a range of 0 to 100. The more you compress a JPEG image, the lower the quality of the image; 100 percent is no compression, 0 percent is no quality (or

Skill 8

at least, very little). Enter a lower number to compress the image more while further reducing the quality, or enter a higher number to improve the quality while also increasing the size of the image file. If you're saving a large JPEG image in a page, you can experiment by lowering the quality setting. See just how much the image is degraded when you later open it in the Editor, and how much time you save from the estimated download time.

A *progressive JPEG* is similar to an interlaced GIF; the image loads in stages, gradually increasing in quality. In the Progressive Passes control, specify the number of stages required to completely load the image. Choosing 0 means the JPEG is not rendered progressively. This is a relatively new enhancement of the JPEG standard, so many browsers still load the entire image at once, regardless of the setting.

Specifying an Alternative for an Image

The Image Properties dialog box lets you specify two alternatives for an image. If the image is large and takes a long time to download, you can specify a second, smaller image file in the Low-Res option (low resolution). Most browsers download and display the Low-Res image first, so the person viewing the page can see the image relatively quickly. The browser then downloads the primary image, and once it's completely downloaded, displays it instead of the low-resolution version.

 NOTE   See *Creating a Thumbnail* later in this Skill for an even slicker way to handle images with long download times.

The second alternative is the Text option. Text you enter here is available to browsers to display when the image is not available or when the browser cannot handle images. For example, most browsers let users suppress downloading and displaying of images to save time online; some browsers can't handle images at all. In these cases, the browser displays the alternative text. The text you enter should describe the image so that the person viewing the page gets an idea of what was supposed to be shown.

Setting Video Properties

The Video page of the Image Properties dialog box has settings that affect video clip images (see Figure 8.6).

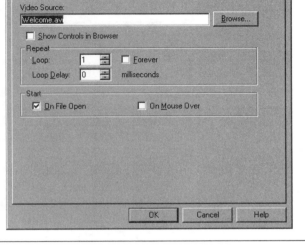

FIGURE 8.6: The Video Page in the Image Properties dialog box.

The Video Source field displays the name of the video clip file. To specify a different file, either enter a new name or click on the Browse button and select a file.

If you select the Show Controls in Browser check box, the browser displays standard video controls beneath the video clip window. The video controls allow the user to start or stop the video at any time.

By default, a video clip plays only once when the page is opened in a browser. You can specify how many times the video should be played by setting the Repeat options. Set the Loop field to the number of times you want the video to play; for infinite looping, enable the Forever checkbox. Specify the amount of time (in milliseconds) between plays in the Loop Delay field. For example, entering 500 puts a half-second pause between playbacks.

Use the Start options to specify that the video should start when the page is opened in a browser (the On File Open check box) or when the reader moves the mouse over the video (the On Mouse Over check box).

Setting Image Alignment and Size

To align an image to the left, center, or right of the page or a table cell, treat the image as you would a paragraph. Select the image, then click on one of the alignment buttons on the Format toolbar.

You can set other image alignment options in the Appearance tab in the Image Properties dialog box (see Figure 8.7). You can also change the size of the image and enclose it within a border.

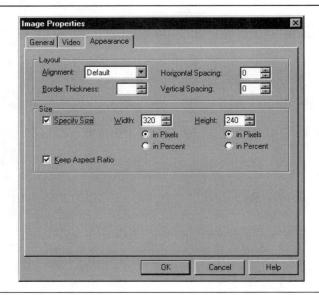

FIGURE 8.7: The Appearance Page in the Image Properties dialog box.

The Layout options include three choices for arranging an image with its surrounding text: Alignment, Horizontal Spacing, and Vertical Spacing. In the Alignment control, choose how the image should align with surrounding text:

- **Absbottom** aligns the image at the bottom of the current line.

- **Absmiddle** aligns the image at the middle of the current line.

- **Baseline** aligns the image at the bottom of the current line; this is the default in most browsers.

- **Bottom** aligns the bottom of the image with the surrounding text.

- **Center** aligns the center of the image with the surrounding text.

- **Default** uses the browser's default settings.

- **Left** aligns the image at the left margin; surrounding text is wrapped at the right side of the image.

- **Middle** aligns the middle of the image with the surrounding text.

- **Right** aligns the image at the right margin; surrounding text is wrapped at the left side of the image.

- **Texttop** aligns the top of the image with the top of the tallest text in the current line.

- **Top** aligns the top of the image with the surrounding text.

In the Horizontal Spacing control, specify the number of pixels of blank space that should separate the image from any text, image, or window edge to its left or right. Use the Vertical Spacing control to specify the number of pixels between the image and any text, image, or window edge above or below it. To enclose the image in a black border, specify a thickness in the Border Thickness field. The default is zero, so no border is displayed.

Use the Size option controls to set the image's width and height. If you want to specify the size of the image, enable the Specify Size checkbox. Then, enter values for image Width, Height, or both in pixels or as a percentage of page size.

If you change the width or height in pixels, you don't have to calculate the other dimension. Make sure the Keep Aspect Ratio checkbox is enabled, and FrontPage maintains the aspect ratio (relationship between the height and width) of the image. As you change the width, FrontPage calculates and changes the height automatically.

Working with the Image Toolbar

If the Editor's Image toolbar is not already displayed, selecting an image displays it. If you deselect the image by clicking elsewhere, the Image toolbar is hidden again.

While you're working intensely with one or more images, choose View ➤ Image Toolbar from the menu to display the Image toolbar all the time. This prevents the page from jumping down or up whenever the toolbar is displayed or hidden.

NOTE   You can position a toolbar anywhere on the screen by pointing to part of the toolbar's gray background and dragging the toolbar to its new location, or by right clicking on the toolbar's title bar when it isn't docked and choosing Move from the shortcut menu.

Making Images Transparent

When you place an image on a page with a background, you'll find that the fill area in the inline images looks pretty tacky; the white fill area surrounds the image, separating it from the background, as shown below. You can easily fix this problem.

 Select the image, click on the Make Transparent button on the Image toolbar, and with the mouse pointer, click on the white fill area of the image. The white fill disappears and the image melds into the page's background.

You can make any single color in an image transparent, and it doesn't have to be the fill color (although that's the usual application). To make a different color transparent, choose the Make transparent tool again and click on a different color in the image. The color you originally selected becomes visible again, and the newly selected color turns transparent. You can only make GIFs transparent, so if you select any other type of image, FrontPage asks you if you want to convert it to a GIF first:

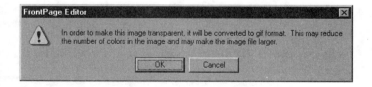

When you alter an image (for instance, by making it transparent), you're prompted to save the image again when you save the page in the Editor.

Adding Text to an Image

One of the new features in FrontPage 98 is the ability to easily add text to an image. First, select the image.

Then, click on the Text button on the image toolbar (if the image isn't a GIF, you're prompted to convert the image), and a text box opens on the image. Enter any text you wish. You can resize the text box by selecting it, then using its handles to resize it.

 NOTE   Adding text to an image doesn't change the image; the text is displayed on top of the image.

Creating a Thumbnail

Thumbnails are alternative images that let users choose whether or not to load large image files. With a thumbnail, a smaller version of the image is loaded before the full image. If a user clicks on the image, the full image is then downloaded. FrontPage 98's *AutoThumbnail* feature creates the thumbnail image and the hyperlink to the original image, so it's very easy to create.

To create a thumbnail, select the image in the Editor and choose Tools ➤ AutoThumbnail from the menu. FrontPage creates a smaller version of the image; the thumbnail image has the same filename as the original, followed by an underscore and the word small. For example, the thumbnail of `cyclone.jpg` is called `cyclone_small.jpg`.

FrontPage replaces the image with the small version, and creates a hyperlink to the full size version. Figure 8.8 shows a section of a page with two thumbnails. Before the images were converted to thumbnails, the page took 94 seconds to load with a modem speed of 28.8. The thumbnail version loads in 11 seconds. Users can then decide whether they wish to click on either thumbnail to load the full-size image.

Skill 8

FIGURE 8.8: These thumbnails load almost nine times faster than the page that contains full size versions of both images.

Changing Thumbnail Options

You can specify how the Editor should create thumbnails on the AutoThumbnail page of the Options dialog box, shown in Figure 8.9. There are three options you can set: Set (size), Border Thickness, and Beveled Edge. You're not setting the options for existing thumbnails or the selected thumbnail, but determining options for new AutoThumbnails you create.

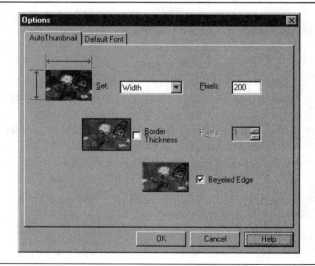

FIGURE 8.9: Set the AutoThumbnail options to change the appearance of new thumbnails you create in the FrontPage Editor.

Use the Set option to specify the size of thumbnails the Editor creates. You only need to specify height or width; FrontPage maintains the aspect ratios of the original image when it creates the thumbnails.

- **Width**   Width of the thumbnail in pixels
- **Height**   Height of the thumbnail in pixels
- **Shortest Side**   Height or width of the shortest dimension in pixels
- **Longest Side**   Height of width of the longest dimension in pixels

Enable the Border Thickness checkbox, then enter a border width in pixels to create borders around thumbnails.

Enable the Beveled Edge checkbox to create thumbnails that have a 3-D look, like buttons. The thumbnails in Figure 8.8 have beveled edges.

Creating Image Maps

You've seen how you can create a hyperlink, and you know how to work with images. Now you'll see how to go one step further by creating an *image map*, which is a single image containing multiple hyperlinks. Each hyperlink is associated with a defined area of the image called a *hotspot*, which, when clicked, activates that link. In a browser, you see only the image; there is no indication it has hotspots until you move your mouse over the hotspot and the pointer changes to a hand.

You've undoubtedly encountered image maps in many, many pages on the Web. They can be informative, attractive, and intuitive, and they can also transcend language, which is an important consideration on the Internet. A typical use of an image map is literally in the form of a map, where you can click on a city, state, or area to display regional information.

 NOTE   Creating an image map from a geographic map works very well when you're defining hotspots for the large areas, like the Canadian provinces or the regularly shaped states in the western U.S.. But the plan doesn't work so well when you try to create hotspots on smaller, irregularly shaped areas like the eastern U.S. states. Make sure you're working with an appropriate map: If all your business is in New England, you'd be better off with a regional map of the eastern United States.

You should also be aware of the following issues when you incorporate an image map in a page:

- The context of the image map must be unambiguous. Users should have no doubt that the image is a place to click to open another resource. If the image isn't completely self-explanatory, add appropriate text.

- A large image can take a long time to download on a dial-up connection (about 3,600 characters, or bytes, per second at 28,800 bps), so use large image maps with caution. Large isn't necessarily tied to the screen size of the image; the map in Figure 8.10 only adds eight seconds to the page's download time. Check the time to download in the status bar before and after adding an image to determine how long it takes to load.

- Hotspots in an image map must be easy to discern, or readers will wind up on pages they had no intention of visiting. The same problem occurs if hotspots are too small or too numerous.

- You can't predict image quality for every browser—or whether the image appears at all. To ensure users can access exactly the right link, you can also include text hyperlinks, or a link to a list of text hyperlinks.

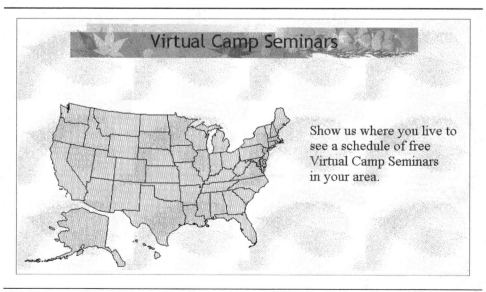

FIGURE 8.10: A geographic map can be a very practical way to implement an image map.

Defining an image map is quite simple:

1. First decide what type of image maps you want to use in your FrontPage web: server-side, client-side, or both.

2. Insert the image that serves as the image map.

3. Define a hotspot in the image for one of the hyperlinks.

4. Define the target of that hyperlink.

5. Define the other hotspots and hyperlink definitions for the rest of the image map.

Choosing the Type of Image Map

You can create one of two types of image maps in a FrontPage web. The difference between them is the way mouse clicks in the image map are handled:

- A *server-side image map* is the traditional type. When a user clicks within an image map, the browser sends the coordinates of the click (relative to the image) to the server. The server looks up the coordinates in a table of hotspots for that image map and processes the appropriate hyperlink target. Different servers have different ways of storing coordinates and targets.

- A *client-side image map* removes the need for server interaction, because the hotspot coordinates for the image map are included in the HTML definition that is sent to the browser. When users click within the client-side image map, the browser locates and opens the target associated with the coordinates.

Client-side image maps not only reduce the processing burden on the server, they are guaranteed to work no matter which server is hosting the page that contains the image map. However, client-side image maps are a fairly recent invention, and not all browsers support them. With FrontPage, though, you can create image maps that use both the server-side and client-side definitions. If a user's browser supports the client-side definition, it uses that definition. Others use the server-side definition.

By default, FrontPage 98 creates client-side code and FrontPage style server-side code for each image map. Image map type is set in the FrontPage Explorer for the entire active web. To change image map types, choose Tools ➤ Web Settings in FrontPage Explorer, then click on the Advanced tab in the FrontPage Web Settings dialog box (see Figure 8.11).

Skill 8

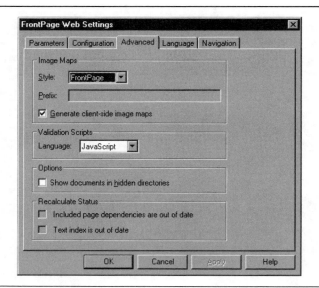

FIGURE 8.11: Specify image map type in the FrontPage Web Settings dialog box's Advanced page.

1. To create client-side HTML code for each image map, enable the Generate Client-Side Image Maps check box (this is the default).

2. If you don't want FrontPage to generate server-side maps, choose <None> in the Style drop-down list. If you select a style other than <None> and leave the client-side check box selected, both types of image map code are created.

3. If you want to create server-side HTML code, select a server from the Style drop-down list. Choose FrontPage from the Style list if the server supports the FrontPage Server Extensions. Otherwise, choose one of the other server types.

 NOTE   If you choose a style other than <None> or FrontPage, you should also enter the path and name of the server's image-map handler (CGI program) that processes coordinates when users click on the map. For example, the default entry in the Prefix field for an NCSA-compatible server is /cgi-bin/imagemap. For help with this, talk to your web server's administrator.

Once you specify the types of image maps you'll create, FrontPage generates the appropriate code whenever you create an image map in this web.

Defining the Hotspots

For this example, you can create an image map from any image in a page appropriate for the job at hand—large enough to contain the hotspots, but not so large that it takes a long time to download to a browser. The image map should also be meaningful to a user. The image we'll use here (see Figure 8.12) was conveniently captured from Sybex's Web site at

```
http://www.sybex.com
```

FIGURE 8.12: The Sybex home page uses an image map that offers hyperlinks to the main areas of the Web site.

This is a spacious image map that uses a desktop metaphor for its hyperlinks: a notepad and pen link to a *FAQ* (frequently asked questions) page, a couple of CDs link to a download page, and a newspaper classified section links to a job listing page. This image works well as an image map, because it is attractive and invites the reader to stay and browse through the site; its pictures are clearly defined and easy to locate in the image; each picture has a short text description next to it that pins down its purpose. Although they're not shown in the figure, there are text hyperlinks below the picture for browsers that can't handle images.

If you'd like to use the image for this exercise, go to the Sybex Web site and either copy the image to the Editor using the clipboard, or save the image, then choose Insert ➤ Image in the Editor to add it to the open page. To save the image, right-click on the image in your browser and choose a Save command from the shortcut menu.

Skill 8

Here's how to define the first hyperlink hotspot in this image, thereby making that image into an image map (with just one hyperlink so far). We'll start with the About Sybex laptop in the center of the image.

1. Select the image.

2. Click on the Rectangle button on the Image toolbar so you can define a rectangular hotspot in the image.

3. Point to the lower-left corner of the laptop computer in the image. Notice that the pointer changes to a pencil.

4. Hold down the mouse button and drag toward the upper-right corner of the laptop's screen. As you drag, a rectangle expands over the image, defining the area of the hotspot. Extend the rectangle to include the About Sybex text above the laptop; this ensures that a user can click on the laptop or the text to activate the link.

5. When the rectangle surrounds the laptop and text, release the mouse button to open the Create Hyperlink dialog box, shown in Figure 8.13.

6. Define the target of the hyperlink just as you would for a normal hyperlink. For this example, you can either link to a file in your active web, or just enter a nonexistent target like About Sybex.htm. Click on OK to create the link.

FIGURE 8.13: Enter a target for the hotspot in the Create Hyperlink dialog box.

Let's define a second hyperlink in this image map. This one is irregularly shaped, over the picture of the open book labeled *Updates* in Figure 8.12. Select the image if it isn't still selected.

1. Click on the Polygon button on the Image toolbar.

2. Click once on the lower-left corner of the Updates book in the image to begin the first line of the polygonal hotspot (this is simply a convenient beginning point).

3. Point to the lower-right corner of the Updates book. A line extends from the first point to the mouse pointer. Click once to end this line and establish the first edge of the hotspot. Try not to overlap the rectangular hotspot you already created; otherwise there could be confusion when a user clicks in that area.

4. Continue from corner to corner, clicking on each one to extend the edges of this hotspot. As long as you don't overlap into another hotspot, try to extend this hotspot a little beyond the edges of the picture of the book so that a click that would otherwise be a "near miss" still activates the link.

5. When you reach the beginning point, double-click to end the definition of this hotspot.

6. Define the target for this hotspot, either to a file on your active web or to a nonexistent file such as `Updates.htm`.

Now this image map has two hotspots. You can continue to create others, as needed, using the appropriate button on the Image toolbar: either Rectangle, Polygon, or Circle. To create a circular hotspot, drag from the center of the circle outward.

Specifying a Default Hyperlink

In many image maps, such as the one in the previous example, there are undefined regions that aren't covered by a hotspot. This presents a problem when a user clicks on the image, ostensibly on a hotspot, and then waits and waits for something to happen that never does.

To avoid this situation, you can define a default hyperlink for the image with a target for all areas of the image that aren't hotspots. This ensures that no matter where a user clicks on the image map, something happens. The default target for an image map might be a page that simply advises the user to return to the previous page and try again.

To define a default hyperlink for an image map, right-click on the image and choose Image Properties from the shortcut menu. In the General page, enter the target for the Default Hyperlink in the Location field.

Viewing Hotspots

When you select an image map in the FrontPage Editor, each of its hotspots is outlined. When the image map is not selected, or when you are viewing it in a browser, you won't notice anything different about the image; the hotspot outlines are invisible. However, when you move your mouse pointer over a hotspot in a client-side image map, the target of that link is displayed in the status line in the Editor (and in most browsers, as well).

Complex graphics can obscure the hotspot outlines, making them difficult to see. You can circumvent this problem by clicking on the Highlight Hotspots button on the Image toolbar. This hides the image completely while still outlining each of its hotspots, as shown in Figure 8.14, so you can get a good idea of where each lies in the image and check for areas of overlap. You can't move or resize a hotspot in this view, but you can change the target of its hyperlink definition.

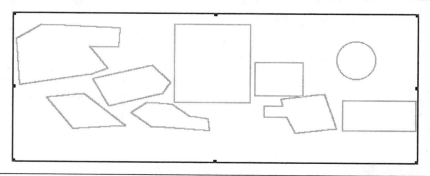

FIGURE 8.14: Highlighting hotspots allows you to check for areas of overlap.

Revising Hotspots

You change an image's hotspots in the Editor. You can also delete a hotspot, change its size and shape, or redefine its hyperlink target. To make changes, first select the image. Then click on the Select button on the Image toolbar and click on the spot you want to change within the hotspot. You'll see selection handles appear around the spot's edges.

WARNING Remember, selecting an image is much the same as selecting text. If, for example, you select an image and then type a single character, you replace the image with that character. So use caution when you are busily working on an image.

Once you've selected a hotspot, you can:

- Move to the next hotspot by pressing Tab.
- Delete the selected hotspot and its hyperlink from the image by pressing Del.
- Change the size of circles and rectangles or the shape of polygon hotspots by dragging any of their selection handles.
- Move the hotspot by dragging it (but not from a selection handle) or by selecting it and using the arrow keys on your keyboard.
- Change the target definition by right-clicking within the hotspot and choosing Image Hotspot Properties from the shortcut menu. This displays the Edit Hyperlink dialog box, which includes the same options as the Create Hyperlink dialog box you used to create the hotspot.

Are You Experienced?

Now you can...

- ☑ **Insert images**
- ☑ **Set image properties**
- ☑ **Make an interlaced image**
- ☑ **Create thumbnails**
- ☑ **Make an image transparent**
- ☑ **Create image maps and hotspots**

Getting Graphic
with Image Composer

- ❑ Using Microsoft Image Composer
- ❑ Creating sprites and compositions
- ❑ Applying effects
- ❑ Saving compositions and sprites
- ❑ Saving for the Web
- ❑ Creating buttons
- ❑ Converting images to JPEGs and GIFs

One of the exciting improvements in FrontPage 98 is the newly updated version of Microsoft Image Composer. With Microsoft Image Composer 1.5, you have hundreds of image-editing tools and effects at your fingertips. Working with Image Composer is challenging, and there's plenty of raw material to practice with. FrontPage 98 includes hundreds of photographic and clip art images for your composing pleasure.

Creating Web Images

Images play a big role in the life of a Web site. The images you incorporate into a page convey information, add snap and pizzazz, serve as hyperlinks, act as image maps for multiple hyperlinks, and generally just make the site a less boring place to visit. Images draw attention to surrounding text, so viewers who only intended to look at the pictures often find themselves reading nearby content. Images also accentuate text by breaking up long text entries, making them easier for users (particularly lower level readers) to read.

Image Composer is just what its name implies: not an image catalog, or image collection, but a powerful tool you can use to create fresh new images for your webs. No small addition to the FrontPage 98 package, Microsoft Image Composer is a powerful image-editing program that can easily stand on its own.

 NOTE   Image Composer is a wonderful tool with a lot of features, but it also has a big appetite for your computer's processing power and RAM. Its official minimum hardware requirements are a 486 processor with 16MB of RAM and a video card that can display at least 256 colors, but you'll want more processing power and memory to work at a decent pace.

Starting Image Composer

Start Microsoft Image Composer in any of the usual ways:

- Start Image Composer from the Windows Start menu to create or revise images, whether or not you're also working in FrontPage.

 - In the FrontPage Explorer, choose Tools ➤ Show Image Editor, or click on the Show Image Editor button on the toolbar to switch to Image Composer. Image Composer will launch it if it isn't already running.

- In either the FrontPage Explorer or Editor, double-click on an image to open it in Image Composer.

If double-clicking on an image file in FrontPage doesn't open the image in Image Composer, that means the image's file format isn't associated with Image Composer. JPEGs and GIFs are automatically associated with Image Composer, so an easy way to open the image is to convert it to a JPEG or GIF. Just save the page that contains the image, and the Editor saves the image in one of the two formats.

If the file type is one you use frequently, you may prefer to associate the image file type with Image Composer. That way, you can place and edit images without saving or converting them. For more information on associating file types with editors, see Skill 5.

In Image Composer, you create customized works of art by combining hand-drawn work, text, scanned images, or the hundreds of sample photographs and drawings that come with Image Composer. Although many image-related programs let you combine various pieces, you'll see this process emphasized in Image Composer—both in the way the program is designed and in the way you build your images.

 NOTE   Microsoft produces two other image editors: Microsoft Photo Editor and Microsoft Picture It!. Although all three programs are image editors, they're used for very different purposes. Image Composer is used to create images, the Photo Editor is used to retouch and enhance existing images, and Picture It! includes image capture utilities and image enhancement tools.

An image you create in Image Composer is called a composition. The basic components of every composition are sprites. For example, the composition in Figure 9.1 includes three sprites: a clip art image inserted from the Clip Gallery, an image copied from another program, and text entered in Image Composer. A composition may include only a single sprite that you import and manipulate with Image Composer's tools.

Skill 9

FIGURE 9.1: You use Image Composer to combine sprites to create compositions.

Image Composer shares the look and feel of the programs in both Microsoft FrontPage and Microsoft Office (see Figure 9.2). Its menus, toolbars, and file-operation dialog boxes look quite familiar, so you won't have any problem finding your way around the program.

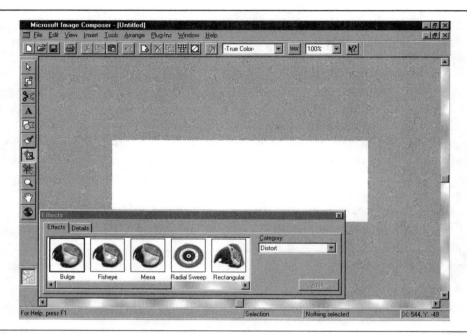

FIGURE 9.2: Image Composer shares the look and feel of FrontPage and Office 97 programs.

You'll recognize the menus and toolbar at the top of the Image Composer's window, and there's a status bar at the bottom that displays pertinent information about your composition and the program. On the left side of the screen is another toolbar called the toolbox; each of its buttons opens a set of image-editing tools displayed in the tool palette near the bottom of the window. In Figure 9.2, the Effects tool palette is displayed. You can also open tool palettes from the Tools menu. The color that's used the next time you apply color to a sprite is displayed in the Color Swatch beneath the toolbox.

The white area beneath the toolbar and to the right of the toolbox is the composition space, where you create your composition. Think of it as a virtual page in Image Composer that serves as the background for your image. You can change its size and color to go with the image you're creating (the default is white). Because its size is in pixels, you can specify the exact size of the images you create.

The gray area around the composition space is the workspace. Use it as a staging area where you can place sprites you need in the image or windows that display other views of your image. The size of the workspace is unlimited, so you'll never run out of room. If you scrolled the window to some far-off realm of the workspace, you can use the View ➤ Center on Composition Space (or press Home) to bring the composition space back into view.

Setting Up Your Work Area

When you save your image, the items in the workspace and composition space are saved (more on this later). Drag one of the composition guides that set the boundaries for the composition space to change its size. You can do this any time, even after you've added sprites to your composition. For more precision, open the Composition Setup dialog box (File ➤ Composition Setup):

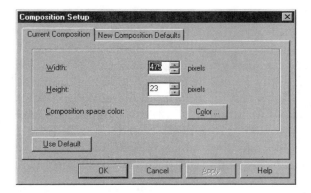

The Composition Setup dialog box has two pages that are nearly identical. Both allow you enter, in pixels, the height and width of the composition space. In the Current Composition page, you can click on the Use Default button to transfer the default settings to the current composition. If you resize the composition space, you can click on the Use Current button in the New Composition Defaults page to change the default to reflect the new height and width. In both pages, you can click on the Color button to open the Color Picker and set the composition space's current or default background color.

Skill 9

Picking Colors for Your Web

Color is one of the most important considerations when you're creating images for display on the Web. In Image Composer, any color you use comes from a palette of colors. A palette can include millions of colors or only a few. Although your first impulse might be to plumb the depths of your artistic talent by using the largest palette possible, there are two important reasons to do exactly the opposite:

- The more colors an image contains, the larger its file becomes and the longer it takes to load.

- No matter how many colors you include in an image, the colors actually displayed in a browser are dependent on the capabilities of the browser and the computer on which it is running.

Using True Color

In the world of computers and in Image Composer, the term true color refers to a palette of a little more than 16 million colors. It is called 24-bit color, because that is how much computer memory is required to display one pixel in any of the 16 million colors. All of your work in Image Composer is saved with 24-bit color, so you'll never lose any colors when you save your work in Image Composer format.

To display all the colors in a true color image, your computer's video adapter and monitor must be able to handle 24-bit color, and Windows must be set up to take advantage of these capabilities. When you display a true color image on an older computer that can't handle true color, the computer will simply approximates the true color by choosing a color from the available colors.

 NOTE   To specify how many colors to display in Windows, choose Start ➤ Settings ➤ Control Panel, and double-click on the Display icon or right click on the Desktop and choose Properties. You'll find a list of available color palettes on the Settings tab in the Display Properties dialog box.

You can choose a color or a color palette in Image Composer from the Composition Setup dialog box, or by clicking the Color Swatch to open the Color Picker dialog box. Select the True Color tab to pick a color from a palette of 16 million-plus colors (see Figure 9.3). Select a color from the palette by clicking on the color, or by entering the exact RGB values in the fields for the Red, Green, and Blue sliders. If you opened the Color Picker from the Composition Setup dialog box, you can click on OK to make the color you chose the current color for the composition space.

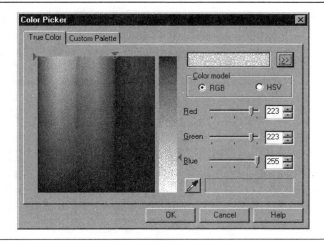

FIGURE 9.3: Use the Color Picker to choose a true color for the composition area.

Using Color Palettes

Unless you are working on an intranet and know most visitors to your site have fast connections and computers that can handle true color images, you should probably limit the images you create to 256 colors, also called *8-bit color*. There are two ways to do this:

- When you save a composition, you can convert the image into a 256-color image (more on this later). Remember that a GIF file is limited to 256 colors, so GIFs automatically use the 8-bit color palettes; only JPEG can handle true color.

- When you create an image, only choose colors from a 256-color palette. This ensures the colors you see on your screen are pretty much like the ones a browser displays.

If you choose the Custom Palette tab in the Color Picker dialog box, you can choose a 256 color palette from the Color Palette drop-down list (see Figure 9.4). Image Composer comes with several palettes; Web (Solid) and Web (Dithered)

are appropriate for color images in your FrontPage webs. If you're converting a true color image, the dithered and ramped palettes create a smoother image than the solid palettes. Once you pick a new palette, it's displayed when you click on the Color Swatch.

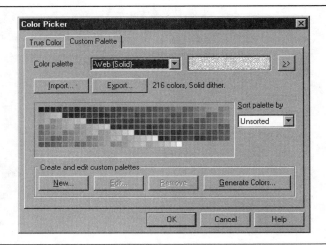

FIGURE 9.4: The Custom Palette tab in the Color Picker lets you choose a color from a 256-color palette, or choose a custom palette.

Even if your computer has true color capabilities, you can view a true color composition in 8-bit color by selecting one of the custom palettes from the Color Format drop-down list on the toolbar. This allows you to see how the image looks when viewed as a 256-color image on your web. Figure 9.5 is the Web (Solid) version of the true color composition in Figure 9.1. The composition background has clear lines of demarcation rather than blending from one color to the next.

The difference between palettes of 16 million to 256 colors isn't as large as it sounds. The human eye cannot even distinguish between several adjacent colors in the true color palette. While richly colored photographs clearly lose quality when displayed in 256 colors, many true color images degrade only slightly.

FIGURE 9.5: The 256 color palettes create lower quality images that load at least three times as fast as true color.

However, the trade off in time is easily quantifiable. Modem transmission speeds are measured in bps: bits per second. If it takes 24 bits to describe one pixel of true color, and 8 bits to describe one pixel created from a 256 color palette, then it takes three times as long to download one true color pixel. Users may not notice the difference in color quality, but they always notice the difference in download time.

Working with Sprites

There are two ways to create a sprite in Image Composer: You can import an existing file or image, or create a sprite from scratch using the Image Composer tools.

Importing Sprites

The default file format for Image Composer files is MIC. FrontPage 98 has a lot of sprite files that are separated into categories. With a typical installation, they're left on the CD. (You can copy them to your hard drive during a custom installation, but they occupy about 190MB.) Image Composer has a sprite catalog with thumbnails of each of the images for easy browsing and selection.

Finding an Image in the Sprite Catalog

To see the thumbnail images of the available sprites, choose Help ➢ Sample Sprites Catalog to open the Sample Sprites Catalog help file. To browse the catalog, begin by selecting Sample Sprites ➢ Photos or Sample Sprites ➢ Web on the Contents page. Double-click on any catalog category to see the thumbnails.

Skill 9

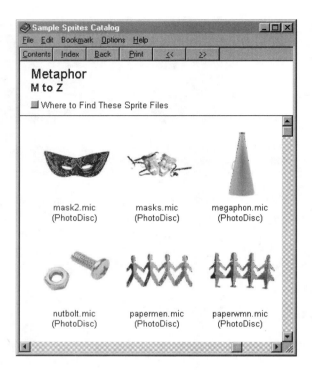

To look for a specific image (for example, an image that includes trees), move to the Index page. Enter text in the search box at the top of the page, then click on the Display button.

When you've found a sprite you want to place in your composition, click on the Where to Find These Sprite Files button at the top of the page. Help gives you the exact location of the file, where, as you can see below, [client] is the drive that contains the CD. Remember the location and file name when you insert this image into Image Composer.

Importing an Image

When you identify the name and location of the sprite or image you want to use, you can import it into Image Composer. Image Composer can import files in most of the common file formats: JPEG, GIF, TIFF, Targa, and others. If you're importing a sprite from Image Composer samples, you need to insert your FrontPage 98 CD into your CD-ROM drive.

Choose Insert ➤ From File or click on the Insert Image File button on the toolbar to open the Inserts an Image File dialog box. Locate the folder where the file is located. Select the file, then click on OK to insert it in the upper left corner of the workspace.

TIP   If you're viewing or inserting several images, you can use the Windows Explorer to find them and drag them into Image Composer.

Sizing and Moving Sprites

When a sprite is selected, it has eight handles. Seven of the handles have arrows and are used for sizing the sprite. Grab one of the handles, and drag it to resize the image. Hold the Shift key while releasing the mouse button to maintain the aspect ratio of the image. The eighth handle in the upper right corner of the image is a rotation handle. Dragging the rotation handle rotates the image around its centerpoint.

To size a sprite precisely (so, for example, it's the same size as the composition space) choose Tools ➤ Arrange, or click on the Arrange button on the toolbox to display the Arrange tool palette, shown in Figure 9.6.

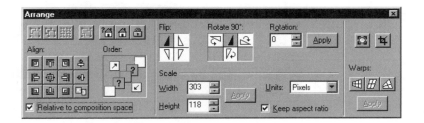

FIGURE 9.6: Use the Arrange tool palette to size and move the selected sprite.

Set the size of the sprite in pixels in the Width and Height controls. You may need to disable the Keep Aspect Ratio check box if you're setting both the width and the height of this sprite, thereby changing its width-to-height aspect ratio. Click on Apply to apply the width and height settings.

Use the Alignment tools at the left end of the palette (see Figure 9.6) to align the sprite in the composition space. Enable the Relative to Composition Space checkbox, then use the 12 alignment buttons to align the sprite. But first, check out the three buttons above the Order control.

The first button, Set Home Position, "memorizes" the sprite's current location as its home position; the second button, Return to Home Position, returns the sprite to its defined home position. This means you can experiment a bit, knowing that you can precisely reposition the sprite if you don't like its new location.

When you think the sprite is where it belongs, lock it in place with the Lock/Unlock Position button so you can't accidentally move it. If you change your mind and want to relocate the sprite, click on the Lock/Unlock Position button again.

You don't have to use the Arrange tool palette to move a sprite; simply drag a selected sprite to a new location. To move a sprite a small distance, use the arrow keys on the keyboard. The default settings move the sprite one pixel in the direction you press. Hold Ctrl and use the arrow keys to move larger distances.

Creating Sprites

While Image Composer has a shapes palette and some basic drawing tools, it's not a paint program. Many of the sprites you create are text sprites, because you can create amazing text effects with Image Composer. To create a text sprite, choose Tools ➤ Text, or click on the Text button in the toolbox (on the left side of the window). This opens the Text tool palette, shown in Figure 9.7.

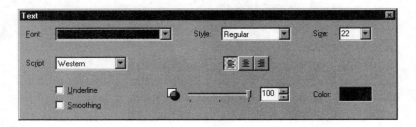

FIGURE 9.7: Use the Text tool palette to create text sprites.

Choose a font, size, and other text attributes using the controls in the palette. The slider bar is used to set opacity: how solid (opaque) or transparent the text is. 100 percent is solid. Click on the Color Swatch to open the Color Picker and select a color for the text.

When all the palette options are set, move the mouse pointer into the workspace, where it changes to a text tool. Hold the mouse button and drag a rectangular text box. When you release the button, the text box opens. Type the text for your sprite, then click outside the text box to create the sprite, as shown in Figure 9.8.

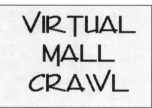

FIGURE 9.8: Text sprites allow you to quickly create distinctive project or department logos.

In FrontPage 98, you can edit text sprites (seems obvious, but it's new in this version). To change the sprite's text or properties, double-click on the sprite. The text box opens for editing, and the Text tool palette displays the current settings for the sprite. The initial text box only has room for one line of text. To enter a second or third line, as shown in Figure 9.8, use the handles to resize the sprite so there's room for additional lines. At the end of a line, hold Ctrl and press Enter to move to the next line.

NOTE   You must double-click to change a sprite's properties. If you simply select the sprite, then open the Text tool palette and change settings, the settings apply to the next sprite you create, not the selected sprite.

Adding an Effect to a Sprite

Now let's put some curves into the text sprite you've just created. Make sure the sprite is selected, and click on the Effects button to open the Effects tool palette.

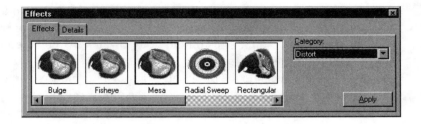

Choose a type of effect from the Category drop-down list. Browse the thumbnail samples of the post-effect macaw to see what the effect does to the selected sprite. When you've selected the effect you wish to use, click on the Details tab and see if you want to change any of the optional settings for the effect. Detail options depend on the effect you select; for example, the Distort Fisheye effect has a single Spread Amount option, while Paint effects have three to five options. When you've set any details you desire, click on the Apply button to apply the effect to the sprite.

 NOTE
You only get one Undo operation in Image Composer. Don't adjust anything until you double check the effect you just applied, in case you want to undo the effect.

Figure 9.9 shows the text sprite in Figure 9.8 with effects from three different categories: Fisheye (Distort), Gray Noise (Patterns), and Stained Glass (Arts and Crafts). For descriptions of effects, see the *Effects Overview* in Image Composer Help.

FIGURE 9.9: Apply Effects to change the appearance of a sprite.

Selecting and Arranging Sprites

There are a number of ways to select sprites:

- Click on a sprite to select it.

- To move from one sprite to the next, press the Tab key.

- To select multiple sprites, select one, then hold Ctrl and select others, or using the selection tool, drag a box around the sprites you wish to select.

- To select all the sprites in the workspace, choose Edit ➢ Select All from the menu, or click on the Select All button on the toolbar.

- To copy the selected sprites, click on the Duplicate button on the toolbar or choose Edit ➢ Duplicate from the menu. The copy is placed on top of the existing sprite. Use the mouse to drag it to its new location.

All the sprites in Image Composer are arranged in a stack, where each sprite is assigned a position relative to the other sprites. For example, when you insert or create a new sprite, it goes to the top of the stack. When you move the sprite, it overlaps any other sprites it encounters.

You can change a sprite's order in the stack by right-clicking on the sprite and choosing one of the stack-related commands. For example, if another sprite overlaps the current one, choose Bring Forward. This places the current sprite one step higher in the stack. You can repeat the command until it is high enough in the stack to overlap the other sprite, or choose Bring to Front to bring the selected sprite to the very front of the stack. If you're going to be arranging a number of sprites, you might prefer to open the Arrange tool palette and use the Order control to restack the sprites.

Saving the Workspace or Composition Space

When you use the File ➢ Save command in Image Composer or click on the Save button on the toolbar, you save the entire workspace, including but not limited to the composition space. You can close Image Composer, then open the file and pick up right where you left off. The file is saved as an Image Composer file, with an .MIC file extension. You can't insert Image Composer files in web pages.

When you're ready to use your image in a FrontPage web (or for any other purpose), you must save the composition in an image format like GIF or JPEG. Note that, when saving in an image format, you can save the entire contents of the composition space, or selected sprites within the workspace or composition space. Image Composer uses a Save for the Web Wizard to help you save your composition as an image. Use the Next and Back buttons to move through the Wizard's steps.

Choose File ➤ Save for the web to open the Wizard. In the first step, indicate whether you want to save selected sprites or the entire composition. Selected sprites don't have to be in the composition space; you can select and save sprites in the workspace. In the second step, shown in Figure 9.10, indicate whether or not the resulting image should be transparent.

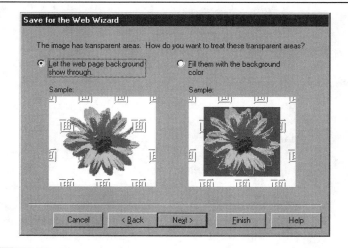

FIGURE 9.10: The Save for the Web Wizard makes it easy to create GIFs and JPEGs for use on your Web pages.

In the third step, specify the background color of the page you intend to place the image on. If you're not sure, leave the default, Tiled Background setting. In the last step, click on Save to open a Save dialog box, shown in Figure 9.11.

Select a file location, then enter a file name. You can change the file type, color format, and transparency if you want. However, the settings in the dialog box are based on the choices you just made in the Wizard. If, for example, you make the image transparent, the dialog box displays only options relevant to GIFs and the transparent color is shown in the Transparent Color swatch. Click on Save to save the file based on the settings you entered.

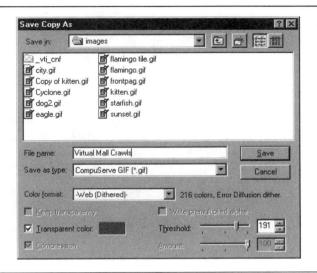

FIGURE 9.11: Specify a file location, name, and type in the dialog box.

When you save to any file format other than MIC, all the sprites are saved as a single image. This is called *flattening* the composition. When you save the composition space instead of the selected sprites option in the Save for the Web wizard, sprites that hang over the composition guides are truncated, and sprites in the workspace are totally ignored.

Saving the workspace and saving sprites or compositions are unrelated operations. You can save a sprite or composition as a GIF, TIFF, JPEG or other standard format, then save the workspace as a MIC. If you close Image Composer without saving the composition, you're prompted to save the Untitled composition, even if you've saved selected sprites from the workspace.

Adding Shapes to a Composition

Image Composer includes a small set of tools you can use to draw ovals, rectangles, arcs, and polygons. You can use shapes as borders for compositions, but you can also fill shape sprites with textures that you want to apply to other sprites (see the next section).

Click on the Shapes button or choose Tools ➢ Shapes to open the Shapes tool palette, shown in Figure 9.12. Click on a shape button in the left end of the palette, set the options for Edge and Opacity, then drag in the workspace to layout the shape.

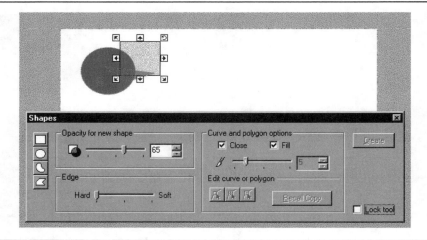

FIGURE 9.12: Use the Shapes tool palette to add regular and irregular shape sprites to your composition.

Click on the Create button or select a different shape tool to create the shape. The shape is filled with the color in the color swatch. If you need to create several shapes, you can enable the Lock Tool checkbox to leave the selected shape tool turned on until you click to turn it off.

After you create a shape, try applying some of the effects from the Effects tool palette. To apply solid colors, click in the Color Swatch and select the new color for the sprite. Select the sprite, then click on the Color Fill button on the toolbar to fill the selected sprite with the color in the Color Swatch.

Transferring Textures between Sprites

One of the many fun and interesting features in Image Composer is its ability to transfer the texture from one sprite to another. (This feature was called Sprite to Sprite in Image Composer 1.0.) In Figure 9.13, for example, the texture from the mint leaves sprite has been transferred to a text sprite. There are five different texture attributes you can transfer from one sprite to another:

- color
- opacity/transparency (0 percent is transparent; 100 percent is opaque)
- shape
- saturation (the fullness of the color)
- intensity (how "pure" the color is)

FIGURE 9.13: You can transfer textures between sprites to create interesting images.

First, move the source sprite (which provides the texture) and destination sprite (the texture's recipient) so they overlap. Then, select both sprites. The sprite you overlap on the other serves as the source. If it's not clear which sprite is the source, it's easy to check: The destination sprite has hollow handles, while the handles on the source sprite are solid. If the source and destination are reversed, just press the Tab key to swap them.

Click on the Texture Transfer button and choose a transfer technique from the thumbnails in the Texture Transfer tools palette. The easiest way to learn about texture transfers is to apply, then undo each of the transfers in turn to see how the transfer applies to real sprites. To really understand the various Map transfers, use a source or destination sprite that contains a gradient. The gradient sprite shown below was created by applying the Gradient effect Grayscale Right to a rectangle shape.

Skill 9

Table 9.1 describes each of the Texture Transfers.

TABLE 9.1: Texture Transfers

Texture Transfer	Description
Glue	Replaces the pixels in the destination sprite with opaque pixels in the source sprite, but only in the area where the two sprites overlap; "glues" the two sprites together.
Map Color	Copies the color values of the source sprite to the overlapping opaque pixels of the destination sprite, without changing the destination sprite's intensity.
Map Intensity	Copies the intensity values of the source sprite to the destination sprite without changing the destination sprite's colors.
Map Saturation	Uses the intensity of the source sprite to change the saturation of the overlapping area of the destination sprite. Saturation works exactly opposite of what you might expect: Where the source sprite is white, the destination sprite pixels becomes more intense.
Map Transparency	Uses the intensity of the source sprite to change the transparency of the destination sprite in the overlap area. Where the color is strongest in the source sprite, the pixels are made more transparent in the destination sprite.
Snip	Deletes opaque pixels from the destination sprite wherever there's an overlapping opaque pixel in the source sprite; use snip to make a silhouette of the source pixel.
Tile	Copies the source sprite's image onto the destination sprite in a tiled manner; this texture transfer does not require the sprites to overlap, as the entire source sprite image is repeated transferred to the entire destination sprite (see Figure 9.13).
Transfer Full	Replaces only the opaque pixels of the destination sprite with the pixels, opaque and transparent, of the source sprite in the overlap area.
Transfer Shape	Replaces only the opaque pixels of the destination sprite with the opaque pixels in the source sprite in the area of overlap; use Transfer Shape to embed a portion of one sprite in another.

Optional settings for each transfer are at the right end of the Texture Transfer tools palette. After you've selected a transfer and set options, click on Apply to transfer the texture from the source sprite to the destination sprite. If you're pleased with the results, click in the workspace, then select one of the sprites and drag it to separate them. Don't forget: Undo is an option.

NOTE   Each Texture Transfer has only one source sprite, but most of the transfers can be made to multiple destination sprites in one operation.

Creating Buttons

When you consider the number of available effects and transfers you can use in Image Composer, it's easy to imagine scores of web developers, chained to desks in dimly lit basements, painstakingly creating, warping, and snipping sprites to create the swarms of custom buttons that appear on commercial Web sites. Image Composer 1.0 was used so often to create buttons that Image Composer 1.5 includes a Button Wizard to help with the process. The buttons in Figure 9.14 were created using the Wizard.

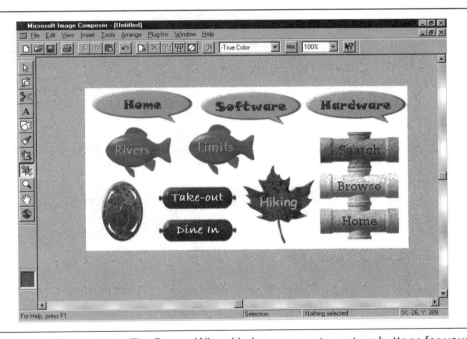

FIGURE 9.14: The Button Wizard helps you create custom buttons for your Web pages.

To create a button, choose Insert ➤ Button from the menu to open the Button Wizard. In the first step, shown in Figure 9.15, select a button style from the list. In the second step, indicate how many buttons you'd like to create using the selected style.

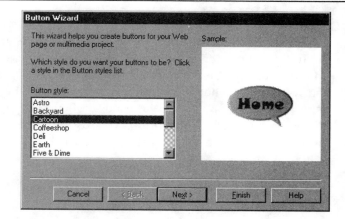

FIGURE 9.15: In the first step of the Wizard, choose a button style.

In the third step, enter text for the first button. You can apply different images to each button you create. Note, however, that you can't add an MIC file to a button because MICs aren't images. When you click on Next, the text for the first button is still in the textbox, but the label above the text box indicates that this is the second button. Enter the text for each button, then click on Next, until all buttons are entered.

In the fourth step of the Button Wizard, decide whether you want all the buttons to be the same size, or have Image Composer size each button according to its contents, as shown in Figure 9.16. (You can enter new dimensions for the buttons later, but you can't resize them by dragging.) If you choose the Same Size for All Buttons option, click on the Preview Size button to find out how large the Same Size actually is. You can change the size using the spinbox controls; you can't make the button smaller than the Minimum to Fit sizes. Click on Next, then on Finish to create the buttons. Image Composer dumps the buttons in a stack in the upper left corner of the screen. You can then drag them into the composition, or select and save each as a separate image.

The Button Wizard offers limited choices: a handful of button shapes, each with a single texture. After you've created a button, however, you can edit it, choosing different shapes, text attributes, and textures. For example, in Figure 9.14, different textures are applied to the three plumbing buttons on the right. To change an existing button, simply right-click on the selected button and choose Edit Button from the shortcut menu to open the Button Editor, shown in Figure 9.17.

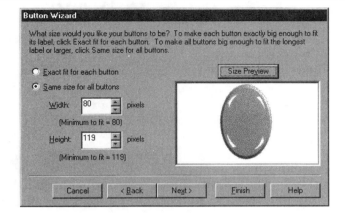

FIGURE 9.16: Choose buttons sized to fit their text, or a consistent size for all the buttons you're creating.

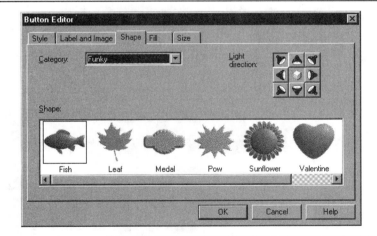

FIGURE 9.17: Use the Button Editor to enhance the buttons you create in the Button Wizard.

You can save individual buttons, or groups of buttons, but it's easiest to simply save the workspace as a MIC file. When you want to place a button in your web, copy it in Image Composer, then paste it in the FrontPage Editor.

Using Image Composer to Convert Files

Earlier in this Skill, you learned how to use the Save for the Web Wizard with a composition or sprite. The Wizard really shines, however, when you use it to convert existing images to JPEGs or GIFs for use in your web. To convert an image, open the image file directly, rather than inserting it on a page. Then, choose File ➤ Save for the Web to launch the Wizard. A progress meter appears to let you know that the Wizard is building previews:

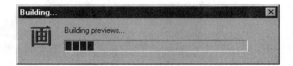

When the previews are completed, you'll find that they were worth the wait. Image Composer creates previews to show you how the file looks when saved as a GIF or JPEG with various options (see Figure 9.18). Each preview's caption includes the file format, file size, and estimated download time based on the modem speed selected in the connection drop-down list. If you change the connection speed, Image Composer recalculates the download times for each preview. After you select a preview, click on the Next button to continue through the Wizard and save the image file.

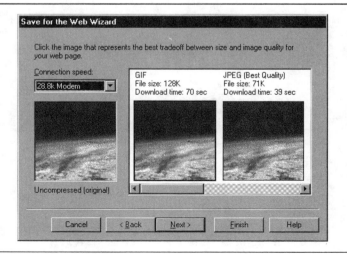

FIGURE 9.18: The Save for the Web Wizard previews allow you to choose an appropriate image format.

Of course there's a tradeoff between image quality and download time, but the Save for the Web Wizard lets you see the tradeoff, and make high quality decisions about the image formats you want to use in your Web site.

Are You Experienced?

Now you can...

- ☑ **Import images and sprites**
- ☑ **Create sprites and compositions with Image Composer**
- ☑ **Apply effects to sprites**
- ☑ **Save compositions, sprites, and the workspace**
- ☑ **Transfer textures**
- ☑ **Create and edit buttons**
- ☑ **Convert images to JPEGs and GIFs**

Creating a Consistent Look for Your Web

❑ Creating a web using wizards and templates

❑ Creating pages using templates

❑ Applying a theme to a web or a page

❑ Creating and linking style sheets

❑ Copying from existing webs and Web pages

As Web sites become more sophisticated and Web design evolves into an art form all its own, Web creators face more pressure to create sites that meet acceptable standards of design. Simply throwing something together to establish a Web presence is no longer considered good business. Today, a Web site must look professional to attract repeat visitors. Although it never hurts to have a computer graphics design artist in the family, you can create a professional looking Web site by yourself as long as you follow some simple design rules and use the built-in tools that come with FrontPage 98.

In this Skill, you learn how to create webs using the FrontPage wizards and templates, apply design style themes to the pages of the web, explore one of the latest HTML enhancements called Cascading Style Sheets, and import pages from existing webs.

Creating a Web Using Wizards and Templates

Now that you know the fundamentals of creating a web and working with Web pages, you'll find that FrontPage's templates and Wizards make creating a web as easy as it gets. Wizards guide you through the process of setting up the structure for the web and adding some basic content before the web is ever created. *Templates* are a little more modest in their approach—they still provide you with a basic structure, but require you to insert all your own content after the web is created.

You already know how to create a new web. The only difference is that this time, you'll choose one of the wizards or templates. In the Explorer, choose File ➤ New ➤ FrontPage Web to display the New FrontPage Web dialog box (shown in Figure 10.1).

 NOTE   When you have a web open in the Explorer, the New FrontPage Web dialog box includes an Add to the Current Web option. If you select the option, all the pages associated with the new web are imported into the current web. If an incoming file has the same name as an existing file, such as INDEX.HTM, you're asked to choose which one you want to keep.

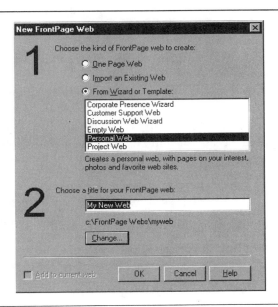

FIGURE 10.1: You can choose a Wizard or a template in the New FrontPage Web dialog box.

By default, FrontPage 98 creates a web based on a template called a Personal Web. There are two wizards and three other templates to choose from. The wizards include:

- **Corporate Presence Wizard**   Helps you design a web that can be the basis for your company's debut on the Web.

- **Discussion Web Wizard**   Helps you design a web that lets visitors leave messages or respond to messages around an identified general topic, and organizes the messages in related threads.

 NOTE

A *thread* is a group of messages that spawns from a message from someone on a particular topic. When someone else responds to that first message with another message, the thread begins. Visitors can read the first message and all of the subsequent responses, then can add their own two cents (even though the responses may no longer have any relevance to the initially identified topic).

When you choose a Wizard in the New FrontPage Web dialog box, the Wizard asks you a series of questions about the content of the new Web site. For example, it may ask you about the type of pages you want in the web, the contents of the home page, and the contents of a feedback form page. It then builds the pages accordingly.

Each FrontPage web template contains a set of pages that can serve as the basis for the web you build (you'll know if a new web is based on a template if its name doesn't end with Wizard). For example, a new web based on the Project Web template, seen in Figure 10.2, can help you and other members of a team oversee a specific project.

- The Members page lets you keep track of who's involved in the project, and includes a place for a picture of each member.

- The Schedule page lets you keep track of the project's schedule.

- The Status page offers you a place to create links to monthly, quarterly, and annual status reports for the project.

- The Search page lets you search all of the pages in the web for text you specify.

- The Archive page is a storehouse of links to related resources that may reside outside of the web.

- The Discussions page provides a central place to link to discussion groups in the web.

The Project Web contains a home page that includes an overview of the web, a What's New section, and an e-mail hyperlink for comments and questions about the web. All pages include shared borders and navigation bars.

Besides the Project Web, here's a quick rundown of the other templates:

- **Customer Support Web**   Creates a web that gives your customers a place to go for information or help with your products, particularly if those products happen to be software (see Figure 10.3).

- **Empty Web**   Contains all the necessary folders for a new FrontPage web, but contains no pages or other resources.

- **Personal Web**   Creates a web you can use to provide personal information for business or personal use.

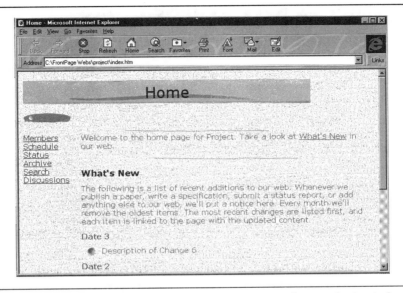

FIGURE 10.2: You can use the Project Web template as the basis for tracking work on a team-assigned project.

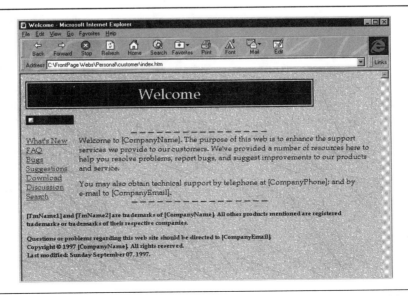

FIGURE 10.3: The Customer Support web includes pages to provide technical assistance and support to users of a company's products.

Getting to Know Your New Web

When you create a web with a wizard or a template, it's important to explore the web in each of the views in the Explorer. The web opens in Navigation view, but be sure to look at the web in Hyperlinks and Folders views at the very least, to get an idea of the web's structure. After you are familiar with the files that make up the new web, open the Home Page in the Editor. Before making any changes, it's a good idea to view the web in your web browser, click on all the internal hyperlinks, and see whether you can understand how a visitor would use the web.

Sometimes the templates and wizards contain advanced elements, such as form fields (see Skill 12) and FrontPage Components (see Skill 11), that may be a trifle disconcerting at first. Once you've seen these elements in operation, it's much easier to determine their purpose so you can decide if you want to include them before you spend time learning how to make them work.

Once you understand how the web works, return to the Editor and follow the instructions in the Comments section to add your content. The Comments are actually FrontPage Components themselves, which you'll learn more about in Skill 11. In the meantime, click on a Comment to select it—the pointer changes to a robot, as seen here. When you begin typing, the Comment is deleted.

Comment: The graphic for this page will be supplied by Tony in Corporate Communications.

When you start a new FrontPage web from a template, you can revise any of the pages, add new pages, or remove pages from the site. The template simply serves as a helpful and convenient way to get started.

You can even combine templates and wizards to add additional functionality to the web you are developing. For example, perhaps you're creating a Corporate Presence web for your company, and want to have a place for your customers to discuss topics related to your products. You can add the Discussion web to the Corporate Presence web. Just run the Corporate Presence wizard first, and when you create the Discussion web, click the Add to Current Web check box at the bottom of the New FrontPage Web dialog box.

Once the new pages are part of the open web, you just have to drag them into the web structure in Navigation view to create hyperlinks between the appropriate pages in the webs (see Skill 5, *"Managing Webs in the Explorer"*).

Adding Pages Using Templates

In addition to the wizards and templates in the Explorer that create entire webs, you can also make use of over 30 additional templates and wizards designed to create individual pages in the Editor. The majority of these templates, shown in Figure 10.4, include tables that provide a well-designed structure for the page, including suggestions for the placement of headings and graphics. All you have to do is enter your content—the design work is taken care of for you. To create a page based on a template, choose File ➤ New in the Editor to open the New dialog box.

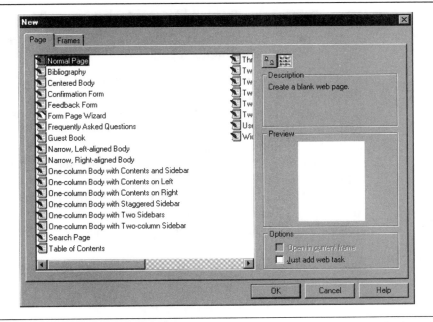

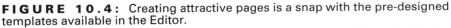

FIGURE 10.4: Creating attractive pages is a snap with the pre-designed templates available in the Editor.

Clicking the New button on the toolbar creates a default new page. You must choose File ➤ New to create a page based on a template.

There are four different types of pages listed here:

- **Structural layout**   Pages such as Centered Body and Narrow, Left-aligned Body, that contain pre-designed tables to provide a standardized structure for a page.

- **Structured content**   Pages, such as the Bibliography and Frequently Asked Questions, that provide structure and suggestions for presenting specific kinds of information.

- **Forms**   Forms, such as the Feedback form and Guest Book, that contain structural layout and FrontPage components that process input from visitors to the site (see Skill 12 for more about Forms).

- **Frames**   Structures to display multiple pages on one screen (see Skill 13 to learn about working with Frames).

Select each template to see a description and a preview of the template. Placing the template into one of the categories listed above helps you decide which page best suits you purpose. When you find a template you want to use, click on OK, or on the Just Add Web Task check box to create the page and put it on your task list to modify later. Adding a task to your Task List is helpful when you're building the skeleton of your web and want to create multiple pages at once.

Figure 10.5 shows a newly created one-column body with a contents and sidebar page. Notice the instructions on the page showing where your headings, titles, and text go. To use the page, select the existing text and type over it. To replace a graphic, select it and insert the new graphic in its place. Once you insert your own content, the page is complete.

To complete several matching pages, just add new pages using the same template.

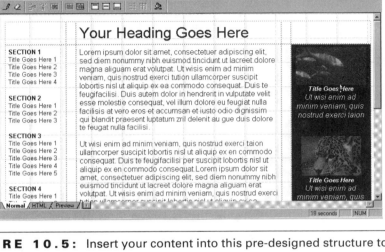

FIGURE 10.5: Insert your content into this pre-designed structure to complete the page.

The page depicted in Figure 10.6, based on the Frequently Asked Questions template, not only provides you with the structural layout but suggests what the content of the page should include. This page includes a comment at the top describing how to use the page, with general instructions for creating additional questions. It's up to you, however, to figure out how to add the additional sections (see Note below), create a bookmark for the new question, and create a hyperlink to the question in the Table of Contents.

NOTE The easiest way to create additional sections on the Frequently Asked Questions page is to copy one of the sections, including the bottom horizontal line, then move the insertion point to the beginning of Author Information and paste the new section. This creates the Back to Top hyperlink for you, but you still have to enter the new question and answer and create the hyperlink to the new question in the Table of Contents.

Just as with the web templates, it's helpful to view the template pages in a browser to see how they look and function before modifying them with your custom content.

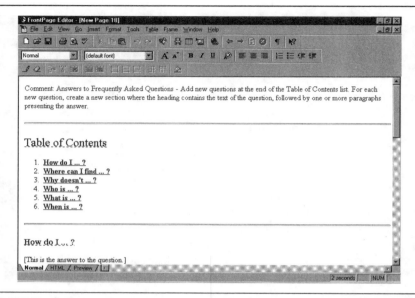

FIGURE 10.6: The Frequently Asked Questions template provides a structure for the page and guidelines for the suggested content.

Saving a Page as a Template

FrontPage doesn't limit you to the pre-existing templates that come with the software. You can save any page as a template. That template is then available in the New dialog box along with all the others.

To save a page you designed as a template, choose File ➤ Save As and click the As Template button at the bottom of the Save As dialog box. This opens the Save as Template dialog box, shown in Figure 10.7.

FIGURE 10.7: Use the Save As Template dialog box to save a page you create as a template.

Complete this dialog box as follows:

- **Title**   Enter the title you want to appear in the New dialog box.

- **Name**   Enter the name you want to use as the file name for the new page. The URL or file name for the page on which you based this template is displayed here when the dialog box opens.

- **Description**   Enter a description of the template to appear in the Description section of the New dialog box.

- **Browse**   Click on Browse to select the name of an existing template that you want to overwrite with this new template.

Click on OK to save the new template. You may want to go to the New dialog box (File ➤ New) to ensure your template made it and that you're satisfied with the name and description you gave it. If you want to make changes, choose File ➤ Save As, click on the As Template button, and revise the information. Click on Browse to select the template you want to overwrite. Click on OK again to save your changes.

Each template file resides in its own folder (named with a .TEM extension) within the Pages folder of the FrontPage program folder, such as

```
C:\Program Files\Microsoft FrontPage\Pages\Employee.tem\Employee.htm
```

To remove a template from the New dialog box, you have to delete the template's folder (using the Windows Explorer or My Computer).

Applying Themes

In Skills 5 and 6, you learned how shared borders and navigation bars add consistency to the pages of a web. Another exciting new feature of FrontPage 98, *themes*, provides the ultimate in consistency. When you apply a theme to a web, FrontPage designs every page with the same background image, color scheme, buttons, navigation bars, fonts, active graphics, and other page elements. Because the theme impacts the entire web, new pages are automatically created with all the design elements of the active web.

When you create a web using a wizard, FrontPage asks you if you want to apply a theme to the web. However, you don't have to use a wizard to have a great looking web—just click on the Themes button on the Explorer Views bar to open the Themes window, shown in Figure 10.8.

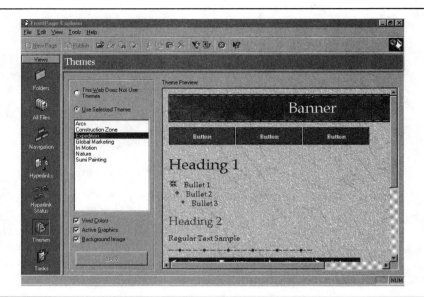

Click on any of the themes to see it previewed in the Theme Preview window. You can modify each theme using the three check boxes on the bottom left. These are:

- **Vivid Colors** brightens the colors for some text and graphics

- **Active Graphics** animates some of the page elements

- **Background Image** adds a textured background to the pages

When you turn off all three options, the background turns white. When Background Image is off and Vivid Colors is on, the background is a solid color.

To apply the theme, click on the Apply button. Switch to another view and open a page in the Editor to see how the theme affects your web.

Changing or Removing a Theme

Once you apply a theme, you can change to another theme or remove the theme completely. To change to another theme, return to the Themes window in the Explorer and select another theme.

To remove a theme, click on the This Web Does Not Use Themes option. The preview window indicates that the current web does not use themes, and the theme is removed.

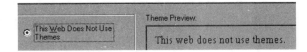

When the This Web Does Not Use Themes option is applied, text returns to the style it had before the theme was applied or becomes Normal. In most cases, you need to do some manual formatting to clean up the text in your web. Of course, if that seems like too much work, you can always change your mind and reapply a theme.

Applying a Theme to a Page

There may be some pages in the web to which you don't want some or all of the theme applied. You can add, modify, and remove themes on individual pages just as easily as you can on entire webs.

From the Editor, right-click and choose Theme from the shortcut menu or choose Format ➤ Theme. This opens a dialog box with the same Choose Theme options you see in the Explorer. There are three options available only to pages:

- **This Page Does Not Use Themes**   A page can be exempted from the theme applied to the rest of the web.

- **Use Theme From Current Web**   The theme used in the rest of the web can be applied to the page.

- **Use Selected Theme**   A different theme can be applied to this page only.

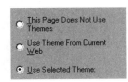

Once you apply a theme to a page, make sure you save the page, or the changes are lost.

Applying Themes to Existing Webs

Although you can apply themes to existing webs, FrontPage warns you that if you apply this theme, all previous formatting is lost. Think carefully before taking this step because there is no way to undo this change. If you spent hours custom formatting a web, it can all be destroyed with one click of the mouse.

Once you apply a theme to a web, your formatting choices are more limited. For example, you can no longer apply a different background unless you remove the theme from individual pages or from the entire web. If you are going to use themes, it's better to decide right from the outset than wait to apply them after you are well into designing your web.

Enhancing Design with Style Sheets

The *World Wide Web Consortium* (W3C), the group that establishes HTML standards for the World Wide Web, is in the midst of developing a new set of standards that will allow Web site developers more control over the precise placement and appearance of elements on a page. FrontPage 98 already provides some support for the standards, called Cascading Style Sheets. However, you need the next generation of Web browsers, Internet Explorer 3.02 or Netscape Navigator 4.0 or higher, to view the results of applying style sheets.

A *cascading style sheet* consists of style definitions or style rules that apply to specific page elements or entire pages. The reason this is valuable is that it gives you more control over how a page appears irrespective of the browser. It still isn't possible to have complete control, but style sheets give web developers many more tools than were possible before.

Let's look at a practical example. Without a style sheet, Heading 1 text appears in a large, bold version of the browser's default font. A style sheet lets you define parameters for the Heading 1 style, including font family, size, and other attributes. You can even define multiple font options to use rather than revert to the browser's default font if your first font choice isn't available on the viewer's browser.

There are three ways of applying style sheets to FrontPage web pages:

- By linking to an *external style sheet* (created in HTML and saved with a .CSS extension). External style sheets are stored as individual pages. By creating an external style sheet, you can link all the pages in your web to that one page. To make a style change to the web, you only have to change one page.

- By creating an *embedded style sheet* on a page in the Editor. With an embedded style sheet, you can create styles that only apply to the active page in your web.

- By applying inline styles to individual elements on a page.

Style sheets are cascading because you can apply multiple styles to a page that are then interpreted by a browser in a specific order. Styles that are applied to individual elements (inline styles) take precedence over styles embedded in the page (embedded styles), and those take precedence over styles included on external style sheets.

 NOTE   FrontPage Themes are based on cascading style sheets. For that reason, you should not apply cascading styles to a page or a web that is already using themes. You should also avoid editing a theme's CSS file, because it may destroy the theme.

You can specify styles for the following properties:

- **Alignment**   Margins, padding, and text wrap

- **Borders**   Style, color, width

- **Colors**   Background, foreground, background image, attachment, repeat, vertical position, horizontal position

- **Font**   Primary font, secondary font, font size

- **Text**   Weight, style, variant, transform, decoration, indent, line height, letter spacing, alignment, vertical alignment

Creating and Linking External Style Sheets

To create an external style sheet, you need to leave the safety of the FrontPage Editor and directly enter the world of HTML code. Open a text editor such as Notepad. Type the style rules you want to define and save the style sheet using a .CSS extension, then import the style sheet into the FrontPage web (see *Importing and Exporting Files* later in this Skill).

NOTE If you're creating a Web site as part of your company's intranet, check with your web administrator to find out if there is a company standard style sheet you should use. Most companies have a standard design they want web authors within the company to follow.

To link an external style sheet to a page, follow these steps:

1. Open the page in the FrontPage Editor.

2. Switch to HTML view.

3. Position the insertion point between the beginning and ending <HEAD> tag and enter an HTML <LINK> tag using the following syntax:

    ```
    <Head>
    <LINK REL=stylesheet  HREF="StyleSheetName.css"
    TYPE="text/css">
    </HEAD>
    ```

    Replace "StyleSheetName" with the name you gave the style sheet when you saved it in Notepad.

4. Switch back to Normal view, save the page, and view it in your browser to see the impact of the style sheet.

If the page contains an embedded style sheet, you need to edit the style rules to reference the external style sheet. To do that, follow these steps:

1. Choose Format ➤ Stylesheet to open the style sheet.

2. Enter an @IMPORT tag immediately following the beginning comment tag (<! - - comment - - >). For example:

    ```
    <style>
    <! - -
    @import URL (/StyleSheetName.css)  ;
    H1 { font - size: x-large;  color:  blue  }
    H2 {  font - size: large;  color: green  }
    - - >
    </style>
    ```

    Replace *StyleSheetName* with the filename you gave the style sheet when you saved it in Notepad.

3. Click on OK to close the Format Stylesheet dialog box.

4. Save the page and view it in your browser to see the impact of the style sheet changes.

NOTE   For up-to-the-minute information about the rules and structure for creating cascading styles, go to the World Wide Web Consortium's site at http://www.htmlhelp.com/reference/css. For help in writing HTML code and applying the standards, see *Mastering HTML 4.0*, 1997, ISBN: 0-7821-2102-0 from Sybex.

Remember that if a page is linked to an external style sheet *and* has an embedded style sheet, the embedded styles are displayed. External styles are only displayed when there is no setting specified on the embedded style sheet.

Creating and Linking Embedded Style Sheets

FrontPage is a little more helpful when it comes to creating embedded styles sheets; however, embedded style sheets only apply to the active page. Not to worry—if you want to apply a style sheet to other pages in your web, save the page as a template. You can then use the template that includes the embedded style sheet as the basis of other new pages in your web. Follow these steps to create an embedded style sheet:

1. Create a new page or open the page in which you want to embed the style sheet in the FrontPage Editor.

2. Choose Format ➢ Stylesheet to open the Format Stylesheet dialog box.

3. Click after the beginning comment tag (<!—) and press Enter.

4. Type the structure tag selector you want to use followed by a space, as shown here.

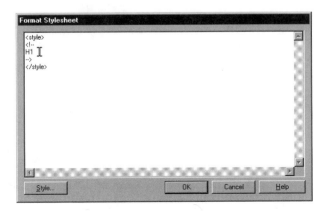

5. Click on the Style button at the bottom of the dialog box to open the Style dialog box shown here.

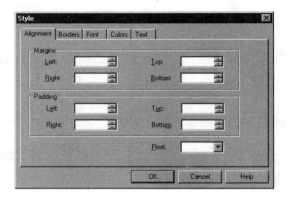

6. Click on the Alignment, Borders, Font, Colors, and Text tabs to access style options related to each category. Set the desired options for the selector.

7. Click on OK.

8. Press End, then Enter and repeat Steps 4 through 7 until you define all the styles you want to set for the page. (Figure 10.9 shows an example of a defined style sheet.)

9. Click OK to close the Format Stylesheet dialog box.

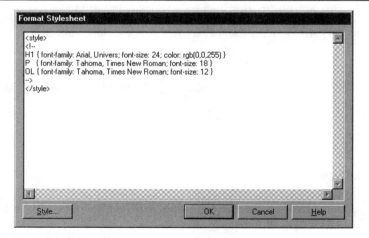

FIGURE 10.9: This Format Stylesheet dialog box shows styles for Heading 1s (H1s), Paragraphs, and Numbered Lists.

Once you define the style sheet, save the page to embed the style sheet. To use the new styles, select the style from the Change Style drop-down arrow on the Format toolbar.

 **WARNING** Remember that not all browsers support Cascading Style Sheets. If a user opens your web with an older browser, your pages may appear as if they have no styles at all. If you produce complex style sheets, you may want to add a notice to users about your use of style sheets. Better yet, include hyperlinks to Microsoft and Netscape to download their latest browsers.

Applying an Inline Style to Page Elements

You can apply *Inline styles* to specific page elements such as tables, graphics, or paragraphs. Inline styles supercede embedded and external style sheets so they allow even more precise formatting of individual elements.

To apply inline styles:

1. Select the element—table, image, or paragraph—to which you want to apply the style.

2. Right-click to open the shortcut menu and choose <element> Properties, where <element> is table, image, or paragraph.

3. Click on the Style button to open the Style dialog box. If you can't apply inline styles to a specific element, there isn't a Style button.

4. Select the desired properties and values from the options available in the tabbed dialog box.

5. Click on OK when you've set all the desired properties.

 NOTE Remember that inline styles only apply to the selected element, not to all the elements in that style. If you apply an inline style to a paragraph formatted as Heading 1, not all Heading 1 text changes to that style—only the selected text changes.

Skill 10

Using Class

When you really want to be specific, you can define a subset of a style and save it in the external or embedded style sheet as a *class*. Think of a class as a new style that you create based on a pre-existing style. For example, you define the Heading 3 style as 14 point, bold, Arial, blue. You want to apply the Heading 3 style to text, but wish to differentiate the headings that contain tips for your users. You can define a Heading 3 Tip style that is 14 point, bold, Arial, green.

To define a class for the embedded style sheet, choose Format ➤ Stylesheet and follow the same steps you use to define any style. The only difference is that instead of using the selector H3 to define this particular style, you use the selector H3.Tip. In Figure 10.10, the H3 style is defined as:

```
font-family: Tahoma; font-size: 18; color: rgb(0,128,0);
font-weight: bold.
```

The H3.Tip style has a different font size (24 rather than 18) and a different color (128,128,0 instead of 0,128,0) from H3. However, because H3.Tip is a class of H3, it inherits the font family and font weight attributes of H3, its parent class, rather than the default properties of the browser.

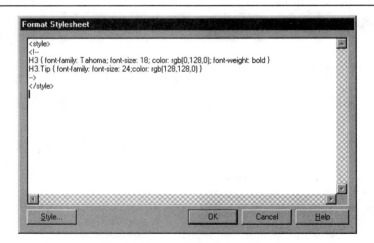

FIGURE 10.10: H3.Tip is defined as a class of H3.

 TIP   Use class names that reflect function rather than attributes. For example, a class that's applied to user tips in the content of the page should be named Tip rather than 16pt, blue.

Using Existing Files to Enhance Your Web

Whenever possible, it is wise to avoid reinventing the wheel. If you create a page or have an existing web you didn't create in FrontPage, but want to use it in your current efforts, there is no reason to start from scratch. You can import pages or entire webs into FrontPage and incorporate them in a new or existing web.

Importing an Existing Web into FrontPage

To import an existing web:

1. Start in the FrontPage Explorer without a web open. If a web is already open, choose File ➤ Close FrontPage Web and then choose Cancel from the Getting Started dialog box when it appears.

2. Choose File ➤ Import to open the New FrontPage Web dialog box with Import an Existing Web selected.

3. Enter a Title for the new web and click on the Change button to change the location, if desired.

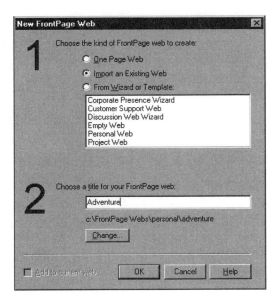

4. Click on OK to create the new web, create the necessary FrontPage folders in the specified location for the incoming web files, and open the *Import Web Wizard* dialog box, shown here.

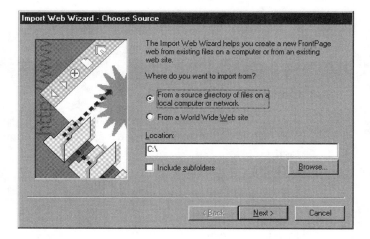

5. The Import Web Wizard prompts you to identify where the existing Web site resides, whether it's on a local or network computer or on the World Wide Web. Select the location and enter the address, or click on the Browse button, select the folder and click on OK. If you want to import subfolders, click on the Subfolders checkbox. Select Next to move on to the next page of the Wizard.

6. Depending on where the site is located, the Import Web Wizard presents you with different options at this point.

   • If you're importing a web from a local computer or network, you see a list of all the files in the existing Web so you can select the ones to import (see Figure 10.11). All the file names displayed are imported; to exclude one or more files, just select them and click on the Exclude button. You can select multiple file names in the usual way—click and Shift+click to select a group of contiguous files, or Ctrl+click to select noncontiguous files. When you are ready, click on the Next button.

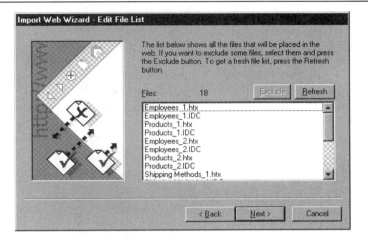

FIGURE 10.11: Choose the files you want to import in the Edit File List step of the Import Web Wizard.

- If you are importing a web from the World Wide Web, the Import Web Wizard asks you to specify how much of the web you want to import (some large sites are over a gigabyte in size!). Figure 10.12 shows that you can specify how many levels of the site you want, how many kilobytes, and if you want to limit the imported files to text and image files. Click on Next to move on to the last step.

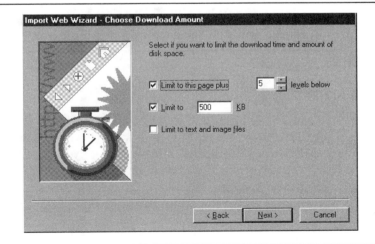

FIGURE 10.12: Indicate how much of the Web site you want to import in the Choose Download Amount step of the Import Web Wizard.

7. The last step offers you the chance to go back to a previous step or cancel the operation, if necessary. Otherwise, choose Finish.

The files from the existing Web site are imported into the new one. If you import a complete site, all the relative hyperlinks should be active, but it's a good idea to click on the Hyperlink Status button to check their status. Hyperlinks that point to files outside the web on a local drive will be broken.

Now that the web is a FrontPage web, you can use all the features of the FrontPage Explorer and Editor that you're already familiar with.

Importing and Exporting Files

In the course of building and maintaining your FrontPage web, you'll need to bring in many different types of files, and incorporate images into your pages, where each image is a separate file. You may also have a page that plays a tune or makes an announcement when that page is opened, which is handled by sound files in your web.

Of course, the beauty of the Internet and the Web is that you can build a Web site whose content (pages and other files) resides anywhere on the Web; all the web's resources need not reside in the same location. Nonetheless, even if a file is accessible outside of your site, if you want to be sure that the file is always available you should save it within the confines of your own site.

TIP You can import files into the active FrontPage web in the Explorer, and you can also export files so that copies of the files are sent to the locations you specify. In the FrontPage Editor, you can open a wide variety of file types that are converted into standard HTML Web pages as they are opened. These types include rich text format (RTF), text, Microsoft Word, and WordPerfect.

Importing Files

In addition to importing webs, you can use the File ➢ Import command to import any file into the active FrontPage web. This is the same command that was discussed earlier in this Skill in *Importing an Existing Web into FrontPage*. In this case, because a web is already open, the command allows you to bring existing files into the active web.

Not only are the imported files copied into the web's location on the server, but FrontPage also examines any incoming HTML pages to keep track of any hyperlinks they contain.

The Explorer warns you if an imported file will overwrite an existing file of the same name. You can choose whether to import the file and replace the existing one. Here's how you import one or more files into the active web:

1. Choose File ➤ Import, which displays the Import File to FrontPage Web dialog box. This is shown in Figure 10.13, with a list of files already in it.

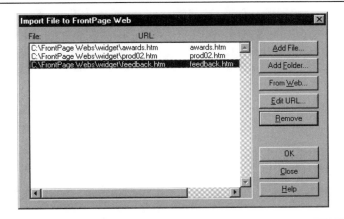

FIGURE 10.13: This dialog box lists the files you have selected to import into the active Web.

2. Click on the Add File button, which displays a standard files dialog box. If you choose the Add Folder button, you can select a folder and all the files and subfolders within it; they are imported into a folder of the same name in your web.

3. Select a folder, then choose the files you want to import from this folder; you can select multiple files with the Shift+Click or Ctrl+Click method.

4. Click on the Open button, which once again displays the Import File to FrontPage Web dialog box.

The files you selected are listed in the dialog box. At this point, there are six different buttons from which you can choose:

- **OK**   All file names that are currently in the dialog box are imported into the active Web.

- **Add File**   Selects more files to add to the import list.

- **Add Folder**   Selects a folder and all the files and subfolders in it to add to the list.

- **Edit URL**   Edits the URL (file name and location) of the selected file; you might need to rename an incoming file so that it does not overwrite an existing file of the same name. You can also add a folder name to the URL of an incoming file so that the file is imported into that folder in the active web.

- **Remove**   Removes the selected file names from the import list, but does not actually delete the files from disk.

- **Close**   Closes the dialog box without importing the files; the list of files is still there and waiting the next time you choose File ➤ Import, until you close the current web or open another.

The Explorer tracks all the links in the HTML pages you import and incorporates them into the FrontPage web. For example, if an incoming page links to a page named SUMMARY.HTM, and a page of that name already exists in the current web, then the incoming page links to the existing page.

All incoming files are placed in the active web's primary folder, unless you edit the URL of an incoming file and specify a different folder or include folders in the import list. Once the files are in the web, you can move them to other folders and let the Explorer automatically adjust links as required. For example, you may want to move all GIF and JPEG image files into the Images folder in the current web.

Exporting Files

You can select a file name or icon in the Explorer's right-hand pane and export it to another location outside of the web. For example, you might want to send a page or image file to a coworker for her to incorporate into the site she is working on.

1. Select the file you want to export.

2. Choose File ➤ Export.

3. In the dialog box, shown in Figure 10.14, choose the location for the file and enter a file name for it.

4. Click on Save to finish the job.

A copy of the file will be created under the name and location you specified. The original file will remain untouched in the current web.

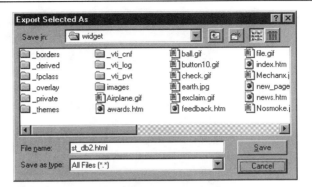

FIGURE 10.14: To export a file, choose the name and location for the file and click on Save.

Opening a Page from outside the Active Web

Usually you open HTML pages in the Editor from the active web in the Explorer. However, you can open pages from other locations, as well. From the Editor's menu, choose File ➤ Open, and then choose the Use Your Web Browser to Select a Page or File or the Select a File on Your Computer button to identify where the file is located. Figure 10.15 shows the Open dialog box.

To open a page from disk, enter the path and file name in the URL field. To open a page from the Web or your intranet, enter the address in URL field. Using this method, you can open any page from any Web site to which you have access, just as you do in your browser. Once open, you can save the page (including its images) to your local disk or web.

Of course, you must work within the constraints of upright behavior and copyright law. But this is a handy way to bring a page from a Web site into the Editor, where you can revise it as necessary and save it to a different location.

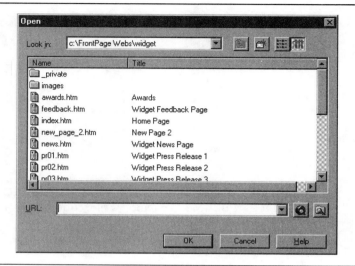

FIGURE 10.15: You can open a page that exist outside the active web by specifying the location in the Open dialog box.

Opening Other File Types

You can open many types of files in the Editor beyond standard HTML Web pages. The Editor converts an incoming file from its native format into an equivalent-looking HTML file. You can then save it as an HTML Web page in the usual way.

When you choose a file to open, the Editor determines what type of file it is and, if it's able to, converts it as it opens it. To make it easier to find a file, and to see the types of files that the Editor can convert, use the Select a File on Your Computer button and look at the Files of Type drop-down list in the Select File dialog box. When you choose one of the file types on the list, only files with the appropriate extension for that type, such as .doc or .xls, are displayed in the dialog box.

There are a wide variety of file types in the list, including several different versions of Microsoft Word, Excel, and Works, and also WordPerfect. The more generic Rich Text Format (RTF) and plain text (TXT) file types are also on the list.

If the incoming file contains any graphic images, the Editor attempts to place them in the document where they belong. Since images are always separate files from the pages in which they appear, when you later save this document as an HTML page, you're asked if you also want to save the images as separate files. By saving the images, they are available the next time you open this page, either in the Editor or in a browser on your web.

If the file you want to open is of an unknown type to the Editor, it displays a dialog box, asking you how it should convert the file—either as an HTML, RTF, or Text file. This is a last-ditch effort on the part of the Editor, and none of the choices may be appropriate. But in some cases, such as when you want to open a text file whose extension is unfamiliar to the Editor, you can choose the appropriate file type and let the Editor proceed.

 TIP   If the Editor can't open a certain file type, you may be able to save that file in the HTML format in the program that created the file. You can then open the HTML file directly into the Editor.

Inserting a File into a Page

You can bring another file into the current page with the Insert ➤ File command. The contents of the other file appear at the insertion point's position within the page.

You'll probably find many occasions to bring another Web page into the current one. For example, suppose you have an online user manual that is spread across multiple pages so that each page downloads pretty quickly. You would also like to have the entire manual in a single page so a visitor to the site can download the complete manual in one operation. You can use the Insert ➤ File command to combine each of the pages into a single page, and then save that page back to the web.

Are You Experienced?

Now you can...

- ☑ **Create a consistent and well-designed web**
- ☑ **Create a variety of different webs using wizards and templates**
- ☑ **Add pages to a web using templates**
- ☑ **Apply a theme to a web and to an individual page**
- ☑ **Create and link external, embedded and inline style sheets**
- ☑ **Import and export files and import webs**
- ☑ **Copy files from existing webs and web pages**
- ☑ **Open other types of pages and pages from other sources**

S K I L L

eleven

11

Automating and Activating Your Web

- ❏ Automating with FrontPage Components
- ❏ Creating Page Banners, Banner Ads, Hover buttons and Marquees
- ❏ Substituting images, text, and pages
- ❏ Creating a table of contents
- ❏ Automatically entering the time or date in a page
- ❏ Pushing content with Channels

Once you've caught a visitor's attention with exciting, up-to-date content in your web, all you have to do is figure out how to get them to come back. This Skill introduces you to the FrontPage components and other active features that make it easy to keep your web interesting, keep your content current, and make sure visitors return to your site. FrontPage 98 includes a number of automated features, from banner ads that appear across the top of pages to hover buttons that respond when a mouse pointer moves over them. There are even a few Web maintenance tricks that can automate many tasks on your web without programming or script writing.

Automating with a FrontPage Component

A *FrontPage component* is a built-in object that executes either when the Web page author saves the page or when the page is opened in a browser. Most FrontPage components automatically generate the appropriate HTML code for their defined tasks. Others work behind the scenes to compete specific tasks, for example saving data that a user inputs into a form.

 NOTE   In previous versions of FrontPage, FrontPage components were referred to as WebBots or Bots. The word is derived from *robot*, which is used in Web-related circles to describe a variety of automated routines. WebBots are a subset of FrontPage components and are referenced in the HTML code when you insert a WebBot component. However, FrontPage 98 consistently uses the broader and more generally accepted name of *component* to refer to these objects.

You have already seen examples of several components in earlier Skills. The webs discussed in Skill 10, created from Wizards and templates, freely use components such as Page Banners and Comments. You learned how themes help provide consistency by including a Page Banner component that displays the same information on each page of the web. The Comment component includes text that is not visible when the page is viewed in a browser—comments are only for the eyes of the web authors. Comments for the page are contained in HTML code within a FrontPage component that tells the Editor to display the comment in a unique color. All the FrontPage components you can insert into a page are described in the next section, *Using The FrontPage Components*. You can incorporate FrontPage components into a page in several ways.

- In the Editor, use the Insert ➤ FrontPage Component command to insert a component.

- Create a new page from a template that uses a component, including Confirmation Form, Search Page, and Table of Contents.

- In the Explorer, FrontPage components are an integral component of the FrontPage webs you create with the wizards and templates, and of Themes you apply to the webs.

NOTE The *Common Gateway Interface (CGI)* has been the traditional way to run auto-mated tasks from Web pages. When you perform tasks with the FrontPage com-ponents on a server configured for FrontPage, you avoid having to write CGI scripts and reference their somewhat arcane parameters.

The FrontPage Editor generally treats components as separate objects in a page. For example, when you insert a FrontPage Comment component, the result is a block of text that's displayed in the page, but is not editable there. If you try to move the insertion point into the block text, it selects the entire component, as shown here.

Comment: This comment is not displayed when this page is viewed in a browser.

You know an object in a page is a FrontPage Component when you click on it with your mouse, because the pointer changes to the FrontPage Component pointer.

Using the FrontPage Components

You can find most of the FrontPage components in the Insert FrontPage Component dialog box (Insert ➢ FrontPage Component), shown here.

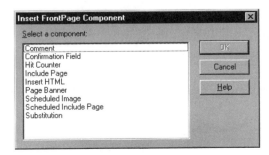

Here is a description of each of the components listed in the Insert FrontPage Component dialog box:

- **Comment** Inserts a comment on a page that is invisible from Web browsers. Use this component to include notes to yourself or instructions for other Web designers who have access to the page that you don't want users to see.

- **Confirmation Field** Displays the results of a specified field in a form, such as when a reader's input is displayed for confirmation in another page.

- **Hit Counter** Displays the number of users who have visited your Web site.

- **Include Page** Displays another Web page within the current page.

- **Insert HTML** Provides a way to enter extended HTML code that is not supported by FrontPage. FrontPage does not verify that the code is valid.

- **Page Banner** Inserts a page banner if the page does not include a theme or shared border.

- **Scheduled Image** Displays an image file for a time period you specify. You can also specify an optional image that's displayed before or after the specified period.

- **Scheduled Include Page** This is the same as the Scheduled Image FrontPage component, but you specify a page instead of an image. The result is the same as Include Page, but only within the specified time period.

- **Substitution** Displays the current value for the FrontPage web configuration variable you choose, such as Page URL, Author, or Description.

When you insert some components into a page in the Editor, you see the complete result of the component immediately—for example, the Hit Counter component displays the numbers of hits on the page. Other components only leave a placeholder in the page to indicate their presence. For example, when the current date is not within the date range for the Scheduled Include Page component, all you see in the Editor is the text Expired Scheduled Include Page. In a browser, however, you see nothing at all.

When the FrontPage component cannot complete its task, it produces an error message. For instance, when you open a page that contains an Include Page component but the file to be included no longer exists, the component displays an appropriate message in the page, such as:

```
Error: Unable to include file: _private\header.htm
```

In the Hyperlinks All Pages pane, you see a red triangle icon next to the name of the page containing the Include Page component, indicating there is an error associated with it. If you right-click on the page and open its Properties dialog box, an Errors tab is available (shown here). It displays any error messages produced for that page, including those from FrontPage components.

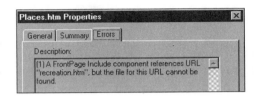

 NOTE The Confirmation Field component is covered in the next Skill on creating forms.

Inserting a FrontPage Component for Your Comments

Whether you are working on a page alone or are sharing responsibility for the development of a page with other people, there are many times when it's helpful to include a comment to document something on the page. Of course, you don't want users to see those comments. Using the FrontPage Comment component, you can place comments within your pages in the Editor that are invisible to users.

 NOTE Never put confidential information in your comments. Even though comments don't appear when the page is viewed in a browser, they are still part of that page's HTML code. Visitors to your site see your comments when they view the underlying code for the page in a browser.

To create a comment, position the insertion point where you want the comment to appear, choose Insert ➢ FrontPage Component, and select Comment from the list of available components. Enter the text of your comment in the Comment dialog box; press Enter after the comment to create a line break when the comment is displayed in the page. Click on OK when you're finished, and your comment appears within the page.

Skill 11

> - **Interest 1** *Provide a description, picture, or perhaps a hyperlink here.*
>
> - **Interest 2** *Provide a description, picture, or perhaps a hyperlink here.*
>
> - **Interest 3** *Provide a description, picture, or perhaps a hyperlink here.*
>
> Comment: This comment is not displayed when this page is viewed in a browser.

HTML has a special tag for comments, and a browser ignores any text within that tag. FrontPage adds its own twist to the comment by displaying it in the Editor in a different color (purple) with whatever formatting has been applied to its displayed text.

Here is the HTML code that FrontPage uses for the comment shown above.

```
<!--webbot bot="PurpleText"
preview="This comment is not displayed when this page is viewed in a
browser." -->
```

The standard HTML tag for a comment is `<! — >`. Comments included in this tag are not displayed in Normal view of the FrontPage Editor, only in HTML view. FrontPage recognizes the FrontPage component in the FrontPage version of the tag and displays the comment in the Editor.

There's also a newer comment tag that you may find in other Web pages, but it is not supported by all browsers. This comment tag looks like this:

```
<COMMENT>This is the text of the comment</COMMENT>
```

Counting Your Visitors

Almost always, the sole reason for publishing a Web site is to attract interest from other people in what you have to say. One of the nerve-racking parts of establishing a Web presence is waiting to see how many visitors find their way to your fabulous site. FrontPage takes care of counting for you with the Hit Counter component, so you can just sit back and watch the numbers grow.

To insert a Hit Counter, follow these steps:

1. In the FrontPage Editor, position the insertion point where you want the Hit Counter to go on your page.

2. Choose Insert ➤ FrontPage Component and select Hit Counter from the list (you'll also find it on the list of Active Elements on the Insert menu). This opens the Hit Counter Properties dialog box, shown here.

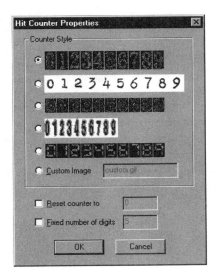

3. Select a counter style or choose a GIF image containing the digits 0 through 9 (You can create your own digits in Image Composer and save them as a grouped GIF image. See Skill 9 for more about Image Composer.)

4. Click on the Reset Counter To checkbox if you want to start the counter at a number other than 0. Enter the number in the adjacent text box. (Just like ordering new checks from the bank, it may be advantageous to start with a slightly higher number.)

5. Select the Fixed Number of Digits checkbox if you want the counter to start over when it reaches a certain number. Enter the maximum number of digits you want to see in the adjacent text box. (For example, if you set the maximum number of digits to 6, when the counter reaches hit number 999,999 it goes back to zero on the next hit.)

6. Click on OK to save the properties and insert the Hit Counter.

You probably want to include some message for your visitors around the Hit Counter like the one shown here.

To edit the Hit Counter, right-click on it and choose FrontPage Component Properties. Make any changes you want and click on OK to save them.

Including Another Web Page Automatically

The Include Page component lets you easily revise many pages in your FrontPage web in only one operation. You saw an application of the Include Page component concept when you learned about shared borders in Skill 6. The actual content of each border is contained in a separate page and is linked to all the pages in the web for a consistent look. The Include Page component works in the same way. When you insert another page into an existing page, the two pages appear as if they are one. However, each page is stored separately. When the included page is revised, changes are reflected on all the pages that are linked to it.

When you select an Include Page component, you can easily tell it is a FrontPage component (see Figure 11.1). In this example, the Include Page component has been selected in the page, so it is highlighted. You can see the image and the Widget Company title are part of the component, and you can clearly see the telltale FrontPage component robot pointer.

FIGURE 11.1: The home page in the Widget Web site takes advantage of the Include Page Component.

NOTE   Remember that the Include Page component offers a double benefit. It gives you a way to display the same information in any pages that reference the same included page. You also get the added benefit of being able to revise the included page and have those changes appear in all the pages that include it. In a web with many pages, this can save you hours and hours of work.

The first step in inserting an Include Page component into a page is to create the page you want to include. Because this page is never viewed directly by users, you may want to save the page in the _private folder of your web. Once you create the page, here's how to place an Include Page component in an active page:

1. In the Editor, open the page in which you want to insert the Include Page component.

2. Position the insertion point where you want the included page to be displayed. In the Widget home page in Figure 11.1, the component was placed at the very top of the page.

3. Choose Insert ➤ FrontPage Component.

4. In the Insert FrontPage Component dialog box, select Include Page and then click on OK.

5. In the Include Page Component Properties dialog box, enter the URL of the page you want displayed in the current page (shown here). The page you want to display must be in the active web; therefore, its URL is relative. For example, in this case the other page is named LOGO.HTM and is located in the web's private folder.

6. Finally, click on OK to insert the Include Page component.

The included page is loaded into the current page and displayed as though it were actually a part of the current page. However, you can't spell-check or edit the text in the included page from the current page. To do that you have to switch to the included page.

Revising a FrontPage Component

You can revise a FrontPage component at any time. For example, with the Include Page component in the previous example, you can change the name of the Web page it references. To revise a component, you can do any of the following:

- Double-click on it.

- Select the component and choose Edit ➤ FrontPage Component Properties (Alt+Enter).

- Right-click on it and choose FrontPage Component Properties from its shortcut menu.

To edit the included page, right-click on the component and choose the Open File option from the shortcut menu shown here.

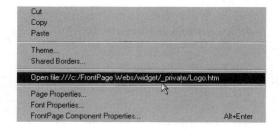

You switch to the included page. Make your editing changes and save the page. When you switch back to the original page, choose View ➤ Refresh and the editing changes you made should be evident.

 TIP   To switch between open pages, open the Window menu and choose the page you want to switch to from the list of open pages.

If you modify the included page, you don't have to worry about updating all the pages that include this page. The Explorer handles that automatically when you save the included page, once again emphasizing the importance of using the Editor and the Explorer together.

Inserting Extended HTML Code

The fast-paced development of HTML means there is always some tags accepted by some browsers, even though those tags have not been accepted and incorporated into the official HTML specification (which is under the auspices of the World Wide Web Consortium).

Whatever the reason for certain tags not being supported by the FrontPage Editor, you can still include any HTML code in your Web pages by choosing Insert ≻ FrontPage Component and choosing Insert HTML from the list. This displays a dialog box with a multi-line edit field in which you enter the HTML code you want to include in the page.

 **WARNING**   FrontPage ignores the HTML code you enter here and does not check it for accuracy. It's up to you to enter the code without mistakes and ensure it's interpreted correctly by a browser.

Click on the OK button to close the HTML Markup dialog box. Even though you can't see how this new material looks in the Editor, you can view this page in a Web browser to see the results.

Creating Page Banners to Share Across Pages

You learned about the Include Page component earlier in this Skill, and you learned about shared borders in Skill 6. Both are examples of elements that allow you to link pages to other pages and have their content included in that page. A top shared border automatically includes a banner that contains the title of the page (as defined in the Explorer), and if you have applied a theme, it also contains a banner image.

FrontPage provides you with a way to manually create a page banner on a particular page by inserting a Page Banner component. When you insert a page banner on a page without a theme or shared borders, the Page Banner component inserts a text-only page banner showing the page title. If you change the page title in the Explorer, the banner automatically changes.

A page banner differs from a shared border in that a page banner only appears on the specific page you apply it to. A shared border appears on every page in the web, except where you have intentionally turned it off.

To insert a page banner, choose Insert ➤ FrontPage Component and choose Page Banner from the list of options. The Page Banner Properties dialog box asks you to indicate whether you want text or an image. Choosing Image has no effect unless a theme has been applied to the page. In that case, the page banner uses the theme's banner image. Otherwise, the text appears on the page by itself in the default font.

Click on the component to select it if you want to apply a heading style—right-click on it to change its font properties or to access themes or shared borders. You can also go back to the Page Banner Properties and change your Appearance selection from Text to Image or vice versa.

Scheduling Changes in Your Web

Keeping the information in a web up-to-date is a challenge even for full-time Web site administrators. FrontPage includes two components that help you keep data current even when you're not there to take care of it. Both of these components, Scheduled Image and Scheduled Include Page, work essentially the same as the Include Page component, except that you can set a starting and an ending date for the image or page to be included. In this way, you could have new pages in your web even when you go on vacation.

To schedule an image or a page to be included automatically, follow these steps:

1.   Choose Insert ➤ FrontPage Component and select either Scheduled Image or Scheduled Include Page from the list of components. Click on OK to open the Scheduled Properties dialog box shown in Figure 11.2.

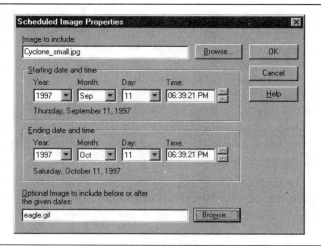

FIGURE 11.2: A Scheduled Include Image appears between the dates you specify.

2. Enter the relative URL of the page or image to include, or click on the Browse button to select from the a dialog box.

3. Select the Year, Month, Day, and Time you want to start including the image or page. To adjust the time, click on the part of the time you want to change (Hours, minutes, seconds, AM/PM) and use the spin box (up and down arrows) to make the change.

4. Select the Year, Month, Day and Time to stop including the image or page.

5. Enter a relative URL to include a different page before or after the given dates. If you don't include another page, [Expired Scheduled Include Page/Image] appears in its place in the Editor and the area is blank when viewed in a browser.

6. Click on OK to schedule the page or image.

If you want to make changes in the component, right-click on it and choose FrontPage Component Properties. To edit an actual included page, right-click on the component and choose the Open [URL] option on the short-cut menu.

TIP   You can insert several Scheduled Include Page/Image components on a single page with different start and end times, but they must occupy different positions on the page.

Automating Text Entry with the Substitution Component

You can display text automatically anywhere you want in a page by taking advantage of two FrontPage features:

- In the Editor, you can insert a Substitution component that references any configuration variable and displays the text that defines that variable.

- In the Explorer, you can create configuration variables that consist of a name (the variable) and a value (the definition of the variable).

This is a very powerful technique for managing information in your FrontPage webs. Its benefits are similar to using the Include Page component: It's a convenient way to display the same information in many different pages, and you can change a configuration variable's definition and have that change reflected throughout your web automatically.

Referencing a Variable in a Page

There are several built-in configuration variables in every FrontPage web. Here's how to reference one of them; the process is the same for variables you create:

1. In the Editor, place the insertion point where you want to display the variable.

2. Choose Insert ≻ FrontPage Component, and select Substitution in the dialog box, then click on OK.

3. In the Substitution Component Properties dialog box, select one of the built-in variables from the drop-down list shown in Figure 11.3. For example, choose Author to display the name of whoever created the current page, or Modified By to display the name of the person who last worked on this page.

4. Click on OK to return to the page.

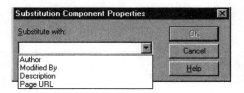

FIGURE 11.3: Using Substitution components you can automatically replace text on a page with other values.

The Substitution component is inserted into the page, and the current value (the text) of the variable you choose is displayed.

For example, in a new page that has not yet been saved, you can create the following sentence that ends with the Page URL variable of the Substitution component:

```
This page's URL is [Page URL].
```

That's how this variable is displayed when there is not yet a value for it. Once you save the page, thereby giving it a URL, the sentence might now look like this:

```
This page's URL is http://www.widget.com/somepage.htm.
```

The actual URL is displayed in place of the Substitution component.

NOTE The display of this variable is not updated until you save the current page. In this case, you have to save the page and either open it again or use the View ➤ Refresh command to see the latest value of the variable. However, if you later move this page in the Explorer when the page is not opened in the Editor, the new URL is updated automatically in the variable in this page.

Creating a Configuration Variable

You can create your own configuration variables in the Explorer and reference them in the pages in that web. In most cases, you create a variable only when that information needs to appear on more than one page, so you save a lot of time when you need to update the information—simply by changing that variable's definition. Here are some typical uses for variables:

- **Webmaster**   Displays the name of whoever maintains the web; if a new person takes over the job, just enter the new name for this variable's definition.

NOTE Webmaster, the term commonly used to signify the person who maintains the web, is falling into disfavor due to a growing number of women who maintain webs. Other names such as Webweaver and Webcrafter are growing in popularity.

- **Phone Voice**   Displays a phone number to call for information.
- **Phone Fax**   Displays a phone number for sending faxes.
- **Company Name**   Displays the name of the company; although this won't change very often (if at all), by using a variable you're assured the name is spelled consistently throughout the web.
- **Company Address**   Displays the company's address.
- **Current**   Displays the most recent stock price; just update the variable's definition when you want to update the displayed price.

NOTE Displaying the value of a configuration variable with the Substitution component is very much like displaying another page with the Include component. The text (value) of a variable, however, can be only a single line long. Even so, it's easier to update a variable in the Explorer than it is to update every page in the Editor.

Skill 11

Let's create a configuration variable named Phone Voice, which displays a day and evening telephone number.

1. Open the web in the Explorer, and choose Tools ➤ Web Settings.

2. Select the Parameters tab in the FrontPage Web Settings dialog box.

3. To create a new configuration variable, choose Add.

4. In the Add Name and Value dialog box, (shown in Figure 11.4), enter Phone Voice as the name of the variable in the Name field.

5. In the Value field, enter the text you want to appear when this variable is inserted into a page, such as 916-555-1212 (day) or 916-555-1213 (eve). Text wraps to the next line as needed; all the text you enter is taken as a single line when it is displayed in the Editor.

6. When you're finished, click on OK, which returns you to the FrontPage Web Settings dialog box.

7. Click Apply to incorporate the new variable into the web, or click OK to apply it and close the dialog box.

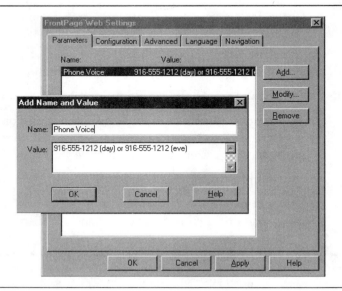

FIGURE 11.4: You can create or revise a configuration variable using the Parameters tab in the Web Settings dialog box.

Once you create a variable for a web, you can insert that variable into any page in that web using the Substitution component. You'll find the new variable name (Phone Voice in this case) on the list of variables in that component's dialog box.

Creating a Table of Contents

Just about every Web site includes some sort of table of contents, whether it's actually called that or not. The multiple pages of a Web site are just too easy to catalog within a single page of hyperlinks to exclude a table of contents from your site. Visitors to the site find such a page a great convenience, and it gives you, the Web author, a practical way to organize the important "stepping stones" in your site.

FrontPage provides a FrontPage component for just such a need. If you insert it into a page, it generates a complete table of contents of all the pages in your FrontPage web. Here's how to build a table of contents:

1. Position the insertion point where you want the table of contents to appear. It might be on the home page of your web or on a page appropriately titled Table of Contents.

2. Choose Insert ➤ Table of Contents.

3. This displays the Table of Contents Properties dialog box, where you define the scope and style of the table of contents (see Figure 11.5).

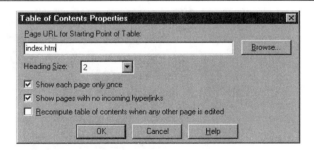

FIGURE 11.5: The Table of Contents Component lets you create a list of hyperlinks to all the pages in your web.

4. First, pick the page that serves as the root of the table of contents. Normally this is the home page, because the hyperlinks it contains should lead you through the chain of hyperlinks to just about every page in the web.

5. Next choose the heading style that's used for each entry in the list. The choices are 1 through 6 (corresponding to the HTML tags <H1> through <H6>). Choose None if you want each item displayed in the default text style.

6. There may be multiple hyperlinks to many pages in the web. If you don't want to see those pages listed multiple times, choose the Show Each Page Only Once option.

7. The table of contents is built from the hyperlinks in the starting point page, but there may be pages in the web to which no other pages link. To display them as well, choose Show Pages with No Incoming Hyperlinks.

 NOTE   The table of contents lists pages it finds in any other folders you may have created in this web. It will not, however, look for pages in any of the FrontPage program's folders in this web, including _private.

8. The last choice, Recompute Table of Contents When Any Other Page is Edited, is deselected by default, so the table of contents is rebuilt only when you open the page containing this FrontPage component. That should be fine in most cases, but if you're willing to put up with delays and put some strain on your server, select this option and the table of contents is updated whenever anyone makes a change to the web.

9. Finally, click on OK and the Table of Contents component is inserted into the active page. Here is an example of the Table of Contents component for the Widget Web.

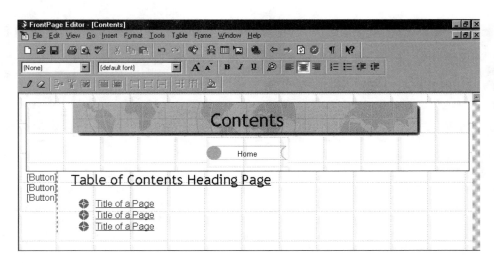

What you see in the table of contents page in the Editor doesn't really look like much, but save the page and preview it in your Web browser. The result looks something like that shown in Figure 11.6 for the Widget Web. Each entry in the table of contents displays the title of a page and is a link to that page.

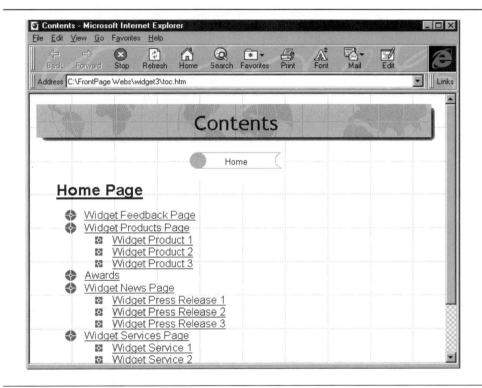

FIGURE 11.6:   The Table of Contents component creates a complete table of contents for the pages in your web.

Pages that are positioned as child pages in Navigation view in the FrontPage Explorer appear indented from their parent pages. Each page listing is a hyperlink to the actual page. Each time you save the table of contents page in your browser, the table of contents is recalculated.

Stamping Your Page with the Date and Time

The Timestamp FrontPage component is a very convenient component that simply displays the date and/or time when the page was last revised. This information is frequently displayed on Web pages to remind you and other authors of when it was last worked on, and also to let your readers know how current the information is. Would you trust pricing information displayed on a page last revised 10 months earlier?

The bottom of a page is often the place for this type of information. You might display a line that looks something like this:

```
This page was last updated on 10/11/97 at 10:15 AM.
```

This display uses two instances of the Timestamp component . Here's how you create them in the Editor:

1. Type the first part of the sentence **This page was last updated on** and end it with a space.

2. Choose Insert ➢ Timestamp.

3. In the Timestamp Properties dialog box, select the option named Date This Page was Last Edited (shown here).

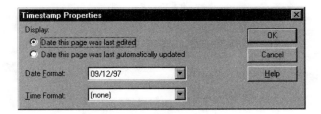

This sets the date or time when someone actually opens this page in the Editor and then saves it back on disk. The other option, Date This Page was Last Automatically Updated, also updates the date or time when the page's HTML is updated by the server. For example, when you revise another page included in this page, this page's code is updated along with the Timestamp.

4. Select an appropriate date style from the Date Format drop-down list.

5. Select (None) in the Time Format drop-down list so this component displays only the date.

6. Choose OK to return to the page in the Editor, and the current date is displayed where you inserted this FrontPage component in the sentence.

7. Type the text that follows this component, starting with a space and continuing with **at** and another space.

8. Once again, choose Insert ➣ Timestamp, but this time set the Date Format option to (None), and then choose an appropriate time style from the Time Format drop-down list.

9. Choose OK to close the dialog box; the current time should be displayed in your sentence.

10. Finish the sentence with a period.

Your completed timestamp should look something like this:

This page was last updated on 09/12/97 at 12:12 AM.

Whenever you save this page, the current date and time are saved along with it in the Timestamp components. When viewed in a browser, a reader knows exactly when the page was last worked on.

 NOTE   If you want to change the font of the entire timestamp sentence, you have to change the font of the text and right-click on each component individually to change the components' Font Properties.

Making Things Move with Active Elements

The Web is becoming more and more lively every day. In the early years of the Web's existence, users were content with text, hyperlinks and a few images thrown in for good measure. It didn't take long for users to demand more images, better color, faster download speeds, sound, and more action. We are a video-oriented society and we won't be satisfied until the Web combines its

Skill 11

flexibility and maneuverability with the video quality of our television sets (high definition television, of course). In the meantime, finding better and more exciting ways to make things move on screen is a major passion of many Web developers.

You've already learned some things about dynamic Web content in Skill 3, with collapsing outlines, and Skill 4 with animated text. Those are just a prelude to the exciting things on the horizon as Web content becomes more action-packed.

In this next section, you learn about a number of features available today that create eye-catching, interest-enhancing movement on your pages.

Hover Buttons

For whatever reason, we like to click buttons. Many of the users of your site choose to click a button over clicking a text-based hyperlink. In Skill 9, you learned how to create exciting looking buttons with Image Composer. FrontPage also gives you a few more ways to have fun with buttons.

Hover buttons are buttons that change in some way when you point to them (without clicking). Hover buttons can change color, bevel in or out, change text, or even become a completely different button. You can use simple rectangles as the buttons and group them together, as shown in Figure 11.7. Or you can use elaborate buttons you create using the Button Wizard in Image Composer. Whatever your choice, hover buttons add just a touch of sparkle.

FIGURE 11.7: You can group simple rectangular Hover buttons together to create a row of buttons.

To create a hover button, follow these steps.

1. Position the insertion point where you want the first button to appear on your page.

 NOTE If you plan to use a custom button, save the button as a GIF file and be able to identify where the GIF is located.

2. Choose Insert ➤ Active Elements ➤ Hover Button to open the Hover Button dialog box, shown here.

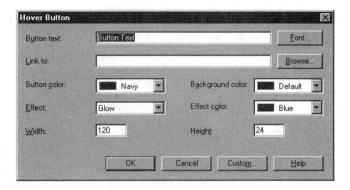

3. Enter the text you want to appear on the button. If you're using a button GIF that already has text on it, delete the text here. Click on the Font button to change the font, font style, size, and color, as shown here. Your choices are limited to four fonts.

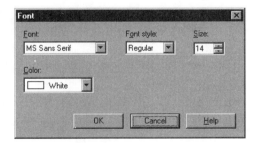

4. Enter the URL you want to link the button to. Click on the Browse button to choose a page from the active web, the World Wide Web, or your computer.

5. Choose a color for the button. You can match the button color to the background color of the page so only the text appears on the page.

6. Choose a background color for the button. Background has little effect on the button.

7. Choose a transition effect for the hover button. Choose from Color Fill, Color Average, Glow, Reverse Glow, Light Glow, Bevel Out, and Bevel In. Experiment with different effects to see which you like best.

8. Choose an effect color—in other words, the color the button transitions to.

9. Select a Width and Height for the button. If you plan to use a custom button, enter the size of the button here in pixels.

10. If you want to use a custom button on your page, click on the Custom button to open the Custom dialog box, shown here.

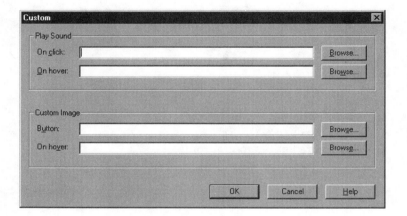

11. Enter the URL of a sound file if you want a sound to play when the button is clicked, or on hover. Browse if you need to locate the file. (You can attach a sound to each event, but that is probably overdoing it.)

12. Enter the location of a GIF you want to use as the button, and one you want to use on hover. If, for example, you use the first button in Figure 11.8 as the button and the second On Hover, the button text and color change when the user points to the button.

FIGURE 11.8: Use two identically shaped buttons with different text and colors to change one button into the other on hover.

13. Click on OK to close the Custom dialog box, and again to close the Hover button dialog box.

14. Save the page and switch to Preview to see your buttons in action.

Now that you have the hang of it, if you want to edit your buttons, right-click on a button and choose Java Applet Properties to reopen the Hover Button dialog box. (For more about Java applets see *Adding Advanced Dynamic Components* later in this Skill.)

If you use the default rectangle button, you can create multiple buttons that appear connected but you have to create them one at a time. Use the same effect on each button for a consistent look. You can also use the opposite effect on alternating buttons—bevel in and bevel out, glow and reverse glow—to create a more complex look.

Banner Ad Manager

If you've spent any time on the Web recently, you've been inundated with advertisements flashing or moving across the top of the screen. Now it's your chance to create your own ads and do your part to contribute to the commercialization of cyberspace.

FrontPage 98 has a feature to create *Banner Ads*, a series of graphic images that transition from one to another at predetermined intervals. Of course, you can use Banner Ads for a lot more than advertising. You can use this feature to present a slide show or to make an announcement that catches users' eyes.

To insert a banner ad, you must first create and or identify the images you want to use in the ad. It's easiest if you copy the images to a folder in the active web so they're available when you need them. Once you've identified the images you want to use, follow these steps to create the banner ad.

1. Choose Insert ➤ Active Elements ➤ Banner Ad Manager to open the Banner Ad Manager dialog box, shown here.

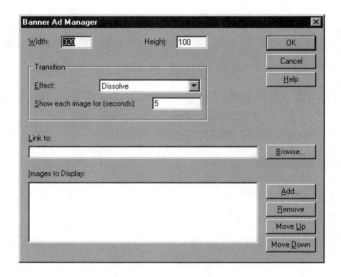

2. Enter the width and height of the largest image.

    It's best to work with images that are all about the same size, so they transition smoothly. Edit the images in Image Composer to make sure the images are the size you want them before you insert them into the Banner Ad Manager. You can't resize them after you insert them.

3. Choose the transition effect—Dissolve, Blinds Horizontal, Blinds Vertical, Box In, Box Out, or None—you want between the images. Dissolve is the default choice.

4. Indicate how long you want each image to appear. The default is five seconds, but you may find that is too long for some images and too short for some text-intense images. If there is a lot of text, make sure you test the transition by reading it out loud slowly. You want to make sure you don't alienate users because the messages are moving too fast.

5. If you want the images to serve as a hyperlink, enter the target of the hyperlink in the Link To text box. You can only assign one link to the entire banner ad—not one for each image.

6. To add images, click on the Add button. This opens the familiar Open dialog box, where you can select an image and click on OK to enter it into the list of Images to Display.

7. Click on Add again to insert a second image, and repeat the process until you add all the images you want to include.

8. Use the Move Up and Move Down buttons to change the order that the images appear in the Banner Ad.

9. Click on the remove button to remove an image from the list.

10. When you complete the settings, click on OK.

   To view the Banner Ad, save the page and switch to the Preview tab or the Preview page in your Web browser. Remember, it takes a few seconds before the second image appears, so don't assume nothing is happening. If it's too long a wait, you can go back in and edit it later (right-click and choose Java Applet Properties).

Troubleshooting Banner Ads

When you close the Banner Ad Manager dialog box, you should see your first image on the page. If all you see is part of the image, as shown in Figure 11.7, the image is larger than the Width and Height settings you entered in the Banner Ad Manager. In Figure 11.9, only a portion of the director's slate is visible.

FIGURE 11.9: The image in this Banner Ad is too large for the Banner Ad property settings.

Skill 11

When this happens, you can either resize the image in Image Composer or resize the banner ad. To resize the banner ad, you have two options:

1. Edit the width and height settings in the Banner Ad Manager.

2. Select one of the handles around the banner ad and drag to expand it to the correct size.

By choosing the second option and dragging the handles, as shown in Figure 11.10, you can make the banner ad the exact size of the image.

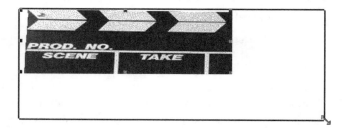

FIGURE 11.10: Drag the handles around the banner ad to make it large enough to fit the image.

NOTE   Remember, you can only see the first image of a banner ad, so if other images are larger than the first one, resizing the banner ad to fit the first image doesn't help the larger images that come later. Your best choice is to make sure all the images are close to the same size before adding them.

Delivering a Message with a Marquee

Microsoft Internet Explorer first introduced the marquee, which is an HTML implementation of the scrolling message you might find on the marquee of a movie theater, where it displays the current schedule, or above a stock brokerage firm, where it displays a live ticker tape.

NOTE   Although the marquee is not yet a part of the HTML standard, the popularity of Internet Explorer (which can display a marquee) may eventually make the marquee an official HTML element. If a browser cannot display a scrolling marquee, it simply displays the text that would have instead scrolled across the screen.

Figure 11.11 shows an example of a marquee in a page in the Editor. The marquee is added to the Widget home page, first shown in Chapter 1. Here the marquee displays a newsy and timely message that you might change every few days.

FIGURE 11.11: A marquee can be an effective way to catch the viewer's attention and display an important message.

Of course, the only problem with the marquee in Figure 11.10 is that you can't see its most important feature— the message scrolling across the marquee from right to left, again and again. To see a marquee in action, you need to open its page in a browser; shown here is a series of views of the same marquee in a browser.

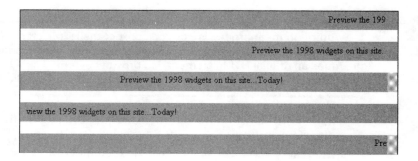

It's easy to create a marquee in the Editor; it's very much like inserting a horizontal line. Here are the steps you can use to create the marquee shown above:

1. Place the insertion point where you want the marquee to appear. As always, you can move the marquee later, if necessary.

2. Choose Insert ➤ Active Elements ➤ Marquee, which displays the Marquee Properties dialog box (see Figure 11.12).

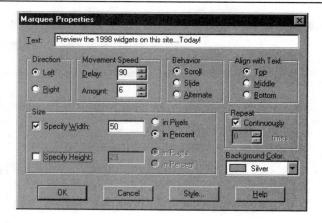

FIGURE 11.12: You can enter the text and define the size, shape, appearance, and behavior of a marquee in the Marquee Properties dialog box.

3. In the Text field, enter the text you want to display in the marquee. In this example, that's **Preview the 1998 widgets on this site....Today!** If you select text in the page before invoking the command, that text appears in this field, and the marquee replaces the text in the page.

By ignoring all the other options at this time and clicking on OK, you create a functioning marquee in your page. However, you can also make a few small modifications to it:

4. To change the color of the marquee's background, select a color in the Background Color option.

5. Select the Specify Width check box, enter **50** for the width, and select In Percent. This sizes the marquee so it is half the width of the window in which this page is displayed.

 NOTE   You can also change the size of a marquee from within the page. Click on it and then drag one of its selection handles, just as you can do with an image or a horizontal line.

6. That's all you need in this dialog box, so click on OK.

The marquee is now half the width of the window but is aligned with the left edge of the window. Its text is in the default size and style, but it should be a little bigger for this purpose. You can change both of these aspects right in the page, treating the marquee like other objects in a page.

7. Select the marquee not by clicking, on it but by pointing to the left of it and clicking. This highlights the marquee as though it were a line of text you had just selected.

8. Now click on the Center button on the Format toolbar to center the marquee on the page.

9. Choose Heading 3 from the Change Style list on the Format toolbar so the marquee's message appears in that heading style.

10. Save the page. Now you're ready to see the marquee in action.

11. Switch to Preview or Preview in Browser. You'll see your message scroll across the marquee from right to left, endlessly repeating.

To modify the marquee, double-click on it to open its Marquee Properties dialog box and adjust its options. Experiment with the Behavior options, which affect the way the message moves across the marquee. Adjusting the Movement Speed options control how fast or how slow the marquee runs. Make sure it's slow enough that your users can read it, but not so slow as to be boring.

Page Transitions

In Skill 4, you saw how FrontPage 98 helps you create animated text similar to the builds in PowerPoint. You can also add transitions to your pages, just like PowerPoint's slide transitions, that are visible in browsers that support Dynamic HTML.

To access page transitions, choose Format ➤ Page Transition. The dialog box, shown here, has only a few options you need to set.

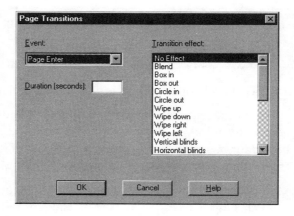

First, choose the event you want to tie the transition to.

- **Page Enter**   Displays when a user opens the page
- **Page Exit**   Displays when a user leaves the page
- **Site Enter**   Displays when a user initially enters the site
- **Site Exit**   Displays when a user leaves the site

Next, choose the transition itself. You have 25 transitions to choose from. You should probably test a few of them out to see how they affect your pages.

Finally, indicate how long you want the transition effect to last. More than a few seconds is typically too long—fewer than two or three seconds is often too short. It depends on the contents of the page, so try different lengths and see how they work.

Once you've set the transition, click on OK and save the page. Preview the page in a browser that supports Dynamic HTML, and remember—the transition is tied to entering or exiting. It's easiest to see the transition if you follow a hyperlink in or out of your page or site.

Adding Advanced Dynamic Components

You can insert other programmable objects into a page in the Editor, although that discussion is beyond the scope of this book. For more information about FrontPage and programmable objects such as Java applets, ActiveX controls, and browser plug-ins, see *Mastering Microsoft FrontPage 98*, also published by Sybex (ISBN 0-7821-2144-6).

 NOTE   A programmer experienced in C, C++, or server-scripting languages, such as Perl or Tcl, can create custom FrontPage components with the FrontPage software developer's kit (SDK). It's available for free on Microsoft's Web site under http://www.microsoft.com/frontpage/.

Signing Up Subscribers with Channels

Despite all the dynamic components you can add to a Web page, the World Wide Web is for the most part, a passive environment. Users are expected to discover for themselves where they want to go, be able to find their way to the site they are looking for, and know how to return to it if they ever want to go back. *Push technology* promises to change all that. One of the latest innovations in Web technology, push allows content providers to send their content directly to the users rather than sitting back and waiting for users to come to them.

At the heart of push is the ability to turn a Web site into a *channel* that users can subscribe to, and then receive content from automatically— just like your favorite premium cable channel. Users can click on a channel button to switch to your channel, or they can receive the content as a screen saver or as a desktop component.

Skill 11

NOTE   A *desktop component* is a feature of Microsoft Internet Explorer 4.0 and other browsers that support channel definitions. It provides a small area of the user's screen to broadcast updated information, such as a stock ticker, sport scores, or other information from a designated Web site.

Push content is updated at regular intervals. Because most people don't have a 24-hour a day Internet connection (yet!), channel-ready browsers automatically connect to the Web at designated times and download the most recent content from the subscribed channels.

To turn your web into a channel so you can enlist your own subscribers, you must first create a *Channel Definition Format (CDF) file*. The CDF file includes an index of the resources, pages, etc. that are available on the channel and a recommended schedule for updating the channel on users' computers. If you only update your web's content once a day, there is no point in users connecting to your channel more often than that. You can edit the CDF file when you want to add new pages to your channel or decide to change content more frequently.

FrontPage 98 makes creating the CDF file easy through the use of a Channel Definition Wizard. Before you start, it's a good idea to prepare a couple of things ahead of time.

Decide which pages of your Web site you want to make available in your channel. You want the channel to include just the few pages that you plan to update regularly; these pages can include links to the other, more static pages in your web. This keeps the channel size under control and makes it easier to keep track of updates.

Open the web in the FrontPage Explorer and create a folder for your channel. Move the pages you decided upon into the folder. If you create more pages for the channel, save them in this folder. (You may also want a subfolder for images.)

The second thing you want to do is prepare two GIF images: The first one you'll use as a logo for the channel button that identifies your channel in a user's Web browser. This image should be exactly 80×32 pixels. The second image is an icon that identifies the pages in your channel. Make this image a 16×16 pixel GIF image. Neither of these images is required, but you'll find that using them makes your channel feel like the real thing. Figure 11.13 shows the channels and their respective buttons that come with Internet Explorer 4.0.

FIGURE 11.13: Internet Explorer 4.0 comes with a group of channels set up for users to subscribe to.

To define a channel for your web, open the web in the FrontPage Explorer and follow the steps below.

1. Choose Tools ➢ Define Channel to launch the Channel Definition Wizard shown here.

2. The first option in the Channel Definition Wizard is whether you want to create a new channel definition or modify an existing one. The default is based on whether a channel for the active web is already defined. If you want to modify the CDF for an existing channel, enter the URL for the web. Click on Next to move to the next step, shown here.

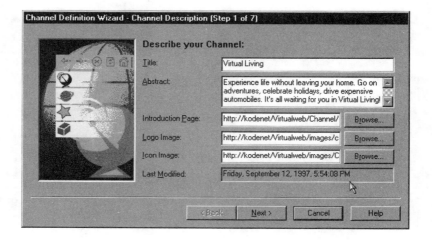

3. Enter the title you want to give your channel. Typically this is the title of your web, but it doesn't have to be.

4. Write a short abstract (summary) of your channel. This is the information users see when they point to your channel logo image, so make it descriptive and enticing. In Figure 11.14 you see an abstract for one of the channels.

5. Enter the URLs for the Introduction Page, Logo Image, and Logo Icon. Click on Browse if you want to locate them in your web. Click on Next.

6. Enter the URL for the source folder—the folder that contains the pages you want to include in your channel—in the text box shown on the next page. Enable the subfolders checkbox if you created an images (or any other) subfolder. Click on Next.

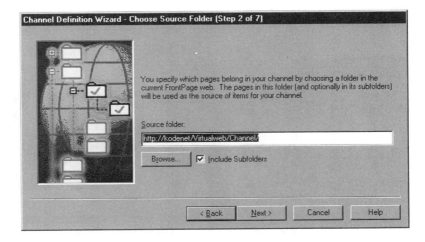

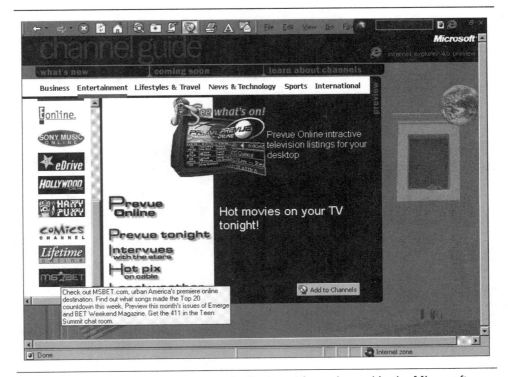

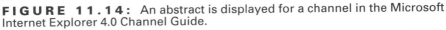

FIGURE 11.14: An abstract is displayed for a channel in the Microsoft Internet Explorer 4.0 Channel Guide.

7. Step 3 asks you to specify any files you do not want to include in your channel. Select the file or files you want to exclude (Shift+Click and Ctrl+Click work here) and click on the Exclude button, shown here.

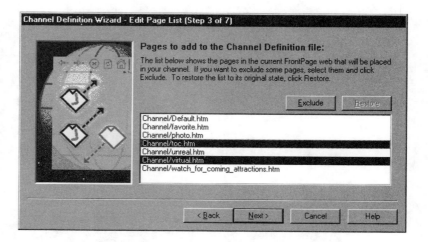

8. Click on Next to move on to Step 4. Here you can set the properties for each page in your channel, including an abstract, page cache, and usage settings. Select a page and enter an abstract or summary of the page.

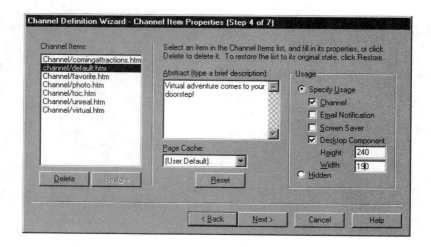

9. Set how you want the page cached on the user's computer. This means whether you want a user to be able to download the page and browse it offline. There are three options: User Default means to use the setting the user establishes in their browser. Don't Use Cache means the user has to be online to view the page. Use Cache means the user can download the page and view it offline.

10. There are five options for how the page should work in a user's browser. Select any or all of the first four options, or choose *Hidden* if you want the page to be a part of the channel list but hidden from view. This may sound a little strange, but is quite useful if you want the user to have a page that is the target of a hyperlink on one of the other pages but you don't want them to access that page directly. The other options work as follows:

   - **Channel**   When the user opens your channel in a browser, the page appears as an item in your channel's list.

   - **E-mail notification**   The user gets an automatic e-mail every time you update or modify the page so they know to check your channel.

   - **Screen saver**   The page is enabled as a screen saver on the user's computer. Of course, the user has to have your screen saver turned on for this to be effective.

   - **Desktop component**   The page is displayed in a small window on the user's screen. You indicate the height and width of the window in pixels. Figure 11.15 shows a desktop component displayed in the top right corner of the Windows desktop.

Skill 11

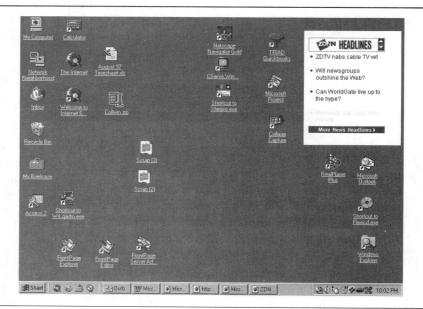

FIGURE 11.15: This desktop component occupies a small area of the screen and brings up-to-date headlines from the world of technology.

11. Click on Next to move on to Step 5. This step, shown below, is where you schedule how often a user's computer should check your channel for updated pages. Indicate the start and end date of your channel, or leave (now) and (forever) if you've made a long-term commitment to your Web presence.

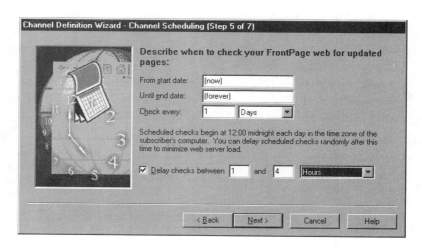

12. To determine how often a user's computer should check for updates, enter the number of minutes, hours, or days and use the drop-down to select the appropriate qualifier.

13. Whether you use the last option on this step depends on how popular you expect your channel to be. Subscribers' computers begin calling your site for updates at midnight each night. If you expect a lot of traffic, you may want to randomize the calls and spread them out over several hours. Click on the Delay Checks checkbox and enter the span of days, hours, or minutes over which you would like the calls spread. Click on Next to go to Step 6.

14. One of the objectives of having subscribers is that it gives you a better idea of who your customers are. In Step 6, shown below, you can identify a log target URL that records the browsing behavior of your subscribers—things like what pages they opened and what links they clicked on give you a lot of information about how to make your site even more interesting. The only way you can use this feature, however, is if you have created a form handler to receive the data (see Skill 12 for information about form handlers). Click on Next to skip this step for now.

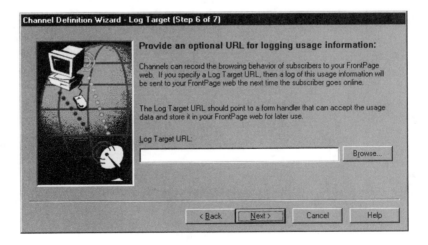

15. The final step, shown on the next page, creates the CDF file, places a button on the Navigation bar of your home page (so users can subscribe) and allows you to publish the channel.

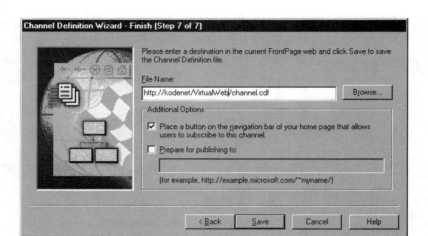

The default file location for the CDF is the top level folder of the active web, and it's a good idea to keep it there. Some browsers look for it there and if they don't find it, users can't access your channel.

If the option for placing a subscribe button on the navigation bar of your home page is gray, it means you don't have shared borders *and* navigation bars turned on in this web. Even though it won't create a button for you, you can still create a hyperlink from your home page to the CDF file. When users click on this link, they subscribe to your channel.

16.   Click on Save to create the Channel Definition File.

Wait to publish your channel until you have tested it locally and know that it is working the way you want it to. When you are ready to publish it, you can send your channel on its way.

Modifying and Publishing Your Channel

After you complete the Channel Definition Wizard, you should be able to locate the *channel.cdf* file in the main folder of your web. If you chose to have the wizard place a button on the navigation bar on your home page, you see the Subscribe node in the Explorer's navigation view, as shown in Figure 11.16.

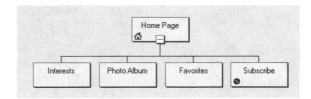

FIGURE 11.16: The Channel Definition Wizard adds a Subscribe node to the web's Navigation view.

If you did not have the wizard insert a button, you need to open your home page and create a hyperlink to the *channel.cdf* file. Open the home page in a channel-ready browser, such as Internet Explorer 4.0, and click on the Subscribe button (or link) to test the subscription.

Double-click on the Subscribe node to reopen the Channel Definition Wizard and make any modifications you want to make.

When you are ready to publish your channel to make it available to other users, click on the Prepare for Publishing to checkbox on the last page of the Channel Definition Wizard. Enter the complete URL of the location to which you want to publish your channel. This can be a World Wide Web location or on your company's intranet server. Click on the Save button to publish the channel.

 NOTE   If you use Microsoft Internet Explorer 4.0, you can learn more about channels by clicking on the View Channels button next to the Start button on the Task Bar.

Are You Experienced?

Now you can...

☑ **Automate your Web sites using FrontPage components**

☑ **Create page banners, banner ads, hover buttons and marquees**

☑ **Substitute images, text, and pages on a scheduled basis**

☑ **Create a table of contents of your web**

☑ **Automatically enter the time or date in a page**

☑ **Push content to your subscribers with Channels**

Letting Users Interact with Forms

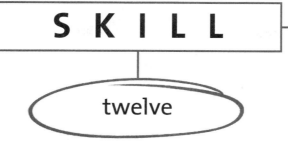

- ❏ Creating forms with templates

- ❏ Creating forms with the Form Page Wizard

- ❏ Choosing a form handler

- ❏ Adding fields to a form

- ❏ Adjusting the properties of form controls

- ❏ Setting data validation for text boxes

- ❏ Using a form

This Skill introduces you to forms, which allow visitors to your Web site to reverse the normal mode of Web browsing by sending information to you. If you've spent much time browsing the Web, you know that forms are being used more often. Many of the sites you visit ask you to register in a guest book or enter personal or company information to download files. And FrontPage 98 includes even more tools to make form creation a snap using form controls like text boxes, radio buttons, check boxes, and drop-down menus.

Creating Forms

A web form lets users of your site enter information, then send it to your server, moving from mere surfing into a two-way communication mode. With forms, you can find out who is visiting your site, what they liked or would like to see improved, and why they visited—user information that's impossible to acquire unless you ask.

You create a form using a variety of *form fields*, like the controls used in Windows dialog boxes, each of which lets the user enter data. Many of your users automatically understand how to use a form, because they've used the same controls to save files, select applications, and install software. Behind the form is a *form handler*, used to collect information from the form and save it in your web. Figure 12.1 shows a form containing some of the standard controls you can include in a form.

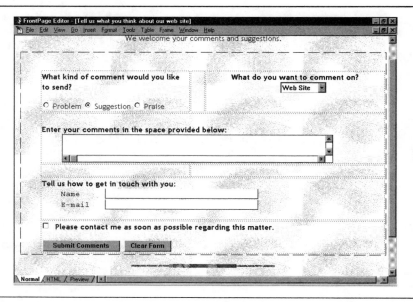

FIGURE 12.1: A form lets the user enter data and then send the data to the server.

FrontPage 98's form fields, and their buttons on the Forms toolbar, are shown in Table 12.1.

TABLE 12.1: Field Forms and Descriptions

Button	Form Field	Description
	One-Line Text Box	A user enters a single line of text, such as a name, street address, or phone number (the Name and E-mail fields in Figure 12.1).
	Scrolling Text Box	An open text box for several lines of text. The window is a fixed size, but scroll bars are displayed (the Comments field in Figure 12.1).
	Check Box	Use check boxes to let a reader select items in the form or make more than one choice from a group of choices (the Please Contact Me field in Figure 12.1).
	Radio Button	Use to present mutually exclusive choices. Users can click one, and only one, radio button in a group to make a single choice from the group (the Kind of Comment choices in Figure 12.1).
	Drop-Down Menu	Lets the user select one or more items (depending on how the field was defined) from a drop-down list (the What Do You Want to Comment On control in Figure 12.1).
	Push Button	Executes an action for the user. In the form shown in Figure 12.1, users click the Submit Comments button to send their entries to the form handler, or the Clear Form button to clear the form.

Form-Building Basics

Creating a form is a three-step process: determining the data you want to collect, including controls appropriate to the data, and setting a form handler to store the data you've collected. Before you start creating the form, decide what data you want users to be able to enter. Then, using a template, wizard or an existing page, insert the form fields you need, like text boxes, radio buttons, and check boxes, as well as any descriptive text or images you want. Whether you use a template or not, FrontPage automatically adds the Submit Form and Clear Form push buttons to the page as soon as you place the first form field.

Finally, decide what to do with the data entered after your server receives it. For example, will it be appended to a database or added to an HTML page and displayed elsewhere on your web? Based on your decision, specify and set options for a form handler so that user data actually arrives at its destination. In most cases, when all the data in the form is sent back to the server, the information entered into

Skill 12

each control (called the control's value) is paired with the name of the control. This name-value pair identifies the data elements so the server can deal with the data appropriately.

> **NOTE**   You can place more than one form on a Web page. The Editor delineates a form with a dark dashed line around it, as you can see in Figure 12.1, which differ from the dotted lines placed around table cells. Any fields you add within the dashed line are part of the form. Each form has its own properties. Each form must also have its own button to submit the data it contains to the server.

Creating a Form from a Template

You don't have to build a form "from scratch," although the process is pretty simple. Instead, when you create a new page, choose a specialized form from the page templates: Confirmation Form, Feedback Form, Guest Book, Search Page, and User Registration. (If none of the templates meet your needs, you can use the Form Page Wizard to create your form page.) You'll probably want to tweak the form that the template constructs, but it gives you a head start by placing form fields that you can copy, modify, or delete to create your finished form. To use a template, choose File ≻ New in the FrontPage Editor to open the New dialog box, shown in Figure 12.2.

Select a template to see a description and a very hard-to-see preview on the right side of the dialog box. To create the form page, select a template and click on OK.

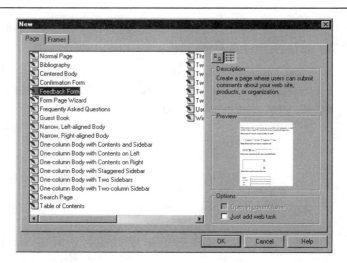

FIGURE 12.2: Choose a template from the New dialog box to quickly create a form.

Creating a Form with the Form Page Wizard

Some forms don't fall into the standard template categories, so FrontPage includes a Form Page Wizard to help you create more unique form pages. To fire up the wizard, choose File ➤ New to open the New dialog box again, but choose Form Page Wizard from the list of templates.

The first page describes the Wizard. In the second page, enter a title and URL for the form page, then click on Next to continue. The third page of the Form Page Wizard, shown here, is rather cryptic.

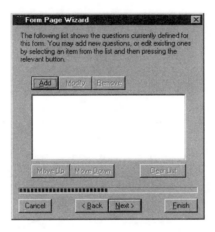

Unless you're editing an existing form, you want to click on the Add button to begin constructing the form's text and controls. You're prompted to choose an input type. The first items in the list create multiple fields. For example, *contact information* asks for name, address, and other similar information. Further down the list are more generic choices like date, one of several options, and paragraph. When you select an input type, a description and sample prompt appear. Enter the prompt that users will see above the form fields.

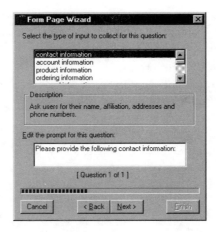

Click on the Next button to see the options associated with the input type you selected. For example, when you choose *contact information*, you can choose whether you'd like users to supply just a first name, first and last, or first, last, and middle names. Do you want their fax number? Home phone? Professional survey designers tell you "the less you ask for, the more you'll get." Only ask for information you really require, so users are more likely to patiently fill in real answers, rather than creating spurious entries for Jabba the Hutt and Winnie the Pooh.

For some questions, you can choose the form field used to collect the data. If users are choosing one option from many, for example, you can present the choices in a drop-down menu or with radio buttons. If you're not sure which control type to use, think about how you've seen similar information presented online. The number of options often decides the issue: a radio button for each U.S. state is simply not a good idea.

Enter a name that's used to describe the data users enter in response to the question, then click on the Next button. You're returned to the list of questions, which includes the question you just entered. Select the question and click on Modify if you want to alter the settings for the first question, or click on Remove to delete the question. To add another question, click on Add. When you have more than one question in the list, you can use the Move Up and Move Down buttons to rearrange the order of the questions. Continue adding and, if necessary, rearranging questions until you've entered all the questions required for the form.

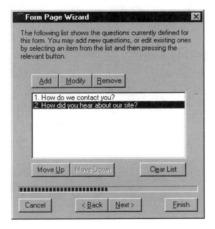

With all the questions entered, click on Next to move to the Presentation Options. Use the radio buttons and checkboxes to indicate how you want to present the questions. If you are asking a number of questions (like an online survey or exam), users often prefer to have a table of contents, so they can jump between questions. Specify whether FrontPage should use tables to format your questions. You can always copy questions and form fields into a table later, or remove the questions from a table. Click on Next to continue.

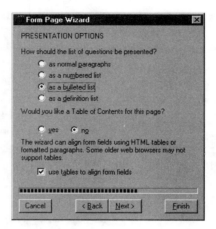

In the Output Options page, specify the form handler you wish to use. FrontPage's form handlers are *CGI (Common Gateway Interface)* scripts. You can save the results to a web page or text file, which uses the default FrontPage form handler, or indicate that you have a custom CGI script to handle this form. In the text box at the bottom of the page, enter the name (without an extension) of the web page or text file that receives the results. FrontPage creates the file if it doesn't exist.

When you've entered output options, click on Next, then click on the Finish button on the final page of the Form Page Wizard to create the form. The form created using the two questions in the example above is shown in Figure 12.3.

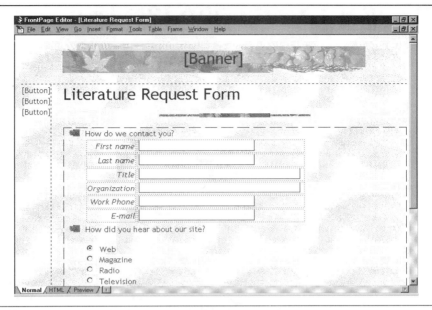

FIGURE 12.3: The Form Page Wizard helps you create a form to collect data from your users.

Aligning Form Fields

When you create a form, you may want to align the various text elements, images, and controls it contains so that users find it easier to progress through the form. The easiest way to align objects in a form is to place them in tables. For example, the field descriptions can be in the left column of a table and the fields themselves in the right column. This method was used in Figure 12.1 to place the first two questions side by side on the page and add space between the other form fields.

You can also align a form's elements by applying the Formatted paragraph style to the entire form (Format ➢ Paragraph). A monospaced font is used, making it easy to align objects on the screen—just press the spacebar to move objects to the right. You can place the main items in the form on separate paragraphs (press Enter) or insert a line break (press Shift+Enter) to separate groups of items. Although it's easier to space objects when you're using a monospaced font, it detracts a bit from the form's graphic appeal.

Telling the Server How to Handle the Data

When you create a form with the Form Page Wizard, you choose your form handler in the Output Options. If you create your form from scratch, you need to specify the form handler that deals with the data when it is sent to the server. Right-click anywhere within the form and choose Form Properties from the shortcut menu to open the Form Properties dialog box (shown in Figure 12.4).

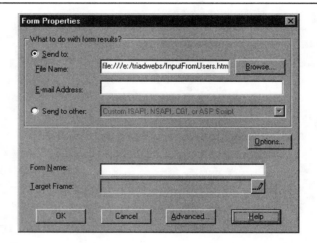

FIGURE 12.4: You specify how the form's data is sent to the server in the Form Properties dialog box.

Choosing a Form Handler

In the Form Properties dialog box, select a form-handling method:

- **Send to Filename**   If you created your form with the wizard, this textbox already contains the filename you entered. Enter a new URL, or Browse to select a file.

- **Send to E-mail**   Enter a valid e-mail address that all user input should be sent to.

- **Send to Other**   Select this option to send user input to a custom form handler or specialized FrontPage form handler. Then, select a handler from the drop down list.

  - **Custom ISAPI, NSAPI, CGI or ASP**   Script sends the form results to a custom form handler created outside FrontPage.

- **Discussion Form Handler**   This FrontPage handler adds the data from the form to a FrontPage discussion group web.

- **Registration Form Handler**   This FrontPage handler allows the user to register for server-provided services.

In the Target Frame section, you can specify a frame to display form results. You'll find out more about frames in Skill 13.

Configuring the Form Handler

After you've selected a form handler, click on the Options button to open the appropriate dialog box for the selected form handler. The Options for Saving Results of Form dialog box shown in Figure 12.5 appears when you send your results to a file or e-mail. These are the most frequently used options, so we'll review them in some depth.

This dialog box has four pages: File Results, E-mail Results, Confirmation Page (which you'll use if you're sending output to a page that appears in the user's browser to confirm the receipt of their data), and Saved Fields, which you'll always want to review.

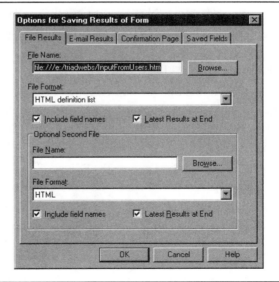

FIGURE 12.5: Use the Options for Saving Results of Form dialog box to configure the default form handler.

If you want to send user results to a file, verify or change the options on the File Results page, shown in Figure 12.5:

- **File Name**   Enter the name of the file where the form's data is saved. If the file doesn't exist, it's created the first time data is submitted from the form. Include the relative URL of the file if it is in the active web (the _private folder might be a good place to store it).

- **File Format**   Select one of the available file formats from the drop-down list. There are several HTML options that save the data in a Web page (you need to specify a Filename with an HTM or HTML extension). There are also several plain text formats; one format, Text Database Using Comma as a Separator, creates a file where a comma is inserted between each piece of data. Most database and spreadsheet programs can read this type of file, so you can easily import it into Excel or Access, or use it as a Word merge file.

- **Include Field Names**   By default, this option is selected so the form's data is returned to the server with each field's name paired with the field's data. Deselect this option to send only the form's data.

- **Latest Results at End**   If you're sending the results to an HTML file, you can deselect this to write the most recent data at the top of the file. With a text file, data is always appended—added to the end.

- **Optional Second File**   Use this group of settings to send the data to two separate files. You might do this if you wanted to have a web-ready HTML file and a text file to import for a database.

The E-mail Results page (see Figure 12.6) includes settings for the e-mail address that should receive the results, and the format that should be used in the e-mail.

Use the following options in the E-mail Message Header section to specify the Subject and Reply To lines of the e-mail message:

- **Subject Line**   Text for the Subject line of the e-mailed form results. For example, if the form is used for a membership registration, the Subject Line might be Our Newest Member or Member Registration Info.

- **Reply-to Line**   Text for the Reply To line of the e-mail message. The recipient of the e-mail clicks on this to reply to the results message. This needs to be an e-mail address, or a form field with an e-mail address as a value.

- **Form Field Name**   Enable this check box to place the results of a control (like the visitor's last name) in the Subject line or Reply To line of the e-mail. Then, type the form field name in the appropriate text box. (Notice that this is enabled by default for the Reply To line. The assumption is that you'll want to include the visitor's e-mail address in the Reply To line so that the e-mail recipient can easily send mail to the visitor.)

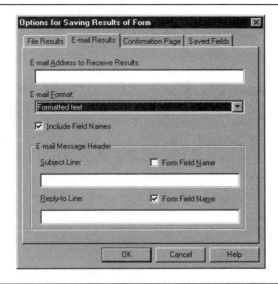

FIGURE 12.6: Format, then e-mail visitor data using the settings on the E-mail Results page.

When a user sends in (submits) the data on a form, the FrontPage form handler returns a Confirmation page to the user. It says "Thanks" and displays the information received from the form. By default, the handler creates a basic vanilla confirmation page. You can specify a page in the Confirmation page of the Options for Saving Results of Form dialog box. The page you specify might be nothing more than a neatly formatted page with the message, "We received your data. Thanks!" But you can personalize the confirmation by including data from selected fields on the form that the user submitted: "Dear Sharon: Thanks for your interest in our organization..." To do this, open the confirmation page you specified in the Editor and insert the Confirmation field component where you want to display the field. (Having the list of field names on hand makes this job easier). Save the Confirmation page, and the next time it is used to confirm the receipt of data from a form, the data in the specified field replaces each Confirmation field component.

The Saved Fields page of the Options for Saving Results of Form dialog box shows the list of fields that are captured on the form. Figure 12.7 is the Saved Fields page from the two question form we created earlier. Each of the contact information fields is preceded by the group name and an underscore: for example, Contact_FirstName. The fields are saved in the order in which they're listed, so if you want to save the e-mail address first, move it to the top of the list. (You can't use the menu or toolbar while you're in this dialog box, but you can use shortcut keys: Ctrl+X or Ctrl+Delete to cut, Ctrl+V or Ctrl+Insert to paste.) Below the list of fields you created are some optional fields you can automatically capture without having the user enter them. Check the fields you wish to include in the data from the user.

FIGURE 12.7: In the Saved Fields page, you can specify other fields to include in the output file.

When you finish setting options, click on OK to close the Options dialog box and return to the Form Properties dialog box.

Adding Fields to a Form

Some web authors prefer to create their forms from scratch. This is easy to do, because the Editor lets you insert any of the controls into a page. If you have not yet placed form controls on a page, when you place one, the Editor creates a new form and add the dashed line that designates the form area. Thereafter, you can add more controls, descriptive text, and images to the form. If you want to create another form on the page, move the insertion point outside of the dashed line that defines the form.

You add a form control with the Insert ➤ Form Field command or by clicking on a button on the Forms toolbar, shown below (View ➤ Forms Toolbar). Browse the toolbar, or refer to Table 12.1 for a review of the form field types.

FrontPage isn't like Visual Basic or Access; you don't drag controls and place them on the screen. Instead, you click and the field appears at the insertion point. So, before you insert a form field, you need to have a place for it. If you want the field to follow text, type the text in first. If you want to place fields in a table, it's easiest to create the table, then place the fields. For example, if you want your form to include the text string "Check here to receive our newsletter" followed by a checkbox, type the string, press the space bar, then choose Insert ➤ Form Field ➤ Check box or click on the Check box button on the Forms toolbar:

Microsoft publishes a large book of standards that specify how you should use product components, including controls. You don't have to read the book to develop web pages, but you should implement controls as your users expect them to be used. This allows visitors to enter information without fumbling around, and is part of what makes a site friendly. For example:

- Radio buttons should always appear in groups of two or more, because they let the reader make only one choice from several choices. If there's only one choice, use a checkbox.

- Only use text boxes if there are a large or unpredictable number of choices. Users would rather choose their modem from a drop-down menu than type its name. And by providing a drop-down menu, you receive consistent data.

- If the answer to a question is Yes or No, you can probably rephrase it to use a Checkbox: "Check here to receive our newsletter" instead of "Would you like to receive our newsletter?"

- Don't ask users to enter data that you can collect automatically. Sophisticated users know that you can get the current date from their computer or your server.

- The default setting for each form field should be the setting most users are likely to choose, making one less control they have to change. Or, in a more Machiavellian worldview, the default setting should be the setting you would *like* them to choose. Some commercial sites have a notice that they offer their e-mail lists to others (for a price, of course), so they offer users the opportunity to "Check here if you don't want us to include your name in these lists." You'll notice that none of these checkboxes are turned on by default.

Changing Form Field Properties

Each control in a form has a set of properties defining its name, default setting, the way it looks, the type of data it accepts (*validation*), and so on. You can adjust the properties after you enter all the fields for a form, or you can modify the properties for each as you create it. To open the properties dialog box for a control, you can do any of the following:

- Double-click on the control.

- Select the control then choose Edit ≻ Form Field Properties or press Alt+Enter.

- Right-click on the control and choose Form Field Properties from the shortcut menu.

In the sections that follow, you learn how to change the properties for each of the form controls that you've seen in this Skill.

One-Line Text Boxes

One-line text boxes have a limited number of properties (see Figure 12.8). The first setting, Name, is found in all the controls except the radio button (which is not individually named). When you insert a control, it is given a short code-like name, such as T1 for the first one-line text box in a form; the Form Page Wizard gives controls the names you specify. As you work your way through the controls, make sure each control has a descriptive name. Don't include spaces in the names—use underscores instead.

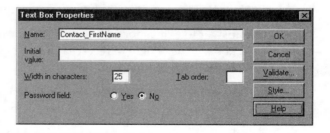

FIGURE 12.8: The Text Box Properties dialog box for a one-line text box field.

Here are the Text Box Properties:

- **Name** Enter a name for the control to help identify the data it contains.

- **Initial Value** Enter the characters you want in this field when the form is opened. In some cases, a default entry can save the user some typing if the default is the typical response entered. A default entry can also serve as an example of what type of data should be entered: *Enter your name here.*

- **Width in Characters** Specify the width of the text box in characters (you can also select the box in the form and drag one of its selection handles to change its size). It's easier to enter data when the field is wide enough to display all or most of the text you're entering. This is not a limitation on the number of characters that can be entered but on the number of characters the user can see; you limit the number of characters through validation.

- **Tab Order** Tab order specifies the order that users move through controls when they press the Tab key. Use numbers from 1-999 to set the order, with 1 being the field that the insertion point appears in when the form opens. If you don't want users to tab to a control, set its tab order value at -1. Newer browsers like IE 4.0 support tab order; others simply use the default tab order.

- **Password Field** If visitors will enter a password in this field, choose Yes. Whatever a user types into this field is displayed as asterisks to hide it from view. You can turn this on for any field, but users are generally not amused.

Data Validation

You can limit the type of data accepted in a one-line text box or scrolling text box by applying data-validation rules to the field. You do so in the Text Box Validation dialog box (see Figure 12.9). To open the dialog box, click on the Validate button in the field's Text Box Properties dialog box, or right-click on the field and choose Form Field Validation.

Skill 12

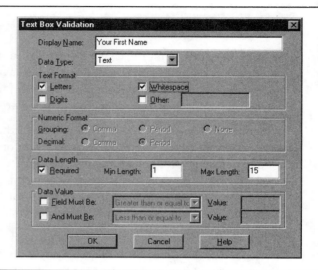

FIGURE 12.9: You can specify the type of data accepted in a one-line or scrolling text box through data validation.

When a user submits the form's data to the server, the entry in each field is checked against any data validation that has been applied to the field. If the data in a field falls outside of the validation criteria, an error message is generated notifying the user of the problem. Whether the error message is generated on the client side or server side depends on the abilities of the browser.

If the browser supports Java, it displays validation messages before the data is ever sent to the server. Otherwise, the browser simply sends the data to the server, and the server checks the data against the validation rules. If some data is invalid, the server generates a page with the appropriate error messages and sends it back to the browser.

Display Name   When a field is mentioned in a validation message, it's identified by the name you entered in the field's Text Box Properties dialog box. The name isn't usually formatted for easy reading. The Display Name is the name that appears in validation messages for the user. Instead of **Contact_FirstName**, you can enter **Your First Name**. This allows you, for example, to use exactly the same name or description that appears next to the field in the form.

Data Type   The Data Type option specifies the type of data allowed in the one-line or scrolling text box:

- **No Constraints**   Allows any type of data in the field.

- **Text**   Allows any characters to be entered into the field.

- **Integer**   Requires a valid whole number, either positive, zero, or negative; ensures users don't enter alphabetic characters where a number is required.

- **Number**   Allows any valid number, with or without a decimal fraction.

Once you select the Data Type, you can limit the acceptable entries for the field even further:

- **Text Format**   When you select Text as the Data Type, you can select the type of characters allowed in the field. For example, for a field in which a membership number is entered, such as 123 45 6789, select the Digits and Whitespace options to allow spaces between the numbers but rule out letters.

- **Numeric Format**   When you choose Integer or Number from the Data Type list, you can specify the Grouping character allowed within the entry to separate every three digits. Choose Comma, Period, or None. When you choose Number from the Data Type list, you can also specify the allowable Decimal character.

- **Data Length**   Choose the Required option to require an entry in this field, no matter what other options have been specified. For example, you might require a first name, last name, and e-mail address from a user requesting information. Use the Min Length and Max Length fields to specify the minimum and maximum number of characters that are allowed in the field.

- **Data Value**   Set a range of acceptable values for an entry. For example, to require a positive whole number greater than 0 but not greater than 100, choose Integer for the Data Type option, select the Required option, choose the Field Must Be option, select Greater Than, and enter 0 in the Value field. Then select the And Must Be option, choose Less Than or Equal To, and enter 100 in its Value field. If the user enters a negative number, a zero, or a number greater than 100, an appropriate error message is generated.

Skill 12

Changing Control Style

Click on the Style button in the Text Box Properties dialog box to open the Style dialog box, shown below. Use the pages in the Style dialog box to set formatting options. For more information on the use of styles, see Skill 10.

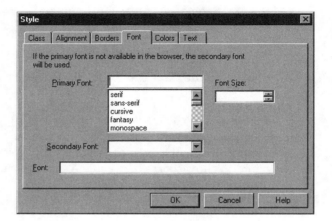

Scrolling Text Boxes

The scrolling text box is essentially the same as a one-line text box, but it allows multiple lines of text. In Figure 12.1, a scrolling text box was used to accept comments from the person filling out the form.

 NOTE   Some browsers automatically wrap text when it reaches the right edge of the scrolling text box. Other browsers, however, let the text extend to the right, so the user has to press Enter to start a new line.

You can specify the width and height of a scrolling text box in its properties dialog box. As with the width of a one-line text box, these settings affect only the size of the field in the form; they do not limit the amount of text that can be entered into the field. You can apply validation rules to a scrolling text box; the choices are the same as those for a one-line text box, as discussed in "Text Box Data Validation" earlier in this chapter.

Drop-Down Menus

The What Do You Want to Comment On field in the form in Figure 12.1 is a drop-down menu. The user can click on the arrow in the control and indicate what they want to comment about. Drop-down menus created by the Wizard or templates include some choices. When you insert a drop-down menu into a form, it is empty. You fill or modify the menu with the Drop-Down Menu Properties dialog box (shown in Figure 12.10).

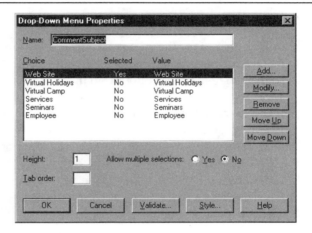

FIGURE 12.10: The Drop-Down Menu Properties dialog box for a drop-down menu form field

To add an item to the menu, click on the Add button to open the Add Choice dialog box. In the dialog box, enter what you want to appear as a choice on the menu.

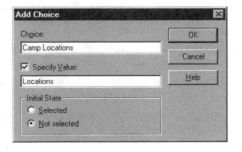

The Name you enter is exactly what's sent to the server when a user selects this item in the menu. Optionally, you can select the Specify Value check box and enter a substitute value to send to the server. For example, you might want **United States** to appear in the list but **USA** sent to the server.

When you're adding an item to a drop-down menu, you can also specify whether the item is selected by default. For example, in Figure 12.1, *Web Site* is selected when the form opens, which is helpful if most users want to comment about the web site. After you've created the new menu item, click OK to close the Add Choice dialog box and return to the Drop-Down Menu Properties dialog box.

The default setting allows a user to select only one item from a drop-down menu; select Yes for the Allow Multiple Selections in the properties dialog box to let a user select more than one by using Ctrl or Shift and clicking.

To rearrange the order of items in the drop-down menu, select the item in the Choice list and then click on the Move Up or Move Down button to change its position in the list. A list should be in a logical order. A list with more than four or five items should be sorted. Don't worry about arranging the list around the default value; the list opens to the Selected item regardless of where it appears on the list. Click on the Remove button to remove it from the list; click on the Modify button to revise its name, value, or selected status.

You can also set validation rules for a drop-down menu in its validation dialog box, shown here.

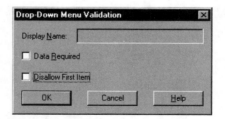

The Disallow First Item setting lets you place an explanatory item first on the list, such as **Choose a State**. This item must be at the top of the list of choices; don't mark any of the other items in the list as Selected, or the item isn't displayed.

Radio Buttons

Radio buttons allow a user to make one choice from a group of choices. In Figure 12.1, three radio buttons let the user choose Problem, Suggestion, or Praise. You define a group of radio buttons by giving each of them the same Group Name in their properties dialog box, as shown here.

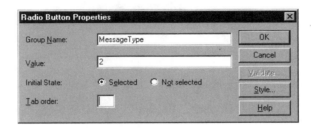

The name MessageType is used for all three radio buttons in Figure 12.1. The value you assign to a radio button is sent to the server when the Submit button is selected by the user. In Figure 12.1, the radio buttons can have the same values as their respective labels. However, we decided to use the value 1 for Problem, 2 for Suggestion, and 3 for Praise; a single digit transmits faster than a string, and takes up less room in a database.

You can select one of the buttons in a group by default, when the form is opened. Again, offering a default choice can be a convenience to the person who's filling out the form. If none of the buttons in a group is a default choice, you can still require the user to select a button in the validation dialog box. Select the Data Required checkbox and, optionally, enter a name for the group of radio buttons in the Display Name field. Applying validation to one radio button in a group applies it to all buttons in the group.

Checkboxes

The checkbox allows a user to select a single item by clicking on the box; clicking on the box again deselects it. A check mark in the box indicates it's selected. In Figure 12.1, users check a box to request immediate contact. The properties of a checkbox consist of its name, value, and whether it's selected or deselected when the form is opened.

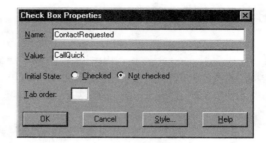

Push Buttons

There are three kinds of push button controls you can insert into a form: Submit, Reset, and Normal. When you add any form field to a page, FrontPage 98 automatically adds the Submit and Reset push buttons, right next to the field you inserted. The Submit and Reset buttons have scripts, based in part on the settings you entered in the Form Properties File Results and E-mail Results pages. Normal push buttons have no attached script, but are generic buttons you can attach scripts to. The Push Button Properties dialog box (shown here) lets you change the text that appears on the face of the button, the button type, and the tab order. Clicking on the Form button opens the Form Properties dialog box so you can choose a form handler.

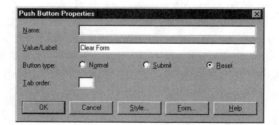

The Image form field is a substitute push button. Specifically, it's a substitute for the Submit button. To insert an Image form field, choose Insert ➤ Form Field ➤ Image. The Image dialog box (see Figure 12.11) opens so you can select the image for the button.

FIGURE 12.11: Select an image for the Image Form Field from the dialog box.

When you click on OK, the selected image is placed in the form as a button, with a narrow border. Choosing either Form Field Properties or Image Properties from the shortcut menu produces the same result: opening the Image Form Field Properties dialog box. You can name the image form field, but you cannot change the image's display properties. If you want to edit the image, open the original image in Image Composer, alter it, then insert the Image Form Field again.

Filling Out the Form in a Browser

Open a page that contains a form in your browser in the same way that you open any other page. No server interaction is involved until you press the button that submits the form's data to the server. The sample form is shown in a browser in Figure 12.12, with data entered in its various controls. At this point, a user can erase the data entered in the form by clicking the Clear Form button, which resets all the controls to their default values. If the user were ready to send the data to the server, a click of the Submit Comments button does the job.

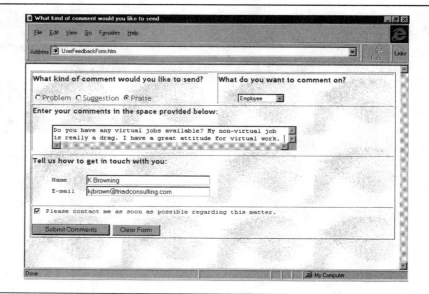

FIGURE 12.12: You open a form in a browser as you would any other page, and fill it out without any server interaction.

When we created this form and specified Send to File, we chose the default form handler. It is this routine that sends the form's data to the server, sends a confirmation page back to the user, and saves the form's data in a file on the server. The confirmation page created by the form handler from the form's data is sent back to the user (shown in Figure 12.13) to verify that the data was received.

FIGURE 12.13: The server returns a confirmation page displaying the information received from the form.

The data from this form is stored on the server in the format specified in the Options for Saving Results of Form dialog box for the form handler, shown below. For the form in Figure 12.1, the file format for the results file is Text Database Using Comma as a Separator; the file is named `feedback.txt`, stored in the web's private folder. A second copy of the data is sent to an HTML file named `feedback.htm`, also located in the web.

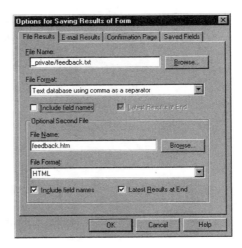

After the data from the form in Figure 12.12 is saved to the file, it contains the entry shown in Figure 12.14. There are no field names in the file, and commas are used to separate the entries from each form field. This is the type of file that most database and spreadsheet programs can easily read. For example, when you open this file in Excel, you can choose to have each control's data fall into a single column.

FIGURE 12.14: The data from the form is saved in a comma-delimited text file.

The HTML file, on the other hand, isn't as readily accessible to other application formats. However, it's easier to open in a browser.

The results files contain data from a single form. Each time the form is filled out and submitted, another line of data is added to each file. They continue to grow until you either delete the files or move them to another location. If you move the text file (say, at the end of the month), the next time the form is submitted, a new feedback.txt file is created.

Are You Experienced?

Now you can...

- ☑ Create forms from scratch, or by using a template or Wizard
- ☑ Select and configure form handlers
- ☑ Add fields to a form
- ☑ Adjust the properties of form controls
- ☑ Set data validation for text boxes and scrolling text boxes
- ☑ Use a form in a browser

Skill 12

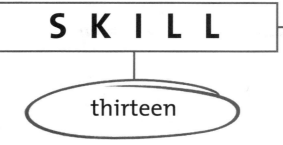

S K I L L

thirteen

13

Getting Fancier with Frames

- ❑ Framing pages in a frames page
- ❑ Using a template to create a frames page
- ❑ Viewing a frames page in your browser
- ❑ Creating a custom frames page
- ❑ Adjusting the size or number of frames
- ❑ Modifying frame and frames page properties

One of the biggest controversies in Web design is in regard to the use of frames, a layout technique in which more than one page is displayed at a time. With adequate forethought, frames can be an exciting and effective design tool. Carelessly applied, they are intrusive and distracting, carving up precious screen space into difficult to see pieces. This Skill shows you when to use frames successfully, how to build a frames page to contain multiple pages, and how to provide users with an option to not use frames, if they prefer.

Dividing a Page into Frames

Frames, an HTML feature that is growing in popularity, allows you to create a single Web page that displays multiple pages. Each page is displayed within a separate window, or *frame*. The page containing these frames is called a *frames page* or *frames set;* when a browser opens a frames page, it opens and displays the page assigned to each frame. Using frames, you can build all sorts of interesting and practical solutions.

Figure 13.1 shows a typical use for a frames page, which you'll build in this Skill. Perhaps without even realizing it, visitors to your frames page see several different pages in their browser:

- A frame in the top-left corner displays a banner and an image.

- A frame on the left side beneath the banner's frame displays a table of contents page, which is built from the Table of Contents component discussed in Skill 11.

- A frame on the right side displays a home page when the frames page is first opened. After that, when you click on a hyperlink in the table of contents frame on the left, the target of the link is displayed in this frame on the right. Therefore, what you see in this frame changes as you click on different links.

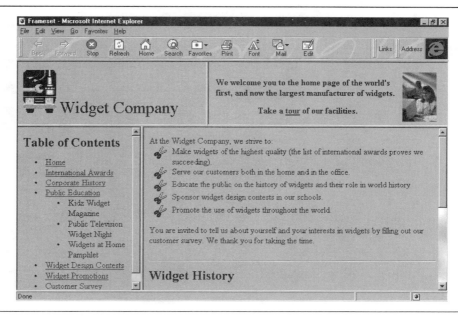

FIGURE 13.1: This frames page displays a banner and an image at the top, a table of contents on the left, and the target of table of contents links on the right.

When you create a frames page in FrontPage 98, you can create new pages to place in the frames or use existing pages from your web. You may want to create the pages that you will display in each frame first before creating the frames page.

It's a good idea to turn off shared borders and navigation bars on any pages you are going to use as part of a frames page. They don't display properly in the frames page and take up valuable display space. The frames provide users with sufficient navigational aids, so additional buttons are unnecessary anyway.

Creating a Frames Page

When you're creating a frames page in the FrontPage Editor, you always start with a Frames template. You can choose from 10 ready-built frames page templates that provide the basic structure for your frames page. You are free to modify that structure after you create the page.

To create the frames page, switch to the FrontPage Editor and choose File ➤ New, and click on the Frames tab of the New dialog box, shown in Figure 13.2.

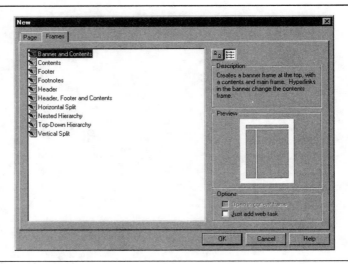

FIGURE 13.2: The Frames page of the New dialog box has 10 frames page templates to choose from.

Click on each of the choices to see a preview of the frames page layout. Choose the layout that is closest to the structure you want for your page, and click on OK to create the frames page.

Each frame has three buttons to help you design your page: Set Initial Page, New Page, and Help. Frames pages have two additional views: No Frames, and Frames Page HTML, so a frames page has five View tabs so you can switch between all the views. When you click on the No Frames tab, you see the page that appears when a users' browser cannot display frames. The Frames Page HTML tab shows you the HTML for the frames page.

The HTML for a typical FrontPage Frames page looks like this:

```
<head>
<meta http-equiv="Content-Type" content="text/html; charset=iso-8859-1">
<title>Widget Company Web</title>
<meta name="GENERATOR" content="Microsoft FrontPage 3.0">
</head>

<frameset framespacing="2" rows="123,*">
  <frameset cols="*,56%">
    <frame name="banner" scrolling="no" noresize target="contents"
src="Banner.htm">
    <frame name="banner1" src="../we_welcome_you_to_the_home_page_.htm"
scrolling="no"
    noresize target="main">
  </frameset>
  <frameset cols="232,*">
    <frame name="contents" target="main" src="table_of_contents.htm">
    <frame name="main" src="index.htm">
  </frameset>
  <noframes>
  <body>
  <p>This page uses frames, but your browser doesn't support them. </p>
  </body>
  </noframes>
</frameset>
</html>
```

The content of each frame is identified between opening and closing
<FRAMESET> tags. The content of the page that is displayed when the
browser doesn't support tags is identified with the <NOFRAMES> tag.

 NOTE   At this point, the No Frames alternative page only contains the default text
"This page uses frames, but your browser doesn't support them." Later in this
Skill you'll learn how to replace this pithy text with another page.

Click on the Normal tab to return to the Frames page.

Creating a New Page to Go into the Frame

To insert a page into a frame, you need to link the page to the corresponding
section of the frames page. If you are creating the pages from scratch, click on the
New Page button in the frame you want to start working in.

The insertion point moves into the frame and all of the normal page editing commands are available to you. If you prefer a larger workspace, right-click in the frame and choose Open Page in New Window from the short-cut menu. When you're finished entering the content for the page, save the page to the active web.

You can close the new page at this point, but it's helpful to actually see the page in the context of the entire frames page—you may want to do some editing to improve how the display. To see your new page, switch to the frames page using the Window menu. The page is displayed in the chosen frame.

Setting the Initial Page from an Existing Page

Set Initial Page

If you already have a page you want to appear in a frame, click on the Set Initial Page button. This opens the same Create Hyperlink dialog box you learned about in Skill 6. By inserting a page into a frame, you create a hyperlink to that page. When you open a frames page, each hyperlink is activated and the target pages, called *initial pages*, appear in the designated frames, as shown in Figure 13.3:

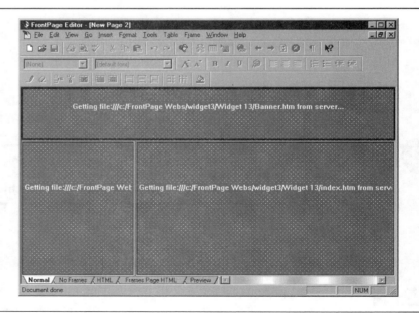

FIGURE 13.3: When a frames page is opened, each of the hyperlinks is activated to open the target pages in the designated frames.

To set the initial page for a frame, you use the Create Hyperlink dialog box, shown in Figure 13.4, in the same way you create other types of hyperlinks. Select the page you want to be the target of the hyperlink and click on OK.

FIGURE 13.4: Create a hyperlink to the page you want to appear in the frame.

The page you select is the page that appears in that frame when the page is opened. If the page is too large for the frame, in most cases horizontal and vertical scroll bars appear by default in the frame. A little later in this Skill, you'll learn how to resize the frame and eliminate unnecessary scroll bars to create a crisper, less cluttered look.

Saving a Frames Page

Saving a frames page is no different than saving any other page, except that you need to remember that you are only saving the page's structure and the hyperlinks to each of the initial pages, not the actual content of the pages themselves. You can still open each page separately from the frames page and make any desired editing changes. The next time you open the frames page, the revised pages are included.

To save the frames page, use File ➢ Save or File ➢ Save As (Figure 13.5).

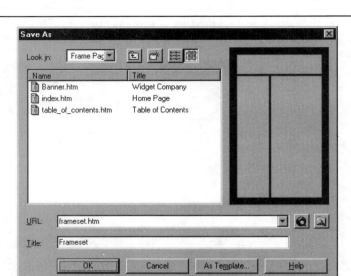

FIGURE 13.5: When you save a frames page, you are only saving the structure of the page with its corresponding hyperlinks.

Enter the URL and Title for the new page. Click on OK to save the new page.

TIP To make a frames page the home page of your web, rename the home page in the FrontPage Explorer before saving the new frames page. When you save the new page, give it the name of your previous home page: `default.htm` or `index.htm`, depending on whether you are using the Microsoft Personal Web Server or the FrontPage Personal Web Server. See Skill 14 for more about web servers.

Editing Pages in Frames

When you click in any of the frames in the Editor, a color-highlighted border appears around the frame indicating that it is the active frame. You can edit the page in its frame or choose Open in New Window from the short-cut menu for more extensive editing.

Resizing a Frame

Whether you create the page from scratch or insert an existing page, you may discover that the frame is not large enough to display the page effectively. Figure 13.6 shows a banner that's too large for the top frame.

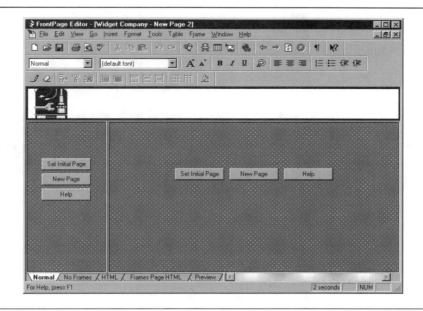

FIGURE 13.6: Only a portion of the banner is displayed in the top window.

This problem is easily rectified by adjusting the size of the frame. To adjust a frame's dimensions, point to the frame border. When the pointer changes to a double-headed arrow, hold down the mouse button and drag the cursor to extend the frame, as shown here.

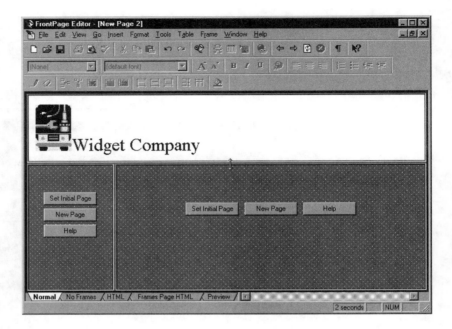

When the frame is the size you want it to be, release the mouse button.

Splitting a Frame

The frames page templates are starting places for any of the frames pages you want to produce. However, you aren't limited to the frame structures that appear in the templates. You can add new frames to existing structures by pointing to a frame's border, holding down the Ctrl key and the mouse button, and dragging the new frame into existence, as shown here.

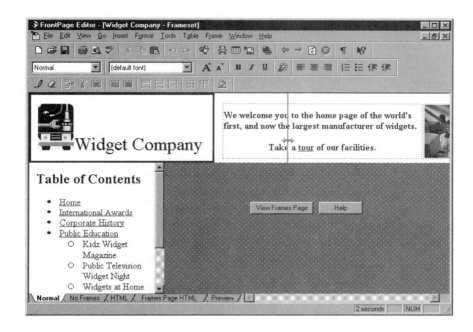

The new frame is created with a Set Initial Page, New Page, and Help button so you can identify or create the target page for the frame.

Creating Hyperlinks to Targeted Frames

When a user clicks on a hyperlink in a page that appears in a frame, you can designate whether you want that page to open in a new window, in the current window, or in a particular frame. By default, the template determines where a page opens. You can change the default in the Edit Hyperlink dialog box.

When you learned to create hyperlinks in Skill 6, there was one option in the Edit Hyperlink dialog box that we didn't discuss. Right-click on a hyperlink in the page you want to re-direct and choose Hyperlink Properties. The Target Frame field is located in the bottom right of the Edit Hyperlink dialog box.

Click on the icon next to the Target Frame field to open the Target Frame dialog box. There's a map of the active frames page on the left side of the dialog box. The right shows a list of common targets. Notice that the default frame in Figure 13.7 is the Main frame. Click on each frame in the Current Frames Page image to see which frame is designated as Main—the name appears in the Target Setting text box.

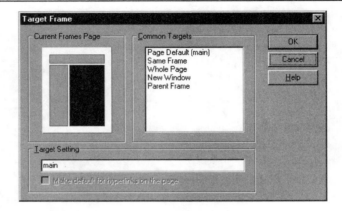

FIGURE 13.7: The Target Frame dialog box lets you designate where you want a hyperlinked page to open.

There are five options, each of which identifies a different possible location:

- **Page Default**   This location is set by the template choice you made, and is the recommended target frame.

- **Same Frame**   Pages replace the original page in the frame—much like standard hyperlink.

- **Whole Page**   Pages replace the entire frames page in the Browser window.

- **New Window**   A second instance of the user's Web browser is launched and the page opens in a new window of the browser.

- **Parent Frame**   Pages are displayed in the frame that contains the current frameset tag. To use this option, you have to be comfortable working directly with HTML.

Any other frame in the Target Frame map is also a possible target. Click on the frame in the map to display the desired frame in the Target Setting text box.

If you want this target to be the new default target for all hyperlinks on this page (this is referring to this page only—not the entire frames page), click on the Make default for hyperlinks on the page checkbox. If you don't do this, the only hyperlink affected by the changed location is the one you right-clicked on to open the dialog box.

NOTE   If you create a form for user input, you can send the output of the form to a frame on a frames page. Open the form's properties and click on the Target Frame button to select a target frame.

Opening a Page in a Frame

You can open any page in a frame in the Editor, make editing changes to it, and save those changes. However, the Editor saves the changes to the page, but doesn't make the page part of the frames page. When you re-open the frames page, the initial page settings are restored. To open a page in a frame, choose File ➢ Open, select the page, and make sure the Open in Current Frame checkbox is checked. Click on OK to open the page.

The only way to close a page that is open in a frame is to open another page in that frame or close the entire frames page and re-open it.

If you want to open a page in a new window while you have a frames page open, click on the Open button on the Standard toolbar or choose File ➢ Open and click the Open in Current Frame checkbox to uncheck it.

Deleting a Frame

If you would like fewer frames than the template provides (or than you created), you can delete a frame by clicking in the frame and choosing Delete Frame from the Frame menu.

Modifying Frame Properties

Every frame has properties and every frames set has a different set of properties. Right-click on a frame and choose Frame Properties to open the dialog box (see Figure 13.8). From there you can access Frame Page Properties.

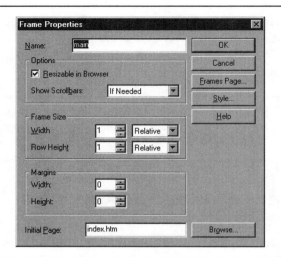

FIGURE 13.8: Use the Frame Properties dialog box to set options for an individual frame.

The five major categories of frame properties are:

- **Name** The name given here is the default name given to the frame by the template. You can leave this the way it is. The names are standard, based on the purpose of the frame within the page. If you decide to ignore this advice and change the name, make sure you don't use a frame name that's already used in the active web, which is easy to do.

- **Options** There are two options related to how the frame appears in the user's browser. The Resizable in Browser checkbox refers to whether you want users to be able to drag the borders of the frame to make it larger or smaller. Although there may be some advantages of this with certain designs, if you allow users to resize the frame display, you give up a lot of control over how your page appears to your users. Test it out first in different browsers and with different size monitors, if possible, to see how resizing affects the page before choosing this option.

  The second option lets you choose whether you want scrollbars to appear. The choices are Never, Always, or If Needed. The If Needed option is probably the most reasonable in most circumstances, but there may be some frames where you want to prohibit scrolling and lock in the contents. The choice of Always rarely makes sense, but there are probably exceptions even for that.

- **Frame Size** Set Width and Row Height for the frame. This is especially important if you clear the Resizable in Browser checkbox above. You can uses pixels to set an exact size, or percent to make the frame variable based on the size of the browser's display.

  If the frame is part of a column that contains at least one other frame, the Column Width and Height options are enabled instead of Width and Row Height. Changes to the column width affect other frames within the same column, and all other columns are adjusted accordingly.

- **Margins** This refers to the indentation of the contents of the frame from the frame borders.

- **Initial Page** If you want to change the page that opens in this frame, enter the new URL here or click on the Browse button to select the file from the Edit Hyperlink dialog box.

In addition to the standard property settings, there is also a Style button to take you to the cascading style sheet settings for this frame. See Skill 10 for more information about cascading style sheets.

When you finish changing the Frame Properties, click on OK to save the changes, or on the Frames Page button to make changes to the properties for the frames page.

Changing Frames Page Properties

Surprisingly, there are only two property settings that affect frames pages. These are on the Page Properties dialog box, which you can access from the Frames Page button on the Frame Properties dialog box or from the Frame menu, where you can choose Frames Page Properties.

There are five pages in the Page Properties dialog box, but only one pertains to frames. Click on the Frames tab, shown in Figure 13.9, to access the frames page options.

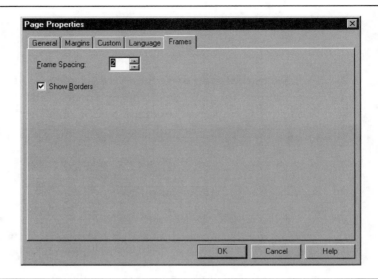

FIGURE 13.9: Set Frame Spacing and Borders in the Page Properties dialog box.

The first option, Frame Spacing, refers to the amount of padding that exists between frames on a page. The default setting is 2 pixels. Use the spin box arrows to increase or decrease this setting.

The second option, Show Borders, is turned on by default, but more and more designers are discouraging the use of borders in order to give pages a cleaner look. Clearing the Show Borders checkbox reduces the Frame Spacing to zero. Figure 13.10 shows the same frames page displayed earlier in Figure 13.1, but this time without borders.

Whether you choose to use borders is a personal design decision. Just be cautious about the number of frames you use on a page. The frames page in Figure 13.10 is actually pretty cluttered with four frames, regardless of whether borders are turned on or off. If you can accomplish your objective in three, or even two frames, there is no reason to add more. A good rule is to keep borders turned on if the content of the frames is so different that you want to keep it separated—turn them off if you want the frames to be more closely tied together.

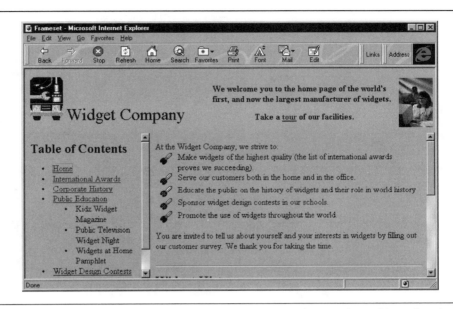

FIGURE 13.10: This page is made up of four frames, but without borders the page appears less divided.

Creating a Frame within a Frame

Just in case you thought your monitor wasn't small enough already, it's possible to set a frames page as the initial page within another frame. FrontPage can't display the frames page within a frames page. Instead you get a View Frames page button in the intended frame, like the one shown in Figure 13.11.

Click on the View Frames Page button to edit the frames page. If you want to see the complete page, click on the Preview tab or click on the Preview in Browser button. Figure 13.12 shows a Vertical Split frames page as part of a Banner and Contents frames page displayed in the Internet Explorer.

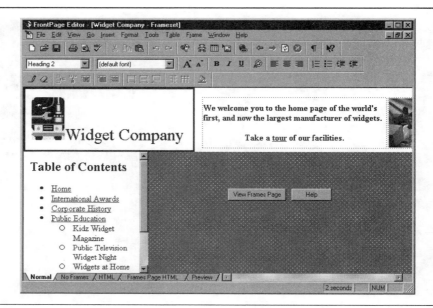

FIGURE 13.11: When you choose a frames page as the initial page of a frame, the frames page is not displayed directly.

FIGURE 13.12: You can preview a frames-within-a-frames page to see how it looks. This Vertical Split frames page is part of a Banner and Contents frames page.

Again, concerns about display size and appearance are paramount when you consider this option.

Designing a No Frames Alternative

There are many people around the world who don't have access to a browser that displays frames. You can take the attitude that it's too bad for them, or you can provide them with a "frameless" way to access your site. HTML has a <NOFRAMES> tag that tells a browser that can't display frames what to do when it encounters your frames page. Click on the No Frames tab at the bottom of the Editor window to see the page that appears by default. It's a simple page with the words: "This page uses frames, but your browser doesn't support them." This page provides no hyperlinks to take users anywhere else in your site, so chances are frames-challenged visitors would click the browser's Back button and you would never see them again.

You can avoid losing an important visitor without frame access by providing a way into your site without having to view frames pages. There are two accepted ways to accomplish this. More designers are creating a front door to their sites—a welcome mat of sorts that gives users some options. The user may be able to decide whether they see graphics or text only. Another common option is a choice between frames or no frames.

Implementing the frames/no frames choice only requires a different target for the hyperlinks from the two buttons. The Frames hyperlink loads a frames page; the No Frames button loads your home page without frames.

NOTE   Providing users with a front door where they can choose a no frames option also accommodates those users who just don't like frames because it divides their screens too much.

Another way to accomplish this same objective is to include a page between opening and closing <NOFRAMES> tags. FrontPage already gives you this page—all you have to do is edit it so it's a bit friendlier than the default. And make sure it includes links to the rest of your web so users aren't stuck there.

Considerations in the Use of Frames

The focus of this Skill is on how to use frames as part of your web design strategy. Now that you know the basics of frames, there are a few important things to consider. We've already mentioned that frames reduce the amount of screen that's available for viewing content. Scroll bars, frame margins, and frame borders all take up critical viewing space. Until the average person accessing the Internet has a 17-inch or larger monitor, frames make a small space uncomfortably cramped for the majority of users. For that reason, many people avoid sites that use frames, especially if the web's designers haven't provided a No Frames alternative.

Even more critical, however, is the fact that people who are visually impaired or require a speech based interface require text-only access to be able to use screen readers and other viewing aids to retrieve information. The use of frames prevents these devices from working effectively, thereby restricting access to your site and denying some people equal access to the information on the Internet.

 NOTE   Decisions about using frames on a company intranet can have larger implications. In the U.S, for example, employers are legally required to make reasonable accommodations for individuals with disabilities and similar legislation is pending in Canada. It's a good idea to discuss company policy on accessibility issues with your personnel or human resources department as part of your intranet development process.

The Internet is an incredible way to make information available to all people across all cultures and all socioeconomic levels. It can only fulfill this purpose, however, if those who are designing Web content keep all people in mind while they are developing sites.

Are You Experienced?

Now you can...

- ☑ **Insert an existing page in a frames page**
- ☑ **Use a template to create a variety of frames pages**
- ☑ **Create a custom frames page**
- ☑ **Resize frames**
- ☑ **Create a hyperlink to targeted frames**
- ☑ **Modify frame and frames page properties**
- ☑ **Include a frames page in frame**
- ☑ **Design a no-frames alternative**

S K I L L

14

fourteen

Publishing Your Web Site

This chapter focuses on how to administer your webs. It begins with some tips on testing your site for reliability and usability. You then learn how to publish your web on a FrontPage server or a server that lacks the FrontPage server extensions. You also find out about user permissions and web administration using the Microsoft Personal Web Server.

Testing and Refining Your Web Site

Before you present your finished Web site to the world, you need be sure everything in it is working perfectly. There's nothing quite so anticlimactic as opening the curtains on your site and then having to close them immediately to make repairs. With that in mind, you'll now see some of the ways you can ensure the dependability of your FrontPage webs. There have been many tips and snippets of testing and maintenance advice throughout this book. Advice relating to keeping a Web site healthy applies to all sites in general, not just FrontPage webs.

In fact, when you build and maintain a web using FrontPage 98, many testing and maintenance chores are either eliminated or vastly simplified. For example, if you rename a file in many webs, the job of finding and revising all the hyperlinks that target the renamed file is a major piece of housekeeping. In the FrontPage Explorer, it happens automatically.

Back Up Your FrontPage Webs

Maintaining current backups is good practice for all of your work on a computer, but it's even more important with your Web publishing. If users rely on your web for access to information, you need to quickly post a backup following a hardware or software failure. And whether you're in the process of building your Web sites or already have them up and running, you'll likely be making changes to them on a daily or weekly basis. Having a previous version of files can be a real lifesaver when you hastily click on OK when asked to confirm a deletion. So be sure your FrontPage webs are included in your regular backups, or back them up separately by copying their root folder. Don't just *create* backups—*verify* your backups to ensure that they contain usable data.

Test Under a Variety of Browsers

The whole purpose of the typical Web site is to deliver content to users. There are many different browsers on the market, all of which produce slightly different results when displaying the same page. Some browsers have more advanced features than others, and some are just plain old outdated. When a browser is pushing a year old, its days seem numbered!

So, have several of the more popular browsers available for testing your FrontPage webs, and try to have both the newest and the previous version of each one. If you want to be really accommodating to visitors to your site, see how your Web pages look in an older browser—one that cannot display frames, for example. If you include newer HTML features in your pages, you're leaving users with older browsers out of the picture. On the other hand, Web browsers aren't exactly expensive or difficult to obtain; many are free and can be downloaded with the click of a button.

Many Web designers feel that it is their responsibility to include the newest, latest features in their Web pages, to push the envelope for the browser companies. If designers don't include new features, they reason, users won't need to download more capable browsers. If users don't demand browsers that support new features, there's no reason for software companies to include support for the latest components in their browsers. If a new technology or HTML extension is the best tool to get your message across, go for it. On the other hand, including a lot of beta components just to prove you can is an easy way to create an annoying Web site; sites that cause computers to crash in the middle of a download are incredibly unpopular.

Use Multiple Testers

It's amazing how one person can discover something that many others have missed. The more people you can corral into testing your site, the better. Each person brings a different perspective, a different interest, and a different set of talents to the job. One person tends to catch grammatical errors, while another might not notice them but finds an empty box that was supposed to display an image.

To ensure a wide range of perspectives, recruit testers with the range of skills representative of potential visitors to your site. For example, if you're creating an intranet that's used throughout the company, recruit a couple of real novices to the Web from outside of your department to help test the site. Novices who work in your department can help you pinpoint usability issues (like the placement of

Skill 14

navigation tools), but it takes an outsider to identify the places that departmental jargon obscures meaning.

Don't just sit testers in front of the computer with paper and pen. You'll learn a lot about your web site by watching testers as they navigate through the pages. For example, three users in a row may click on an image that doesn't have a link, rather than the nearby text link. By watching, you'll know that it's a good idea to either move or change the picture, or use it as a hyperlink.

Test Your Sites With and Without Color

Although monochrome monitors are becoming rare, it's still a little early to assume everyone who visits your site is using a color monitor. If your site is heavy with color graphics and, especially, backgrounds, you may want to develop an alternative for those who don't have color.

If you feel there are just too few people who would benefit from this to make the extra work worthwhile, at least take the time to see how your pages look when viewed on a monochrome monitor. If they're unreadable or just plain impossible, you might consider providing a simple, pared-down alternate page.

Offer a Text-Only Page

There was a time when text-only browsers were the norm, but not any more. Nonetheless, some users may turn off the graphical image capabilities of their browsers to trim download time, to cut costs or simply to make the Web tolerable when connection speeds are slow.

Other users can't choose a better browser. Many of the free browsers available in public libraries are text only. Blind and visually impaired visitors use Lynx or other screen reader software, to interpret and read the text on your site. If all your pages use frames or many of your links are hotspots instead of textual, the site isn't accessible. To create a site that the largest percentage of visitors can load and enjoy, offer a text-only alternative page (or series of alternate pages for the site) that users open through a `Text only` link on the home page.

 NOTE   For more information on the issues involved in designing speech-friendly sites for users with screen readers, see "A List of Resources for Making Your Web Accessible" at `http://www2.cdepot.net/~mist/access.htm`.

Test Your Pages at Different Screen Resolutions

One of the more frustrating aspects of creating a Web page is trying to compromise on an "average" screen size. You can design your pages compactly so they nicely fill a monitor at a resolution of 640 by 480, but they might leave a lot of blank space on the right side when viewed at 800 by 600. If you design your pages for that higher resolution, a visitor working at a lower resolution might have to scroll the screen right and left to see the entire page.

 NOTE One way to avoid resolution problems is to design your pages with a tall orientation rather than a wide one. Let the visitor scroll down through a page instead of having to scroll to the right and back again. Better yet, put some of your content on another page and add a link. The majority of users don't bother to scroll, so content that exceeds page size is never seen by most of your visitors.

No matter how you design your pages, you should certainly test them at different screen resolutions. That's why the FrontPage Editor's File ➤ Preview in Browser command lets you specify a size for the browser. The command doesn't change your screen's resolution, it simply adjusts the size of the browser's window to show the equivalent amount of screen at the given resolution. Of course, this only works if your own screen is running at a resolution that's equal to or higher than the one you choose for the preview.

Test Your Sites at Different Connection Speeds

When you test your Web site on your local computer running one of the Personal Web Servers, you don't know what it's like to access the site over a slow network connection, let alone over a dial-up connection at modem speeds. So do yourself and visitors to your site a favor, and test your site over a slower, real-world connection. You might be shocked at how slowly that seemingly small image downloads at 28,800 bits per second (about 3,600 bytes, or characters, per second). When you've browsed through your site or others at modem speeds, you'll start to get a feel for how fast large pages or images are transferred. If pages download slowly, make use of some of the techniques you learned in earlier Skills:

- Create links to pages with multiple images or video, and make users aware of the approximate download time.

- Use thumbnails to link to large images.

- Use progressive JPEGs rather than regular JPEGs.

- Convert JPEGs to interlaced GIFs.

Don't forget to check the download estimates in the Editor's status bar as you're constructing your pages. And if your pages are published on a high volume server, remember to test the site at peak times as well as off hours to determine real download speeds that users experience.

Test Your Hyperlinks

As emphasized in Skill 6, you must test the hyperlinks in your site on a regular basis to ensure they still connect to target URLs, and that the targets are the files you expect them to be. The Explorer's Tools ➤ Verify Hyperlinks command can do the first part of this job by testing to see if a link actually has a valid target URL.

The second part is a little more difficult, however. There's really no automated way to confirm the target of an external hyperlink is still *relevant* to you and your site. When a link goes outside of your Web site and your control, you have to click on the link and see what the server returns. Having multiple testers go through your site on an ongoing basis is one way to find broken links. Large corporate web sites often have full time Web gardeners, who have the job of following each link and "rooting out" dead links and orphaned pages.

Provide an Opportunity for Feedback

Browsing a Web site is often a read-only process, where visitors to a site get a lot of information without returning any. It's important to give visitors the opportunity to let you know how things are going so they can report problems, leave comments, or ask questions.

In fact, on a busy site the visitors are actually doing a lot more testing of the site than you ever will! Therefore, you should either have a form on a page for accepting their comments or simply include an e-mail hyperlink on your home page, such as "Please e-mail any questions or comments to webcrafter@widget.com."

Visit Other Sites

Some of your best ideas about what works, and what doesn't work, come from browsing other sites. The following sites contain links to the "top" or "best" web sites:

PC Magazine's Top 100 Web Sites: `http://www.wizvax.net/alfalfa/ pcmag100.htm`

Best of the Web Awards: `http://www.botw.org/index.html`

Another site worth visiting is the W3 site: `http://www.w3.org`. W3 is the organization responsible for HTML, and their site contains numerous resources on HTML usage and information on changing language standards. For example, the W3 site includes Tim Berners-Lee's Style Guide for online hypertext: `http://www .w3.org/Provider/Style/Overview.html`.

Publishing a Web to a Server

After you've finished creating and testing your web site, you need to give it some wider distribution, putting it on a Web server where users can access it. You can publish your web on the Internet, or on a local intranet. In FrontPage lingo, *publishing* a web means copying it either to a different server or with a different name on the same server. You use the File ➤ Publish FrontPage Web command to do the job.

 NOTE   If you create your FrontPage web on the same server that is hosting it, then the world might be seeing your work virtually as you do it. This isn't a good idea, because users are browsing in a construction zone. You should either create your webs on another server, like one of the personal web servers, or in a private folder.

All the Internet Web pages you view in your browser are stored on a Web server. Many Internet service providers (ISPs) offer Web hosting services for customer's Web pages at a minimal charge. ISPs are also called WPPs: Web Presence Providers. Before you can publish your web, speak to your web server's administrator at the ISP/WPP and ask for:

- The protocol used at the ISP, such as FTP or HTTP Post

- The URL for the Web server, including the folder where you are to publish your files

- A connection to your ISP when you're actually publishing the Web

Before you publish your web on an intranet, speak with the web server's administrator. Ask about conventions for naming webs and folders, see if the FrontPage server extensions are installed on the server, and get the name of the folder your web should be published in.

Publishing your web is a convenient way to back up the entire web with all its folders and files. The resulting copy is a fully functional FrontPage web, so you can make changes and perform tests on that web while leaving the original up and running for users. Often, site maintenance begins and ends with publishing: Publish a copy to an internal server to work on, make changes or corrections, then publish the copy back to the public server.

Publishing a Web to a FrontPage Server

It's easy to publish a Web to a FrontPage server—either one of the Personal Web Servers, or another server that includes the FrontPage Server Extensions. For example, when you've finished building a Web site on a local PC using a Personal Web Server, you can use the Explorer to publish the entire site to the Internet or intranet server that hosts this site. If you've pulled a copy of a web for maintenance, you can just publish the updated files. Follow the steps below to publish your web:

1. In the Explorer, open the web you want to publish.

2. Choose File ➤ Publish FrontPage Web, or click on the Publish button on the toolbar.

3. In the Publish dialog box, shown in Figure 14.1 below, select the server, or a folder on disk, to which you want to copy the web. Enter a name for the web in the Name of Destination FrontPage Web field. Remember that the web's name is also used to name the folder in which it resides, so the name must follow the naming conventions used on the server.

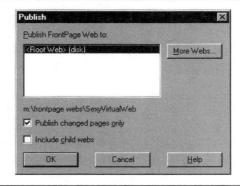

FIGURE 14.1: Specify a server or folder destination and a name in the Publish dialog box.

4. Click on the More Webs button if you need to select another location.

5. If you are only updating the files in an existing web, select the Publish Changed Pages Only checkbox. This is the option to choose if you've been doing maintenance work on a copy of a web.

6. If you are publishing a FrontPage root web, you can select the Include Child Webs checkbox so that all webs within the root web are also created at the destination.

7. When you're ready, click on OK.

If the destination web name you enter doesn't exist within the server's root web, a new folder of that name is created and the web is copied there. All the files and folders within the published web are duplicates of the current web.

Publishing a Web to a Non-FrontPage Server

You can publish a FrontPage web from the Explorer to a server that does not have the FrontPage Server Extensions. You can do so either with the traditional File Transfer Protocol (FTP), or with Microsoft's Web Publishing Wizard.

Of course your Web site won't offer all the FrontPage features that are available under a server with the FrontPage Server Extensions, as discussed in "The FrontPage Server Extensions" in Skill 1.

Using the Web Publishing Wizard

You can publish your web to a server that doesn't include the FrontPage server extensions using Microsoft's Web Publishing Wizard. This tool helps you copy your web to just about any of the popular Web servers, as long as they're able to run an FTP session. The Web Publishing Wizard is a separate program that you can start either from within the FrontPage Explorer or as a stand-alone program. You need some specific information to publish your web using the Wizard.

- The name of your Internet Service Provider (ISP), if you use one to access the WWW. The list of choices includes AOL, CompuServe, and GNN; choose Other Internet Provider if yours is not listed.

- The URL of your ISP, such as `http://www.host.com`, so the Web Publishing Wizard can find the site.

- The type of connection you make to access the destination Web server, either Network or Dial-Up Networking. If you choose the latter, you then select the connection settings to use.

- The protocol that the Web Publishing Wizard should use to send your web files: FTP or Windows File Transfer. Select FTP if you're not sure.

- Your username and password for the destination Web server.

- The name of the FTP server on the destination server.

- The name of the destination subfolder on the server, as well as your own root folder on that server (which usually is restricted only to you).

 NOTE   If you have not yet installed the Web Publishing Wizard, you can do so from the setup program on your FrontPage disk. You can also download it for free from Microsoft's Web site. Go to `http://www.microsoft.com`, and search for it by name.

Start in the Explorer and open the web you wish to publish. Follow all the steps for publishing to a FrontPage server that were described in the previous section, "Publishing a Web to a FrontPage Server." When you click on OK in the Publish dialog box, the Explorer connects with the server you specified. When it finds that the FrontPage Server Extensions are not installed on that server, the Explorer automatically starts the Web Publishing Wizard and passes control to it:

The Web Publishing Wizard walks you through the process of copying your web to the server. It starts by letting you select the folder or just a file that you want to copy (shown in Figure 14.2).

FIGURE 14.2: The Web Publishing Wizard starts by letting you select the folder and files you want to copy to another server.

You can either type in the name of the folder or file that you want to copy, click on the Browse Folders button and select a folder, or Browse Files and select a single file. If you selected a folder, you probably want to select the Include Subfolders checkbox in the Web Publishing Wizard dialog box to include your Images and private folders in the published Web. Click on the Next button to continue. In the Descriptive name text box, type a name for the Web server.

If you use a particular protocol to publish to an Internet service provider's server (or to your intranet), click on Advanced to select the provider from the list, shown in Figure 14.3. If the provider you need is listed, select it. Otherwise, choose Automatically Select Service Provider before you click on Next.

Specify the URL for the server you're publishing to, including any specific folder your ISP has assigned to you. For example, if your company's intranet administrator assigns you the folder with your name on the server www.mycompany.com, you would enter http://www.mycompany.com/myname as the URL. Make sure the local folder is the folder you wish to publish.

FIGURE 14.3: Specify a provider, or let the Wizard determine the provider.

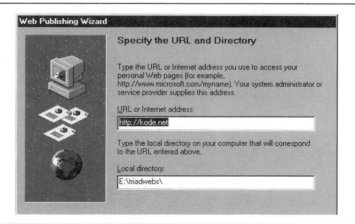

FIGURE 14.4: Enter the URL for your Web server.

If you haven't published to the selected server in the past, identify how you connect with the server in the next step of the Wizard, shown in Figure 14.5. (This page doesn't appear if the server you selected in the previous step has already been configured.) If you choose Dial-Up Networking, select the connection from the list or choose New Dial-Up Connection to open the Dial-up Networking Make New Connection dialog box.

FIGURE 14.5: Select a local area network or a dial-up connection to the server.

The Web Publishing Wizard begins to copy the folder or file you selected to the destination server if the server is on a network. If the URL you designated is an Internet Service Provider's server or otherwise requires a dial-up connection, the Microsoft Connection Wizard opens, and locates the server you indicated. If the Wizard can't find the server, it displays an error message:

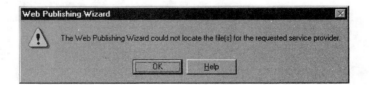

After the Wizard connects with the server, a progress meter appears to keep you posted on the progress. After it successfully publishes your web, the Web Publishing Wizard closes.

NOTE If you know that you're publishing to a server without the FrontPage server extensions, you can run the Web Publishing Wizard as a stand-alone program, outside of FrontPage. Launch the Wizard from the Windows Start menu: Programs ➤ Accessories ➤ Internet Tools.

Publishing a Web with FTP

You can copy your FrontPage web to any server that supports FTP, just as you can copy any other files to that server. Windows 95 and NT have FTP built-in, but the command-line interface is all too reminiscent of the dog days of DOS.

You'll find an easy-to-use interface on many FTP programs on the market. They can make copying files from your system to another virtually painless. Some of these programs are even available free of charge; you can find many FTP programs listed on Yahoo if you search for "FTP software." When you publish a FrontPage web to a server that is not running the FrontPage Server Extensions, you need not include any folders whose names begin with _VTI_. These are used only by FrontPage and are not needed outside of it.

Renaming, Moving, or Deleting a Web Site

You can perform several Web management tasks on the active web from within the Explorer. You should *only* perform these procedures from within the FrontPage Explorer so it can complete the entire job and update its own indexes of your web.

Renaming a Web Site

When you create a web, the name you give it is also used to name the actual folder on the disk where the web resides. You can rename your web at any time within the FrontPage Explorer.

Select Tools ➤ Web Settings, and choose the Configuration tab in the FrontPage Web Settings dialog box, shown in Figure 14.6.

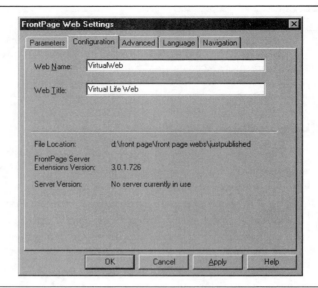

FIGURE 14.6: Change a web's name or title in the FrontPage Web Settings dialog box.

You'll find two edit fields:

- **Web Name** The actual name of the web's folder on the server. Any name you enter here must be compatible with the file-naming conventions on that server.

- **Web Title** The descriptive title of the web that is used only by FrontPage.

You can change the web's title at any time, but because a web's name is part of its URL, you should avoid changing the name once the web is in service. Users who have added your site to their Favorites or Bookmarks won't be able to find your page if you change the URL.

Moving a Web Site

There is no specific command for moving a web to another location, but you can do so in two steps. First, copy the web to the new location with the File ➤ Publish FrontPage Web command. Then use File ➤ Delete FrontPage Web to delete the original Web site.

Deleting a Web Site

You can delete a FrontPage web from its server by opening that web in the FrontPage Explorer and choosing File ➤Delete FrontPage Web. You're asked to confirm your decision—for the obvious reasons! If you choose Yes, the web, with all its folders and files, are erased from the server's disk—completely and irrevocably. So use caution, and be sure you really want to delete a web before you proceed.

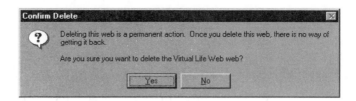

Keeping Your Web Secure

After your webs are published, there is always at least one person, an *administrator*, who has full access rights to FrontPage's root web: the server folder that contains all other FrontPage webs. The administrator can create or delete FrontPage webs, create or delete files within a web, and assign access rights (permission) for those webs to others, either as browsers, authors, or other administrators. Unless your server has been set up to restrict access to a FrontPage web, anyone can browse through the files in all FrontPage webs by default, although they are not allowed to make changes to those files.

When you install FrontPage, you are asked for the name of a person who serves as administrator. If the name you give is not already a registered user on your server, you're also prompted for a password. The name you provide is then an administrator of the FrontPage root web and, by definition, all FrontPage webs within it. This administrator can then restrict or assign access rights to others as needed.

The security restrictions and access rights for your FrontPage webs are dependent on the host server. The rest of this skill assumes your server has the FrontPage Server Extensions installed or that you are using the Microsoft Personal Web Server. Your rights to access your web once it's published are dependent on the host server's administrator. Some administrators give you full permission to administer your own web site within the larger site, but most give you limited permissions: author permissions or, perhaps, only browser permissions unless you notify the administrator of a pending update.

NOTE   Administering and securing a public or corporate web site are beyond the scope of this book. However, you should have a basic understanding of user permissions, how they are assigned, and how to secure your web. For more information on web site administration, see Mastering Microsoft FrontPage 98 from Sybex (ISBN 0-7821-2144-6).

Assigning Permissions

To change permission settings for the active FrontPage web, choose Tools ➤ Permissions in the Explorer, which displays the Permissions dialog box. When you are running the Microsoft Personal Web Server (PWS), there are three tabs in this dialog box for defining the access rights to this web:

- **Settings**   Choose to let the active web inherit all permission settings from the root web, or set unique permissions for the active web (you won't find this tab when the FrontPage root web is the active web).

- **Users**   When you are setting unique permissions for a web, you can specify the users who have access to this web.

- **Groups**   When you are setting unique permissions for a web, you can specify a group of users who all have the same access to this web. You cannot create new groups in FrontPage—you must do so in the Microsoft PWS administration tool. See your system administrator for more information on creating groups or adding users.

You can assign one of three levels of access rights to an individual, a computer, or a group for each FrontPage web on a server:

- **Browser**   In this context, a browser is a user who has read-only rights in a web and cannot make any changes to it (cannot open a web in the Explorer, for example). In most cases, a person with browsing rights is accessing that web in a Web browser.

- **Author**   An author has all the rights of a browser, *and* can view or make changes to the files in a web, but cannot create or delete entire webs or change permission settings. Therefore, if you have logged in with only author permissions, you can't invoke the Tools ➤ Permissions command in the Explorer.

- **Administrator**   An administrator has all the rights of an author, *and* can do just about anything in the way of editing or viewing webs and their files and can also grant or revoke access rights to a web.

Assigning Unique Permissions for a Web

Each new FrontPage web inherits the permission settings of the root web by default, so anyone who has access rights in the root web has those same rights in a new web within the root, unless you specify otherwise. To assign unique permissions for a web, open that web in the Explorer and choose Tools ➤ Permissions, then choose the Settings tab in that web's Permissions dialog box (shown in Figure 14.7). Remember that this tab is not available for the FrontPage root web.

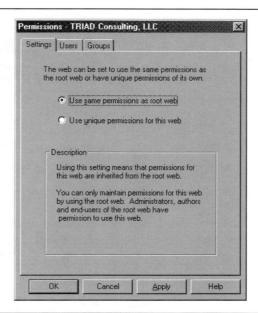

FIGURE 14.7: Assign unique access rights for the active web in the Settings tab of the Permissions dialog box.

The two options in the Settings tab let you specify how the permissions are set for this web. By default, the Use Same Permissions as Root Web option is selected so whatever permissions have been set for the root web also applies to this web. To apply different permission settings to this web, you must select the Use Unique Permissions for This Web option, which allows you to make changes in the other two tabs in the dialog box. Then, click on the Apply button to proceed to the other two pages in the dialog box. If there are no unique permissions assigned for this web, you can't make changes in the other two tabs in the Permissions dialog box.

At this point, if you make no other changes in the Permissions dialog box, the access rights in this web are still the same as those in the root web. You use the other two tabs in the dialog box to restrict access to the site further or specify permission settings for other users.

Assigning Permissions to Users

When you Use Unique Permissions for This Web, you can assign access rights for the active web in the Users tab (shown in Figure 14.8).

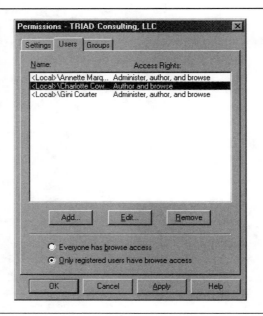

FIGURE 14.8: Specify the type of access that users have to the active web in the Users tab of the Permissions dialog box.

If you do not want to restrict browsing rights in this web, leave the default setting: Everyone Has Browse Access. That way, anyone can view pages and other files in this web (this is the default setting). If you want to limit browsing only to those you specify, select the Only Registered Users Have Browse Access option. Now when anyone tries to open a file on this site, their browser displays a dialog box prompting them for their name and password. Only those users whose names appear in the list in the Permissions dialog box can browse this web (assuming they remember their passwords).

To add a new user to the list of registered users for the active web, click on the Add button. You can only add users and groups that are already registered with the server, so if users you wish to add aren't on the list, contact your server administrator.

Select the type of access for this user, either as a browser, an author, or an administrator. Remember, an author's access rights include the rights to browse the web, and an administrator's rights include all the rights of an author. Click on OK to close the dialog box, and you'll see the new username in the list in the Users tab of the Permissions dialog box.

To change the access level of a user, an administrator can select a name in the list in the Users tab in the Permissions dialog box and click on the Edit button. Then choose one of the three permission settings for this user (see Figure 14.9) and click on OK. To remove a user from the list, thereby excluding that user from working on this web, an administrator can select a name in the list and click on the Remove button.

FIGURE 14.9:   To change a user's access level, use the Edit Users dialog box.

Working with the Personal Web Servers

If you already had FrontPage 1.1 installed on your computer when you installed FrontPage 98, you probably have both the FrontPage Personal Web Server (PWS) and the Microsoft PWS on your computer. If this is the first time you've installed FrontPage, then you have only the Microsoft PWS installed unless you chose both servers in a Custom installation. You can run FrontPage 98 with either PWS, although the FrontPage PWS is being phased out in favor of the more robust Microsoft PWS, which is a subset of Microsoft's popular Internet Information Server (IIS). The rest of this section addresses working with the Microsoft PWS.

Running the Microsoft Personal Web Server

The Microsoft PWS starts each time you start Windows 95 or 98 by default; therefore, it's available to the FrontPage Explorer at all times. When it's running, you'll see an icon for it on the right side of the Windows taskbar.

You really don't see any interaction with the Microsoft PWS while you're working in FrontPage; the server is pretty transparent. You can stop or start the Microsoft PWS at any time via its Properties dialog box, where you can also adjust a few settings and access its administration utility:

- Right-click on its icon on the taskbar and choose Properties.

- From the Windows Start menu, choose Settings ➤ Control Panel and open the Personal Web Server.

The General tab of the Microsoft Personal Web Server Properties dialog box (shown in Figure 14.10) shows you the Internet address of your computer and the URL of the root web's home page. If you click on either the Display Home Page or the More Details button, your Web browser starts and opens the appropriate pages for the Microsoft PWS.

On the Startup tab in this dialog box, you can stop the server by clicking on the Stop button. When stopped, a Start button is enabled. You can also choose whether the Microsoft PWS starts each time Windows starts, and whether its icon appears on the taskbar when it is running.

FIGURE 14.10: The dialog box where you can adjust the settings for the Microsoft Personal Web Server

NOTE   Taking care of administration duties in the Microsoft PWS is outside the scope of this book. If you're in charge of administering all aspects of the server, you might want to read Sybex's *Mastering Microsoft FrontPage 98*.

On the Administration tab, you can click the Administration button to change user access rights on the server , the folders (directories) that the server uses, its default home page name, and more. Again, this opens appropriate pages in your Web browser, where you perform administration duties via Web pages. Finally, on the Services tab, you can enable or disable HTTP and FTP on the server, and adjust related properties.

This concludes the discussion of Web site management in the FrontPage Explorer and the Microsoft Personal Web Server, and this is also the last Skill in this book. Your head is undoubtedly brimming over with ideas for creating sites, pages, hyperlinks, tables, images, frame sets, image maps, and all the other myriad Web and HTML features you can produce in FrontPage. Don't forget to visit the Microsoft FrontPage site for themes, tips, and information:

```
http://www.microsoft.com/frontpage
```

Good luck with all your projects on the Web!

Are You Experienced?

Now you can...

- ☑ **Test your web site**
- ☑ **Publish your web on a server with FrontPage server extensions**
- ☑ **Publish you web on other servers using the Web Publishing Wizard**
- ☑ **Set user permissions in the Microsoft Personal Web Server**

APPENDIX

A

Installing and Starting FrontPage

- ❑ Learning about RAM and disk space requirements
- ❑ Installing FrontPage
- ❑ Installing additional FrontPage software
- ❑ Starting FrontPage
- ❑ Getting help

Installing FrontPage and its additional software does not take long, but it does involve several choices and considerations. If you have already installed FrontPage and have it up and running under a Web server, you may not need to read this appendix. For further help with FrontPage, be sure to check out Microsoft's Web site:

```
http://www.microsoft.com/frontpage/
```

Running the Setup Program

Most of these programs require a computer with at least a 486 processor and 16MB of RAM, although more RAM is recommended for some of them. Let's take a quick look at the programs and their RAM and disk space requirements. The requirements listed are for Windows 95; additional memory is required with Windows NT.

- **FrontPage 98**   Create and manage Web sites and their pages with the Explorer, Editor, Task List, and the FrontPage Personal Web Server (16MB RAM; 36MB disk space).

- **Image Composer**   Create images for your Web sites or other uses; it offers a huge collection of photographs and clip art, as well as a dazzling array of image-editing tools and effects. (16MB RAM; 28MB+ disk space).

- **Microsoft Personal Web Server**   Allows you to develop your FrontPage webs under Web server control and host your sites while they are actually up and running for public access. This Web server was derived from the Microsoft Internet Information Server (IIS) and is more robust and better integrated with Windows 95 than the FrontPage Personal Web Server (16MB RAM when used with FrontPage; 1MB of disk space).

- **Internet Explorer**   Browse the Web with Microsoft's Web browser (8MB RAM; 11MB disk space).

- **Web Publishing Wizard**   Helps you upload your FrontPage webs to another server when that server does not have the FrontPage Server Extensions installed and is not FrontPage-aware (8MB RAM; 1MB disk space; also requires that Microsoft Internet Explorer 3+ already be installed).

Each of these components is a separate program you can install at any time, although when you install FrontPage you're asked if you also want to install Microsoft Personal Web Server. You should answer yes to this option.

If you have an earlier version of FrontPage installed on your computer, you can either overwrite the earlier version by installing FrontPage 98 in the same folder, or you can install FrontPage 98 in its own folder and leave FrontPage 1.1 or 97 untouched and still available. You don't need to keep earlier versions; your existing FrontPage webs work fine in FrontPage 98.

Installing FrontPage 98

Here are the steps to install FrontPage:

1. When you insert the FrontPage 98 CD into your computer's CD-ROM drive, the setup program should start automatically. If you do not have AutoStart enabled in Windows, go to Windows Explorer and double-click on the program SETUP.EXE on your CD drive.

2. If you do not already have a Web server installed, you're asked if you want to install the Microsoft Personal Web Server as soon as you begin the FrontPage installation (see Figure A.1.) If you installed Windows 98 with a typical installation, you already have the Microsoft Personal Web Server on your computer. You need the Web server to use FrontPage to its fullest, so unless you are using another Web server, choose OK.

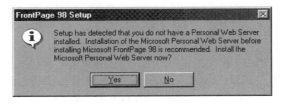

FIGURE A.1: If you haven't already installed the Personal Web Server, you'll be prompted to install it.

3. Windows asks for any other disks or CDs that the PWS installation requires. You must then reboot the computer to continue. After your PC boots, you're prompted to put the FrontPage CD back in the drive.

4. The setup program displays its opening screen, where you click on a title to install FrontPage or one of the other programs (shown in Figure A.2).

FIGURE A.2: Install the FrontPage applications using the Setup program.

5. From the FrontPage setup program, choose Install FrontPage 98. The InstallShield wizard loads and displays a Welcome screen.

6. Enter and confirm your name and company name, then read and agree to the End User License Agreement (EULA). You don't have to agree, but clicking on No terminates the installation.

7. Choose Typical or Custom installation. If you're not familiar with FrontPage 98 *and* your computer's current configuration, choose Typical, as shown in Figure A.3. The default destination directory (folder) for FrontPage, C:\Program Files\Microsoft FrontPage, is displayed at the bottom of the page. Either choose Next to accept this default, or click on Browse, select another folder, then choose Next. The following instructions assume you chose Typical installation; if you need the instructions that follow, you probably should have.

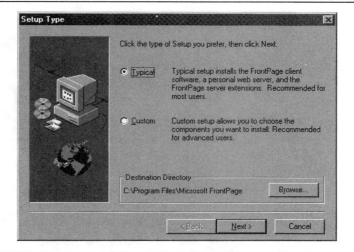

FIGURE A.3: Select a Typical installation unless you are familiar with FrontPage and your computer's current configuration.

8. InstallShield displays four progress meters to let you know how the installation is going. The three meters on the left show progress on individual files, all the files that have to be copied, and remaining space on the drive that FrontPage is being installed on (see Figure A.4).

9. After FrontPage 98 is installed, the Setup Complete dialog box appears. If you're ready to run FrontPage now, leave the Start the FrontPage Explorer Now checkbox enabled. If you want to install Image Composer or Internet Explorer, turn the checkbox off before you click on Finish.

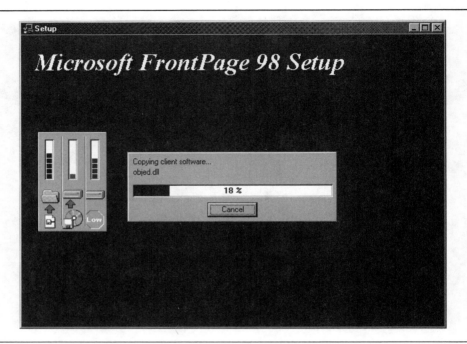

FIGURE A.4: Progress meters keep you informed about the installation.

Installing Image Composer

Setting up Image Composer is much like installing FrontPage 98. Choose Install Image Composer from the FrontPage Setup page and enter your personal and organizational information. When the Setup dialog box appears, accept the default or browse and select another directory for Image Composer. After you accept the license agreement, you'll see the installation options shown in Figure A.5.

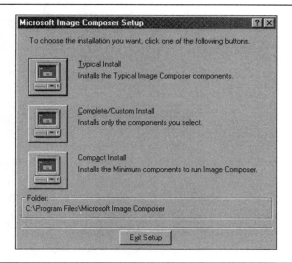

FIGURE A.5: Choose from Typical, Complete/Custom, or Compact installations.

The three installations require differing amounts of space on your computer's hard drive, as indicated below:

> **Typical** requires 41MB+ on your drive, and includes all Image Composer program files, WordArt, and Microsoft GIF Animator. Typical installation does NOT include the photo samples and web art samples from the FrontPage CD.
>
> **Complete** requires 250MB on your drive, because it also includes all the photo samples and web art samples.
>
> **Compact** includes just the Image Composer program files, and requires 24MB of hard drive space.

If you choose Complete/Custom installation, you can select which files you wish to install, as shown in Figure A.6. For example, you may choose to skip the Impressionist Plug-Ins for now, but have the Image Composer web art samples on hand. (The selections shown in Figure A.6 are the items installed in a Typical installation.) At the bottom of the page, you can see the space your selected files require and the kilobytes available on the drive you selected. After you've selected the files you wish to install, click on Continue.

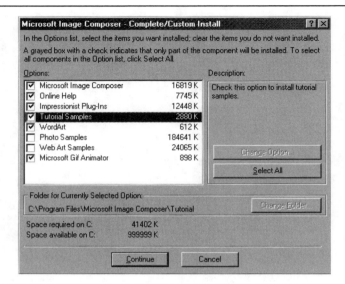

FIGURE A.6: Use Custom to choose specific programs, add-ins, and image files.

In the Choose Program Group dialog box, click on Continue to create the Microsoft Image Composer program group, or select another Start Menu group from the Existing Groups list. When you click on Continue, Setup installs Image Composer.

Starting FrontPage

You normally work with FrontPage by starting its Explorer—choose Programs ➤ Microsoft FrontPage from the Windows Start menu. This opens the FrontPage Explorer, where you can create a new FrontPage web, open an existing one, or start the Editor to create or revise Web pages.

Keep in mind that you should use the FrontPage Explorer and Editor in concert with a Web server—such as the Microsoft PWS—that is running the FrontPage Server Extensions. You can then work on any FrontPage web and make changes as needed. When you modify a Web page in the FrontPage Editor, the changes you make, such as the addition of new links, are tracked by the Explorer and the site is updated accordingly.

So you should become accustomed to starting the Explorer, opening a FrontPage web, and *then* working on its pages in the Editor as needed. You should close the Editor *before* you close the Explorer so the final changes you make in the Editor are recorded by the Explorer.

 NOTE The first time you start the Explorer, FrontPage examines your computer system to determine information about the computer's host name for the Personal Web Server. Click on OK to continue. When FrontPage has determined your computer's host name and TCP/IP connection information (on a network), it displays a message to let you know you can now work in FrontPage 98.

Getting Help

You'll find plenty of help available in FrontPage 98, which you can access in several ways:

- Choose a topic from the Help menu.

- Press F1 to open a context-sensitive Help screen based on your current activities in the program.

- Click on the Help button on the toolbar, then click on a command on the menu or toolbar that you'd like to know about.

- Choose Help ➤ Microsoft on the Web. This will open your Web browser and connect you with Microsoft's Web site, where you can choose from a variety of FrontPage topics, browse the answers to FAQs, and download files.

You should definitely set aside some time to run through the FrontPage tutorial in the user manual. It walks you through the process of building a small Web site from the Learning FrontPage template. It is a step-by-step process that introduces you to many of the tools in FrontPage and gives you a feeling for the way the individual resources interact and contribute to a Web site.

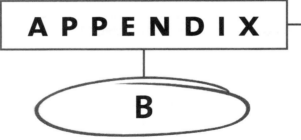

APPENDIX

B

B

HTML Reference

Welcome to the HTML Reference. Here you'll find the low-down on each and every tag from the HTML 4 Document Type Definition. The information includes each tag's attributes, what other tags they can work with legally, style tips, and samples of HTML markup. The reference also includes Internet Explorer and Netscape Navigator extensions, which are marked with (IE) or (N) respectively. For more information on coding HTML, see *HTML 4.0: No experience required* (ISBN 0-7821-2143-8) or *Mastering HTML 4.0* (ISBN 0-7821-2102-0), both published by Sybex.

WHAT'S ONLINE

The best source of up-to-date information about HTML is the World Wide Web Consortium site at http://www.w3.org. The current draft of the HTML 4.0 standard is available at http://www.w3.org/TR/WD-html40-970708.

To show how these tags relate to one another and to make them easier to remember, we've grouped them by type and function. Here's a quick overview of what you'll find in a typical tag description:

<TAG> (...</TAG>)   This is a formal HTML tag as it should be used in an HTML document. The large majority of tags come in pairs—for example, the boldface tags <B>...</B>, with an opening tag and a closing tag comprising the pair. Some tags are singletons, like the hard or horizontal rule tag <HR>, which does not require a closing tag. Any tag written as <TAG> (...</TAG>) means that the tag can be used correctly either as a singleton or as a pair. Underneath each tag name you'll find a brief, plain-English description of its purpose and capabilities.

Style Tip   Here we offer brief comments about how to use the tag properly, in accordance with good Web style. While Style Tips are suggestions, they represent our experience as Webmasters and Web citizens as well. We promise they won't lead you astray.

Attributes   Here you'll find a complete listing of all the attributes associated with each tag, their values, and a description of their effect on how the tag is rendered.

Parent Tags   This is a list of all the tags within which the present tag may be legally enclosed. This relationship derives from HTML syntax; while it's a little technical, it can affect the way a tag is rendered. It's included to indicate which tags may include the current tag, so as to keep you out of syntax trouble.

Content Tags   These are the opposite of parent tags; they represent those tags the current tag may contain legally. As with parent tags, this is a syntax thing. It's important to recognize that you shouldn't use any tag that does not appear in this list within the current tag.

Sample HTML   Real-life examples go further in showing how HTML is used than anything we can write or say. To that end we've included some sample markup for each and every tag, so you can see how all these tags work.

In the HTML 4.0 specification, several tags have become obsolete because they have been replaced by other markup; these tags will probably be phased out of HTML entirely in the next version. The majority of these tags have been *deprecated* (meaning that they are no longer recommended for use) in favor of style sheet rules. We have marked each of these tags or attributes as *[Deprecated]*. You may use these tags but we recommend that you look for other ways to achieve their effects, so you won't have to go back and remove them from your documents once they've been removed from the specification.

Finally, we have included style sheet tags in this reference. These use somewhat different conventions than standard HTML tags; we have noted those differences in that section.

That's the rundown on the HTML Master's Reference. Let the tags begin!

Global Structure Tags

The global structure tags (also called document structure) help define the structure of HTML documents. They give each document as a whole an HTML label and divide it into head and body sections. These tags also provide a way to include information about a document's contents. This markup does not produce much visible output, but it's vital for the construction of a well-designed Web page. FrontPage automatically inserts most of these tags into HTML documents, after prompting you for specific information, such as a document's title.

<!DOCTYPE>

The <!DOCTYPE> tag is an SGML (Standardized General Markup Language, a standard that includes HTML) identifier, not an HTML tag. It defines which version of the HTML DTD should be used to interpret its tags. Every document should include <!DOCTYPE> as its first element. To create DTD-compliant documents, every HTML document must include a <!DOCTYPE> declaration.

Style Tip

Supplying a DTD declaration not only conforms to HTML standards but ensures compatibility with Web document tools such as validators, HTML editors, index tools, and even browsers.

Attributes

HTML PUBLIC "version name"

Defines the DTD to be used for this document. This is the only attribute for this tag.

WHAT'S ONLINE

The "version name" must comply with a list of allowed names, known as *defined names*. You can find a list of defined names at http://www.webtechs .com/html-tk/src/lib/catalog.

Parent Tags

This tag must appear first in any HTML document, therefore it has no parents.

Content Tags

None.

Sample HTML

```
<!DOCTYPE HTML PUBLIC "-//W3C//DTD HTML 4.0//EN">
<HTML>
<HEAD>
<TITLE>Cogs of Chicago</TITLE>
</HEAD>
<BODY>
...
</BODY>
</HTML>
```

\<ADDRESS\>...\</ADDRESS\>

The ADDRESS tag pair is like a signature; it appears at the end of the Web page and contains contact, copyright, address, and other information.

Style Tip

Address information is an important component of any page because it gives you a place in your document to identify yourself and provide readers with other important document-specific information. Recommended information includes the date the page was last revised, an e-mail link to the person responsible for the page, and a copyright notice.

Attributes

None.

Parent Tags

<BLOCKQUOTE>, <BODY>, <BUTTON>, <CENTER>, <DD>, <DIV>, <FIELDSET>, <FORM>, <IFRAME>, <LI>, <NOFRAMES>, <NOSCRIPT>, <OBJECT>, <TD>, <TH>

Content Tags

<A>, <ACRONYM>, <APPLET>, <B>, <BASEFONT>, <BDO>, <BIG>, <BR>, <BUTTON>, <CITE>, <CODE>, <DFN>, <EM>, <FONT>, <I>, <IFRAME>, <IMG>, <INPUT>, <KBD>, <LABEL>, <MAP>, <OBJECT>, <P>, <Q>, <S>, <SAMP>, <SCRIPT>, <SELECT>, <SMALL>, <SPAN>, <STRIKE>, <STRONG>, <SUB>, <SUP>, <TEXTAREA>, <TT>, <U>, <VAR>

Sample HTML

```
<BODY>
<ADDRESS>
URL:http://www.mysite.com/home.html<BR>
Webmaster: <A HREF="mailto:bill@mysite.com">Bill "BBQ" Baker</A>
Revised: June 23, 1997
</ADDRESS>
</BODY>
```

<BODY>...</BODY>

The BODY tags block out an HTML document's body.

Style Tip

All of the content and HTML markup that will be displayed by a browser should be included within the BODY tags. While some browsers will display text placed outside of the BODY tags, others will not. Adding BODY tags before adding any body content helps eliminate forgotten tags.

Attributes

ALINK=(#RRGGBB|colorname)

Defines the color for any links in a document that are currently selected, or active. #RRGGBB is the RGB value defined by two-digit hex codes from 00 to FF (0–256). Colorname is a known color name. The standard 16 colors and their corresponding RGB values are shown in Table B.1.

TABLE B.1: Color Codes and the Colors They Represent

RGB Code	The Color It Represents
#000000	Black
#000080	Navy
#0000FF	Blue
#008000	Green
#008080	Teal
#00FF00	Lime
#00FFFF	Aqua
#800000	Maroon
#800080	Purple
#808000	Olive
#808080	Gray
#C0C0C0	Silver
#FF0000	Red
#FF00FF	Fuchsia
#FFFF00	Yellow
#FFFFFF	White379

These color values are used by all color attributes.

BACKGROUND="URL"
Points to the location of the image that is to be used as the background of the document. Usually this image is tiled.

BGCOLOR=(#RRGGBB|colorname)
Specifies the background color for a document. (See Table B.1.)

BGPROPERTIES="URL"
Specifies the location of an image to use as a watermark. The *watermark* is an image that appears behind the other elements on the page and does not scroll.

LEFTMARGIN=number
Sets the left margin for the entire page.

LINK=(#RRGGBB|colorname)

Specifies color of all hyperlinks within a document. (See Table B.1.)

TEXT=(#RRGGBB|colorname)

Specifies the color of all the regular text within a document. (See Table B.1.)

TOPMARGIN=number

Sets the top margin for the top of the page.

VLINK=(#RRGGBB|colorname)

Defines the color of all links within a document that have already been visited. (See Table B.1.)

Parent Tags

```
<HTML>, <NOFRAMES>
```

Content Tags

```
<A>, <ACRONYM>, <ADDRESS>, <APPLET>, <B>, <BASEFONT>, <BDO>, <BIG>,
<BLOCKQUOTE>, <BR>, <BUTTON>, <CENTER>, <CITE>, <CODE>, <DFN>, <DIR>,
<DIV>, <DL>, <EM>, <FIELDSET>, <FONT>, <FORM>, <H1>, <H2>, <H3>, <H4>,
<H5>, <H6>, <HR>, <I>, <IFRAME>, <IMG>, <INPUT>, <ISINDEX>, <KBD>,
<LABEL>, <MAP>, <MENU>, <NOFRAMES>, <NOSCRIPT>, <OBJECT>, <OL>, <P>,
<PRE>, <Q>, <S>, <SAMP>, <SCRIPT>, <SELECT>, <SMALL>, <SPAN>, <STRIKE>,
<STRONG>, <SUB>, <SUP>, <TABLE>, <TEXTAREA>, <TT>, <U>, <UL>, <VAR>
```

Sample HTML

```
<HTML>
<HEAD><TITLE>Insert the title of your document here.</TITLE>
</HEAD>
<BODY BGCOLOR="white" ALINK="teal" TEXT="navy">
Let's see, what goes here? The body of your document.
</BODY>
</HTML>
```

<DIV> (...</DIV>)

This tag defines divisions of an HTML document. <DIV> is a block-level element, and other block-level elements can be grouped with this tag.

Style Tip

When align attributes occur within tags grouped by the <DIV> tag, the grouped tags alignment takes precedence over any alignment set in the <DIV> tag. <DIV> cannot be used to group elements within a paragraph since it will cause the paragraph to terminate. Use the <SPAN> tag to group within a paragraph without forcing termination. HTML defines <DIV ALIGN=CENTER> and <CENTER> as identical, but the <CENTER> tag is the preferred method of alignment.

Attributes

ALIGN=(LEFT|CENTER|RIGHT|JUSTIFY)

Defines the default horizontal alignment for the contents of the <DIV> tags.

STYLE="text"

Defines special style settings for the grouped elements. Refer to the <STYLE> tag for syntax of style markup.

Parent Tags

<BLOCKQUOTE>, <BODY>, <BUTTON>, <CENTER>, <DD>, <DIV>, <FIELDSET>, <FORM>, <IFRAME>, <LI>, <NOFRAMES>, <NOSCRIPT>, <OBJECT>, <TD>, <TH>

Content Tags

<A>, <ACRONYM>, <ADDRESS>, <APPLET>, <B>, <BASEFONT>, <BDO>, <BIG>, <BLOCKQUOTE>, <BR>, <BUTTON>, <CENTER>, <CITE>, <CODE>, <DFN>, <DIR>, <DIV>, <DL>, <EM>, <FIELDSET>, <FONT>, <FORM>, <H1>, <H2>, <H3>, <H4>, <H5>, <H6>, <HR>, <I>, <IFRAME>, <IMG>, <INPUT>, <ISINDEX>, <KBD>, <LABEL>, <MAP>, <MENU>, <NOFRAMES>, <NOSCRIPT>, <OBJECT>, <OL>, <P>, <PRE>, <Q>, <S>, <SAMP>, <SCRIPT>, <SELECT>, <SMALL>, <SPAN>, <STRIKE>, <STRONG>, <SUB>, <SUP>, <TABLE>, <TEXTAREA>, <TT>, <U>, <UL>, <VAR>

Sample HTML

```
<BODY>
<DIV>
<OL>
<LI>stop
<LI>drop
<LI>roll
</OL>
Section 1.
```

```
</DIV>
<DIV ALIGN=CENTER>
Section 2 centered.
</DIV>
</BODY>
```

<HEAD>...</HEAD>

The document HEAD tags define the part of a Web page that contains the document's header information.

Style Tip

This header tag is another required tag pair and should be used in every Web page. Although the text included in <HEAD>...</HEAD> tags does not show up in the browser window, important information, such as the document's title, META tags, and base URL, is included here.

Attributes

Profile="URL"

Specifies the location of a meta profile or interpretation dictionary.

Parent Tags

```
<HTML>
```

Content Tags

```
<BASE>, <ISINDEX>, <LINK>, <META>, <SCRIPT>, <STYLE>, <TITLE>
```

Sample HTML

```
<HTML>
<HEAD>
<TITLE>Insert the title of your document here.</TITLE>
</HEAD>
</HTML>
```

<H*n*>...</H*n*>

The H*n* tags create a series of headings, numbered from 1 to 6 (H1 through H6). H1 is the top-most head level while H6 is the bottom-most level. Most browsers render headings in decreasing font sizes, although this can be overcome using either the FONT tag within the H*n* tag or with style sheets.

Style Tip

Headings should not be used for text formatting but rather to convey page and content organization. As a general rule, headings should be used in descending order.

Attributes

ALIGN=(LEFT|CENTER|RIGHT|JUSTIFY)
Specifies the alignment of the heading text.

Parent Tags

```
<BLOCKQUOTE>, <BODY>, <BUTTON>, <CENTER>, <DD>, <DIV>, <FIELDSET>,
<FORM>, <IFRAME>, <LI>, <NOFRAMES>, <NOSCRIPT>, <OBJECT>, <TD>, <TH>
```

Content Tags

```
<A>, <ACRONYM>, <APPLET>, <B>, <BASEFONT>, <BDO>, <BIG>, <BR>, <BUTTON>,
<CITE>, <CODE>, <DFN>, <EM>, <FONT>, <I>, <IFRAME>, <IMG>, <INPUT>,
<KBD>, <LABEL>, <MAP>, <OBJECT>, <Q>, <S>, <SAMP>, <SCRIPT>, <SELECT>,
<SMALL>, <SPAN>, <STRIKE>, <STRONG>, <SUB>, <SUP>, <TEXTAREA>, <TT>,
<U>, <VAR>
```

Sample HTML

```
<BODY>
<H1>Heading 1</H1>
<H2>Heading 2</H2>
<H3>Heading 3</H3>
<H4>Heading 4</H4>
<H5>Heading 5</H5>
<H6>Heading 6</H6>
</BODY>
```

<HTML>...</HTML>

The HTML tags define an HTML document. In other words, these tags surround all markup and text that comprise a Web document.

Style Tip

The <HTML> tag pair is required and should be used to begin and end every HTML document you create.

Attributes

VERSION="URL"

Specifies the location of a DTD that should be used to interpret the enclosed markup. This attribute performs the same function as the <!DOCTYPE> tag.

Parent Tags

There are no parent tags for <HTML>...</HTML>.

Content Tags

```
<BODY>, <FRAMESET>, <HEAD>
```

Sample HTML

```
<HTML>
<HEAD>
<TITLE>The Title of Your Document</TITLE>
</HEAD>
<BODY>
Everything else you wish to include in your Web page.
</BODY>
</HTML>
```

<META>

The META tag provides *meta* information—that is, information about information—for an entire document.

Style Tip

Meta information provides both search engines and users a description of the content in your Web pages; it also provides keywords that a search engine can use for indexing content in its database. You can also use META tags to force the browser to automatically load a page after a certain amount of time has passed.

Attributes

NAME="text"
Specifies the name of the meta information contained within this particular META tag.

CONTENT="text"
Supplies a value for the named property.

HTTP-EQUIV="text"
Used to control some special meta information that is sent automatically by the Web server when a page is viewed. For example, this attribute can be used to force a browser to reload a page at a given interval of time.

Parent Tags

```
<HEAD>
```

Content Tags

None.

Sample HTML

```
<META HTTP-EQUIV="KEYWORDS" CONTENT="internet, vrml, books, networking,
intranets, windows nt, netware, html">
<META NAME="Copyright" CONTENT= "LANWrights, Inc. ">
```

<SPAN>...</SPAN>

Similar to <DIV>, these tags group nonblock elements together. Their most common usage is to apply style to sections of text.

Style Tip

<SPAN>, unlike <DIV>, can be used within a paragraph since it is an inline division element. This means it does not prematurely terminate a paragraph.

Attributes

ALIGN=(LEFT|CENTER|RIGHT|JUSTIFY)
Specifies the horizontal alignment of the enclosed elements.

STYLE="text"

Used to define special style settings for the grouped elements. Refer to the
<STYLE> tag for syntax of style markup.

Parent Tags

<A>, <ACRONYM>, <ADDRESS>, <APPLET>, <B>, <BDO>, <BIG>, <BLOCKQUOTE>,
<BODY>, <BUTTON>, <CAPTION>, <CENTER>, <CITE>, <CODE>, <DD>, <DEL>,
<DFN>, <DIV>, <DT>, <EM>, <FIELDSET>, <FONT>, <FORM>, <H1>, <H2>, <H3>,
<H4>, <H5>, <H6>, <I>, <IFRAME>, <INS>, <KBD>, <LABEL>, <LEGEND>, <LI>,
<NOFRAMES>, <NOSCRIPT>, <OBJECT>, <P>, <PRE>, <Q>, <S>, <SAMP>,
<SMALL>, <SPAN>, <STRIKE>, <STRONG>, <SUB>, <SUP>, <TD>, <TH>, <TT>,
<U>, <VAR>

Content Tags

<A>, <ACRONYM>, <APPLET>, <B>, <BASEFONT>, <BDO>, <BIG>, <BR>, <BUTTON>,
<CITE>, <CODE>, <DFN>, <EM>, <FONT>, <I>, <IFRAME>, <IMG>, <INPUT>,
<KBD>, <LABEL>, <MAP>, <OBJECT>, <Q>, <S>, <SAMP>, <SCRIPT>, <SELECT>,
<SMALL>, <SPAN>, <STRIKE>, <STRONG>, <SUB>, <SUP>, <TEXTAREA>, <TT>,
<U>, <VAR>

Sample HTML

```
<BODY>
<SPAN STYLE="margin-left: .3in"> This paragraph is styled to create a
.3 inch margin on the left.<SPAN>
...
</BODY>
```

<TITLE>...</TITLE>

The TITLE tags supply the title for the entire HTML document—this is the title
that appears in the browser window title bar.

Style Tip

A good title should be less than 260 characters and is descriptive rather than general. Many search engines list pages by title, so it is often the first impression a user
gets of your page. While "My Home Page" is concise and to the point, it doesn't tell
a user much about your document. "Bill's BBQ Home Page" is still concise and
gives the user a good idea of what to expect from the page.

Attributes

None.

Parent Tags

<HEAD>

Content Tags

None.

Sample HTML

```
<HEAD>
<TITLE>Bill's BBQ Home Page </TITLE>
</HEAD>
```

<!—...—>

The comment tag indicates a comment, which is not seen by the browser.

Style Tip

Comment tags have many purposes, including to remind yourself why you used a certain tag construction, to leave messages for others who may also be working on the document, to identify authorship or revision dates, and to label sections of a document. A browser will not display commented text, but anyone looking at your HTML source will see it.

Attributes

None.

Parent Tags

All.

Content Tags

All.

Sample HTML

```
<!-The browser won't include this text in the displayed content.->
```

Language Information Tags

Language information tags define the language to be used to interpret and display text. They also provide clues as to which direction the language runs (remember, some languages, like Arabic and Japanese, run right to left, not left to right).

<BDO>...</BDO>

The BDO (bi-directional algorithm) tags are used to define the language type and display direction of all enclosed text.

Style Tip

These tags should be used when displaying sections of text from languages other than the default.

Attributes

LANG=*language-code*

Defines the language to be used for the enclosed elements. The *language-code* values are determined by RFC 1766.

WHAT'S ONLINE

You can retrieve a copy of RFC 1766 from http://ds.internic.net/rfc/rfc1766.txt. A list of the actual country codes is available at http://www.sil.org/sgml/iso639a.html or ftp://ftp.ripe.net/iso3166-countrycodes.

DIR=LTR|RTL

Used to define the direction of the language, left-to-right or right-to-left. This is a mandatory attribute.

Parent Tags

<A>, <ACRONYM>, <ADDRESS>, <APPLET>, <B>, <BDO>, <BIG>, <BLOCKQUOTE>, <BODY>, <BUTTON>, <CAPTION>, <CENTER>, <CITE>, <CODE>, <DD>, <DEL>, <DFN>, <DIV>, <DT>, <EM>, <FIELDSET>, <FONT>, <FORM>, <H1>, <H2>, <H3>, <H4>, <H5>, <H6>, <I>, <IFRAME>, <INS>, <KBD>, <LABEL>, <LEGEND>, <LI>, <NOFRAMES>, <NOSCRIPT>, <OBJECT>, <P>, <PRE>, <Q>, <S>, <SAMP>, <SMALL>, <SPAN>, <STRIKE>, <STRONG>, <SUB>, <SUP>, <TD>, <TH>, <TT>, <U>, <VAR>

Content Tags

<A>, <ACRONYM>, <APPLET>, <B>, <BASEFONT>, <BDO>, <BIG>, <BR>, <BUTTON>, <CITE>, <CODE>, <DFN>, <EM>, <FONT>, <I>, <IFRAME>, <IMG>, <INPUT>, <KBD>, <LABEL>, <MAP>, <OBJECT>, <Q>, <S>, <SAMP>, <SCRIPT>, <SELECT>, <SMALL>, <SPAN>, <STRIKE>, <STRONG>, <SUB>, <SUP>, <TEXTAREA>, <TT>, <U>, <VAR>

Sample HTML

```
<BODY>
<P>This is an English sentence.
<P><BDO LANG="FR" DIR="RTL">This is a French sentence.</BDO>
</BODY>
```

Text Tags

Text tags affect how text looks when displayed within your browser. Text tags are meant to reflect the content, or its place within the document. These tags differ from presentation tags, covered later, because presentation tags change text's appearance, but do not reflect its meaning or role within the document. Use text tags whenever possible, rather than presentation tags.

<ACRONYM>...</ACRONYM>

The ACRONYM tags mark the text they contain as an acronym.

Style Tip

Be sure to include the acronym's fully spelled out version in the TITLE= attribute so users can learn what it stands for.

Attributes

TITLE="text"

Provides an acronym's expanded form that appears in a highlighted box next to the acronym when a user runs his or her mouse over it.

Parent Tags

```
<A>, <ACRONYM>, <ADDRESS>, <APPLET>, <B>, <BDO>, <BIG>, <BLOCKQUOTE>,
<BODY>, <BUTTON>, <CAPTION>, <CENTER>, <CITE>, <CODE>, <DD>, <DEL>,
<DFN>, <DIV>, <DT>, <EM>, <FIELDSET>, <FONT>, <FORM>, <H1>, <H2>, <H3>,
<H4>, <H5>, <H6>, <I>, <IFRAME>, <INS>, <KBD>, <LABEL>, <LEGEND>, <LI>,
<NOFRAMES>, <NOSCRIPT>, <OBJECT>, <P>, <PRE>, <Q>, <S>, <SAMP>,
<SMALL>, <SPAN>, <STRIKE>, <STRONG>,<SUB>, <SUP>, <TD>, <TH>, <TT>,
<U>, <VAR>
```

Content Tags

```
<A>, <ACRONYM>, <APPLET>, <B>, <BASEFONT>, <BDO>, <BIG>, <BR>, <BUTTON>,
<CITE>, <CODE>, <DFN>, <EM>, <FONT>, <I>, <IFRAME>, <IMG>, <INPUT>,
<KBD>, <LABEL>, <MAP>, <OBJECT>, <Q>, <S>, <SAMP>, <SCRIPT>, <SELECT>,
<SMALL>, <SPAN>, <STRIKE>, <STRONG>, <SUB>, <SUP>, <TEXTAREA>, <TT>,
<U>, <VAR>
```

Sample HTML

```
<BODY>
<ACRONYM TITLE="Hypertext Markup Language> HTML </ACRONYM> is used to
create Web pages.
</BODY>
```

<BLOCKQUOTE>... </BLOCKQUOTE>

BLOCKQUOTE tags set off long quotations or citations from other sources.

Style Tip

BLOCKQUOTE tags are intended to set off longer passages. They indent all lines of enclosed text to the left. While multiple sets of BLOCKQUOTE tags can be used to create a series of indentations, this is a misuse of the tag. Use style sheet properties instead.

Attributes

CITE="text"
Provides additional information about the source of the quoted text.

Parent Tags

```
<BLOCKQUOTE>, <BODY>, <BUTTON>, <CENTER>, <DD>, <DIV>, <FIELDSET>,
<FORM>, <IFRAME>, <LI>, <NOFRAMES>, <NOSCRIPT>, <OBJECT>, <TD>, <TH>
```

Content Tags

```
<A>, <ACRONYM>, <ADDRESS>, <APPLET>, <B>, <BASEFONT>, <BDO>, <BIG>,
<BLOCKQUOTE>, <BR>, <BUTTON>, <CENTER>, <CITE>, <CODE>, <DFN>, <DIR>,
<DIV>, <DL>, <EM>, <FIELDSET>, <FONT>, <FORM>, <H1>, <H2>, <H3>, <H4>,
<H5>, <H6>, <HR>, <I>, <IFRAME>, <IMG>, <INPUT>, <ISINDEX>, <KBD>,
<LABEL>, <MAP>, <MENU>, <NOFRAMES>, <NOSCRIPT>, <OBJECT>, <OL>, <P>,
<PRE>, <Q>, <S>, <SAMP>, <SCRIPT>, <SELECT>, <SMALL>, <SPAN>, <STRIKE>,
<STRONG>, <SUB>, <SUP>, <TABLE>, <TEXTAREA>, <TT>, <U>, <UL>, <VAR>
```

Sample HTML

```
<BLOCKQUOTE CITE="Julius Caesar">
Friends, Romans, Countryman, lend me your ears!
</BLOCKQUOTE>
```


The BR (line break) tag causes a line of text to break wherever the tag is placed.

Style Tip

The line break tag is best used to create short lines of text, as often seen in poetry. It guarantees a break in the text regardless of the size of the browser window.

Attributes

CLEAR=(LEFT|ALL|RIGHT|NONE)

Specifies how the text should flow in relation to any floating images it may follow. LEFT causes the text to be aligned directly under a left-floating image and to the left side of the screen. ALL positions the text after any floating images. RIGHT causes the text to be aligned directly under a right-floating image and to the right side of the screen. NONE, the default, allows the text to flow naturally based on the other elements on the page.

Parent Tags

\<A>, \<ACRONYM>, \<ADDRESS>, \<APPLET>, \<B>, \<BDO>, \<BIG>, \<BLOCKQUOTE>, \<BODY>, \<BUTTON>, \<CAPTION>, \<CENTER>, \<CITE>, \<CODE>, \<DD>, \<DEL>, \<DFN>, \<DIV>, \<DT>, \<EM>, \<FIELDSET>, \<FONT>, \<FORM>, \<H1>, \<H2>, \<H3>, \<H4>, \<H5>, \<H6>, \<I>, \<IFRAME>, \<INS>, \<KBD>, \<LABEL>, \<LEGEND>, \<LI>, \<NOFRAMES>, \<NOSCRIPT>, \<OBJECT>, \<P>, \<PRE>, \<Q>, \<S>, \<SAMP>, \<SMALL>, \<SPAN>, \<STRIKE>, \<STRONG>, \<SUB>, \<SUP>, \<TD>, \<TH>, \<TT>, \<U>, \<VAR>

Content Tags

None.

Sample HTML

```
This line will break here <BR>
and this text moved to the next line.
```

\<CITE>...\</CITE>

The CITE tags mark a citation or bibliographic reference.

Style Tip

Whenever you include other people's content within your Web pages, always be sure to give them proper credit enclosed in CITE tags.

Attributes

None.

Parent Tags

```
<A>, <ACRONYM>, <ADDRESS>, <APPLET>, <B>, <BDO>, <BIG>, <BLOCKQUOTE>,
<BODY>, <BUTTON>, <CAPTION>, <CENTER>, <CITE>, <CODE>, <DD>, <DEL>,
<DFN>, <DIV>, <DT>, <EM>, <FIELDSET>, <FONT>, <FORM>, <H1>, <H2>, <H3>,
<H4>, <H5>, <H6>, <I>, <IFRAME>, <INS>, <KBD>, <LABEL>, <LEGEND>, <LI>,
<NOFRAMES>, <NOSCRIPT>, <OBJECT>, <P>, <PRE>, <Q>, <S>, <SAMP>,
<SMALL>, <SPAN>, <STRIKE>, <STRONG>, <SUB>, <SUP>, <TD>, <TH>, <TT>,
<U>, <VAR>
```

Content Tags

```
<A>, <ACRONYM>, <APPLET>, <B>, <BASEFONT>, <BDO>, <BIG>, <BR>, <BUTTON>,
<CITE>, <CODE>, <DFN>, <EM>, <FONT>, <I>, <IFRAME>, <IMG>, <INPUT>,
<KBD>, <LABEL>, <MAP>, <OBJECT>, <Q>, <S>, <SAMP>, <SCRIPT>, <SELECT>,
<SMALL>, <SPAN>, <STRIKE>, <STRONG>, <SUB>, <SUP>, <TEXTAREA>, <TT>,
<U>, <VAR>
```

Sample HTML

```
<BODY>
All statistical references in this document are from <BR>
<CITE>Statistics Daily, Volume 3, Issue 2; March, 1994. </CITE>
</BODY>
```

<CODE>...</CODE>

The CODE tags are used to identify text that represents programming code and is most often displayed in a monospaced font.

Style Tip

Any text that represents programming or computer code should be included within CODE tags so users recognize it as such. Also, the monospaced font will preserve code formatting, often an essential part of a program.

Attributes

None.

Parent Tags

```
<A>, <ACRONYM>, <ADDRESS>, <APPLET>, <B>, <BDO>, <BIG>, <BLOCKQUOTE>,
<BODY>, <BUTTON>, <CAPTION>, <CENTER>, <CITE>, <CODE>, <DD>, <DEL>,
```

<DFN>, <DIV>, <DT>, <EM>, <FIELDSET>, <FONT>, <FORM>, <H1>, <H2>, <H3>,
<H4>, <H5>, <H6>, <I>, <IFRAME>, <INS>, <KBD>, <LABEL>, <LEGEND>, <LI>,
<NOFRAMES>, <NOSCRIPT>, <OBJECT>, <P>, <PRE>, <Q>, <S>, <SAMP>,
<SMALL>, <SPAN>, <STRIKE>, <STRONG>, <SUB>, <SUP>, <TD>, <TH>, <TT>,
<U>, <VAR>

Content Tags

<A>, <ACRONYM>, <APPLET>, <B>, <BASEFONT>, <BDO>, <BIG>, <BR>, <BUTTON>,
<CITE>, <CODE>, <DFN>, <EM>, <FONT>, <I>, <IFRAME>, <IMG>, <INPUT>,
<KBD>, <LABEL>, <MAP>, <OBJECT>, <Q>, <S>, <SAMP>, <SCRIPT>, <SELECT>,
<SMALL>, <SPAN>, <STRIKE>, <STRONG>, <SUB>, <SUP>, <TEXTAREA>, <TT>,
<U>, <VAR>

Sample HTML

```
<CODE>
The following HTML markup must be included in every page: <BR>
<CODE>
<!DOCTYPE HTML PUBLIC &quot;-//IETF//DTD HTML 4.0//EN&quot;>
<HTML>
<HEAD>

<TITLE></TITLE>

</HEAD>
<BODY>

</BODY>
</HTML>
</CODE>
```

<DEL>...</DEL>

DEL (deletion) tags set off text that was included in previous versions of a document but has been deleted in the new version.

Style Tip

The DEL tags, and their companion INS (insertion) tags, are very useful tools for showing how a Web document has been revised over time. These are similar to the revision tools found in many word processors.

Attributes

CITE="url"

Provides a link to another Web document that contains information about why the text was deleted from the document.

DATETIME=YYYY-MM-DDThh:mm:ssTZD

Specifies when the enclosed text was deleted, using standard date and time notation. YYYY indicates the year, MM the two-digit month, and DD the two-digit day. T is the time indicator. HH stands for the two-digit hour (in military time), mm the two-digit minute, and ss the two-digit seconds. TZD is used to specify the time zone.

Parent Tags

```
<BODY>
```

Content Tags

```
<A>, <ACRONYM>, <APPLET>, <B>, <BASEFONT>, <BDO>, <BIG>, <BR>, <BUTTON>,
<CITE>, <CODE>, <DFN>, <EM>, <FONT>, <I>, <IFRAME>, <IMG>, <INPUT>,
<KBD>, <LABEL>, <MAP>, <OBJECT>, <Q>, <S>, <SAMP>, <SCRIPT>, <SELECT>,
<SMALL>, <SPAN>, <STRIKE>, <STRONG>, <SUB>, <SUP>, <TEXTAREA>, <TT>,
<U>, <VAR>
```

Sample HTML

```
<BODY>
<DEL CITE="changes.html" DATETIME=1994-09-21T23:10:15Z>
<H1>Introduction</H1>
...
</DEL>
<H1>Introduction</H1>
...
</BODY>
```

<DFN>...</DFN>

The DFN (definition) tags are used to mark the first use of term within a Web document.

Style Tip

If you are introducing new terminology for the first time in a Web document or series of documents, it is important to insure that users recognize the term as new, understand its meaning, and know that it will be used again in the document. Text enclosed within DFN tags is usually rendered in italics so it stands out for users.

Attributes

None.

Parent Tags

<A>, <ACRONYM>, <ADDRESS>, <APPLET>, <B>, <BDO>, <BIG>, <BLOCKQUOTE>, <BODY>, <BUTTON>, <CAPTION>, <CENTER>, <CITE>, <CODE>, <DD>, <DEL>, <DFN>, <DIV>, <DT>, <EM>, <FIELDSET>, <FONT>, <FORM>, <H1>, <H2>, <H3>, <H4>, <H5>, <H6>, <I>, <IFRAME>, <INS>, <KBD>, <LABEL>, <LEGEND>, <LI>, <NOFRAMES>, <NOSCRIPT>, <OBJECT>, <P>, <PRE>, <Q>, <S>, <SAMP>, <SMALL>, <SPAN>, <STRIKE>, <STRONG>, <SUB>, <SUP>, <TD>, <TH>, <TT>, <U>, <VAR>

Content Tags

<A>, <ACRONYM>, <APPLET>, <B>, <BASEFONT>, <BDO>, <BIG>, <BR>, <BUTTON>, <CITE>, <CODE>, <DFN>, <EM>, <FONT>, <I>, <IFRAME>, <IMG>, <INPUT>, <KBD>, <LABEL>, <MAP>, <OBJECT>, <Q>, <S>, <SAMP>, <SCRIPT>, <SELECT>, <SMALL>, <SPAN>, <STRIKE>, <STRONG>, <SUB>, <SUP>, <TEXTAREA>, <TT>, <U>, <VAR>

Sample HTML

```
<DFN>TCP/IP</DFN> stands for Transfer Control Protocol/Internet
Protocol. TCP/IP is the universal translator for the Internet.
```

<EM>...</EM>

The EM (emphasis) tags indicate that the enclosed text has a special importance and should be noted by the reader.

Style Tip

As with all text-altering tags, do not overuse the EM tags, or their effectiveness will be reduced.

Attributes

None.

Parent Tags

<A>, <ACRONYM>, <ADDRESS>, <APPLET>, <B>, <BDO>, <BIG>, <BLOCKQUOTE>, <BODY>, <BUTTON>, <CAPTION>, <CENTER>, <CITE>, <CODE>, <DD>, <DEL>, <DFN>, <DIV>, <DT>, <EM>, <FIELDSET>, <FONT>, <FORM>, <H1>, <H2>, <H3>, <H4>, <H5>, <H6>, <I>, <IFRAME>, <INS>, <KBD>, <LABEL>, <LEGEND>, <LI>, <NOFRAMES>, <NOSCRIPT>, <OBJECT>, <P>, <PRE>, <Q>, <S>, <SAMP>, <SMALL>, <SPAN>, <STRIKE>, <STRONG>, <SUB>, <SUP>, <TD>, <TH>, <TT>, <U>, <VAR>

Content Tags

<A>, <ACRONYM>, <APPLET>, <B>, <BASEFONT>, <BDO>, <BIG>, <BR>, <BUTTON>, <CITE>, <CODE>, <DFN>, <EM>, <FONT>, <I>, <IFRAME>, <IMG>, <INPUT>, <KBD>, <LABEL>, <MAP>, <OBJECT>, <Q>, <S>, <SAMP>, <SCRIPT>, <SELECT>, <SMALL>, <SPAN>, <STRIKE>, <STRONG>, <SUB>, <SUP>, <TEXTAREA>, <TT>, <U>, <VAR>

Sample HTML

"I <EMP>don't</EMP> want to go to school today," the little boy said.

<INS>...</INS>

The INS (insertion) tags set off text that was not included in previous versions of a document but has been added in the new version.

Style Tip

The INS tags, and their companion DEL (deletion) tags, are very useful tools for showing how a Web document has been revised over time. These are similar to the revision tools found in many word processors.

Attributes

CITE="url"

Provides a link to another Web document that contains information about why the text was added to the document.

DATETIME=YYYY-MM-DDThh:mm:ssTZD

Specifies when the enclosed text was added, using standard date and time notation. YYYY indicates the year, MM the two-digit month, and DD the two-digit day. T is the time indicator. HH stands for the two-digit hour (in military time), mm the two-digit minute, and ss the two-digit seconds. TZD is used to specify the time zone.

Parent Tags

```
<BODY>
```

Content Tags

```
<A>, <ACRONYM>, <APPLET>, <B>, <BASEFONT>, <BDO>, <BIG>, <BR>, <BUTTON>,
<CITE>, <CODE>, <DFN>, <EM>, <FONT>, <I>, <IFRAME>, <IMG>, <INPUT>,
<KBD>, <LABEL>, <MAP>, <OBJECT>, <Q>, <S>, <SAMP>, <SCRIPT>, <SELECT>,
<SMALL>, <SPAN>, <STRIKE>, <STRONG>, <SUB>, <SUP>, <TEXTAREA>, <TT>,
<U>, <VAR>
```

Sample HTML

```
<BODY>
<INS CITE="changes.html" DATETIME=1994-09-21T23:10:15Z>
<H1>Summary</H1>
...
</INS>
</BODY>
```

<KBD>...</KBD>

The KBD (keyboard text) tags are used around text that should be typed in at a computer keyboard by the user.

Style Tip

KBD tags display text in a monospaced font, in the same way the CODE tags do.

Attributes

None.

Parent Tags

<A>, <ACRONYM>, <ADDRESS>, <APPLET>, <B>, <BDO>, <BIG>, <BLOCKQUOTE>,
<BODY>, <BUTTON>, <CAPTION>, <CENTER>, <CITE>, <CODE>, <DD>, <DEL>,
<DFN>, <DIV>, <DT>, <EM>, <FIELDSET>, <FONT>, <FORM>, <H1>, <H2>, <H3>,
<H4>, <H5>, <H6>, <I>, <IFRAME>, <INS>, <KBD>, <LABEL>, <LEGEND>, <LI>,
<NOFRAMES>, <NOSCRIPT>, <OBJECT>, <P>, <PRE>, <Q>, <S>, <SAMP>,
<SMALL>, <SPAN>, <STRIKE>, <STRONG>, <SUB>, <SUP>, <TD>, <TH>, <TT>,
<U>, <VAR>

Content Tags

<A>, <ACRONYM>, <APPLET>, <B>, <BASEFONT>, <BDO>, <BIG>, <BR>, <BUTTON>,
<CITE>, <CODE>, <DFN>, <EM>, <FONT>, <I>, <IFRAME>, <IMG>, <INPUT>,
<KBD>, <LABEL>, <MAP>, <OBJECT>, <Q>, <S>, <SAMP>, <SCRIPT>, <SELECT>,
<SMALL>, <SPAN>, <STRIKE>, <STRONG>, <SUB>, <SUP>, <TEXTAREA>, <TT>,
<U>, <VAR>

Sample HTML

```
<BODY>
When you get to the login prompt type in your <KBD>username</KBD> and
<KBD>password</KBD>
</BODY>
```

<P>...(</P>)

The P (paragraph) tags separate paragraphs of text within a Web document by
inserting a line break and a blank line just before the P tag.

Style Tip

Paragraph markup can be used as either a singleton tag or a pair. Paragraphs are
especially useful for applying style sheet rules to sections of text using the tag pair.
Multiple instances of the singleton paragraph tag cannot be used to create large
blocks of white space as most browsers will only display one blank line at a time,
regardless of the number of paragraph tags.

Attributes

ALIGN=(LEFT|CENTER|RIGHT|JUSTIFY) *[Deprecated]*
Specifies the horizontal alignment of the enclosed elements.

Parent Tags

<ADDRESS>, <BLOCKQUOTE>, <BODY>, <BUTTON>, <CENTER>, <DD>, <DIV>, <FIELDSET>, <FORM>, <IFRAME>, <LI>, <NOFRAMES>, <NOSCRIPT>, <OBJECT>, <TD>, <TH>

Content Tags

<A>, <ACRONYM>, <APPLET>, <B>, <BASEFONT>, <BDO>, <BIG>, <BR>, <BUTTON>, <CITE>, <CODE>, <DFN>, <EM>, <FONT>, <I>, <IFRAME>, <IMG>, <INPUT>, <KBD>, <LABEL>, <MAP>, <OBJECT>, <Q>, <S>, <SAMP>, <SCRIPT>, <SELECT>, <SMALL>, <SPAN>, <STRIKE>, <STRONG>, <SUB>, <SUP>, <TEXTAREA>, <TT>, <U>, <VAR>

Sample HTML

```
<BODY>
This is the first paragraph of my document.<P>
This is the second paragraph of my document.
</BODY>
```

<PRE>...</PRE>

PRE (preformatted text) tags force the browser to display the enclosed text exactly as it appears in HTML.

Style Tip

Because preformatted text is displayed exactly as it is written in HTML, multiple spaces, hard returns, and character spacing will show up in the browser window. Use preformatted text to create large blocks of white space where multiple paragraph tags will not. The biggest drawback of preformatted text is that it is rendered in a monospaced font and is limited in the other HTML markup it can contain.

Attributes

WIDTH=number

Indicates the maximum number of characters that should appear on a line. Based on this number, the browser selects an appropriate font size and indentation.

Parent Tags

<BLOCKQUOTE>, <BODY>, <BUTTON>, <CENTER>, <DD>, <DIV>, <FIELDSET>, <FORM>, <IFRAME>, <LI>, <NOFRAMES>, <NOSCRIPT>, <OBJECT>, <TD>, <TH>

Content Tags

<A>, <ACRONYM>, <APPLET>, <B>, <BASEFONT>, <BDO>, <BIG>, <BR>, <BUTTON>, <CITE>, <CODE>, <DFN>, <EM>, <FONT>, <I>, <IFRAME>, <IMG>, <INPUT>, <KBD>, <LABEL>, <MAP>, <OBJECT>, <Q>, <S>, <SAMP>, <SCRIPT>, <SELECT>, <SMALL>, <SPAN>, <STRIKE>, <STRONG>, <SUB>, <SUP>, <TEXTAREA>, <TT>, <U>, <VAR>

Sample HTML

```
<BODY>
Class schedule:
<PRE>
Monday/Wednesday      Tuesday/Thursday
12:00  Chemistry      12:00  English
 1:30  Physics         1:30  Math
</PRE>
</BODY>
```

<Q>...</Q>

Q (quotation) tags enclose short quotations within a line of text.

Style Tip

Unlike the BLOCKQUOTE tags that set off large amounts of text from other text in the document, the Q tags should be used to highlight bits of text that remain inline.

Attributes

CITE="text"

Provides additional information about the source of the quoted text.

Parent Tags

<A>, <ACRONYM>, <ADDRESS>, <APPLET>, <B>, <BDO>, <BIG>, <BLOCKQUOTE>, <BODY>, <BUTTON>, <CAPTION>, <CENTER>, <CITE>, <CODE>, <DD>, <DEL>, <DFN>, <DIV>, <DT>, <EM>, <FIELDSET>, <FONT>, <FORM>, <H1>, <H2>, <H3>, <H4>, <H5>, <H6>, <I>, <IFRAME>, <INS>, <KBD>, <LABEL>, <LEGEND>, <LI>, <NOFRAMES>, <NOSCRIPT>, <OBJECT>, <P>, <PRE>, <Q>, <S>, <SAMP>, <SMALL>, <SPAN>, <STRIKE>, <STRONG>, <SUB>, <SUP>, <TD>, <TH>, <TT>, <U>, <VAR>

Content Tags

<A>, <ACRONYM>, <APPLET>, <B>, <BASEFONT>, <BDO>, <BIG>, <BR>, <BUTTON>, <CITE>, <CODE>, <DFN>, <EM>, <FONT>, <I>, <IFRAME>, <IMG>, <INPUT>, <KBD>, <LABEL>, <MAP>, <OBJECT>, <Q>, <S>, <SAMP>, <SCRIPT>, <SELECT>, <SMALL>, <SPAN>, <STRIKE>, <STRONG>, <SUB>, <SUP>, <TEXTAREA>, <TT>, <U>, <VAR>

Sample HTML

```
<BODY>
Julius Caesar said <Q>Et Tu, Brute?</Q> when he was stabbed on the
steps of the Forum.
</BODY>
```

<SAMP>...</SAMP>

The SAMP (sample) tags are used to highlight text that represents output from a program or other literal text.

Style Tip

While the CODE tags are used to mark up the actual code for a program, use the SAMP tags to show what the output from the code should look like.

Attributes

None.

Parent Tags

<A>, <ACRONYM>, <ADDRESS>, <APPLET>, <B>, <BDO>, <BIG>, <BLOCKQUOTE>, <BODY>, <BUTTON>, <CAPTION>, <CENTER>, <CITE>, <CODE>, <DD>, <DEL>, <DFN>, <DIV>, <DT>, <EM>, <FIELDSET>, <FONT>, <FORM>, <H1>, <H2>, <H3>, <H4>, <H5>, <H6>, <I>, <IFRAME>, <INS>, <KBD>, <LABEL>, <LEGEND>, <LI>, <NOFRAMES>, <NOSCRIPT>, <OBJECT>, <P>, <PRE>, <Q>, <S>, <SAMP>, <SMALL>, <SPAN>, <STRIKE>, <STRONG>, <SUB>, <SUP>, <TD>, <TH>, <TT>, <U>, <VAR>

Content Tags

<A>, <ACRONYM>, <APPLET>, <B>, <BASEFONT>, <BDO>, <BIG>, <BR>, <BUTTON>, <CITE>, <CODE>, <DFN>, <EM>, <FONT>, <I>, <IFRAME>, <IMG>, <INPUT>, <KBD>, <LABEL>, <MAP>, <OBJECT>, <Q>, <S>, <SAMP>, <SCRIPT>, <SELECT>, <SMALL>, <SPAN>, <STRIKE>, <STRONG>, <SUB>, <SUP>, <TEXTAREA>, <TT>, <U>, <VAR>

Sample HTML

```
<BODY>
The output from my first program ever was:<BR>
<SAMP>Hello world!</SAMP>
</BODY>
```

<STRONG>...</STRONG>

STRONG tags indicate that the enclosed text is very important and should clearly stand out from the surrounding text. Strong text is usually formatted in boldface type.

Style Tip

This tag pair provides the strongest possible emphasis on text without changing its font size or separating it from the text. Be careful not to overuse these tags or your emphasized text will lose its effect.

Attributes

None.

Parent Tags

<A>, <ACRONYM>, <ADDRESS>, <APPLET>, <B>, <BDO>, <BIG>, <BLOCKQUOTE>, <BODY>, <BUTTON>, <CAPTION>, <CENTER>, <CITE>, <CODE>, <DD>, <DEL>, <DFN>, <DIV>, <DT>, <EM>, <FIELDSET>, <FONT>, <FORM>, <H1>, <H2>, <H3>, <H4>, <H5>, <H6>, <I>, <IFRAME>, <INS>, <KBD>, <LABEL>, <LEGEND>, <LI>, <NOFRAMES>, <NOSCRIPT>, <OBJECT>, <P>, <PRE>, <Q>, <S>, <SAMP>, <SMALL>, <SPAN>, <STRIKE>, <STRONG>, <SUB>, <SUP>, <TD>, <TH>, <TT>, <U>, <VAR>

Content Tags

<A>, <ACRONYM>, <APPLET>, <B>, <BASEFONT>, <BDO>, <BIG>, <BR>, <BUTTON>, <CITE>, <CODE>, <DFN>, <EM>, <FONT>, <I>, <IFRAME>, <IMG>, <INPUT>, <KBD>, <LABEL>, <MAP>, <OBJECT>, <Q>, <S>, <SAMP>, <SCRIPT>, <SELECT>, <SMALL>, <SPAN>, <STRIKE>, <STRONG>, <SUB>, <SUP>, <TEXTAREA>, <TT>, <U>, <VAR>

Sample HTML

```
<BODY>
"I <STRONG>really don't</STRONG> want to go to school today," the
little boy said.</BODY>
```

_{...}

The SUB (subscript) tags are used to mark text that should be displayed as subscript.

Style Tip

Although SUB tags can be nested within other SUB tags and SUP (superscript) tags, the final browser rendering is unpredictable and will vary from browser to browser.

Attributes

None.

Parent Tags

<A>, <ACRONYM>, <ADDRESS>, <APPLET>, <B>, <BDO>, <BIG>, <BLOCKQUOTE>, <BODY>, <BUTTON>, <CAPTION>, <CENTER>, <CITE>, <CODE>, <DD>, <DEL>, <DFN>, <DIV>, <DT>, <EM>, <FIELDSET>, <FONT>, <FORM>, <H1>, <H2>, <H3>, <H4>, <H5>, <H6>, <I>, <IFRAME>, <INS>, <KBD>, <LABEL>, <LEGEND>, <LI>, <NOFRAMES>, <NOSCRIPT>, <OBJECT>, <P>, <Q>, <S>, <SAMP>, <SMALL>, <SPAN>, <STRIKE>, <STRONG>, <SUB>, <SUP>, <TD>, <TH>, <TT>, <U>, <VAR>

Content Tags

<A>, <ACRONYM>, <APPLET>, <B>, <BASEFONT>, <BDO>, <BIG>, <BR>, <BUTTON>, <CITE>, <CODE>, <DFN>, <EM>, <FONT>, <I>, <IFRAME>, <IMG>, <INPUT>, <KBD>, <LABEL>, <MAP>, <OBJECT>, <Q>, <S>, <SAMP>, <SCRIPT>, <SELECT>, <SMALL>, <SPAN>, <STRIKE>, <STRONG>, <SUB>, <SUP>, <TEXTAREA>, <TT>, <U>, <VAR>

Sample HTML

```
<BODY>
CO<SUB>2</SUB> is a dangerous gas that can cause death if inhaled in
large quantities; in smaller quantities, it is used to carbonate soft
drinks!
</BODY>
```

^{...}

The SUP (superscript) tags are used to mark text that should be displayed as superscript.

Style Tip

Although SUP tags can be nested within other SUP tags and SUB (subscript) tags, the final browser rendering is unpredictable and will vary from browser to browser.

Attributes

None.

Parent Tags

<A>, <ACRONYM>, <ADDRESS>, <APPLET>, <B>, <BDO>, <BIG>, <BLOCKQUOTE>, <BODY>, <BUTTON>, <CAPTION>, <CENTER>, <CITE>, <CODE>, <DD>, <DEL>, <DFN>, <DIV>, <DT>, <EM>, <FIELDSET>, <FONT>, <FORM>, <H1>, <H2>, <H3>, <H4>, <H5>, <H6>, <I>, <IFRAME>, <INS>, <KBD>, <LABEL>, <LEGEND>, <LI>, <NOFRAMES>, <NOSCRIPT>, <OBJECT>, <P>, <Q>, <S>, <SAMP>, <SMALL>, <SPAN>, <STRIKE>, <STRONG>, <SUB>, <SUP>, <TD>, <TH>, <TT>, <U>, <VAR>

Content Tags

<A>, <ACRONYM>, <APPLET>, <B>, <BASEFONT>, <BDO>, <BIG>, <BR>, <BUTTON>, <CITE>, <CODE>, <DFN>, <EM>, <FONT>, <I>, <IFRAME>, <IMG>, <INPUT>, <KBD>, <LABEL>, <MAP>, <OBJECT>, <Q>, <S>, <SAMP>, <SCRIPT>, <SELECT>, <SMALL>, <SPAN>, <STRIKE>, <STRONG>, <SUB>, <SUP>, <TEXTAREA>, <TT>, <U>, <VAR>

Sample HTML

```
<BODY>
When I was little, my dad and I went to M<SUP>c</SUP>Dougall's House of
Pancakes every Saturday for breakfast.
</BODY>
```

<VAR>...</VAR>

VAR (variable) tags mark text that represents a placeholder for user-supplied text. Most browsers display variable text in italics.

Style Tip

When writing instructions that require users to supply their own information, use VAR tags to highlight where this information should be placed.

Attributes

None.

Parent Tags

<A>, <ACRONYM>, <ADDRESS>, <APPLET>, <B>, <BDO>, <BIG>, <BLOCKQUOTE>, <BODY>, <BUTTON>, <CAPTION>, <CENTER>, <CITE>, <CODE>, <DD>, <DEL>, <DFN>, <DIV>, <DT>, <EM>, <FIELDSET>, <FONT>, <FORM>, <H1>, <H2>, <H3>, <H4>, <H5>, <H6>, <I>, <IFRAME>, <INS>, <KBD>, <LABEL>, <LEGEND>, <LI>, <NOFRAMES>, <NOSCRIPT>, <OBJECT>, <P>, <PRE>, <Q>, <S>, <SAMP>, <SMALL>, <SPAN>, <STRIKE>, <STRONG>, <SUB>, <SUP>, <TD>, <TH>, <TT>, <U>, <VAR>

Content Tags

<A>, <ACRONYM>, <APPLET>, <B>, <BASEFONT>, <BDO>, <BIG>, <BR>, <BUTTON>, <CITE>, <CODE>, <DFN>, <EM>, <FONT>, <I>, <IFRAME>, <IMG>, <INPUT>, <KBD>, <LABEL>, <MAP>, <OBJECT>, <Q>, <S>, <SAMP>, <SCRIPT>, <SELECT>, <SMALL>, <SPAN>, <STRIKE>, <STRONG>, <SUB>, <SUP>, <TEXTAREA>, <TT>, <U>, <VAR>

Sample HTML

```
<BODY>
To change directories in DOS, type the following command:<BR>
<KBD>cd <VAR>dir</VAR></KBD>
</BODY>
```

List Tags

List tags define lists of elements that may be displayed as bulleted or numbered lists, glossary entries with definitions, and menu formats. All of these layouts are useful when organizing lists of items or elements to improve their readability.

<DD> (...</DD>)

The DD (definition description) tags mark the descriptive piece of a definition list.

Style Tip

Definition descriptions can be entire paragraphs, if necessary to define the definition term. Other markup, such as paragraphs and line breaks, can be used within <DD> markup.

Attributes

None.

Parent Tags

<DL>

Content Tags

<A>, <ACRONYM>, <ADDRESS>, <APPLET>, <B>, <BASEFONT>, <BDO>, <BIG>, <BLOCKQUOTE>, <BR>, <BUTTON>, <CENTER>, <CITE>, <CODE>, <DFN>, <DIR>, <DIV>, <DL>, <EM>, <FIELDSET>, <FONT>, <FORM>, <H1>, <H2>, <H3>, <H4>, <H5>, <H6>, <HR>, <I>, <IFRAME>, <IMG>, <INPUT>, <ISINDEX>, <KBD>, <LABEL>, <MAP>, <MENU>, <NOFRAMES>, <NOSCRIPT>, <OBJECT>, <OL>, <P>, <PRE>, <Q>, <S>, <SAMP>, <SCRIPT>, <SELECT>, <SMALL>, <SPAN>, <STRIKE>, <STRONG>, <SUB>, <SUP>, <TABLE>, <TEXTAREA>, <TT>, <U>, <UL>, <VAR>

Sample HTML

```
<BODY>
<DL>
<DT>SGML
<DD>Standardized General Markup Language
<DT>HTML
<DD>Hypertext Markup Language
</DL>
```

<DIR>...</DIR>

The DIR (directory list) tags render a plain list for short items, such as filenames. The items in the list must be labeled with the <LI> tag.

Style Tip

Directory lists are best for short groups of items that need to be set away from the text but not bulleted or numbered.

Attributes

None.

Parent Tags

<BLOCKQUOTE>, <BODY>, <BUTTON>, <CENTER>, <DD>, <DIV>, <FIELDSET>, <FORM>, <IFRAME>, <LI>, <NOFRAMES>, <NOSCRIPT>, <OBJECT>, <TD>, <TH>

Content Tags

```
<LI>
```

Sample HTML

```
<BODY>
Grocery List:
<DIR>
<LI>Pizza
<LI>Ice Cream
<LI>Dr. Pepper
</DIR>
</BODY>
```

<DL>...</DL>

DL (definition list) tags are used to mark glossary terms and their associated definitions.

Style Tip

Definition lists are not limited to terms and definitions. Use this list type for items with associated descriptions, such as article titles and related information. The definition description, marked by the <DD> tag, appears one line down, indented to the right of the definition term, marked by the <DT> tag.

Attributes

COMPACT

Indicates a list should be tightly spaced to make it more compact.

Parent Tags

```
<BLOCKQUOTE>, <BODY>, <BUTTON>, <CENTER>, <DD>, <DIV>, <FIELDSET>,
<FORM>, <IFRAME>, <LI>, <NOFRAMES>, <NOSCRIPT>, <OBJECT>, <TD>, <TH>
```

Content Tags

```
<DT>, <DD>
```

Sample HTML

```
<BODY>
<DL>
<DT>SGML
<DD>Standardized General Markup Language
<DT>HTML
<DD>Hypertext Markup Language
</DL>
```

<DT>

The DT (definition term) tag marks the word actually being defined in a definition list.

Style Tip

Definition terms can be a single word or a string of words.

Attributes

None.

Parent Tags

```
<DL>
```

Content Tags

None.

Sample HTML

```
<BODY>
<DL>
<DT>SGML
<DD>Standardized General Markup Language
<DT>HTML
<DD>Hypertext Markup Language
</DL>
```

<LI>

The LI (list item) tag marks a list item in every type of list except the definition list.

Style Tip

Any element in a list, except a definition list, must be preceded by an LI tag. While list tags without list items render contained text as indented, that is invalid HTML syntax and should be avoided.

Attributes

TYPE=(DISC|SQUARE|CIRCLE) or (1|a|A|i|I)

When the <LI> element is used in an ordered list (<OL>), a number will appear before the list item. With the TYPE attribute, you can change the style of the number or letter that appears before the listed item. (See Table B.2.)

T A B L E   B . 2 : Numbering Systems: Both Roman and Arabic

Use This	To Do This
1	Label the listed items with standard numbers (1, 2, 3, etc.) This is the default.
a	Provide a lowercase letter as the label (a, b, c, etc.)
A	Provide an uppercase letter as the label (A, B, C, etc.)
i	Provide a lowercase Roman numeral as the label (i, ii, iii, iv, etc.)
I	Provide an uppercase Roman numeral as the label (I, II, III, IV, etc.)

In an unordered list (<UL>), you can choose what type of bullet is displayed. (See Table B.3.)

T A B L E   B . 3 : Types of Bullets

Use This	To Get This
DISC	A closed circular bullet
SQUARE	An open square bullet
CIRCLE	An open circular bullet

VALUE=number

Changes the counting order of the list.

Parent Tags

<DIR>, <MENU>, <OL>, <UL>

Content Tags

None.

Sample HTML

```
<BODY>
<OL>
<LI VALUE=2>List item 1, numbered 2
<LI>List item 2, numbered 3
<LI>List item 3, number 4
</OL>
</BODY>
```

<MENU>...</MENU>

The MENU tags are used for short lists of items or short paragraphs. It is necessary to use the <LI> tag within the menu list.

Style Tip

Menu lists and directory lists are interchangeable and are usually rendered the same by most major browsers.

Attributes

COMPACT

Indicates a list should be tightly spaced to make it more compact.

Parent Tags

<BLOCKQUOTE>, <BODY>, <BUTTON>, <CENTER>, <DD>, <DIV>, <FIELDSET>, <FORM>, <IFRAME>, <LI>, <NOFRAMES>, <NOSCRIPT>, <OBJECT>, <TD>, <TH>

Content Tags

<LI>

Sample HTML

```
<BODY>
For Dessert:
<MENU>
<LI>Chocolate cake
<LI>Ice cream
<LI>Cherry pie
</MENU>
</BODY>
```

<OL>...</OL>

The OL (ordered list) tags render a numbered list. Items in the list must be labeled with the <LI> tag.

Style Tip

Ordered list items always include a number before the item. The lists will always start with 1, and at this time there is no standard way to define the starting number as anything other than 1.

Attributes

TYPE= (1|a|A|i|I)

Changes the style of the number or letter that appears before the listed item. (See Table B.2.)

COMPACT

Indicates a list should be tightly spaced to make it more compact.

START="value"

Specifies where in the list to begin the numbering or lettering.

Parent Tags

```
<BLOCKQUOTE>, <BODY>, <BUTTON>, <CENTER>, <DD>, <DIV>, <FIELDSET>,
<FORM>, <IFRAME>, <LI>, <NOFRAMES>, <NOSCRIPT>, <OBJECT>, <TD>, <TH>
```

Content Tags

```
<LI>
```

Sample HTML

```
<BODY>
Things to do today:
<OL>
<LI>Wash the car
<LI>Grocery shopping
<LI>Clean house
</OL>
</BODY>
```

<UL>...</UL>

The UL (unordered list) tags render a bulleted list.

Style Tip

Bulleted lists set items away from the text and include a bullet before each element. Use this list type when items should be grouped where order or rank is unimportant. Internet Explorer and Netscape Navigator currently support the TYPE attribute to change how bullets appear in a list. This attribute is not standard nor is it backward compatible with earlier browsers.

Attributes

COMPACT

Indicates a list should be tightly spaced to make it more compact.

TYPE=(DISC|SQUARE|CIRCLE)

Specifies the type of bullet used in the list. (See Table B.3.)

Parent Tags

```
<BLOCKQUOTE>, <BODY>, <BUTTON>, <CENTER>, <DD>, <DIV>, <FIELDSET>,
<FORM>, <IFRAME>, <LI>, <NOFRAMES>, <NOSCRIPT>, <OBJECT>, <TD>, <TH>
```

Content Tags

```
<LI>
```

Sample HTML

```
<BODY>
Cars I have owned:
<UL>
<LI>Saturn SL1
<LI>Ford Contour
<LI>Ford Probe
</UL>
</BODY>
```

Table Tags

Table tags are used to create HTML tables and their constituent elements: captions, rows, individual cells, and column and row groups. Tables allow you to add more organization to text by separating page content into rows and columns. Tables are more versatile than regular HTML because they provide more precision when placing text and images, both in relation to the page and to each other. Tables can also add interesting horizontal elements to HTML pages.

<CAPTION>...</CAPTION>

The CAPTION tags are used to attach a caption either before or after a table.

Style Tip

CAPTION tags help identify a table and its contents for users, but should be brief and to the point, like HTML document titles. Any text-level markup may appear within CAPTION tags.

Attributes

ALIGN=(LEFT|RIGHT|TOP|BOTTOM)

The default alignment for a caption is centered. With this attribute you can set the alignment to the left, right, top, or bottom.

Parent Tags

```
<TABLE>
```

Content Tags

```
<A>, <ACRONYM>, <APPLET>, <B>, <BASEFONT>, <BDO>, <BIG>, <BR>, <BUTTON>,
<CITE>, <CODE>, <DFN>, <EM>, <FONT>, <I>, <IFRAME>, <IMG>, <INPUT>,
<KBD>, <LABEL>, <MAP>, <OBJECT>, <Q>, <S>, <SAMP>, <SCRIPT>, <SELECT>,
<SMALL>, <SPAN>, <STRIKE>, <STRONG>, <SUB>, <SUP>, <TEXTAREA>, <TT>,
<U>, <VAR>
```

Sample HTML

```
<BODY>
<TABLE WIDTH="75%" ALIGN=CENTER>
<CAPTION>
This is a sample table
</CAPTION>
... table data ...
</TABLE>
</BODY>
```

<COL>

The COL (column) tag is used to set the properties for a column or a set of columns within a column group.

Style Tip

While the COLGROUP (column group) tag sets the properties for an entire group of columns, the COL tag can be used within a column group to provide specific information about one or more of the columns within the group.

Attributes

ALIGN=(LEFT|RIGHT|CENTER|JUSTIFY|CHAR)

Indicates how the text within the column's cells should be horizontally aligned. The CHAR value indicates that the text should be aligned to a specific character, as defined by the CHAR attribute (described next).

CHAR="text"

Identifies the character that text should be aligned horizontally with if the value of ALIGN is CHAR.

CHAROFF="number"

Specifies how many pixels the rest of the text in a line should be offset from the character defined by the value of the CHAR attribute.

SPAN="number"
Identifies how many columns the column tag properties apply to.

VALIGN= TOP|MIDDLE|BOTTOM|BASELINE
Specifies how the text within the column's cells should be vertically aligned.

WIDTH="number"
Specifies how wide each column controlled by the column tag should be.

Parent Tags
```
<COLGROUP>, <TABLE>
```

Content Tags
None.

Sample HTML
```
<TABLE>
<COLGROUP>
  <COL ALIGN=CENTER>
  <COL ALIGN=LEFT>
<COLGROUP>
  <COL ALIGN=RIGHT>
<TBODY>
  <TR>
  <TD>This is the first column in the group and is centered.</TD>
  <TD>This is the second column in the group and is left-aligned.</TD>
  <TD>This column is in a new group and is right-aligned.</TD>
  </TR>
</TABLE>
```

<COLGROUP>

The COLGROUP (column group) tag is used to set the properties for a group of columns.

Style Tip

Use the COLGROUP tag to identify general properties for a large group of columns, and then include the COL tag to set specific properties for individual columns or smaller groups of columns within the large group.

Attributes

ALIGN=(LEFT|RIGHT|CENTER|JUSTIFY|CHAR)

Indicates how the text within the column's cells should be horizontally aligned. The CHAR value indicates that the text should be aligned to a specific character, as defined by the CHAR attribute (described next).

CHAR="text"

Identifies the character that text should be aligned with horizontally if the value of ALIGN is CHAR.

CHAROFF="number"

Specifies how many pixels the rest of the text in a line should be offset from the character defined by the value of the CHAR attribute.

SPAN="number"

Identifies the number of columns to which the column tag properties apply.

VALIGN= TOP|MIDDLE|BOTTOM|BASELINE

Specifies how text within the columns' cells should be aligned vertically.

WIDTH="number"

Specifies how wide each column within the column group should be.

Parent Tags

```
<TABLE>
```

Content Tags

```
<COL>
```

Sample HTML

```
<TABLE>
<COLGROUP ALIGN=CENTER>
<COLGROUP SPAN=4 ALIGN=RIGHT>
<TBODY>
  <TR>
  <TD>This column is in the first group and is centered.</TD>
  <TD>This column is in the second group and is right-aligned.</TD>
<TD>This column is in the second group and is right-aligned.</TD>
<TD>This column is in the second group and is right-aligned.</TD>
<TD>This column is in the second group and is right-aligned.</TD>
  </TR>
</TABLE>
```

<TABLE>...</TABLE>

The TABLE tags create the table to which the following rows and cells belong.

Style Tip

The precise rendering of table markup varies from browser to browser. Always view complex tables using different browsers to make sure your content isn't confused or altered when another browser displays it differently. Also, text-only browsers do not support tables, and may make your content inaccessible to those users who use them. Generally, text-only browsers present table information from left to right and top to bottom. Always check tables with non-graphical browsers.

Attributes

ALIGN=(LEFT|RIGHT|CENTER)

Assigns alignment to the table in relationship to the page. (See Table B.4.)

TABLE B.4: Options for Alignment

Use This	To Do This
LEFT	Align the table to the left. (This is the default alignment.)
RIGHT	Align the table to the right. If there is any available space, the text will wrap along the left of the table.
CENTER	Place the table in the middle of the window.

BGCOLOR=colorname *[Deprecated]*

Provides the color of the background that is either a hexadecimal, red-green-blue color value, or a predefined color name. (See Table B.1.)

BORDER=number

Sets the table border. The default border size is 0; any other number creates a border equal to the number in pixels.

CELLPADDING=number

Specifies the amount of space (measured in pixels) between the sides of a cell and the text or graphics within the cell.

CELLSPACING=number

Sets the amount of space (measured in pixels) between the exterior of the table and the cells inside the table. In addition, it also sets the space that is between the cells themselves.

COLS=number

Defines the number of columns in a table.

FRAME=(VOID|ABOVE|BELOW|HSIDES|LHS|RHS|VSIDES|BOX|BORDER)

Specifies which sides of the outer border of the table should be displayed. (See Table B.5.)

TABLE B.5: Options for Outside Borders

Use This	To Get This
VOID	No outside borders
ABOVE	A border on the top of the table
BELOW	A border on the bottom of the table
HSIDES	A border both on the top and bottom of the table
LHS	A border on the left side of the table
RHS	A border on the right side of the table
VSIDES	A border on both the left and right sides of the table
BOX	A complete border around all sides of the table
BORDER	A complete border around all sides of the table (This produces the same result as BOX.)

RULES=(NONE|GROUPS|ROWS|COLS|ALL)

Specifies which of the inner border lines of a table are displayed. (See Table B.6.)

TABLE B.6: Options for Inside Borders

Use This	To Get This
NONE	No interior borders
GROUPS	Horizontal borders between all table groups (THEAD, TBODY, TFOOT, and COLGROUP elements designate a group.)
ROWS	Horizontal borders between all table rows
COLS	Vertical borders between all table columns
ALL	Borders on all rows and columns

WIDTH=(pixels|"*n*%")
Determines the width of the table in pixels or as a percentage of the window. The *n* must end with the percent (%) sign and be contained within quotation marks to set a percentage.

Parent Tags
<BLOCKQUOTE>, <BODY>, <BUTTON>, <CENTER>, <DD>, <DIV>, <FIELDSET>, <FORM>, <IFRAME>, <LI>, <NOFRAMES>, <NOSCRIPT>, <OBJECT>, <TD>, <TH>

Content Tags
<CAPTION>, <COL>, <COLGROUP>, <TBODY>, <TFOOT>, <THEAD>

Sample HTML
```
<BODY>
<TABLE WIDTH="75%" ALIGN=CENTER>
... table data ...
</TABLE>
</BODY>
```

<TBODY> (...</TBODY>)

The TBODY (table body) tags are used to define the table body information and distinguish it from the rows of the table header or footer.

Style Tip
If the THEAD and TFOOT tags have not been used in a table, then the TBODY tag is optional. You can include more than one TBODY tag to create logical divisions within your document.

Attributes
None.

Parent Tags
<TABLE>

Content Tags
<TR>

Sample HTML

```
<BODY>
<TABLE WIDTH="75%" ALIGN=CENTER>
<CAPTION>
This is a sample table
</CAPTION>
<THEAD>
<TR> ... </TR>
<TBODY>
<TR> ... </TR>
</TABLE>
</BODY>
```

<TD>...</TD>

These TD (table cell) tags create individual cells within table rows.

Style Tip

As with TR (table row) tags, it is important to close each TD tag before beginning a new cell, or your table may not be displayed correctly. All browsers render empty cells a little differently, so test your table with a variety of browsers to see the different displays. Cell attributes and specifications override those previously defined by the row or table settings.

Attributes

ALIGN=(CENTER|LEFT|RIGHT)

Specifies the alignment. The default horizontal alignment of the text is centered.

AXIS="text"

Allows you to provide an abbreviated version of the cell's contents.

AXES="text"

Allows you to provide a list of keywords, separated by commas, that list a set of row and column headers related to the contents of the cell.

BGCOLOR=colorname *[Deprecated]*

Provides the color of the background that is either a hexadecimal, red-green-blue color value, or a predefined color name. (See Table B.1.)

CHAR="text"

Identifies the character that text should be aligned horizontally with if the value of ALIGN is CHAR.

CHAROFF="number"

Specifies how many pixels the rest of the text in a line should be offset from the character defined by the value of the CHAR attribute.

COLSPAN=number

Specifies how many columns the cell overlaps.

NOWRAP *[Deprecated]*

Shows that the contents of the cell are not to be wrapped; they will appear as a single line unless the <BR> tag is used.

ROWSPAN=number

Specifies how many rows the cell overlaps.

VALIGN=(TOP|MIDDLE|BOTTOM|BASELINE)

Designates the vertical alignment of text within a cell. The default text alignment is in the middle. (See Table B.7.)

T A B L E B . 7 : Options for Vertical Alignment in Tables

Use This	To Get This
TOP	Text aligned at the top of each cell
MIDDLE	Text aligned in the middle of each cell
BOTTOM	Text aligned at the bottom of each cell
BASELINE	Text in cells in adjoining rows aligned along a common baseline

WIDTH=number

Designates the width of the cell in pixels.

Parent Tags

<TR>

Content Tags

<A>, <ACRONYM>, <ADDRESS>, <APPLET>, <B>, <BASEFONT>, <BDO>, <BIG>, <BLOCKQUOTE>, <BR>, <BUTTON>, <CENTER>, <CITE>, <CODE>, <DFN>, <DIR>, <DIV>, <DL>, <EM>, <FIELDSET>, <FONT>, <FORM>, <H1>, <H2>, <H3>, <H4>, <H5>, <H6>, <HR>, <I>, <IFRAME>, <IMG>, <INPUT>, <ISINDEX>, <KBD>, <LABEL>, <MAP>, <MENU>, <NOFRAMES>, <NOSCRIPT>, <OBJECT>, <OL>, <P>, <PRE>, <Q>, <S>, <SAMP>, <SCRIPT>, <SELECT>, <SMALL>, <SPAN>, <STRIKE>, <STRONG>, <SUB>, <SUP>, <TABLE>, <TEXTAREA>, <TT>, <U>, <UL>, <VAR>

Sample HTML

```
<BODY>
<TABLE WIDTH="75%" ALIGN=CENTER>
<CAPTION>
This is a sample table
</CAPTION>
      <TR>
              <TH>Number</TH>
              <TH>Color</TH>
      </TR>
              <TD>One Fish</TD>
              <TD>Red Fish</TD>
      <TR>
              <TD>Two Fish</TD>
              <TD>Blue Fish</TD>
      </TR>
      <TR>
      </TR>
</TABLE>
</BODY>
```

<TFOOT>

The TFOOT (table footer) tag is used to define the table footer information and distinguish it from the rows of the table header or body text.

Style Tip

As with THEAD, you can only include one TFOOT section in any given table.

Attributes

None.

Parent Tags

<TABLE>

Content Tags

```
<TR>
```

Sample HTML

```
<BODY>
<TABLE WIDTH="75%" ALIGN=CENTER>
<CAPTION>
This is a sample table
</CAPTION>
<THEAD>
<TR> ... </TR>
<TBODY>
<TR> ... </TR>
<TFOOT>
<TR>... </TR>
</TABLE>
</BODY>
```

<TH>...</TH>

The TH (table head/column head) tags format column header information in a table.

Style Tip

Whereas a table caption provides information for an entire table, table row headers provide specific information related to data in each column. Use multiple table row headers within a single table to create logical divisions, and to group similar content.

Attributes

ALIGN=(CENTER|LEFT|RIGHT)

Specifies the alignment. The default horizontal alignment of the text is centered.

AXIS="text"

Allows you to provide an abbreviated version of the cell's contents.

AXES="text"

Allows you to provide a list of keywords, separated by commas, that list a set of row and column headers related to the contents of the cell.

BGCOLOR=colorname *[Deprecated]*

Provides the color of the background that is either a hexadecimal, red-green-blue color value, or a predefined color name. (See Table B.1.)

CHAR="text"

Identifies the character that text should be aligned horizontally with if the value of ALIGN is CHAR.

CHAROFF="number"

Specifies how many pixels the rest of the text in a line should be offset from the character defined by the value of the CHAR attribute.

COLSPAN=number

Specifies how many columns the row header overlaps.

NOWRAP *[Deprecated]*

Shows that the contents of the cell are not to be wrapped; they will appear as a single line unless the <BR> tag is used.

ROWSPAN=number

Specifies how many rows the row header overlaps.

VALIGN=(TOP|MIDDLE|BOTTOM|BASELINE)

Designates the vertical alignment of text within the header. The default text alignment is in the middle. (See Table B.7.)

WIDTH=number

Designates the width of the row header in pixels.

Parent Tags

<TR>

Content Tags

<A>, <ACRONYM>, <ADDRESS>, <APPLET>, <B>, <BASEFONT>, <BDO>, <BIG>, <BLOCKQUOTE>, <BR>, <BUTTON>, <CENTER>, <CITE>, <CODE>, <DFN>, <DIR>, <DIV>, <DL>, <EM>, <FIELDSET>, <FONT>, <FORM>, <H1>, <H2>, <H3>, <H4>, <H5>, <H6>, <HR>, <I>, <IFRAME>, <IMG>, <INPUT>, <ISINDEX>, <KBD>, <LABEL>, <MAP>, <MENU>, <NOFRAMES>, <NOSCRIPT>, <OBJECT>, <OL>, <P>, <PRE>, <Q>, <S>, <SAMP>, <SCRIPT>, <SELECT>, <SMALL>, <SPAN>, <STRIKE>, <STRONG>, <SUB>, <SUP>, <TABLE>, <TEXTAREA>, <TT>, <U>, <UL>, <VAR>

Sample HTML

```
<BODY>
<TABLE WIDTH="75%" ALIGN=CENTER>
<CAPTION>
This is a sample table
</CAPTION>
      <TR>
              <TH>Number</TH>
              <TH>Color</TH>
      </TR>
</TABLE>
</BODY>
```

<THEAD>...</THEAD>

The THEAD (table header) tags define the header of the table and distinguish it from the rows in the footer or the main body text.

Style Tip

If you choose to use these tags in your tables, only one table head is allowed.

Attributes

None.

Parent Tags

```
<TABLE>
```

Content Tags

```
<TR>
```

Sample HTML

```
<BODY>
<TABLE WIDTH="75%" ALIGN=CENTER>
<CAPTION>
This is a sample table
</CAPTION>
<THEAD>
<TR> ... </TR>
</TABLE>
</BODY>
```

<TR>...</TR>

The TR tags create a row in the table.

Style Tip

Table rows are the first component you will create when building tables. Rows are then divided into cells. It's important to close one table row before you begin another or the table may not display properly.

Attributes

ALIGN=(CENTER|LEFT|RIGHT)

Determines how the text within a row should be aligned horizontally. The default alignment is centered.

BGCOLOR=colorname *[Deprecated]*

Provides the color of the background for the row that is either a hexadecimal, red-green-blue color value, or a predefined color name. (See Table B.1.)

CHAR="text"

Identifies the character that text should be aligned horizontally with if the value of ALIGN is CHAR.

CHAROFF="number"

Specifies how many pixels the rest of the text in a line should be offset from the character defined by the value of the CHAR attribute.

VALIGN=(TOP|MIDDLE|BOTTOM|BASELINE)

Designates the vertical alignment of text within the row's cells. The default text alignment is MIDDLE. (See Table B.7.)

Parent Tags

<TBODY>, <TFOOT>, <THEAD>

Content Tags

<TD>, <TH>

Sample HTML

```
<BODY>
<TABLE WIDTH="75%" ALIGN=CENTER>
<CAPTION>
This is a sample table
</CAPTION>
      <TR>
              <TH>Number</TH>
              <TH>Color</TH>
      </TR>
      <TR>
      </TR>
      <TR>
      </TR>
</TABLE>
</BODY>
```

Link Tags

Link tags provide a mechanism in HTML to create links to other Web resources. Hyperlinks, those underlined, clickable links found in most Web pages, are the most common type of link. However, links can be made to style sheets, to previous and next pages within a document, and to a base URL to which all documents within a collection are tied. Links make the Web hyper and enable Web designers to provide resources outside of their own domains to users.

\<A\>...\</A\>

The A (anchor) tags provide the essential hypertext link capabilities within HTML. They are used to create links to other resources and to name specified locations within a document.

Style Tip

Use hyperlinks liberally throughout your HTML pages to create links to related resources and to information on your own site as well as other sites. For long documents, use anchors within the document to help users navigate. The TITLE attribute is particularly useful to give users a sneak peek at a linked resource.

Attributes

ACCESSKEY="text"
Identifies a character to be used to create a keyboard shortcut to activate the link.

CHARSET="text"
Specifies what character set the linked Web resource uses. The default is ISO-8859-1.

COORDS="X1, Y1, X2, Y2, etc."
Provides the coordinates that define the shapes of a hot spot within a client-side image map. See the SHAPE attribute for details.

HREF="URL"
URL is the uniform resource locator, which specifies the location of a resource that is typically another HTML file. In addition, it can also specify other types of Internet resources such as files, Telnet, e-mail, FTP, or Gopher services.

NAME="text"
Marks a specific place within an HTML document. FrontPage calls these *bookmarks*.

REL="text"
Indicates the relationship between the current document and the document it is linked to. Some common relations are REL="NEXT" to indicate that the link points to the next page in a sequence and REL="PREVIOUS" to indicate that the link points to the previous page in a sequence. REL="STYLESHEET" tells the browser that the linked document is a style sheet.

REV="text"
The opposite of the REL attribute. Defines the relationship between the linked document and the current document.

SHAPE=(RECT|CIRCLE|POLY|DEFAULT)
Specifies the shape of the region. (See Table B.8.)

TABLE B.8: Shapes That Can Be Used As Hot Spots in an Image Map

Use This	To Get This
RECT	A rectangle, which is defined by the coordinates of its top left corner and its bottom right corner. For example, <AREA SHAPE=rect COORDS="0,0,9,9"> defines a rectangle 10 by 10 pixels in size, starting in the top left corner of the image.
CIRCLE	A circle, which is defined by the coordinates of its center and radius. The coordinates of the circle's center are defined first, and then the radius, in pixels. For example, <AREA SHAPE=circle COORDS="10,10,5"> defines a circle with radius of five pixels at location (10,10) in the image.

TABLE B.8 CONTINUED: Shapes That Can Be Used As Hot Spots in an Image Map

Use This	To Get This
POLY	A polygon, which is built from a list of coordinates, all connected in the order listed, with the last coordinate pair connected to the first. The POLY value allows you to build arbitrary figures with multiple sides. For example, <AREA SHAPE=POLY COORDS="10,50,15,20,20,50"> would specify a triangle, with edge locations (10,50), (15,20), and (20,50).
DEFAULT	The default URL is defined for those areas on an image map that are not otherwise linked with an <AREA> specification. It should be used only once within each image map.

TABINDEX="number"

Specifies the link's place in the tabbing order.

TARGET="window"

Specifies that the link should be loaded into the targeted frame or window. Use this attribute when the targeted frame or window is different from the frame or window the current document resides in. The attribute can target a <FRAMESET> where a frame has been created and given a name using the <FRAME> element or an entire browser window. The targeted frame or window can be specified using the information shown in Table B.9.

TABLE B.9: Options for Specifying Whether a Linked Document Will Appear in a Frame or a New Window

What It's Called	What It Does
window name	Identifies the name of the specific frame or window the document should be opened in. The frame name must begin with an alphanumeric character to be valid. The following four special names are an exception to this rule and provide explicit directions for loading a linked page into a frame or window.
_blank	Creates a new, unnamed window and loads the document into it.
_parent	Loads the linked file into the parent frame or window of the current frame or window. If the link is located in a window without a parent, then this will behave the same as specifying _self.
_self	Loads the linked file in the same window as the document containing the link. A link that specifies this target behaves the same as a link that does not specify a target.
_top	Overrides and erases the entire frame configuration and loads the document into the full body of the current window.

Parent Tags

<ACRONYM>, <ADDRESS>, <APPLET>, <B>, <BDO>, <BIG>, <BLOCKQUOTE>, <BODY>, <CAPTION>, <CENTER>, <CITE>, <CODE>, <DD>, <DEL>, <DFN>, <DIV>, <DT>, <EM>, <FIELDSET>, <FONT>, <FORM>, <H1>, <H2>, <H3>, <H4>, <H5>, <H6>, <I>, <IFRAME>, <INS>, <KBD>, <LABEL>, <LEGEND>, <LI>, <NOFRAMES>, <NOSCRIPT>, <OBJECT>, <P>, <PRE>, <Q>, <S>, <SAMP>, <SMALL>, <SPAN>, <STRIKE>, <STRONG>, <SUB>, <SUP>, <TD>, <TH>, <TT>, <U>, <VAR>

Content Tags

<A>, <ACRONYM>, <APPLET>, <B>, <BASEFONT>, <BDO>, <BIG>, <BR>, <BUTTON>, <CITE>, <CODE>, <DFN>, <EM>, <FONT>, <I>, <IFRAME>, <IMG>, <INPUT>, <KBD>, <LABEL>, <MAP>, <OBJECT>, <Q>, <S>, <SAMP>, <SCRIPT>, <SELECT>, <SMALL>, <SPAN>, <STRIKE>, <STRONG>, <SUB>, <SUP>, <TEXTAREA>, <TT>, <U>, <VAR>

Sample HTML

```
<A HREF="http://www.mysite.com/">A hyperlink to my site. </A>
<A HREF="#body5">A hyperlink to body paragraph 5 in the current
document.</A>
Body text
More body text
Even more body text
Some more body text
<A NAME="body5"></A>Paragraph 5 of my body text
```

<BASE>

The BASE tag gives you an opportunity to define specific server and folder location information for the current document and others that are linked to it.

Style Tip

When you use relative addressing to link files that reside on the same server, a base URL provides the common file location information. Base URLs are not required but can be useful when managing large document collections.

Attributes

HREF="URL"
Defines the base URL.

TARGET="window"

Specifies that the link should be loaded into the targeted frame or window. Use this attribute when the targeted frame or window is different from the frame or window the current document resides in. The attribute can target a <FRAMESET> where a frame has been created and given a name using the <FRAME> element or an entire browser window. The targeted frame or window can be specified using the information shown in Table 9.

Parent Tags

<HEAD>

Content Tags

None.

Sample HTML

```
<BASE URL="http://www.mysite.com/webdocs/" TARGET=body>
```

<LINK>

The LINK tag provides the information that sets the relationship between the current document and other documents or URL resources.

Style Tip

The <LINK> tags are best used for linking to externally referenced style sheets and other documents. Large document collections benefit from the use of <LINK> tags because they establish relationships among related documents, making them easier to rename and move as necessary.

Attributes

HREF = "URL"

Works the same as the anchor tags (<A>...</A>). It supplies the address of the current link destination.

MEDIA=SCREEN|PRINT|PROJECTION|BRAILLE|SPEECH|ALL

Used to identify the presentation method the style sheet is best suited for. Screen is the most common presentation method and the default, but style sheets can also be created specifically for print, projection, Braille, speech, or all types of media.

REL="text"

Indicates the source end of a link and identifies the link's type. REL="STYLESHEET" tells browser that the linked document is a style sheet.

REV="text"

Defines the destination end of a link and its type.

TARGET="window"

Specifies that the link should be loaded into the targeted frame or window. Use this attribute when the targeted frame or window is different from the frame or window the current document resides in. The attribute can target a <FRAMESET> where a frame has been created and given a name using the <FRAME> element or an entire browser window. The targeted frame or window can be specified using the information shown in Table B.9.

TYPE="text"

Specifies the specific style sheet language used to create the style rules. The type for Cascading Style Sheets (CSS1), the most common style sheet language, is text/css.

Parent Tags

<HEAD>

Content Tags

None.

Sample HTML

```
<LINK HREF="style/css/mystyle.css/" TYPE=text/css>
```

Inclusion Tags

Inclusion tags are used to incorporate non-HTML objects into a document. Such objects may be images, applets, image maps, programming controls, or even other HTML documents.

<APPLET>...</APPLET>

The APPLET tags are used to incorporate Java applets into HTML documents.

Style Tip

Java applets can add interactivity and a few bells and whistles to your pages. Remember that users with older browsers, or those who have turned Java off in newer browsers, will not be able to see your Java content nor use any Java-based controls. Always include alternate access to Java-based information for these users.

Attributes

ALIGN="(LEFT|RIGHT|TOP|MIDDLE|BOTTOM)"

Defines the default horizontal alignment of the applet.

ALT="text"

If the applet cannot run, this alternate text will be displayed.

ARCHIVE="text"

A string of comma-delimited archive names that point to class files or other resources that are to be "preloaded."

CODE="URL"

Specifies the URL of a compiled subclass for an applet. The browser looks for the specific applet location within the server and file hierarchy defined in the CODEBASE attribute.

CODEBASE="URL"

Defines the server and folder information for all of the applets within an HTML document (similar to the BASE tag).

HEIGHT=number

Sets the height of the applet's window.

HSPACE=number

Controls the horizontal blank space that appears around the applet.

NAME="text"

Points to the name of the applet.

OBJECT="text"

Defines the resource name which contains the applet in a serialized version.

VSPACE=number

Controls vertical blank space that appears around the applet.

WIDTH=(number|"%")

Sets the width of the applet's window.

Parent Tags

<A>, <ACRONYM>, <ADDRESS>, <APPLET>, <B>, <BDO>, <BIG>, <BLOCKQUOTE>, <BODY>, <BUTTON>, <CAPTION>, <CENTER>, <CITE>, <CODE>, <DD>, <DEL>, <DFN>, <DIV>, <DT>, <EM>, <FIELDSET>, <FONT>, <FORM>, <H1>, <H2>, <H3>, <H4>, <H5>, <H6>, <I>, <IFRAME>, <INS>, <KBD>, <LABEL>, <LEGEND>, <LI>, <NOFRAMES>, <NOSCRIPT>, <OBJECT>, <P>, <PRE>, <Q>, <S>, <SAMP>, <SMALL>, <SPAN>, <STRIKE>, <STRONG>, <SUB>, <SUP>, <TD>, <TH>, <TT>, <U>, <VAR>

Content Tags

<A>, <ACRONYM>, <APPLET>, <B>, <BASEFONT>, <BDO>, <BIG>, <BR>, <BUTTON>, <CITE>, <CODE>, <DFN>, <EM>, <FONT>, <I>, <IFRAME>, <IMG>, <INPUT>, <KBD>, <LABEL>, <MAP>, <OBJECT>, <PARAM>, <Q>, <S>, <SAMP>, <SCRIPT>, <SELECT>, <SMALL>, <SPAN>, <STRIKE>, <STRONG>, <SUB>, <SUP>, <TEXTAREA>, <TT>, <U>, <VAR>

Sample HTML

```
<APPLET CODEBASE="http://www.mysite.com/extras/applets/"
CODE="applet1.class" HEIGHT=50 WIDTH=100> </APPLET>
```

<AREA>

Image map areas can be rectangles, circles, polygons, or single pixels. It is usually best to avoid linking URLs to single pixels because it's difficult for users to locate the exact spot within the image. Numerous mapping applications are available that provide coordinates for areas within an image. Most common graphics programs also have mechanisms to determine the coordinates of any specific area.

Style Tip

Use this to drive image-based selections with buttons or labeled graphics. Remember to provide text alternatives for those users who've turned graphics support off in their browsers. (People do this for faster loading of pages, or to avoid seeing ads, or because they are visually impaired and can't see the images anyway.)

 NOTE   Providing a phrase to describe each graphic makes your pages much friendlier to visually impaired visitors. Some Web browsers can even be configured to *speak* the text of a page, and they will speak out the phrase you've provided!

Attributes

ACCESSKEY="character"

Defines a hot-spot activation key, not case-sensitive.

ALT="text"

Furnishes an alternate string of text for text browsers to present the image map's URLs in a manner that is easier to read.

COORDS="X1, Y1, X2, Y2, etc."

Defines the coordinates of a shape within a clickable image. See the SHAPE coordinate for more information.

HREF="URL"

Links the hot spot on the image map to the appropriate Internet resource.

NOHREF

Indicates that the image area does not have an associated hyperlink.

SHAPE=(RECT|CIRCLE|POLY|DEFAULT)

Specifies the shape of the region. The possible region shapes are shown in Table B.8.

TABINDEX=number

Defines the order of tab navigation for each hot spot. The value can be a positive or negative integer.

TARGET="window"

Specifies that the link should be loaded into the targeted frame or window. Use this attribute when the targeted frame or window is different from the frame or window the current document resides in. The attribute can target a <FRAMESET> where a frame has been created and given a name using the <FRAME> element or an entire browser window. The targeted frame or window can be specified using the information shown in Table B.9.

Parent Tags

<MAP>

Content Tags

None.

Sample HTML

```
<BODY>
<IMG SRC="image.gif" HEIGHT=50 WIDTH=100 HSPACE=25 VSPACE=25
USEMAP="imagemap1" ALIGN=MIDDLE>
<MAP NAME="imagemap1">
<AREA SHAPE="RECT" COORDS= "0,0,25,50" HREF="home.html">
<AREA SHAPE="RECT" COORDS= "26,0,50,50" HREF="toc.html">
<AREA SHAPE="RECT" COORDS= "51,0,75,50" HREF="products.html">
<AREA SHAPE="RECT" COORDS= "76,0,100,50" HREF="contact.html">
</MAP>
</BODY>
```

<IMG>

The IMG (image) tag inserts an image into your document. The tag is a singleton and has many associated attributes you may use to control its placement.

Style Tip

Use images in your Web pages to add splashes of color as well as meaning to content. You should make your image files as small as possible, preferably 30K or less, and always remember to include descriptive alternative text for those users who surf with graphics turned off or with non-graphical browsers. It is important to remember that images are secondary to content and should play a supporting role in your pages, not take the lead.

Attributes

ALT="text"

Provides an alternative text string that describes the image. Users with non-graphical browsers or browsers with graphics turned off will see text in place of the image. Internet Explorer 3 and Navigator 4 also display this text when the user points at a graphic.

ALIGN=LEFT|RIGHT|TOP|MIDDLE|BOTTOM

Specifies the alignment of the image in relation to the surrounding text. (See Table B.10.)

TABLE B.10: Options for Aligning Images

Use This	To Get This
LEFT	An image aligned to the left margin with the text displayed in the space to its right
RIGHT	An image aligned to the right margin with the text displayed in the space to its left
TOP	The top of the image and the top of the text aligned with each other
MIDDLE	The middle of the image and the baseline of the surrounding text aligned with each other
BOTTOM	The bottom of the image and the baseline of the surrounding text aligned with each other

BORDER=number

Indicates what size the border around the image should be. If the image is a hyperlink, the border will rendered in the designated hyperlink color. If the image is not a hyperlink, the border is transparent (invisible).

HEIGHT=pixels

Used with WIDTH=, it specifies the image's height. If the image has different dimensions than those specified using the HEIGHT and WIDTH attributes, the image will be sized accordingly.

HSPACE=number

Used with VSPACE=, the horizontal space attribute assigns the blank space or margins that are created to the left and right of the image.

ISMAP

Indicates that the image is a server-side clickable map and has an associated CGI script for translating the image regions into Web resource addresses.

SRC="URL"

Specifies the location of the file you wish to incorporate into your Web page. This is a mandatory attribute.

USEMAP=map-name

Marks the image as a client-side image map and references the inline map information defined with the <MAP> tag that will translate the image areas into Web resource addresses.

VSPACE=number

Used with HSPACE=, the vertical space attribute assigns the blank space or margins that are displayed at the top and bottom of the image.

WIDTH=pixels

Used with HEIGHT=, it specifies the image's width. If the image has different dimensions than those specified using the HEIGHT and WIDTH attributes, the image will be sized accordingly.

Parent Tags

<A>, <ACRONYM>, <ADDRESS>, <APPLET>, <B>, <BDO>, <BIG>, <BLOCKQUOTE>, <BODY>, <BUTTON>, <CAPTION>, <CENTER>, <CITE>, <CODE>, <DD>, <DEL>, <DFN>, <DIV>, <DT>, <EM>, <FIELDSET>, <FONT>, <FORM>, <H1>, <H2>, <H3>, <H4>, <H5>, <H6>, <I>, <IFRAME>, <INS>, <KBD>, <LABEL>, <LEGEND>, <LI>, <NOFRAMES>, <NOSCRIPT>, <OBJECT>, <P>, <Q>, <S>, <SAMP>, <SMALL>, <SPAN>, <STRIKE>, <STRONG>, <SUB>, <SUP>, <TD>, <TH>, <TT>, <U>, <VAR>

Content Tags

None.

Sample HTML

```
<BODY>
<IMG SRC="image.gif" HEIGHT=50 WIDTH=100 HSPACE=25 VSPACE=25
USEMAP="imagemap1" ALIGN=MIDDLE>
</BODY>
```

<MAP>...</MAP>

The MAP tags work in conjunction with an image designated as a client-side image map to translate the image regions into associated URLs.

Style Tip

Client-side image maps save time and server resources because all map information resides within the HTML document itself. The client does not have to send a request to a CGI script stored on a server to get the URL associated with a specific region. You can include more than one map file per page, as long as each one has a unique identifier so it can be referenced by name. Users who view without images or with non-graphical browsers will not be able to see image maps at all. It's important to supply alternative navigation aids when using image maps.

Attribute

NAME="text"

Names the MAP so it can be referred to at a later time by the USEMAP tag.

Parent Tags

<A>, <ACRONYM>, <ADDRESS>, <APPLET>, <B>, <BDO>, <BIG>, <BLOCKQUOTE>, <BODY>, <BUTTON>, <CAPTION>, <CENTER>, <CITE>, <CODE>, <DD>, <DEL>, <DFN>, <DIV>, <DT>, <EM>, <FIELDSET>, <FONT>, <FORM>, <H1>, <H2>, <H3>, <H4>, <H5>, <H6>, <I>, <IFRAME>, <INS>, <KBD>, <LABEL>, <LEGEND>, <LI>, <NOFRAMES>, <NOSCRIPT>, <OBJECT>, <P>, <PRE>, <Q>, <S>, <SAMP>, <SMALL>, <SPAN>, <STRIKE>, <STRONG>, <SUB>, <SUP>, <TD>, <TH>, <TT>, <U>, <VAR>

Content Tags

<AREA>

Sample HTML

```
<BODY>
<IMG SRC="image.gif" HEIGHT=50 WIDTH=100 HSPACE=25 VSPACE=25
USEMAP="imagemap1" ALIGN=MIDDLE>
<MAP NAME="imagemap1">
... Map information ...
</MAP>
</BODY>
```

<OBJECT>...</OBJECT>

The OBJECT tags insert a non-HTTP object, such as an audio or video file, into an HTML document.

Style Tip

The OBJECT tags allow you to incorporate audio, video, and other multimedia files into your HTML pages. This allows you to go beyond plain text and graphics to make your pages more interactive and exciting. As with Java applets, some older browsers do not support this tag and their users will not be able to see any content you include in an embedded non-HTTP object. Always provide an alternative way for users to get at any information you present in this way.

Attributes

ALIGN=(BASELINE|CENTER|LEFT|MIDDLE|RIGHT|TEXTBOTTOM|TEXTMIDDLE| TEXTTOP)

Sets the alignment of the object. The ALIGN value can be one of those shown in Table B.11.

T A B L E   B . 1 1 : Options for Aligning Objects

Use This	To Get This
BASELINE	The bottom of the object aligned with the baseline of the surrounding text
CENTER	The object centered between the left and right margins, with any following text beginning on the next line after the object
LEFT	The object aligned with the left margin, with any following text wrapped along the right side of the object
MIDDLE	The middle of the object aligned with the baseline of surrounding text
RIGHT	The object aligned with the right margin, with any following text wrapped along the left side of the object
TEXTBOTTOM	The bottom of the object aligned with the bottom of surrounding text
TEXTMIDDLE	The middle of the object aligned with the midpoint between the baseline and the x-height of the surrounding text
TEXTTOP	The top of the object aligned with the top of surrounding text

BORDER=number

Specifies the width of the border in pixels.

CLASSID="URL"

Defines (with the associated URL) how the object should be implemented. The actual form the URL takes is based entirely on the object's type.

CODEBASE="URL"

Defines the server and folder information for all of the objects within an HTML document (similar to the BASE tag).

CODETYPE=codetype

Designates the Internet media type for code.

DATA="URL"

Defines the URL of the object's data source. The actual syntax of the URL is determined by the object's type.

DECLARE

Used to load an object without actually activating it. Use this attribute to reference and activate an object later in the page.

HEIGHT=number

Specifies the proposed height for the object in pixels. Some objects have the capability to violate this parameter.

HSPACE=n

Controls the horizontal blank space that appears around the applet.

NAME="URL"

Gives the object a name so it can be referenced by other objects and forms later on in the document.

SHAPES

Indicates to the browser that the object is an image, has been divided into shaped regions, and is being used for an image map.

STANDBY=message

Provides a message that will show while the object is loading.

TYPE=type

Provides the object's Internet media type.

USEMAP="URL"

Specifies the image map file that will translate the clickable regions on an image map into the addresses of Web resources.

VSPACE=number

Controls the vertical blank space that appears around the applet.

WIDTH=number

Specifies the proposed width for the object in pixels. Some objects have the capability to violate this parameter.

Parent Tags

<A>, <ACRONYM>, <ADDRESS>, <APPLET>, <B>, <BDO>, <BIG>, <BLOCKQUOTE>, <BODY>, <BUTTON>, <CAPTION>, <CENTER>, <CITE>, <CODE>, <DD>, <DEL>, <DFN>, <DIV>, <DT>, <EM>, <FIELDSET>, <FONT>, <FORM>, <H1>, <H2>, <H3>, <H4>, <H5>, <H6>, <I>, <IFRAME>, <INS>, <KBD>, <LABEL>, <LEGEND>, <LI>, <NOFRAMES>, <NOSCRIPT>, <OBJECT>, <P>, <PRE>, <Q>, <S>, <SAMP>, <SMALL>, <SPAN>, <STRIKE>, <STRONG>, <SUB>, <SUP>, <TD>, <TH>, <TT>, <U>, <VAR>

Content Tags

<A>, <ACRONYM>, <ADDRESS>, <APPLET>, <B>, <BASEFONT>, <BDO>, <BIG>, <BLOCKQUOTE>, <BR>, <BUTTON>, <CENTER>, <CITE>, <CODE>, <DFN>, <DIR>, <DIV>, <DL>, <EM>, <FIELDSET>, <FONT>, <FORM>, <H1>, <H2>, <H3>, <H4>, <H5>, <H6>, <HR>, <I>, <IFRAME>, <IMG>, <INPUT>, <ISINDEX>, <KBD>, <LABEL>, <MAP>, <MENU>, <NOFRAMES>, <NOSCRIPT>, <OBJECT>, <OL>, <P>, <PARAM>, <PRE>, <Q>, <S>, <SAMP>, <SCRIPT>, <SELECT>, <SMALL>, <SPAN>, <STRIKE>, <STRONG>, <SUB>, <SUP>, <TABLE>, <TEXTAREA>, <TT>, <U>, <UL>, <VAR>

Sample HTML

```
<OBJECT CODEBASE="http://www.mysite.com/objects/audio/" TYPE=Audio/.avi
DATA="sound1.avi" STANDBY="Thank you for your patience while the audio
file loads.">
```

<PARAM>

This tag provides page-specific parameters for applets and non-HTTP objects such as scripts.

Style Tip

Because they are stored separately from HTML pages, a single Java applet and objects can be used by many different pages. Each use of the applet or object may be a little different, so the PARAM tag allows you to provide page-specific variables for the applet to use when it is called and run from the page. Reusing applets can save you time and programming costs.

Attributes

NAME="text"

Specifies the name of the parameter.

VALUE=number|"text"

Assigns a value to the named parameter. The value supplied here is not altered before it is passed to the applet unless it contains alphanumeric characters that must be replaced with character equivalents.

VALUETYPE=(DATA|REF|OBJECT)

Specifies how the value is interpreted. The type can be one of those shown in Table B.12.

TABLE B.12: Options for Specifying the Type of Data

Use This	When
DATA	The value is data, which is the default value type.
REF	The value is a URL.
OBJECT	The value is the URL of an object that is in the same document.

TYPE=type

Specifies the Internet Media Type [MIMETYPE]. See `ftp://ftp.isi.edu/in-notes/iana/assignments/media-types/`.

Parent Tags

`<APPLET>`, `<OBJECT>`

Content Tags

None.

Sample HTML

```
<APPLET CODEBASE="http://www.mysite.com/extras/applets/"
CODE="applet1.class" HEIGHT=50 WIDTH=100>
<PARAM NAME="booktitle" VALUE="frontpage">
<PARAM NAME= "publisher" VALUE="sybex">
</APPLET>
```

Style Sheets

Style sheets do not contain HTML tags but rather create style rules to modify the way HTML tags appear. Many deprecated HTML tags should be replaced with style sheet properties and values to give Web designers more control over their Web pages. But there is one HTML tag pair associated with style sheets—namely, the STYLE tags. In this section, we include standard tag information for the STYLE tags, and provide a complete rundown on all style sheet property families, their individual properties, and the values they take.

<STYLE>...</STYLE>

Use STYLE tags to include style sheet rules within the Web pages they affect.

Style Tip

Because style sheets are now part of the HTML specification, it's important to use them to replace deprecated STYLE tags.

Attributes

MEDIA= SCREEN|PRINT|PROJECTION|BRAILLE|SPEECH|ALL

Identifies what presentation method the style sheet is suited to support. Screen is the most common presentation method, and the default, but style sheets can be created specifically for print, projection, Braille, speech, or all types of media.

TYPE="text"

Specifies a specific style sheet language used to create the style rules. The type for Cascading Style Sheets (CSS1), the most common style sheet language, is `text/css`.

Parent Tags

```
<HEAD>
```

Content Tags

None.

Sample HTML

```
<HEAD>
<TITLE>Company Homepage</TITLE>
<STYLE>
BODY {background-color: navy;}
H1 {font: 24pt Verdana bold}
P {font: 12 Arial;
   text-align: right;
   }
</STYLE>
</HEAD>
```

Box Properties

The box properties are used with a box-model method of page layout to specify margin, border, height and width, and white space information for HTML elements. Use box properties with text and image "boxes" to strictly control their placement in relation to each other and the page.

Style Tip

Always remember that style sheets are not backward compatible with older versions of HTML and older browsers. While the text affected by style sheets will still be displayed by the browser, your formatting will not apply. Since box properties control the margin and placement characteristics of text and image boxes, always check your pages using older browsers to insure that your content remains readable.

Properties and Values

 NOTE

Style sheet tags, such as these, define layout in style sheets (see Chapter 13). They are unlike other tags in that they are not surrounded by angle brackets, they usually include hyphenated words, and they are always followed by a colon. Convention has it that they are shown in lowercase, again unlike standard HTML tags, which are usually shown in uppercase.

margin-top: <length>|<percentage>|auto

Defines an element's top margin. (See Table B.13.)

TABLE B.13: Units of Measurement Recognized in the Use of Style Sheets

Units	What It Means
No units specified	The current font size
Em	The width of the letter m in the current font
Ex	The height of the letter x in the current font

margin-bottom: <length>|<percentage>|auto

Defines an element's bottom margin. (See Table B.13.)

margin-left: <length>|<percentage>|auto

Defines an element's left margin. (See Table B.13.)

margin-right: <length>|<percentage>|auto

Defines an element's right margin. (See Table B.13.)

margin: [<length>|<percentage>|auto]

Defines all of the margins for an element. (See Table B.13.)

padding-top: ‹length›|‹percentage›

Specifies the amount of white space that should be included between the top border of an element and its contents. (See Table B.13.)

padding-bottom: ‹length›|‹percentage›

Specifies the amount of white space that should be included between the bottom border of an element and its contents. (See Table B.13.)

padding-left: ‹length›|‹percentage›

Specifies the amount of white space that should be included between the left border of an element and its contents. (See Table B.13.)

padding-right: ‹length›|‹percentage›

Specifies the amount of white space that should be included between the right border of an element and its contents. (See Table B.13.)

padding: [‹length›|‹percentage›|auto]

Specifies the padding for all sides of an element. (See Table B.13.)

border-top-width: ‹length›|thin|medium|thick

Defines the thickness of an element's top border. (See Table B.13.)

border-bottom-width: ‹length›|thin|medium|thick

Defines the thickness of an element's bottom border. (See Table B.13.)

border-right-width: ‹length›|thin|medium|thick

Defines the thickness of an element's right border. (See Table B.13.)

border-left-width: ‹length›|thin|medium|thick

Defines the thickness of an element's top border. (See Table B.13.)

border-right-width: ‹length›|thin|medium|thick

Specifies the thickness of an element's left border. (See Table B.13.)

border-width: [‹length›|thin|medium|thick]

Specifies the thickness of an element's borders. (See Table B.13.)

border-color: ‹color/#RRGGBB›

Specifies the color of an element's borders. (See Table B.1.)

border-style: none|dotted|dashed|solid|double|groove|ridge|inset|outset

Specifies the style of an element's borders.

border-top: <border-width>|<border-style>|<color>

Specifies the width, style, and color (see Table B.1) of an element's top border.

border-bottom: <border-width>|<border-style>|<color>

Specifies the width, style, and color (see Table B.1) of an element's bottom border.

border-left: <border-width>|<border-style>|<color>

Specifies the width, style, and color (see Table B.1) of an element's left border.

border-right: <border-width>|<border-style>|<color>

Specifies the width, style, and color (see Table B.1) of an element's right border.

border: <border-width>|<border-style>|<color>

Specifies the width, style, and color (see Table B.1) of an element's borders.

width: <length>|<percentage>|auto

Specifies the width of an element. (See Table B.13.)

height: <length>|<percentage>|auto

Specifies the height of an element. (See Table B.13.)

clear: none|left|right|both

Indicates whether or not other elements may be wrapped around the element as well as to which side.

float: left|right|none|both

Defines what direction text and other elements should be wrapped around an element.

Sample HTML

```
<STYLE>
P.body {margin: .75in;
        padding: 20%;
        border-width: thin;
        border-style: dashed;
        color: navy;
        }
</STYLE>
```

Classification Properties

The classification properties provide specifics about the display of white space, list numbers, and list bullets.

Style Tip

Always be sure to include alternate text, such as "*", when substituting an image for a list marker. This allows those users with text-only browsers or images turned off to still see a marker of some type.

Properties and Values

display: block|inline|list-item|none

Defines how an element should be displayed. (See Table B.14.)

TABLE B.14: Options for the Appearance of Elements

Use This	To Do This
block	Create a line break and space both before and after the element
inline	Remove all line breaks
list-item	Include a bullet with the item without using list markup
none	Disable any display already defined for the item

white-space: normal|pre|nowrap

Defines how an element's white space should be displayed. (See Table B.15.)

TABLE B.15: Options for the Appearance of White Space

Use This	To Do This
normal	Use the browser's standard display
pre	Interpret every space and hard return literally (like the PRE tag does)
nowrap	Prevent lines from being broken until a tag is inserted

list-style-type: disc|circle|square|decimal|lower-roman|upper-roman|lower-alpha|upper-alpha|none

Identifies the type of bullet to be used with list items.

list-style-image: URL

Defines the URL for a graphic to be inserted instead of a standard bullet in a list.

list-style-position: inside|outside

Identifies how a list marker, such as a bullet, image, or number, is placed relative to the text in the list. (See Table B.16.)

TABLE B.16: Options for the Location of List Markers

Use This	To Do This
inside	Wrap text underneath the marker
outside	Indent all lines of text to the right of the marker

list-style: <list-style-type>|<list-style-position>|<list-style-image>

Specifies the style, position, and image source of a list's markers.

Sample HTML

```
<STYLE>
P.list {display: list-item;
        white-space: normal;
        list-style: url(bullet.gif) inside;
        }
</STYLE>
```

Font Properties

The font properties are used to specify information specific to the font used to display text, such as face, color, and size.

Style Tip

Be careful when using a wide variety of font sizes as they may make your pages difficult to read.

Properties and Values

font-family: <family-name>|<generic family>

Identifies the specific font face that should be applied to the text display. Some examples of family names include Times, Helvetica, and Arial. The generic families are not specific font faces, but rather describe the type of font, i.e. serif, sans-serif, cursive, fantasy, or monospaced.

font-size: [xx-small|x-small|small|medium|large|x-large|xx-large]|\<length\>|\<percentage\>|[larger | smaller|\<relative-size\>]

Specifies the font size. (See Table B.13.)

font-style: normal|italic|oblique

Defines the style in which a font should be displayed.

font-variant: normal|small-caps

Identifies a font variant.

font-weight: normal|bold|100|200|300|400|500|600|700|800|900|lighter|bolder

Defines the thickness of the text. 400 is normal text while 700 is boldface text.

line-height: normal|\<number\>|\<length\>|\<percentage\>

Defines the amount of space between lines of text. (See Table B.13.)

font: \<font-weight\>|\<font-style\>|\<font-variant\>|\<font-size\>|\<line-height\>|\<font-family\>

Combines all the modifiable aspects of text into one property.

Sample HTML

```
<STYLE>
P.byline {font-family: Helvetica sans-serif;
          font-size: large;
          font-weight: bold;
          font-variant: small-caps;
          line-height: 35%;
          }
</STYLE>
```

Text Properties

Text properties provide information about how text should be rendered, including color, spacing, case, decoration, and alignment specifics.

Style Tip

Be careful when using a variety of text colors, because they can make your pages hard to read.

Properties and Values

color: <colorname|#RRGGBB>

Defines the text color. (See Table B.1.)

text-align: left|right|center|justify

Defines the alignment of the text.

text-indent: <length>|<percentage>

Specifies an indentation for the text. (See Table B.13.)

word-spacing: normal|<length>

Defines the amount of space that should be included between words. (See Table B.13.)

letter-spacing: normal|<length>

Defines the amount of space that should be included between letters. (See Table B.13.)

text-transform: capitalize|uppercase|lowercase|none

Defines how the enclosed text should be displayed regardless of how the text is typed.

text-decoration: none|underline|overline|line-through|blink

Specifies a decoration for the text.

vertical-align: base-line|sub|super|top|text-top|middle|bottom|text-bottom|<percentage>

Defines the text's vertical alignment.

Sample HTML

```
<STYLE>
P.article {color: navy:
        letter-spacing: 4px;
        word-spacing: 12px;
        text-transform: none;
        text-align: justify;
        }
</STYLE>
```

Background Properties

Use background properties to include backgrounds, and to define the placement and scrolling of background images.

Style Tip

Use different backgrounds to separate groups of text. You can also use the vertical or horizontal alignment properties to create a frame or color border for an entire page or a few sections of a page.

Properties and Values

background-color: transparent|<colorname>

Specifies the background color for an element. If the value is transparent, the background color of the element's parent will show through. (See Table B.1.)

background-image: none|<url>

Identifies the location of a background image using this notation: url(image.gif).

background-repeat: repeat|repeat-x|repeat-y|no-repeat

Defines how a background should be tiled. (See Table B.17.)

T A B L E   B . 1 7 : Options for the Appearance of Background Images

Use This	To Do This
repeat	Tile the image in the standard way
repeat-x	Repeat the image in a single line horizontally
repeat-y	Repeat the image in a single line vertically
no-repeat	Include the image without repeating it

background-attachment: scroll|fixed

Specifies whether a background image should scroll with its element or remain fixed on the screen.

background-position: <percentage>|<length>|top|center|bottom

Identifies the position of an element relative to both its element and the browser window. (See Table B.13.)

Sample HTML

```
<STYLE>
P.body1 {background-image: url(topborder.gif);
        background-repeat: repeat-x;
        background-attachment: fixed;
        }
</STYLE>
```

Presentation Tags

Presentation tags govern how text is displayed within a browser, but without the content or contextual implications that come with text tags. Hard rules are also included with presentation tags to provide a graphical division within an HTML page without actually using an inline image that can take time to download. Half of these presentation tags have been deprecated in favor of style sheets.

<B>...</B>

The boldface tags render the enclosed text in boldface type.

Style Tip

Boldface adds emphasis to words and makes them stand out from the surrounding text.

Attributes

None.

Parent Tags

```
<A>, <ACRONYM>, <ADDRESS>, <APPLET>, <B>, <BDO>, <BIG>, <BLOCKQUOTE>,
<BODY>, <BUTTON>, <CAPTION>, <CENTER>, <CITE>, <CODE>, <DD>, <DEL>,
<DFN>, <DIV>, <DT>, <EM>, <FIELDSET>, <FONT>, <FORM>, <H1>, <H2>, <H3>,
<H4>, <H5>, <H6>, <I>, <IFRAME>, <INS>, <KBD>, <LABEL>, <LEGEND>, <LI>,
<NOFRAMES>, <NOSCRIPT>, <OBJECT>, <P>, <PRE>, <Q>, <S>, <SAMP>,
<SMALL>, <SPAN>, <STRIKE>, <STRONG>, <SUB>, <SUP>, <TD>, <TH>, <TT>,
<U>, <VAR>
```

Content Tags

```
<A>, <ACRONYM>, <APPLET>, <B>, <BASEFONT>, <BDO>, <BIG>, <BR>, <BUTTON>,
<CITE>, <CODE>, <DFN>, <EM>, <FONT>, <I>, <IFRAME>, <IMG>, <INPUT>,
<KBD>, <LABEL>, <MAP>, <OBJECT>, <Q>, <S>, <SAMP>, <SCRIPT>, <SELECT>,
<SMALL>, <SPAN>, <STRIKE>, <STRONG>, <SUB>, <SUP>, <TEXTAREA>, <TT>,
<U>, <VAR>
```

Sample HTML

```
I bet you're <B>really</B> tired of staring at HTML tags.
```

<BASEFONT>

*[Deprecated]*The BASEFONT tag sets the default font for any unformatted text.

Style Tip

Use BASEFONT to establish font style, including size and color, for the regular, unformatted text on a page. Users may choose to override or ignore font settings you specify in favor of their own—don't count on such settings to provide total font control.

Attributes

COLOR=colorname *[Deprecated]*
Assigns a color to the base font. (See Table B.1.)

NAME=name *[Deprecated]*
Allows you to give a name to your base font style.

SIZE="number" *[Deprecated]*
Defines the size of the base font using a number between 1 and 7. The default base font size is 3 and the largest is 7. The relative font size settings are determined according to this value all the way through the document.

Parent Tags

```
<A>, <ACRONYM>, <ADDRESS>, <APPLET>, <B>, <BDO>, <BIG>, <BLOCKQUOTE>,
<BODY>, <BUTTON>, <CAPTION>, <CENTER>, <CITE>, <CODE>, <DD>, <DEL>,
<DFN>, <DIV>, <DT>, <EM>, <FIELDSET>, <FONT>, <FORM>, <H1>, <H2>, <H3>,
<H4>, <H5>, <H6>, <I>, <IFRAME>, <INS>, <KBD>, <LABEL>, <LEGEND>, <LI>,
<NOFRAMES>, <NOSCRIPT>, <OBJECT>, <P>, <PRE>, <Q>, <S>, <SAMP>,
<SMALL>, <SPAN>, <STRIKE>, <STRONG>, <SUB>, <SUP>, <TD>, <TH>, <TT>,
<U>, <VAR>
```

Content Tags

None.

Sample HTML

```
<HEAD>
<BASEFONT SIZE=4 COLOR="navy">
</HEAD>
```

<BIG>...</BIG>

The BIG tags render the enclosed text one size bigger than the standard type size.

Style Tip

While many browsers support nesting <BIG> tags to increase text sizes correspondingly, this is not part of the actual HTML specification. Use <FONT SIZE=+*n*> where *n* is a number between 1 and 7, in place of the <BIG> tag.

Attributes

None.

Parent Tags

<A>, <ACRONYM>, <ADDRESS>, <APPLET>, <B>, <BDO>, <BIG>, <BLOCKQUOTE>, <BODY>, <BUTTON>, <CAPTION>, <CENTER>, <CITE>, <CODE>, <DD>, <DEL>, <DFN>, <DIV>, <DT>, <EM>, <FIELDSET>, <FONT>, <FORM>, <H1>, <H2>, <H3>, <H4>, <H5>, <H6>, <I>, <IFRAME>, <INS>, <KBD>, <LABEL>, <LEGEND>, <LI>, <NOFRAMES>, <NOSCRIPT>, <OBJECT>, <P>, <Q>, <S>, <SAMP>, <SMALL>, <SPAN>, <STRIKE>, <STRONG>, <SUB>, <SUP>, <TD>, <TH>, <TT>, <U>, <VAR>

Content Tags

<A>, <ACRONYM>, <APPLET>, <B>, <BASEFONT>, <BDO>, <BIG>, <BR>, <BUTTON>, <CITE>, <CODE>, <DFN>, <EM>, <FONT>, <I>, <IFRAME>, <IMG>, <INPUT>, <KBD>, <LABEL>, <MAP>, <OBJECT>, <Q>, <S>, <SAMP>, <SCRIPT>, <SELECT>, <SMALL>, <SPAN>, <STRIKE>, <STRONG>, <SUB>, <SUP>, <TEXTAREA>, <TT>, <U>, <VAR>

Sample HTML

```
I <BIG>know</BIG> I am.
```

\<CENTER>...\</CENTER>

[Deprecated] The CENTER tags center the text horizontally across the display window.

Style Tip

Centered text is especially nice for document and section titles because it sets them off from the remainder of the text that is usually left or double justified. Used centered text sparingly as it can be hard to read in large quantities.

Attributes

None.

Parent Tags

\<BLOCKQUOTE>, \<BODY>, \<BUTTON>, \<CENTER>, \<DD>, \<DIV>, \<FIELDSET>, \<FORM>, \<IFRAME>, \<LI>, \<NOFRAMES>, \<NOSCRIPT>, \<OBJECT>, \<TD>, \<TH>

Content Tags

\<A>, \<ACRONYM>, \<ADDRESS>, \<APPLET>, \<B>, \<BASEFONT>, \<BDO>, \<BIG>, \<BLOCKQUOTE>, \
, \<BUTTON>, \<CENTER>, \<CITE>, \<CODE>, \<DFN>, \<DIR>, \<DIV>, \<DL>, \<EM>, \<FIELDSET>, \<FONT>, \<FORM>, \<H1>, \<H2>, \<H3>, \<H4>, \<H5>, \<H6>, \<HR>, \<I>, \<IFRAME>, \<IMG>, \<INPUT>, \<ISINDEX>, \<KBD>, \<LABEL>, \<MAP>, \<MENU>, \<NOFRAMES>, \<NOSCRIPT>, \<OBJECT>, \<OL>, \<P>, \<PRE>, \<Q>, \<S>, \<SAMP>, \<SCRIPT>, \<SELECT>, \<SMALL>, \<SPAN>, \<STRIKE>, \<STRONG>, \<SUB>, \<SUP>, \<TABLE>, \<TEXTAREA>, \<TT>, \<U>, \<UL>, \<VAR>

Sample HTML

```
<BODY>
<CENTER>
This is my title. It is centered.
</CENTER>
This is my body. It is not centered.
</BODY>
```

\<FONT>...\</FONT>

[Deprecated] The font tags allow you to designate the font, size, and color of the text within the tags.

Style Tip

While BASEFONT sets font size and color for an entire document, the FONT tag applies formatting only to text contained within the FONT tags. You can draw user attention to selected text by changing its size, color, or face. As with BASEFONT, keep in mind that this is a non-standard tag and can be ignored by users. Also, be careful to choose sensible font combinations. No matter how useful or valuable your content is, bright yellow text on a white background is difficult to read and may cause users to leave your pages before they read a word.

Attributes

SIZE="number" *[Deprecated]*

Allows you to set font size between 1 and 7 where 7 is largest. If you put a plus or a minus sign before a number it gives you a font that much bigger or smaller than the current size.

FACE="name [,name2[,name3]]" *[Deprecated]*

Specifies the font in which the text should be displayed. If you list several font face names separated by commas, the browser will try each one in turn if the first font is not available, until it finds one it can use. If none of the fonts you have specified is available, a default font is used.

COLOR="(#RRGGBB|colorname)" *[Deprecated]*

Sets the font color. (See Table B.1.)

Parent Tags

<A>, <ACRONYM>, <ADDRESS>, <APPLET>, <B>, <BDO>, <BIG>, <BLOCKQUOTE>, <BODY>, <BUTTON>, <CAPTION>, <CENTER>, <CITE>, <CODE>, <DD>, <DEL>, <DFN>, <DIV>, <DT>, <EM>, <FIELDSET>, <FONT>, <FORM>, <H1>, <H2>, <H3>, <H4>, <H5>, <H6>, <I>, <IFRAME>, <INS>, <KBD>, <LABEL>, <LEGEND>, <LI>, <NOFRAMES>, <NOSCRIPT>, <OBJECT>, <P>, <Q>, <S>, <SAMP>, <SMALL>, <SPAN>, <STRIKE>, <STRONG>, <SUB>, <SUP>, <TD>, <TH>, <TT>, <U>, <VAR>

Content Tags

<A>, <ACRONYM>, <APPLET>, <B>, <BASEFONT>, <BDO>, <BIG>, <BR>, <BUTTON>, <CITE>, <CODE>, <DFN>, <EM>, <FONT>, <I>, <IFRAME>, <IMG>, <INPUT>, <KBD>, <LABEL>, <MAP>, <OBJECT>, <Q>, <S>, <SAMP>, <SCRIPT>, <SELECT>, <SMALL>, <SPAN>, <STRIKE>, <STRONG>, <SUB>, <SUP>, <TEXTAREA>, <TT>, <U>, <VAR>

Sample HTML

```
<BODY>
<FONT SIZE=+3 COLOR="teal" FACE="Times, Garamond, Arial">This font will
be three sizes larger than the default font, and displayed in teal
Times.</FONT>
</BODY>
```

<HR>

The horizontal rule tag inserts a plain line across the width of the page.

Style Tip

Horizontal rules are particularly useful to emphasize divisions and transitions in page content. Avoid overuse of this tag since this can clutter up a page and distract readers' attention from the content.

Attributes

ALIGN=(LEFT|CENTER|RIGHT)

Lets you decide if you want the line left-aligned, right-aligned, or centered. The default is centered.

NOSHADE

Renders the rule without any 3-D shading.

SIZE=number *[Deprecated]*

Allows you to set the height (thickness) of your rule in pixels. The smallest you can make the rule is 2, which is the default.

WIDTH=(number|"%") *[Deprecated]*

Allows you to specify the width of the rule. You can do this either in pixels or as a percentage of the window width. If you choose to do it as a percentage, you must end the number with the percent (%) sign. The default is 100%.

Parent Tags

```
<BLOCKQUOTE>, <BODY>, <BUTTON>, <CENTER>, <DD>, <DIV>, <FIELDSET>,
<FORM>, <IFRAME>, <LI>, <NOFRAMES>, <NOSCRIPT>, <OBJECT>, <TD>, <TH>
```

Content Tags

None.

Sample HTML

```
<BODY>
This is the document title.
<HR>
Section 1
...
<HR>
Section 2
</BODY>
```

<I>...</I>

The I tags render the enclosed text in italics.

Style Tip

Large amounts of italics are difficult to read. Employ this tag to make a brief point or to set the contained text apart from surrounding text.

Attributes

None.

Parent Tags

<A>, <ACRONYM>, <ADDRESS>, <APPLET>, <B>, <BDO>, <BIG>, <BLOCKQUOTE>, <BODY>, <BUTTON>, <CAPTION>, <CENTER>, <CITE>, <CODE>, <DD>, <DEL>, <DFN>, <DIV>, <DT>, <EM>, <FIELDSET>, <FONT>, <FORM>, <H1>, <H2>, <H3>, <H4>, <H5>, <H6>, <I>, <IFRAME>, <INS>, <KBD>, <LABEL>, <LEGEND>, <LI>, <NOFRAMES>, <NOSCRIPT>, <OBJECT>, <P>, <PRE>, <Q>, <S>, <SAMP>, <SMALL>, <SPAN>, <STRIKE>, <STRONG>, <SUB>, <SUP>, <TD>, <TH>, <TT>, <U>, <VAR>

Content Tags

<A>, <ACRONYM>, <APPLET>, <B>, <BASEFONT>, <BDO>, <BIG>, <BR>, <BUTTON>, <CITE>, <CODE>, <DFN>, <EM>, <FONT>, <I>, <IFRAME>, <IMG>, <INPUT>, <KBD>, <LABEL>, <MAP>, <OBJECT>, <Q>, <S>, <SAMP>, <SCRIPT>, <SELECT>, <SMALL>, <SPAN>, <STRIKE>, <STRONG>, <SUB>, <SUP>, <TEXTAREA>, <TT>, <U>, <VAR>

Sample HTML

```
Gee, it is <I>hot</I> in Texas.
```

<S>...</S>

[Deprecated] The S tags render the enclosed text in strikethrough format.

Style Tip

Strikethrough text usually represents a correction or text that has been removed. As with italics, large amounts of struck text can be difficult to read, so keep use of the S tag at a minimum.

Attributes

None.

Parent Tags

<A>, <ACRONYM>, <ADDRESS>, <APPLET>, <B>, <BDO>, <BIG>, <BLOCKQUOTE>, <BODY>, <BUTTON>, <CAPTION>, <CENTER>, <CITE>, <CODE>, <DD>, <DEL>, <DFN>, <DIV>, <DT>, <EM>, <FIELDSET>, <FONT>, <FORM>, <H1>, <H2>, <H3>, <H4>, <H5>, <H6>, <I>, <IFRAME>, <INS>, <KBD>, <LABEL>, <LEGEND>, <LI>, <NOFRAMES>, <NOSCRIPT>, <OBJECT>, <P>, <PRE>, <Q>, <S>, <SAMP>, <SMALL>, <SPAN>, <STRIKE>, <STRONG>, <SUB>, <SUP>, <TD>, <TH>, <TT>, <U>, <VAR>

Content Tags

<A>, <ACRONYM>, <APPLET>, <B>, <BASEFONT>, <BDO>, <BIG>, <BR>, <BUTTON>, <CITE>, <CODE>, <DFN>, <EM>, <FONT>, <I>, <IFRAME>, <IMG>, <INPUT>, <KBD>, <LABEL>, <MAP>, <OBJECT>, <Q>, <S>, <SAMP>, <SCRIPT>, <SELECT>, <SMALL>, <SPAN>, <STRIKE>, <STRONG>, <SUB>, <SUP>, <TEXTAREA>, <TT>, <U>, <VAR>

Sample HTML

When we went out to eat, <S>Donna</S> Amy ordered the steak.

<SMALL>...</SMALL>

SMALL tags render enclosed text one size smaller than the standard type size.

Style Tip

While many browsers support nesting <SMALL> tags to make text sizes increasingly smaller, this isn't part of the HTML specification. Use <FONT SIZE=-*n*> where *n* is a number between 1 and 7, instead of the <SMALL> tag.

Attributes

None.

Parent Tags

<A>, <ACRONYM>, <ADDRESS>, <APPLET>, <B>, <BDO>, <BIG>, <BLOCKQUOTE>, <BODY>, <BUTTON>, <CAPTION>, <CENTER>, <CITE>, <CODE>, <DD>, <DEL>, <DFN>, <DIV>, <DT>, <EM>, <FIELDSET>, <FONT>, <FORM>, <H1>, <H2>, <H3>, <H4>, <H5>, <H6>, <I>, <IFRAME>, <INS>, <KBD>, <LABEL>, <LEGEND>, <LI>, <NOFRAMES>, <NOSCRIPT>, <OBJECT>, <P>, <Q>, <S>, <SAMP>, <SMALL>, <SPAN>, <STRIKE>, <STRONG>, <SUB>, <SUP>, <TD>, <TH>, <TT>, <U>, <VAR>

Content Tags

<A>, <ACRONYM>, <APPLET>, <B>, <BASEFONT>, <BDO>, <BIG>, <BR>, <BUTTON>, <CITE>, <CODE>, <DFN>, <EM>, <FONT>, <I>, <IFRAME>, <IMG>, <INPUT>, <KBD>, <LABEL>, <MAP>, <OBJECT>, <Q>, <S>, <SAMP>, <SCRIPT>, <SELECT>, <SMALL>, <SPAN>, <STRIKE>, <STRONG>, <SUB>, <SUP>, <TEXTAREA>, <TT>, <U>, <VAR>

Sample HTML

```
That was the <SMALL>smallest</SMALL> monkey I've ever seen.
```

<STRIKE>...</STRIKE>

[Deprecated] The STRIKE tags render enclosed text in strikethrough format.

Style Tip

Strikethrough text usually represents a correction or text that has been removed. As with italics, large amounts of struck text can be difficult to read, so use STRIKE tags sparingly.

Attributes

None.

Parent Tags

<A>, <ACRONYM>, <ADDRESS>, <APPLET>, <B>, <BDO>, <BIG>, <BLOCKQUOTE>, <BODY>, <BUTTON>, <CAPTION>, <CENTER>, <CITE>, <CODE>, <DD>, <DEL>, <DFN>, <DIV>, <DT>, <EM>, <FIELDSET>, <FONT>, <FORM>, <H1>, <H2>, <H3>, <H4>, <H5>, <H6>, <I>, <IFRAME>, <INS>, <KBD>, <LABEL>, <LEGEND>, <LI>, <NOFRAMES>, <NOSCRIPT>, <OBJECT>, <P>, <PRE>, <Q>, <S>, <SAMP>, <SMALL>, <SPAN>, <STRIKE>, <STRONG>, <SUB>, <SUP>, <TD>, <TH>, <TT>, <U>, <VAR>

Content Tags

<A>, <ACRONYM>, <APPLET>, <B>, <BASEFONT>, <BDO>, <BIG>, <BR>, <BUTTON>, <CITE>, <CODE>, <DFN>, <EM>, <FONT>, <I>, <IFRAME>, <IMG>, <INPUT>, <KBD>, <LABEL>, <MAP>, <OBJECT>, <Q>, <S>, <SAMP>, <SCRIPT>, <SELECT>, <SMALL>, <SPAN>, <STRIKE>, <STRONG>, <SUB>, <SUP>, <TEXTAREA>, <TT>, <U>, <VAR>

Sample HTML

The cat <S>dog</S> ate my homework.

<TT>...</TT>

The TT (teletype text) tags render text in a monospaced font.

Style Tip

Teletype script logically represents typewriter style text. Physically it is displayed in the same way as code, keyboard, and sample text.

Attributes

None.

Parent Tags

<A>, <ACRONYM>, <ADDRESS>, <APPLET>, <B>, <BDO>, <BIG>, <BLOCKQUOTE>, <BODY>, <BUTTON>, <CAPTION>, <CENTER>, <CITE>, <CODE>, <DD>, <DEL>, <DFN>, <DIV>, <DT>, <EM>, <FIELDSET>, <FONT>, <FORM>, <H1>, <H2>, <H3>, <H4>, <H5>, <H6>, <I>, <IFRAME>, <INS>, <KBD>, <LABEL>, <LEGEND>, <LI>, <NOFRAMES>, <NOSCRIPT>, <OBJECT>, <P>, <PRE>, <Q>, <S>, <SAMP>, <SMALL>, <SPAN>, <STRIKE>, <STRONG>, <SUB>, <SUP>, <TD>, <TH>, <TT>, <U>, <VAR>

Content Tags

```
<A>, <ACRONYM>, <APPLET>, <B>, <BASEFONT>, <BDO>, <BIG>, <BR>, <BUTTON>,
<CITE>, <CODE>, <DFN>, <EM>, <FONT>, <I>, <IFRAME>, <IMG>, <INPUT>,
<KBD>, <LABEL>, <MAP>, <OBJECT>, <Q>, <S>, <SAMP>, <SCRIPT>, <SELECT>,
<SMALL>, <SPAN>, <STRIKE>, <STRONG>, <SUB>, <SUP>, <TEXTAREA>, <TT>,
<U>, <VAR>
```

Sample HTML

```
Type <TT>myfile.doc</TT> in the Find box.
```

<U>...</U>

[Deprecated] The U tags render underlined text.

Style Tip

Use underlined text judiciously as users may mistake it for the underlined hyperlinks they have become accustomed to clicking on.

Attributes

None.

Parent Tags

```
<A>, <ACRONYM>, <ADDRESS>, <APPLET>, <B>, <BDO>, <BIG>, <BLOCKQUOTE>,
<BODY>, <BUTTON>, <CAPTION>, <CENTER>, <CITE>, <CODE>, <DD>, <DEL>,
<DFN>, <DIV>, <DT>, <EM>, <FIELDSET>, <FONT>, <FORM>, <H1>, <H2>, <H3>,
<H4>, <H5>, <H6>, <I>, <IFRAME>, <INS>, <KBD>, <LABEL>, <LEGEND>, <LI>,
<NOFRAMES>, <NOSCRIPT>, <OBJECT>, <P>, <PRE>, <Q>, <S>, <SAMP>,
<SMALL>, <SPAN>, <STRIKE>, <STRONG>, <SUB>, <SUP>, <TD>, <TH>, <TT>,
<U>, <VAR>
```

Content Tags

```
<A>, <ACRONYM>, <APPLET>, <B>, <BASEFONT>, <BDO>, <BIG>, <BR>, <BUTTON>,
<CITE>, <CODE>, <DFN>, <EM>, <FONT>, <I>, <IFRAME>, <IMG>, <INPUT>,
<KBD>, <LABEL>, <MAP>, <OBJECT>, <Q>, <S>, <SAMP>, <SCRIPT>, <SELECT>,
<SMALL>, <SPAN>, <STRIKE>, <STRONG>, <SUB>, <SUP>, <TEXTAREA>, <TT>,
<U>, <VAR>
```

Sample HTML

```
By George, I think we're <U>underlined.</U>
```

Frame Tags

Frame tags create multipart display areas within a browser window. Each area, called a frame, can contain a separate document. This permits authors to create unique layouts with static navigation and logo areas. With properly attributed hyperlinks, actions in one frame can affect content displayed in another frame.

WHAT'S ONLINE

Creating good frames is complicated and takes practice. To learn all about frames from folks who've been there, visit these tutorials: `http://www.w3` `.org/TR/WD-html40/present/frames.html` and `http://home.netscape` `.com/assist/net_sites/frames.html`.

\<FRAME\>

This tag defines a single frame within a FRAMESET pair.

Style Tip

Frames are popular, but are not fully supported by all browsers. Therefore, it's good practice to create a nonframed version of a site, or to use NOFRAME tags to offer alternate unframed content to "frame-disadvantaged" users.

Attributes

FRAMEBORDER=(1|0)

Turns the 3-D frame border on (1, the default) or off (0).

MARGINHEIGHT=(number|"%")

Defines the vertical margin within the frame in pixels.

MARGINWIDTH=(number|"%")

Defines the horizontal margin within the frame in pixels.

NAME="text"

Defines a name for the frame, used as a reference by the TARGET attribute.

NORESIZE

Prevents users from resizing the frame.

SCROLLING=(yes|no|auto)

Sets the scrolling abilities of the frame to yes (force display of scroll bar), no (never display scroll bar), or auto (default, display scroll bar if needed).

SRC="URL"

Specifies the URL of the file to be displayed within the frame.

Parent Tags

```
<FRAMESET>
```

Content Tags

None.

Sample HTML

```
<HTML>
<HEAD>
<TITLE>Sproket Sprinklers</TITLE>
</HEAD>
<FRAMESET COLS="30%,*, 10%">
<FRAME SCROLLING=YES SRC="nav_menu.htm">
<FRAME SRC="main.htm">
<FRAME SCROLLING=NO SRC="ss_logo.htm">
</FRAMESET>
</HTML>
```

<FRAMESET>...</FRAMESET>

These tags define the size and number of frames to be created.

Style Tip

Frames can be constructed in rows or columns with the appropriate attributes. A grid of frames can be established by including both ROWS and COLS attributes in the same FRAMESET tag. FRAMESET tag pairs can be nested to construct complicated shapes and arrangements of frames.

Attributes

COLS="col-widths|%|*"

Defines columns of frames in exact pixels, percentage (%), or a relative size (*).

ROWS="row-height|%|*"

Defines rows of frames in exact pixels, percentage (%), or a relative size (*).

Parent Tags

```
<FRAMESET>, <HTML>
```

Content Tags

```
<FRAME>, <FRAMESET>, <NOFRAMES>
```

Sample HTML

```
<HTML>
<HEAD>
<TITLE>Sproket Sprinklers</TITLE>
</HEAD>
<FRAMESET COLS="30%,*, 10%">
<FRAME SCROLLING=YES SRC="nav_menu.htm">
<FRAME SRC="main.htm">
<FRAME SCROLLING=NO SRC="ss_logo.htm">
</FRAMESET>
</HTML>
```

<IFRAME>...</IFRAME>

These tags define inline or floating frames. They operate in a manner similar to FRAMESET. Inline frames cannot be resized by the user.

Style Tip

Inline or floating frames offer intriguing design elements previously unavailable to Web authors. Considerable experimentation is required to master this tag.

Content enclosed by IFRAME tags is used only when a browser does not support inline frames. Always include alternate versions of your content with this feature.

Attributes

ALIGN=(LEFT|CENTER|RIGHT|TOP|MIDDLE|BOTTOM)

This attribute specifies the alignment of the inline frame in relation to the surrounding text. (See Table B.10.)

FRAMEBORDER=(1|0)

Turns the 3-D frame border on (1, the default) or off (0).

HEIGHT=(number|"%")

Specifies the pixel height of the frame.

MARGINHEIGHT=(number|"%")

Defines the vertical margin within the frame in pixels.

MARGINWIDTH=(number|"%")

Defines the horizontal margin within the frame in pixels.

NAME="text"

Defines a name for the frame, used as a reference by the TARGET attribute of the A tag.

SCROLLING=(yes|no|auto)

Sets the scrolling abilities of the frame to yes (force display of scroll bar), no (never display scroll bar), or auto (default, display scroll bar if needed).

SRC="URL"

Specifies the URL of the file to be displayed within the frame.

WIDTH=(number|"%")

Specifies the pixel width of the frame.

Parent Tags

<A>, <ACRONYM>, <ADDRESS>, <APPLET>, <B>, <BDO>, <BIG>, <BLOCKQUOTE>, <BODY>, <BUTTON>, <CAPTION>, <CENTER>, <CITE>, <CODE>, <DD>, <DEL>, <DFN>, <DIV>, <DT>, <EM>, <FIELDSET>, <FONT>, <FORM>, <H1>, <H2>, <H3>, <H4>, <H5>, <H6>, <I>, <IFRAME>, <INS>, <KBD>, <LABEL>, <LEGEND>, <LI>, <NOFRAMES>, <NOSCRIPT>, <OBJECT>, <P>, <PRE>, <Q>, <S>, <SAMP>, <SMALL>, <SPAN>, <STRIKE>, <STRONG>, <SUB>, <SUP>, <TD>, <TH>, <TT>, <U>, <VAR>

Content Tags

<A>, <ACRONYM>, <ADDRESS>, <APPLET>, <B>, <BASEFONT>, <BDO>, <BIG>, <BLOCKQUOTE>, <BR>, <BUTTON>, <CENTER>, <CITE>, <CODE>, <DFN>, <DIR>, <DIV>, <DL>, <EM>, <FIELDSET>, <FONT>, <FORM>, <H1>, <H2>, <H3>, <H4>, <H5>, <H6>, <HR>, <I>, <IFRAME>, <IMG>, <INPUT>, <ISINDEX>, <KBD>, <LABEL>, <MAP>, <MENU>, <NOFRAMES>, <NOSCRIPT>, <OBJECT>, <OL>, <P>, <PRE>, <Q>, <S>, <SAMP>, <SCRIPT>, <SELECT>, <SMALL>, <SPAN>, <STRIKE>, <STRONG>, <SUB>, <SUP>, <TABLE>, <TEXTAREA>, <TT>, <U>, <UL>, <VAR>

Sample HTML

```
<HTML>
<HEAD>
<TITLE>Inline Frames</TITLE>
</HEAD>
<IFRAME SCROLLING=NO SRC="float_main.htm">
Your browser does not support floating frames (IFRAME), click
<A HREF="http://www.domain.com/stuff/noif-nav.htm">
here to view the data without frames.</A>
</IFRAME>
</HTML>
```

<NOFRAMES>...</NOFRAMES>

These tags provide content to be used when a browser is unable to display frame-based information.

Style Tip

Frames are very popular, but are not fully supported by all browsers. It's good practice to create a nonframed version of your site, or to use NOFRAME tags to offer alternate content.

Attributes

None.

Parent Tags

<BLOCKQUOTE>, <BODY>, <BUTTON>, <CENTER>, <DD>, <DIV>, <FIELDSET>, <FORM>, <FRAMESET>, <IFRAME>, <LI>, <NOFRAMES>, <NOSCRIPT>, <OBJECT>, <TD>, <TH>

Content Tags

<A>, <ACRONYM>, <ADDRESS>, <APPLET>, <B>, <BASEFONT>, <BDO>, <BIG>, <BLOCKQUOTE>, <BODY>, <BR>, <BUTTON>, <CENTER>, <CITE>, <CODE>, <DFN>, <DIR>, <DIV>, <DL>, <EM>, <FIELDSET>, <FONT>, <FORM>, <H1>, <H2>, <H3>, <H4>, <H5>, <H6>, <HR>, <I>, <IFRAME>, <IMG>, <INPUT>, <ISINDEX>, <KBD>, <LABEL>, <MAP>, <MENU>, <NOFRAMES>, <NOSCRIPT>, <OBJECT>, <OL>, <P>, <PRE>, <Q>, <S>, <SAMP>, <SCRIPT>, <SELECT>, <SMALL>, <SPAN>, <STRIKE>, <STRONG>, <SUB>, <SUP>, <TABLE>, <TEXTAREA>, <TT>, <U>, <UL>, <VAR>

Sample HTML

```
<HTML>
<HEAD>
<TITLE>Sproket Sprinklers</TITLE>
</HEAD>
<FRAMESET COLS="30%,*, 10%">
<FRAME SCROLLING=YES SRC="nav_menu.htm">
<FRAME SRC="main.htm">
<FRAME SCROLLING=NO SRC="ss_logo.htm">
<NOFRAMES>
<EM>Your browser does not support frames.</EM>
</NOFRAMES>
</FRAMESET>
</HTML>
```

Form Tags

Use form tags to create HTML forms to solicit user feedback or add interactivity to Web pages. Form tags provide a variety of graphical and text items, as well as pick lists, that allow users to choose from different input options.

<BUTTON>...</BUTTON>

Use the BUTTON tags to create graphically interesting form input controls that provide more variety than standard submit and reset buttons.

Style Tip

If creating input objects that include images, use BUTTON tags instead of INPUT tags. Resulting images appear as raised buttons that depress when selected.

Attributes

DISABLED

Disables the button.

NAME="name"

Defines a name for the button.

TABINDEX="number"

Specifies the element's place in the tabbing order.

TYPE=BUTTON|SUBMIT|RESET

Defines the type of button. (See Table B.18.)

TABLE B.18: Options for the Function of Buttons

Use This	To Get This
BUTTON	A button that calls a script.
SUBMIT	A button that sends the contents of the form to a specified URL. The button name and value are also sent.
RESET	A button that resets the contents of a form.

VALUE="value"

Defines the button's value.

Parent Tags

<A>, <ACRONYM>, <ADDRESS>, <APPLET>, <B>, <BDO>, <BIG>, <BLOCKQUOTE>, <BODY>, <CAPTION>, <CENTER>, <CITE>, <CODE>, <DD>, <DEL>, <DFN>, <DIV>, <DT>, <EM>, <FIELDSET>, <FONT>, <FORM>, <H1>, <H2>, <H3>, <H4>, <H5>, <H6>, <I>, <IFRAME>, <INS>, <KBD>, <LABEL>, <LEGEND>, <LI>, <NOFRAMES>, <NOSCRIPT>, <OBJECT>, <P>, <PRE>, <Q>, <S>, <SAMP>, <SMALL>, <SPAN>, <STRIKE>, <STRONG>, <SUB>, <SUP>, <TD>, <TH>, <TT>, <U>, <VAR>

Content Tags

<A>, <ACRONYM>, <ADDRESS>, <APPLET>, <B>, <BASEFONT>, <BDO>, <BIG>, <BLOCKQUOTE>, <BR>, <BUTTON>, <CENTER>, <CITE>, <CODE>, <DFN>, <DIR>, <DIV>, <DL>, <EM>, <FIELDSET>, <FONT>, <FORM>, <H1>, <H2>, <H3>, <H4>, <H5>, <H6>, <HR>, <I>, <IFRAME>, <IMG>, <INPUT>, <ISINDEX>, <KBD>, <LABEL>, <MAP>, <MENU>, <NOFRAMES>, <NOSCRIPT>, <OBJECT>, <OL>, <P>, <PRE>, <Q>, <S>, <SAMP>, <SCRIPT>, <SELECT>, <SMALL>, <SPAN>, <STRIKE>, <STRONG>, <SUB>, <SUP>, <TABLE>, <TEXTAREA>, <TT>, <U>, <UL>, <VAR>

Sample HTML

```
<FORM METHOD=POST ACTION="http://www.mysite.com/bin/form">
...
<BUTTON TYPE=SUBMIT NAME="FORM1" VALUE="FORM1">
<IMG SRC="button.gif">
</BUTTON>
</FORM>
```

<FIELDSET>...</FIELDSET>

The FIELDSET tags are used to divide similar form controls into groups.

Style Tip

Always include LEGEND tags with FIELDSETs to help users understand the form and the data it is requesting.

Attributes

None.

Parent Tags

<BLOCKQUOTE>, <BODY>, <CENTER>, <DD>, <DIV>, <FIELDSET>, <FORM>, <IFRAME>, <LI>, <NOFRAMES>, <NOSCRIPT>, <OBJECT>, <TD>, <TH>

Content Tags

<A>, <ACRONYM>, <ADDRESS>, <APPLET>, <B>, <BASEFONT>, <BDO>, <BIG>,
<BLOCKQUOTE>, <BR>, <BUTTON>, <CENTER>, <CITE>, <CODE>, <DFN>, <DIR>,
<DIV>, <DL>, <EM>, <FIELDSET>, <FONT>, <FORM>, <H1>, <H2>, <H3>, <H4>,
<H5>, <H6>, <HR>, <I>, <IFRAME>, <IMG>, <INPUT>, <ISINDEX>, <KBD>,
<LABEL>, <LEGEND>, <MAP>, <MENU>, <NOFRAMES>, <NOSCRIPT>, <OBJECT>,
<OL>, <P>, <PRE>, <Q>, <S>, <SAMP>, <SCRIPT>, <SELECT>, <SMALL>,
<SPAN>, <STRIKE>, <STRONG>, <SUB>, <SUP>, <TABLE>, <TEXTAREA>, <TT>,
<U>, <UL>, <VAR>

Sample HTML

```
<FORM METHOD=POST ACTION="http://www.mysite.com/bin/form">
<FIELDSET>
<INPUT TYPE=TEXT NAME="PET" VALUE="pet">
<INPUT TYPE=TEXT NAME="CAR" VALUE="car">
<INPUT TYPE=TEXT NAME="MUSIC" VALUE="music">
<BUTTON TYPE=SUBMIT NAME=ABOUT1 VALUE="about11">
<IMG SRC="button.gif">
</BUTTON>
</FIELDSET>
</FORM>
```

<FORM>...</FORM>

The FORM tags create the region on a page that holds the elements for soliciting
user input.

Style Tip

Forms are the only built-in mechanism available in HTML to solicit feedback from
and provide interactivity for users. Remember that a CGI script of some sort is
usually needed to process the form's data, so you may need to enlist the assistance
of a programmer to respond to data delivered via HTML forms.

Attributes

ACCEPT="Internet media type"
Defines a list of MIME types recognized by the server that processes the form.

ACCEPT-CHARSET="text"
Defines a list of character sets recognized by the server that processes the form.

ACTION="URL"

Specifies the location of a resource for the browser to execute once a form has been completed and submitted. This is generally some sort of CGI script that translates data into a usable format, and that may process it further to return more information to users.

METHOD=("GET"|"POST")

This attribute lets the browser know how it should work with the resource identified by the ACTION attribute. If the value of METHOD is GET, the browser creates a query that includes the page URL, a question mark, and the values generated by the form. The browser then returns the query to the URL specified by ACTION for processing. The POST method returns the form data to the URL specified by ACTION as a block of data rather than a query string.

ENCTYPE="MIME type"

Specifies the type and format of the submitted form data. If the data is submitted using the POST method, this attribute is defined as a MIME type.

TARGET="window"

Specifies that the link should be loaded into the targeted frame or window. Use this attribute when the targeted frame or window is different from the frame or window the current document resides in. The attribute can target a <FRAMESET> where a frame has been created and given a name using the <FRAME> element or an entire browser window. The targeted frame or window can be specified using the information shown in Table 9.

Parent Tags

```
<BLOCKQUOTE>, <BODY>, <CENTER>, <DD>, <DIV>, <FIELDSET>, <IFRAME>,
<LI>, <NOFRAMES>, <NOSCRIPT>, <OBJECT>, <TD>, <TH>
```

Content Tags

```
<A>, <ACRONYM>, <ADDRESS>, <APPLET>, <B>, <BASEFONT>, <BDO>, <BIG>,
<BLOCKQUOTE>, <BR>, <BUTTON>, <CENTER>, <CITE>, <CODE>, <DFN>, <DIR>,
<DIV>, <DL>, <EM>, <FIELDSET>, <FONT>, <FORM>, <H1>, <H2>, <H3>, <H4>,
<H5>, <H6>, <HR>, <I>, <IFRAME>, <IMG>, <INPUT>, <ISINDEX>, <KBD>,
<LABEL>, <MAP>, <MENU>, <NOFRAMES>, <NOSCRIPT>, <OBJECT>, <OL>, <P>,
<PRE>, <Q>, <S>, <SAMP>, <SCRIPT>, <SELECT>, <SMALL>, <SPAN>, <STRIKE>,
<STRONG>, <SUB>, <SUP>, <TABLE>, <TEXTAREA>, <TT>, <U>, <UL>, <VAR>
```

Sample HTML

```
<BODY>
<FORM ACTION="http://www.mysite.com/cgis/form1.pl" METHOD="POST">
... form data ...
</FORM>
```

<INPUT>

The INPUT tag defines type and appearance for input widgets.

Style Tip

The <INPUT> tag is a key element for any form because it supplies the mechanism through which users can provide you with data. Input widgets can take several different forms, from checkboxes, to radio buttons, to text fields. Think carefully about what kind of information you want to solicit from your readers, and match it with the appropriate input widget.

Attributes

ACCEPT="Internet media type"

Defines a list of MIME types recognized by the server that processes the form.

ALIGN=(LEFT|CENTER|RIGHT) *[Deprecated]*

Specifies how the widget will be aligned relative to the page.

CHECKED

Specifies that a checkbox or radio button should appear selected when the form is displayed by the browser.

DISABLED

Disables the input control.

NAME="text"

Names the input widget.

MAXLENGTH=number

Sets the maximum number of characters a user can enter into a text field.

READONLY

Prevents the user from altering the widget's contents.

SIZE="width|(width, height)"

Sets the width and height of a text input widget.

SRC="URL"

When TYPE=IMAGE is used, this attribute specifies the URL for the image.

TYPE=(TEXT|PASSWORD|CHECKBOX|RADIO|SUBMIT|RESET|FILE|HIDDEN|IMAGE|BUTTON)

Indicates which type of input widget to display. The default is text, and your options include those shown in Table B.19.

TABLE B.19: Options for the Appearance of Input Boxes

Use This	To Do This
TEXT	Generate a text input field where MAXLENGTH limits how many characters a user can enter, and the field size is defined with the SIZE attribute.
PASSWORD	Create a text input field the same way the TYPE=TEXT attribute does, but any character entered by the user is replaced by a bullet or similar character.
CHECKBOX	Create a checkbox. When checked and a form is submitted, the browser automatically returns a value of NAME=on. If it is unchecked, no value is sent.
RADIO	Generate a radio button. Radio buttons are created in groups, each with the same name but with different values. When a form is returned, the name and value of the selected radio button is returned and the others ignored.
SUBMIT	Create the SUBMIT button that causes all of the form data to be returned to the URL specified by the ACTION attribute. You may have more than one submit button, but each should have a different name to differentiate between the data they are returning.
RESET	Create a RESET button that restores the form to its original, clean state to allow users to begin entering data again.
FILE	Permit a user to upload a file from his or her computer to your server. This option is not yet widely implemented, however, and should be used sparingly.
HIDDEN	Generate form data that is necessary for the correct processing of the form, but that you don't want users to see.
IMAGE	Create a SUBMIT button that uses the image specified by the SRC attribute.
BUTTON	Create a button that calls a script.

VALUE=value

For nontext field input elements, this attribute specifies the value that should be returned to the server when the form is submitted.

Parent Tags

<A>, <ACRONYM>, <ADDRESS>, <APPLET>, <B>, <BDO>, <BIG>, <BLOCKQUOTE>, <BODY>, <CAPTION>, <CENTER>, <CITE>, <CODE>, <DD>, <DEL>, <DFN>, <DIV>, <DT>, <EM>, <FIELDSET>, <FONT>, <FORM>, <H1>, <H2>, <H3>, <H4>, <H5>, <H6>, <I>, <IFRAME>, <INS>, <KBD>, <LABEL>, <LEGEND>, <LI>, <NOFRAMES>, <NOSCRIPT>, <OBJECT>, <P>, <PRE>, <Q>, <S>, <SAMP>, <SMALL>, <SPAN>, <STRIKE>, <STRONG>, <SUB>, <SUP>, <TD>, <TH>, <TT>, <U>, <VAR>

Content Tags

None.

Sample HTML

```
<BODY>
<FORM ACTION="http://www.mysite.com/cgi/form1.pl" METHOD="POST">
<INPUT TYPE=CHECKBOX NAME="ch1">Checkbox 1
<INPUT TYPE=CHECKBOX NAME="ch2" CHECKED>Checkbox 2
<INPUT TYPE=TEXT SIZE=25 MAXLENGTH=25 NAME="FNAME" VALUE="fname">First
Name
<INPUT TYPE=TEXT SIZE=25 MAXLENGTH=25 NAME="LNAME" VALUE="lname">Last
Name
<INPUT TYPE=SUBMIT VALUE="Send">
<INPUT TYPE=RESET VALUE="Clear">
</FORM>
```

<ISINDEX>

[Deprecated] The ISINDEX (document index) tag requires the user input a single line of text, usually to perform a search of the site's documents.

Style Tip

Because site searches are miniforms anyway, the ISINDEX tag has been deprecated in favor of a standard form and the INPUT tag.

Attributes

PROMPT="text" *[Deprecated]*

This attribute's value specifies the text that will appear next to the search field box.

Parent Tags

<BLOCKQUOTE>, <BODY>, <CENTER>, <DD>, <DIV>, <FIELDSET>, <FORM>, <HEAD>, <IFRAME>, <LI>, <NOFRAMES>, <NOSCRIPT>, <OBJECT>, <TD>, <TH>

Content Tags

None.

Sample HTML

```
<ISINDEX ACTION="/cgis/search.pl" PROMPT="Enter a key word or search
string here to search our site."
```

<LABEL>...</LABEL>

Use LABEL tags to provide additional information about a form control, just like the TITLE attribute does for other HTML elements.

Style Tip

Use labels to provide specific information about how users should enter data into a form control.

Attributes

ACCESSKEY="text"

Identifies a character to be used to create a keyboard shortcut to activate the link.

DISABLED

Disables the input control.

FOR="text"

Specifically associates the label with a form control using the ID name provided in the control's markup.

TABINDEX="number"

Specifies the link's place in the tabbing order.

Parent Tags

<A>, <ACRONYM>, <ADDRESS>, <APPLET>, <B>, <BDO>, <BIG>, <BLOCKQUOTE>, <BODY>, <CAPTION>, <CENTER>, <CITE>, <CODE>, <DD>, <DEL>, <DFN>, <DIV>, <DT>, <EM>, <FIELDSET>, <FONT>, <FORM>, <H1>, <H2>, <H3>, <H4>, <H5>, <H6>, <I>, <IFRAME>, <INS>, <KBD>, <LEGEND>, <LI>, <NOFRAMES>, <NOSCRIPT>, <OBJECT>, <P>, <PRE>, <Q>, <S>, <SAMP>, <SMALL>, <SPAN>, <STRIKE>, <STRONG>, <SUB>, <SUP>, <TD>, <TH>, <TT>, <U>, <VAR>

Content Tags

<A>, <ACRONYM>, <APPLET>, <B>, <BASEFONT>, <BDO>, <BIG>, <BR>, <BUTTON>, <CITE>, <CODE>, <DFN>, <EM>, <FONT>, <I>, <IFRAME>, <IMG>, <INPUT>, <KBD>, <LABEL>, <MAP>, <OBJECT>, <Q>, <S>, <SAMP>, <SCRIPT>, <SELECT>, <SMALL>, <SPAN>, <STRIKE>, <STRONG>, <SUB>, <SUP>, <TEXTAREA>, <TT>, <U>, <VAR>

Sample HTML

```
<FORM METHOD=POST ACTION="http://www.mysite.com/bin/form">
<FIELDSET>
<LABEL FOR="PET">Your Favorite Pet</LABEL>
<INPUT TYPE=TEXT NAME="PET" VALUE="pet" ID=PET>
<BUTTON TYPE=SUBMIT NAME=ABOUT1 VALUE="about11">
<IMG SRC="button.gif">
</BUTTON>
</FIELDSET>
</FORM>
```

<LEGEND>...</LEGEND>

LEGEND tags provide labels for field sets that explain their capabilities or contents.

Style Tip

Use legends to instruct users how to enter data into a form control.

Attributes

ALIGN=(LEFT|RIGHT|TOP|BOTTOM)

Sets the alignment of the legend with respect to the field set.

ACCESSKEY="text"

Identifies a character to be used to create a keyboard shortcut to bring the field set into focus.

Parent Tags

```
<FIELDSET>
```

Content Tags

```
<A>, <ACRONYM>, <APPLET>, <B>, <BASEFONT>, <BDO>, <BIG>, <BR>, <BUTTON>,
<CITE>, <CODE>, <DFN>, <EM>, <FONT>, <I>, <IFRAME>, <IMG>, <INPUT>,
<KBD>, <LABEL>, <MAP>, <OBJECT>, <Q>, <S>, <SAMP>, <SCRIPT>, <SELECT>,
<SMALL>, <SPAN>, <STRIKE>, <STRONG>, <SUB>, <SUP>, <TEXTAREA>, <TT>,
<U>, <VAR>
```

Sample HTML

```
<FORM METHOD=POST ACTION="http://www.mysite.com/bin/form">
<FIELDSET>
<LEGEND ALIGN=CENTER>Tell Us About Yourself</LEGEND>
<INPUT TYPE=TEXT NAME="PET" VALUE="pet">
<INPUT TYPE=TEXT NAME="CAR" VALUE="car">
<INPUT TYPE=TEXT NAME="MUSIC" VALUE="music">
<BUTTON TYPE=SUBMIT NAME=ABOUT1 VALUE="about11">
<IMG SRC="button.gif">
</BUTTON>
</FIELDSET>
</FORM>
```

<OPTION>

The OPTION tag assigns a value or default to an input item in a select menu.

Style Tip

Use the OPTION tag with a selection menu to provide a series of choices for users. Drop-down menus usually take up less space than radio or checkbox lists.

Attributes

DISABLED

Disables the input control.

SELECTED

Indicates that the option should be the default choice that appears in the menu window.

VALUE="text"

Sets the value for the individual option.

Parent Tags

<SELECT>

Content Tags

None.

Sample HTML

```
<BODY>
<FORM ACTION="http://www.mysite.com/cgis/form1.pl" METHOD="POST">
<SELECT NAME="dogs" MULTIPLE SIZE="2">
<OPTION VALUE="lab">Labrador
<OPTION VALUE="shep">German Shepherd
<OPTION VALUE="wiener">Dachshund
</SELECT>
<INPUT TYPE=SUBMIT VALUE="Send">
<INPUT TYPE=RESET VALUE="Clear">
</FORM>
```

<SELECT>...</SELECT>

The SELECT tags create a menu or scrolling list of input items.

Style Tip

This input widget creates list of items users can choose from. This allows you to provide specific choices to match the data types you need. Using the MULTIPLE tag, users can select more than one option from a list, or you can restrict them to a single choice by default.

Attributes

DISABLED

Disables the input control.

MULTIPLE

Allows users to choose more than one item from the set of <OPTION> values supplied within the <SELECT>...</SELECT> tag pair.

NAME="text"

Associates a name with the list.

SIZE="number"

Sets the number of choices visible within the drop-down menu.

TABINDEX="number"

Specifies the control's place in the tabbing order.

Parent Tags

<A>, <ACRONYM>, <ADDRESS>, <APPLET>, <B>, <BDO>, <BIG>, <BLOCKQUOTE>, <BODY>, <CAPTION>, <CENTER>, <CITE>, <CODE>, <DD>, <DEL>, <DFN>, <DIV>, <DT>, <EM>, <FIELDSET>, <FONT>, <FORM>, <H1>, <H2>, <H3>, <H4>, <H5>, <H6>, <I>, <IFRAME>, <INS>, <KBD>, <LABEL>, <LEGEND>, <LI>, <NOFRAMES>, <NOSCRIPT>, <OBJECT>, <P>, <PRE>, <Q>, <S>, <SAMP>, <SMALL>, <SPAN>, <STRIKE>, <STRONG>, <SUB>, <SUP>, <TD>, <TH>, <TT>, <U>, <VAR>

Content Tags

<OPTION>

Sample HTML

```
<BODY>
<FORM ACTION="http://www.mysite.com/cgis/form1.pl" METHOD="POST">
<SELECT NAME="dogs" MULTIPLE SIZE="2">
... menu data ...
</SELECT>
<INPUT TYPE=SUBMIT VALUE="Send">
<INPUT TYPE=RESET VALUE="Clear">
</FORM>
```

<TEXTAREA>...</TEXTAREA>

The TEXTAREA tags create a text input box usually used for multiline text input.

Style Tip

Text areas in forms allow users to provide information that does not conform to strict input limitations. Open-ended comments and suggestions are best solicited using text areas.

Attributes

COLS="number"

Specifies the width of the text box in columns. Convention limits this number to 72.

DISABLED
Disables the input control.

NAME="text"
Associates a name with the data entered in the text box for processing by an associated CGI script.

READONLY
Prevents the user from altering the text area's contents.

ROWS="number"
Specifies the height of the text box in rows.

TABINDEX="number"
Specifies the text area's place in the tabbing order.

Parent Tags

<A>, <ACRONYM>, <ADDRESS>, <APPLET>, <B>, <BDO>, <BIG>, <BLOCKQUOTE>, <BODY>, <CAPTION>, <CENTER>, <CITE>, <CODE>, <DD>, <DEL>, <DFN>, <DIV>, <DT>, <EM>, <FIELDSET>, <FONT>, <FORM>, <H1>, <H2>, <H3>, <H4>, <H5>, <H6>, <I>, <IFRAME>, <INS>, <KBD>, <LABEL>, <LEGEND>, <LI>, <NOFRAMES>, <NOSCRIPT>, <OBJECT>, <P>, <PRE>, <Q>, <S>, <SAMP>, <SMALL>, <SPAN>, <STRIKE>, <STRONG>, <SUB>, <SUP>, <TD>, <TH>, <TT>, <U>, <VAR>

Content Tags

None.

Sample HTML

```
<BODY>
<FORM ACTION="http://www.mysite.com/cgis/form1.pl" METHOD="POST">
<TEXTAREA NAME="comments" ROWS="10" COLS="60">
</TEXTAREA>
<INPUT TYPE=SUBMIT VALUE="Send">
<INPUT TYPE=RESET VALUE="Clear">
</FORM>
```

Script Tags

Script tags invoke inline programming scripts that execute on the client side within a Web document. These client-side scripts can be embedded directly into HTML or loaded from separate files. You will need to be adept in some specific programming language—such as C, JavaScript, VBScript, etc.—to benefit from these tags.

<NOSCRIPT>...</NOSCRIPT>

The NOSCRIPT tags define alternate content to use when the browser is unable to use the data defined by the SCRIPT tag.

Style Tip

Not all browsers support scripting or the specific scripting language used in a particular script; therefore, providing alternate content for these users is a good idea.

Attributes

None.

Parent Tags

<BLOCKQUOTE>, <BODY>, <BUTTON>, <CENTER>, <DD>, <DIV>, <FIELDSET>, <FORM>, <IFRAME>, <LI>, <NOFRAMES>, <NOSCRIPT>, <OBJECT>, <TD>, <TH>

Content Tags

<A>, <ACRONYM>, <ADDRESS>, <APPLET>, <B>, <BASEFONT>, <BDO>, <BIG>, <BLOCKQUOTE>, <BR>, <BUTTON>, <CENTER>, <CITE>, <CODE>, <DFN>, <DIR>, <DIV>, <DL>, <EM>, <FIELDSET>, <FONT>, <FORM>, <H1>, <H2>, <H3>, <H4>, <H5>, <H6>, <HR>, <I>, <IFRAME>, <IMG>, <INPUT>, <ISINDEX>, <KBD>, <LABEL>, <MAP>, <MENU>, <NOFRAMES>, <NOSCRIPT>, <OBJECT>, <OL>, <P>, <PRE>, <Q>, <S>, <SAMP>, <SCRIPT>, <SELECT>, <SMALL>, <SPAN>, <STRIKE>, <STRONG>, <SUB>, <SUP>, <TABLE>, <TEXTAREA>, <TT>, <U>, <UL>, <VAR>

Sample HTML

```
<HEAD>
<SCRIPT LANGUAGE="VBScript">
{script statements and instructions}
</SCRIPT>
<NOSCRIPT>
Your browser does not support our script, please follow this <A
HREF="http://www.domain.com/special/noscript.htm">link to an alternate
form of the same content.</A>
</NOSCRIPT>
</HEAD>
```

<SCRIPT>...</SCRIPT>

The SCRIPT tag informs the browser that the text contained within the tags should be rendered as script instead of as content for the Web page.

Style Tip

Scripts provide an easy way to add interactivity to pages without accessing external applets or programs. Use scripts to display messages based on user URL choices, to create customized pages, and more. Keep in mind that not all browsers can execute scripts—always provide alternative content to match material contained within scripts.

WHAT'S ONLINE

HTML 4 allows developers to use scripts to create such effects as the highlighting of items as the mouse moves over them. Find out more at http://www.w3.org/TR/WD-html40/interact/scripts.html.

Attributes

TYPE="scripting language"

Defines the scripting language type for the script text enclosed by the tag pair. The value of scripting language must be an Internet Media Type (MIME); see ftp://ftp.isi.edu/in-notes/iana/assignments/media-types.

LANGUAGE="scripting language"

Specifies what scripting language the enclosed script was written in, such as "JavaScript" and "VBScript."

SRC="URL"

Specifies the URL of an external script. If this attribute is used, all text enclosed by the tag pair is ignored.

Parent Tags

<A>, <ACRONYM>, <ADDRESS>, <APPLET>, <B>, <BDO>, <BIG>, <BLOCKQUOTE>, <BODY>, <BUTTON>, <CAPTION>, <CENTER>, <CITE>, <CODE>, <DD>, <DEL>, <DFN>, <DIV>, <DT>, <EM>, <FIELDSET>, <FONT>, <FORM>, <H1>, <H2>, <H3>, <H4>, <H5>, <H6>, <HEAD>, <I>, <IFRAME>, <INS>, <KBD>, <LABEL>, <LEG-END>, <LI>, <NOFRAMES>, <NOSCRIPT>, <OBJECT>, <P>, <PRE>, <Q>, <S>, <SAMP>, <SMALL>, <SPAN>, <STRIKE>, <STRONG>, <SUB>, <SUP>, <TD>, <TH>, <TT>, <U>, <VAR>

Content Tags

None.

Sample HTML

```
<HEAD>
<SCRIPT LANGUAGE="VBScript">
{script statements and instructions}
</SCRIPT>
</HEAD>
```

HTML Extensions

The HTML 4 DTD is not the only brand of HTML you can use in your Web documents. Rogue tags and attributes abound, including proprietary markup from Microsoft and Netscape. We've gathered a list of these extensions to provide you with the most extensive possible HTML coverage.

However, as we wrote this section, both Netscape's Communicator and Microsoft's Internet Explorer were still in flux. Therefore, those extensions that were clearly defined in the current version of their browsers remain the only documentation available. While most of this information should remain consistent, check with both vendors for the latest details on their proprietary HTML.

WHAT'S ONLINE

Get the scoop on developing sites to be viewed with Microsoft Internet Explorer and Netscape Navigator at `http://www.microsoft.com/sitebuilder` and `http://developer.netscape.com`.

In the sections that follow, only those tags or extensions that do not appear in the HTML 4 DTD are listed. They are identified by (N) for Netscape and (IE) for Microsoft by the tag name or the attribute. If details are not provided, they did not differ from the 4 DTD, or they were not available.

<BGSOUND> (IE)

The BGSOUND (background sound) tag links a sound file of .WAV, .AU or .MID/.MIDI to a document. The sound plays when the page is accessed.

Attributes

SRC=URL

Defines the URL of the sound file.

LOOP=number/INFINITE

Specifies how many times a sound will repeat or loop. If INFINITE is specified, it loops indefinitely.

<BLINK>...</BLINK> (N)

The BLINK tags cause enclosed text to blink on and off.

<COMMENT>...</COMMENT> (IE)

The COMMENT tags are the same as the <!- ... -> tag.

<FRAME>

The FRAME tag defines the contents of a single frame.

Attributes

BORDERCOLOR="#RRGGBB|colorname" (N, IE)

Defines the frame border's color. (See Table B.1.)

LANGUAGE=JAVASCRIPT|JSCRIPT|VBSCRIPT|VBS (IE)

Defines the language of the current script and loads the scripting engine.

HEIGHT=number|"%"

Specifies the height of the frame in pixels or percentages.

WIDTH=number|"%" (IE)

Specifies the width of the frame in pixels or percentages.

<FRAMESET>...</FRAMESET>

The FRAMESET tag splits up the browser window into different frames; each frame can have a separate document within it.

Attributes

BORDER="number" (N, IE)

Specifies the thickness of frame borders for all frames in a frameset. If BORDER="0", frames have no visible border. The default is 5 pixels. The BORDER attribute can be used only on an outermost FRAMESET tag.

BORDERCOLOR="#RRGGBB|colorname" (N, IE)

Specifies the frame's border color. (See Table B.1.)

FRAMEBORDER=1|o (N, IE)

Displays the 3-D border (1, the default), or no border (0).

FRAMESPACING=spacing (IE)

Places additional space between frames, in pixels.

LANGUAGE=JAVASCRIPT|JSCRIPT|VBSCRIPT|VBS (IE)

Defines the language of the current script and loads the scripting engine.

<IFRAME>

The IFRAME tag inserts a frame within a block of text so that you can insert a second HTML document there.

Attributes

NORESIZE (IE)
Prevents the user from resizing the frame.

<MARQUEE>...</MARQUEE> (IE)

The MARQUEE tags create a scrolling text marquee.

Attributes

ALIGN=TOP/MIDDLE/BOTTOM
Defines how text wraps around the marquee.

BEHAVIOR= SCROLL/SLIDE/ALTERNATE
Sets the scrolling behavior.

BGCOLOR="#RRGGBB|colorname"
Sets the color of marquee text. (See Table B.1.)

DIRECTION=LEFT/RIGHT
Sets the direction of scrolling.

HEIGHT=number|"%"
Sets the height of the marquee in pixels or as a percentage.

WIDTH=number|"%"
Sets the width of the marquee in pixels or as a percentage.

HSPACE=number
Sets blank space in pixels to the left and right of the marquee.

VSPACE=number
Sets blank space in pixels above and below the marquee.

LOOP=number/INFINITE
Sets the number of times the message repeats.

SCROLLAMOUNT=number
Sets the number of pixels between repeated messages.

SCROLLDELAY=number
Sets the delay in number of milliseconds before the next display.

<MULTICOL>...</MULTICOL> (N)

The MULTICOL (multiple column) formatting tag creates a multiple column display of text.

Attributes

COLS="number"
Defines the number of text columns.

GUTTER="gwidth"
Defines the space between columns. The default is 10 pixels.

WIDTH="colwidth"
Defines the width of the columns.

<NOBR>...</NOBR> (N, IE)

The NOBR (no break) tags turn off line breaking and renders text without line breaks.

<NOEMBED>...</NOEMBED> (N)

The NOEMBED tags provide alternate content for browsers that do not support the plug-in required for an inline media type.

<SPACER>...</SPACER> (N)

The SPACER tags are used to control spacing by forcing white space around the enclosed elements.

Attributes

ALIGN="LEFT|RIGHT|TOP|ABSMIDDLE|ABSBOTTOM|TEXTTOP|MIDDLE|BASE-LINE|BOTTOM"
Defines alignment of external text. Only applies when TYPE=BLOCK. Default is BOTTOM.

HEIGHT="number"
Defines the height in pixels. Applies only when TYPE=BLOCK.

SIZE="number"

When TYPE=HORIZONTAL, specifies the absolute width of blank space. When TYPE=VERTICAL, specifies the absolute height of blank space.

TYPE="HORIZONTAL"|"VERTICAL"|"BLOCK"

Determines the action of the spacer—space between words (HORIZONTAL), space between lines of text (VERTICAL), or as an invisible image (BLOCK).

WIDTH="number"

Defines the width in pixels. Applies only when TYPE=BLOCK.

<WBR> (N, IE)

The WBR (word break) tag inserts a line break in a block of <NOBR> text.

APPENDIX C

Glossary of Terms

absolute URL   A complete address on the Internet's World Wide Web that points precisely to one file (see also *relative URL* and *URL*).

active web   The web currently open in the FrontPage Explorer. When you save a new page in the Editor, it's saved to the active web unless you specify a different location. Also called the *current web*.

ActiveX control   A programmable object that can be placed in a Web page and executed after someone opens the page in a browser. For example, an ActiveX control in a page allows you to enter an interest rate and principal amount in two form fields and then calculate a loan payment, all without having to invoke a program on the server.

administrator   Person who has full access rights to a Web site and can modify the pages and files in a site, create new files or delete existing ones, and assign access rights to others; the permissions that give administrative rights to a person.

All Files view   The FrontPage Explorer view that displays all the files in a web in a list.

All Folders pane   The left pane in FrontPage Explorer's Folders view.

All Pages pane   The left pane in FrontPage Explorer's Hyperlinks view.

anchor   The source (the text or image) of a hyperlink in a page, as defined in the HTML anchor tag, <A> (see *bookmark*).

applet   A compiled Java program (normally with a CLASS file name extension) that you can reference in a Web page to produce effects that would otherwise be difficult or impossible to create in HTML. Instead of the server executing the program, the browser's computer executes it.

aspect ratio   The relationship between the height and width of an image or object.

attribute   A parameter added to an HTML tag that affects the way the tag is interpreted in a browser. For example, the paragraph tag, <P>, can take the ALIGN attribute, which defines its alignment. When you center a paragraph in the FrontPage Editor, the resulting HTML code looks like this: <P ALIGN="CENTER">.

author   Individual who has *permission* to edit, delete, or add pages to a web; permission level for authors.

AutoThumbnail   A new feature in FrontPage 98 that creates a smaller thumbnail version of the selected image, replaces the image with the thumbnail, and creates a hyperlink from the thumbnail to the original image.

Banner Ad   A series of graphic images that transition from one to another at a predetermined interval.

bit   The smallest piece of information that a computer can handle, represented by either the number 0 or 1. Transmission speeds are often stated in the number of bits per second, so a 28.8k modem can theoretically handle 28,800 bits per second.

bitmap   An image, such as a picture or a character in a bitmapped font, created from many tiny dots (or pixels on a computer screen). Each dot's color and position defines the image. The two most common types of bitmapped image file formats used in Web sites are GIF and JPEG (see also *GIF, JPEG,* and *TIFF*).

bookmark   A named location within a page that you can specify as the target of a hyperlink by preceding its name with a pound sign; also known as a "destination," "named target," or "named anchor."

browse   To navigate through a Web site with a browser; permission level that allows browsing.

browser   A viewer or reader program that can request files over the World Wide Web or an intranet and display HTML Web pages.

bulleted lists   Lists that begin with the <UL> tag and have bullets or images marking each item; also called unordered lists.

byte   A collection of eight bits that can represent a single character, such as a letter, punctuation mark, or symbol.

cascading   Modifier that describes a style or property that can be specified in a resource, or inherited from the resource's container. For example, you can specify the background property for a table cell. If none is specified, then the background for the table is used. If there is no table background specified, then the page background is used in the cell.

cascading style sheets   A cascading style sheet consists of style definitions or style rules that apply to specific page elements or to entire pages.

CD-ROM   A CD (compact disc)-ROM (read-only memory) is a data-storage disk that can store hundreds of megabytes of data but, unlike a floppy disk, can only be written to once.

CGI   The Common Gateway Interface is a standard that allows a browser to execute a program on a server. The program, called a *CGI script,* processes the data and returns the results to the browser.

channel   Push technology that allows users to receive automatic updates of Web content.

Channel Definition Format (CDF) file   File that contains an index of the resources that are available on the channel and a recommended schedule for updating the channel on users' computers.

checkbox   Form field used to collect Boolean (yes/no, true/false) data from users. Clicking on the checkbox turns it on.

child page   A page that is subordinate to another page, called the parent page.

class   A class is a new style you create based on an existing style. The class inherits the attributes of the existing style.

client   A computer program that requests data from another program called the "server."

client-side image map   A client-side image map removes the need for server interaction because the hotspot coordinates for the image map are included in the HTML definition that is sent to the browser. When users click within the client-side image map, the browser locates and opens the target associated with the coordinates.

Comment   FrontPage component that includes text that is not visible when the page is viewed in a browser.

Common Gateway Interface   See *CGI*.

component   A built-in object that executes when the page is opened in a browser.

composition   The image you create in Microsoft Image Composer from a variety of elements, including text, hand-drawn art, and clip art.

composition space   In Image Composer, the white area where you create compositions.

compression ratio   A compression ratio relates the size of a file before and after compression. For example, if an image that occupies 400KB of the computer's memory is saved as a 100KB GIF file, then the compression ratio is 4:1.

confirmation   A message sent from the server to the user to indicate that a submitted form has been received.

Confirmation Field   FrontPage component that displays the value from a specified form field.

controls   Input areas you use to create a form on a page. Each control lets the person reading the form either enter data, such as their name, or make a choice, such as selecting their country of residence from a drop-down menu.

current web   See *active web*.

desktop component   Feature of Microsoft Internet Explorer 4.0 and other browsers that support channel definitions. Uses part of the desktop to broadcast updated information, such as a stock ticker, sports scores, or other information from a designated Web site.

domain   The network or server name, including the site name and domain, associated with a specific organization; for example, `sybex.com`, `uua.org`, `att.net`. The portion of a URL that indicates the type of organization that owns the host server, for example, COM, EDU, ORG, GOV, is the root domain.

download   The process of receiving data; a browser downloads data from a server (see also *upload*).

Drop-down menu   A form field designed to allow users to choose from a set of defined values. Drop-down menus can allow a single choice or multiple choices.

8-bit color   Color palettes that include 256 colors.

element   An HTML feature in a page, such as a heading, horizontal line, table, or bulleted list (see also *tag*).

embedded style sheet   A style sheet embedded in a single page. With an embedded style sheet, you can create styles that only apply to the active page in your web.

external link   A hyperlink that targets a file outside of its Web site.

external style sheet   External style sheets are stored as individual pages with the .CSS file extension. By creating an external style sheet, you can link all the pages in your web to that one style sheet page. To make a style change to the web, you only have to change one page.

FAQ   Frequently Asked Questions; a common page on a Web site.

file format   A definition that specifies how information is saved in a file.

Files pane   The right pane in the FrontPage Explorer's Folders view.

firewall   Software that creates a barrier between a private network and the Internet.

flattening   Saving a multi-layered composition as a single image file.

Folders view   FrontPage Explorer view that displays the web's resources based on location; similar to the Windows Explorer.

form   An HTML feature consisting of controls for entering data and making choices. A user can fill out the form in a browser and then push a button to send that data to the server. You can use this data, for example, to compile a mailing list of all visitors to your site who fill out the form.

form field   A form page control used to capture data entered by the user.

form handler   A server-side program that executes when the user submits a form.

frame   A separate window within a page that displays another page.

frame set   An HTML feature that lets you display multiple pages in a single page; each is displayed in its own window.

frames page   A FrontPage template with a defined frame set.

freeware   Any software available for free, with no obligation to pay for it and, consequently, no guarantee of its precision or reliability. Often includes small utility programs created by amateur programmers or by professionals who are either being magnanimous or simply can't be bothered to try to charge for a small piece of work (see *shareware*).

FrontPage 98   Microsoft's suite of programs, including the Editor, Explorer, Image Composer, server extensions, and Personal Web Server, that you use to create a Web site.

FrontPage component   A built-in object that executes when the page is opened in a browser. Most FrontPage components automatically generate the appropriate HTML code for their defined tasks.

FrontPage Editor   The word processor–like program in the FrontPage package in which you create Web pages.

FrontPage Explorer   The FrontPage program in which you work with webs. You can create new webs, delete or copy a web, manage the files and hyperlinks in a web, assign access rights to a web, and much more. In general, when you want to do any work in your web, you start in the Explorer, then open the page in the FrontPage Editor. For example, when you want to edit a page in a web, you open that site in the Explorer and double-click on the page in question to open it in the FrontPage Editor.

FrontPage Personal Web Server   Available as part of the custom FrontPage installation, the FrontPage PWS hosts your site while you build, test, and maintain it.

FrontPage Server Extensions   See *server extensions*.

FrontPage web   A Web site you created or are managing under FrontPage.

FTP   The File Transfer Protocol is an Internet protocol for transferring files from one computer to another.

GIF   The Graphics Interchange Format is a file format for image files. The image is limited to 256 colors and is compressed in the file (without any loss of quality) to decrease transmission time over a network. It is a popular file format (with a .GIF file name extension) supported by almost all browsers on the World Wide Web (see also *JPEG*).

Hit Counter   FrontPage component that displays the number of users who have visited a Web site.

home page   Default page for a Web site; the first page that a user sees when accessing a Web site, typically containing hyperlinks that can lead the user to all the other pages in that web. The home page is normally the first page opened when a browser accesses a Web site without requesting a specific file.

host   A computer that controls access to a Web site and responds to requests for files on that site (host server) or a computer that runs (hosts) client software locally.

hotspot   Text or an image in a page that you can click on to activate a hyperlink and open its target. The term is often used to refer to a defined hyperlink region in an image map (see also *hyperlink* and *image map*).

hover button   A button that visibly changes when a user points at it in a browser.

HTML   The WWW formatting language, interpreted by browsers. You create Web pages in the Hypertext Markup Language using tags to define structural or formatting features in the page.

HTTP   The Hypertext Transfer Protocol is the protocol of the World Wide Web by which a browser requests and opens pages or other files.

hyperlink   Also called a "link." In a Web page, text or a graphic image that you can click on to access the target resource of that link anywhere on the Web. Most browsers signify text links by underlining them and displaying them in a different color.

Hyperlinks pane   The right pane in the Explorer's Hyperlinks view.

Hyperlinks view   The FrontPage Explorer view that displays a model of the resources and links in the web.

Hypertext Markup Language   See *HTML*.

Hypertext Transfer Protocol   See *HTTP*.

image   A graphics object displayed in a Web page. Line drawings, photographs, geometric shapes, and textures suitable for page backgrounds are all images.

Image Composer   The image composition application included with FrontPage. It is particularly well-suited for creating and manipulating images destined to be displayed on a computer screen, such as in a Web site (see also *composition* and *sprite*). Version 1.5 of Image Composer is included in FrontPage 98.

image map   An image in a page that contains hidden hyperlinks called "hotspots." A client-side image map contains all the necessary information to make the link to the target, while a server-side image map requires the server to process the link from the coordinates of the map (see also *hotspot*).

Import Web Wizard   The FrontPage 98 Wizard used to import an existing Web site.

Include Page   FrontPage component that displays another Web page within the current page.

i*net   A general term that includes intranets and the Internet.

initial page   The page that is displayed in a frame when the frames page opens.

inline image   An image that appears within a Web page; the image is actually stored in its own file, separate from the HTML of the page.

inline style   Inline styles can be applied to specific page elements such as tables, graphics, or paragraphs. Inline styles supercede embedded and external style sheets, so they allow even more precise formatting of individual elements.

Insert HTML   Component used to enter extended HTML code that is not supported by FrontPage. FrontPage does not verify that the code is valid.

interlaced image   A GIF image file in which the order of its scan lines have been rearranged. When the image is opened in a browser, it seems to come into focus within its box, rather than appearing line by line from top to bottom.

internal link   A link that targets a file within the same Web site.

Internet   A network of countless smaller networks, all of which use the same protocol—TCP/IP—to communicate. The World Wide Web is one method of communicating on the Internet, along with FTP, Gopher, Telnet, and e-mail.

Internet Information Server (IIS)   Microsoft's server software for commercial Web sites.

Internet Explorer   A Web browser produced by Microsoft; you may often simply see it called *IE*.

intranet   A private network that functions much like the Internet; the same client and server software can be used on both.

ISDN   The Integrated Services Digital Network is a telephone service based on digital instead of analog signals. A computer can transmit data at a much higher rate (up to 128,000 bits per second) over an ISDN phone line than it can over a regular phone line (currently about 56,000 bits per second).

Java   A programming language that allows you to create mini-programs that are executable on a Web client instead of a server. For example, when you open a Web page in your browser, a Java program might be downloaded along with it (much as images are). The program can then run automatically when the page is opened, or it might instead run when you point to an object on the page. Once the Java program is on the client computer, it's available the next time a page calls for that program.

JavaScript   A scripting language for creating programs within a Web page. When someone with a JavaScript-aware browser opens a page, the commands run on that computer, not on the server.

JPEG   The Joint Photographic Expert Group file format is a highly compact way to store true-color (24-bit) images with up to 16.7 million colors in a file. The method used to compress the image actually lowers the overall image quality, but it does so only slightly compared to the huge savings in file size. It is a popular file format, which uses a .JPG file name extension, supported by just about all browsers on the World Wide Web.

link   See *hyperlink*.

lossless   Description of an image file format, such as GIF, in which the image information is compressed in the file while losing none of the image's information (see also *lossy* and *GIF*).

lossy   An image file format, such as JPEG, that actually throws away some of the image's information so that the image can be compressed more, with only a small decrease in image quality (see also *lossless* and *JPEG*).

marquee   A FrontPage scrolling message component, not yet part of the HTML standard.

Microsoft Personal Web Server   One of the two PWSs included with FrontPage 98. A scaled-down version of the Internet Information server that allows you to create a Web site in FrontPage, test the site, revise it, and even host the site while under the server's control. See *FrontPage Personal Web Server*.

modem   An electronic device that allows one computer to exchange data with another over ordinary phone lines by using sound (analog signals) instead of a strictly digital network connection. The name is derived from the fact that a computer sends data by modulating it into an analog signal, while the receiving computer demodulates the signal back into digital data.

navigation bars   A set of buttons located on each page that allow visitors to move to another page in the current web.

Navigation view   FrontPage Explorer view that displays your web like an organizational chart.

Net   Slang or a nickname for the Internet.

Netscape Navigator   A Web browser produced by Netscape Communications Corporation.

network   Multiple computers that can communicate with one another, such as clients requesting and receiving data from a server. The communication may be via copper wire, coaxial cable, fiber-optic cable, microwave relay, satellite transmission, and so on. The network includes the computers, software, interconnections, and is often defined to include all the people using the network.

numbered lists   A list where each item is prefaced by a number. Numbered lists are preceded with the <OL> tag, and are also called ordered lists.

one-line text box   Form field that allows users to enter a single line of text.

online   Used to refer to being connected to a network and able to share its resources. You might say, "When I go online, I'll visit your Web site."

ordered list   See *numbered list*.

orphan, orphaned page   File that is not linked to any other files in a web.

page   An HTML document (file) that you can view in a Web browser, much as you can view a word processing document in a word processor.

Page Banner   FrontPage component used to insert a page banner. Normally only used if the page does not include a theme or shared border.

parent page   A page with links to subordinate pages, called child pages.

permissions   Rights to browse, author, or administer a web. Permissions are set by a web's administrator.

Personal Web Server   See *Microsoft Personal Web Server* and *PWS*.

pixel   An individual display element on a screen, based on the current resolution setting for the screen. For example, if your monitor's display resolution is 640 × 480, there are 640 pixels across and 480 pixels down the screen.

plug-in   Any of a variety of programs designed to work with a Web browser and give it enhanced capabilities. For example, a plug-in might give a browser the ability to display a non-standard file. Plug-ins usually work behind the scenes, so the user does not even realize they are working with the browser.

point   A typesetting measurement. One point is ½", so 12 point type is ⅙" high. (This also means that with 12 point type, there are six lines of text to a vertical inch.)

progressive JPEG   Similar to an interlaced GIF; the image loads in stages, gradually increasing in quality.

protocol   A method of communication among computers on a network, such as TCP/IP on the Internet.

publish   To copy a Web site or portion of a site to a Web server.

push technology   Communications technology that allows Web content providers to send their content directly to the users on a preset schedule or when content changes.

PWS   A Web server you can run locally while building and testing your Web site. See *Microsoft Personal Web Server*.

radio button   A control that can have two values: on or off. Also called option buttons, radio buttons are used in groups to provide a single choice from a group of options.

relative URL reference   An address on the Internet's World Wide Web based on another address. If a hyperlink in a page references the target <u>Images/picture.gif</u>, then it is assumed this folder and file are in the same folder as the page that contains the hyperlink. In terms of street addresses, it's the equivalent of a friend giving you his address but supplying only a street, house number, and his name, in which case you would assume that this address must be in the same city and country you are in.

resolution   The density of the dots that make up an image. On a computer screen, this refers to the number of pixels per square inch or centimeter, or in the entire screen. In general, higher resolution (higher dot or pixel density) makes for higher quality images. A computer screen set at a resolution of 800 by 600 has a higher resolution, and therefore higher quality images, than the same monitor set at 640 by 480.

resource   Any file within a Web site, such as an HTML Web page, an image, a video clip, or an executable program or script. A URL is a resource's address.

root web, FrontPage   The folder that serves as the default FrontPage web on a server. FrontPage refers to it as <root web>. All other FrontPage webs on that server reside within the root web.

RTF   The Rich Text Format is a file format for storing a text document and its formatting in a text-only file. It's one way to transfer documents between different word processors; the FrontPage Editor can open RTF files, as well.

Scheduled Image   FrontPage component that displays an image file for a time period you specify.

Scheduled Include Page   FrontPage component used to include a page within the current page for a specified time period.

scrolling text box   Form field that allows users to enter multiple lines of text.

server   A computer program that makes data available to other programs on the same computer or on other computers—it "serves" them (see also *client*).

server extensions   Add-on programs that extend the capabilities of a server. The FrontPage Server Extensions allow a server to provide additional services to a FrontPage web.

server-side image map   A traditional image map. When a user clicks within an image map, the browser sends the coordinates of the click (relative to the image) to the server. The server looks up the coordinates in a table of hotspots for that image map and processes the appropriate hyperlink target.

SGML   Standard Generalized Markup Language, the superset of languages that HTML belongs to.

shareware   Software available for free, but that nonetheless comes with a license agreement describing how you may use the software, how many copies you can make of it, and so on. Usually, the license also states that if you continue to use the software after a trial period, such as 30 days, you have to pay for it (see also *freeware*).

shared border   A page area that displays the same content on each page in the web, unless superseded by settings on individual pages.

site map   An org chart style view of your web displayed in the FrontPage Explorer's Navigation View.

sprite   The basic components of every composition in Microsoft Image Composer.

Substitution   FrontPage component that displays the current value for the FrontPage web configuration variable you choose, such as Page URL, Author, or Description.

table   An HTML feature that lets you create a grid of rows, columns, and cells for organizing information on a page. You can also take advantage of the structure of a table while hiding its borders so, for example, you can easily create three columns of text on a page by entering the text in a three-column by one-row table.

tag   An HTML code, always surrounded by angle brackets, that defines an element in a Web page. For example, the single tag <HR> creates a horizontal line in the page; the tag <H1> and its closing tag </H1> display the text within them in the level-one heading style.

Tasks List   A FrontPage feature that helps you keep track of the work that needs to be completed on a web.

target   The object that is opened or accessed when a hyperlink is activated. For example, a Web page can be the target of a hyperlink, so when the link is clicked, the target page is opened in the browser. A target can also include a named bookmark in a page, so when the target page is opened, the bookmark is displayed at the top of the browser's window (see also *bookmark*, *browser*, and *hyperlink*).

TCP/IP   Transmission Control Protocol specifies how messages should be split up into packets for transmission. Internet Protocol addresses the packets and routes them to their destination.

template   A model from which you can make many copies. You create new FrontPage webs from templates in the Explorer, and you can create new pages from templates in the Editor.

theme   When you apply a theme to a web, FrontPage designs every page with the same background image, color scheme, buttons, navigation bars, fonts, active graphics, and other page elements. Because the theme impacts the entire web, new pages are automatically created with all the design elements of the active web.

thread   A group of messages that spawns from a message on a particular topic. When someone else responds to that first message with another message, the thread begins. Visitors can read the first message and all of the subsequent responses, then can add their own two cents (even though the responses may no longer have any relevance to the initially identified topic).

thumbnail   A smaller version of an image, used as a hyperlink to the full size version.

TIFF   The Tagged Image File Format is a bitmapped image file format (usually with a .TIF file name extension). Most Web browsers cannot display TIFF images, so to display a TIFF image in a Web page, you normally convert the image file into either a GIF or JPEG image file (see also *bitmap*, *GIF*, and *JPEG*).

toolbox   The Image Composer toolbar used to open the tool palettes.

transition   An animation applied to a page or page element.

transparent   A color hidden in a GIF image, so whatever is behind the image in the page will show through.

true color   A palette of a little more than 16 million colors. Also called 24-bit color, because that is how much computer memory is required to display one pixel in any of the 16 million colors.

Uniform Resource Locator   See *URL*.

unordered list   A bulleted list.

upload   The process of sending data. A server uploads requested data to a browser (see also *download*).

URL   The Uniform Resource Locator identifies the address of a file on the World Wide Web, as well as the protocol by which to reach it. An absolute URL is the complete address, while a relative URL defines the address in relation to another address. For example, if a hyperlink in a page targets a relative URL that is only a file name, then the target is assumed to be in the same location as the current page.

validate   To limit the range of acceptable choices in a form field, and return error messages when user input is not within the range.

WC3   The World Wide Web Consortium, the group that establishes HTML standards for the World Wide Web.

Web Publishing Wizard   FrontPage program used to publish webs to the Internet or a local area network.

Web site   A collection of files hosted by a server and accessed with a Web browser.

WebBot   A FrontPage web automation feature that you insert in a page (or is inserted automatically) to create the appropriate HTML code for its defined task. Renamed to FrontPage component in FrontPage 98.

Wizard   A Microsoft application feature that helps you create new sites or Web pages by asking you relevant questions, accepting your responses, and then proceeding to the next step.

workspace   The gray area surrounding the composition guide in Image Composer.

World Wide Web   The network on the Internet that uses HTTP to distribute files from servers to clients. It is also known as the "WWW" or simply the "Web."

WWW   See *World Wide Web*.

WYSIWYG   An acronym meaning "What you see is what you get."

Index

Note to the Reader: First level entries are in **bold**. Page numbers in bold indicate the principal discussion of a topic or the definition of a term. Page numbers in *italic* indicate illustrations.

Numbers and Symbols

8-bit color palettes, 193–195, *194, 195,* **499**

24-bit (true color) palette, 192–193, *193,* 194–195, **508**

<!-...-> comment tags, 388–389

~- (minus signs) in FrontPage Explorer, 85, *88,* 89, 92

+ (plus signs) in FrontPage Explorer, 85, *88,* 89, 92

 # (pound signs) in HTML bookmark references, 124, *125*

A

<A>...</A> link tags, 429–432

absolute URLs, 114–115, **495**

ACCEPT= HTML attribute of forms, 474, 476

ACCEPT-CHARSET= HTML attribute of forms, 474

access rights in webs, 355–359, *357–359,* 361

ACCESSKEY= HTML attribute
of forms, 479–480
of image maps, 437
of links, 430

<ACRONYM>...</ACRONYM> text tags, 390–391

ACTION= HTML attribute of forms, 475

Active Elements, 263–275. *See also* automating and activating webs
Banner Ads, 267–270, *269, 270,* **496**
hover buttons, 264–267, *264, 267,* **501**
marquees, 270–274, *271, 272,* **504**
overview of, 263–264
page transitions, 274–275, **508**

active webs, 18, 23, **495**

Add Task command in FrontPage Explorer, 96

adding. *See also* inserting
captions to tables, 145–146
effects to sprites, 199–200, *199, 200*
fields to forms, 300–301
headings, 44–46
horizontal lines, 42–44

items to lists, 48
linked Web pages to webs, 81
navigation bars, 129
page transitions, 274–275
table cells, 153
tables of contents to webs, 259–261, *259, 261*
tasks, 107–108, *107*
text to images, 175
time and date stamps to webs, 262–263

add-on software in FrontPage 98, 366–367

<ADDRESS>...</ADDRESS> global structure tags, 378–379

addresses of Web sites, 4–5

Administration tab in Personal Web Server Properties dialog box, 361

administrators, 355, 356–357, **495**

advanced dynamic components, 275

Advanced tab in FrontPage Web Settings dialog box, 179–180, *180*

ALIGN= HTML attribute
of applets, 435
of columns, 416
of form labels, 480
of form widgets (deprecated), 476
of frames, 468
of headings, 384
of horizontal rules, 460
of images, 438–439
of marquees, 490
of objects, 442
of paragraphs (deprecated), 400
of table captions, 415
of table column headers, 425
of table text, 416–418, 422, 428
of tables, 419
of text, 382, 386
of white space, 491

aligning
form fields, *288,* 295, 476
horizontal lines, 43, 460

B

C

R

S